There's a feature in the *Bleach* PSP video game that lets you increase the trust between you and your partner character. I decided to build trust with Rangiku, but I soon found that I have no idea what she's thinking. It's scary how often she gets mad at me when I answer one of her questions. And I created her!

–Tite Kubo

*BLEACH* is author Tite Kubo's second title. Kubo made his debut with *ZOMBIEPOWDER.*, a four-volume series for *WEEKLY SHONEN JUMP.* To date, *BLEACH* has been translated into numerous languages and has also inspired an animated TV series that began airing in the U.S. in 2006. Beginning its serialization in 2001, *BLEACH* is still a mainstay in the pages of *WEEKLY SHONEN JUMP.* In 2005, *BLEACH* was awarded the prestigious Shogakukan Manga Award in the *shonen* (boys) category.

**BLEACH**
**Vol. 24: Immanent God Blues**
**SHONEN JUMP Manga Edition**

This volume contains material that was originally published in SHONEN JUMP #66-68. Artwork in the magazine may have been altered slightly from what is presented in this volume.

STORY AND ART BY
TITE KUBO

English Adaptation/Lance Caselman
Translation/Joe Yamazaki
Touch-Up Art & Lettering/Mark McMurray
Design/Sean Lee
Editor/Pancha Diaz

Published by VIZ Media, LLC
P.O. Box 77010
San Francisco, CA 94107

10 9 8 7 6 5 4 3
First printing, September 2008
Third printing, April 2013

www.viz.com

THE WORLD'S MOST POPULAR MANGA
www.shonenjump.com

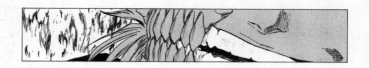

Break down, every single one of you.

# BLEACH24 IMMANENT GOD BLUES

# STARS AND

**Tôshirô Hitsugaya**

**Renji Abarai**

**Ichigo Kurosaki**

plot

When Ichigo Kurosaki meets Soul Reaper Rukia Kuchiki his life is changed forever. Soon Ichigo is a Soul Reaper himself, cleansing lost souls called Hollows.

Ichigo and his friends travel to the Soul Society to rescue Rukia, and uncover a sinister plot orchestrated by Sôsuke Aizen. Aizen and his cohorts are forced to flee, but they are far from neutralized. When deadly Arrancars begin to appear in the world of the living, Rukia and a team of Soul Reapers are sent to stop them. But they soon find themselves fighting for their lives against powerful enemies who will stop at nothing to achieve their terrible ends.

# BLEACH ALL

Grimmjow

Rangiku
Matsumoto

Shawlong

# STORIES

# BLEACH 24

## IMMANENT GOD BLUES

## Contents

## 206. ¡Mala Suerte! 5 [LUCKY]

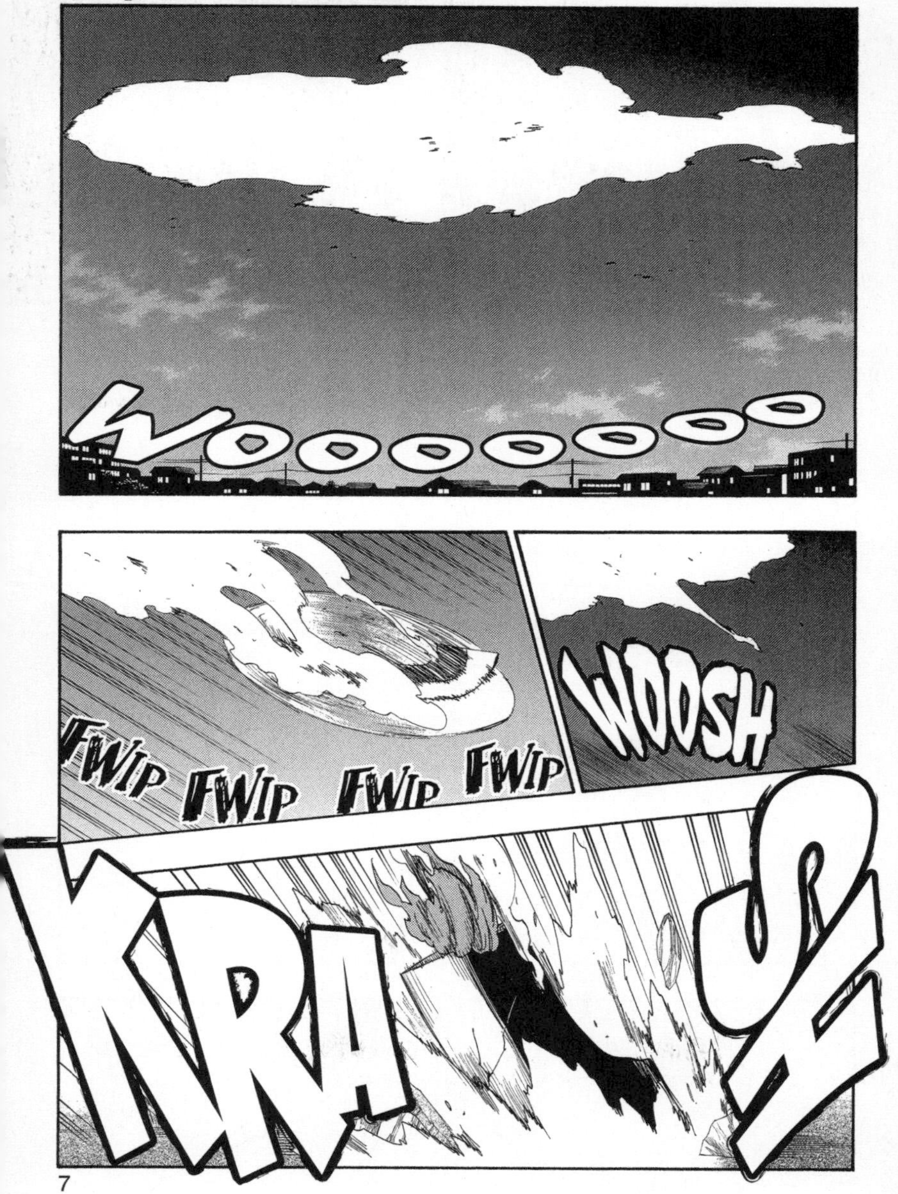
WOOOOOOO
WOOSH
FWIP FWIP FWIP FWIP
KRA

FWOOO

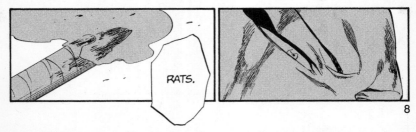

RATS.

8

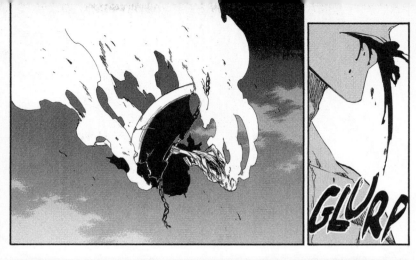

GLURP

KROO M

IKKAKU ...

MADA-RAME...

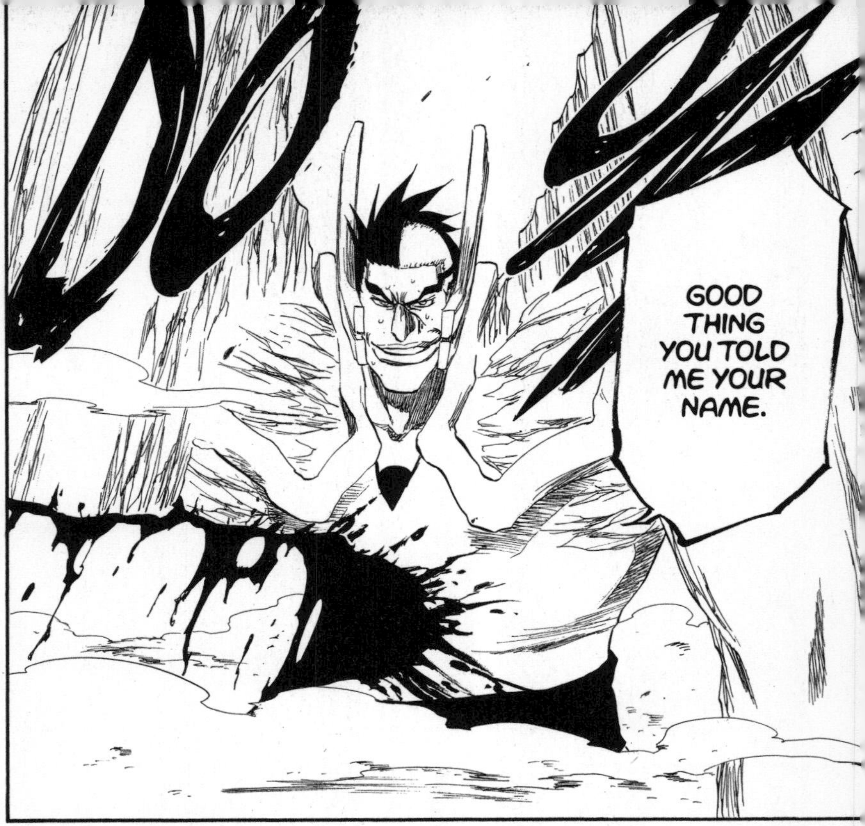
GOOD THING YOU TOLD ME YOUR NAME.

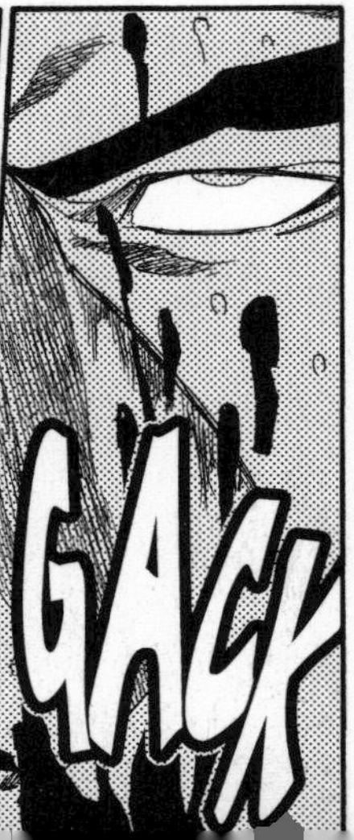
GACK

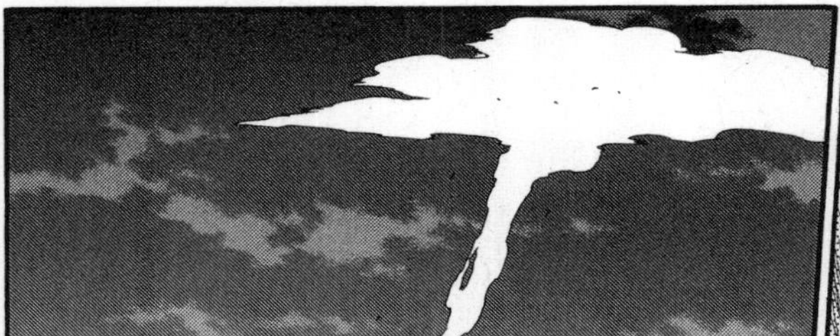
SHOOM

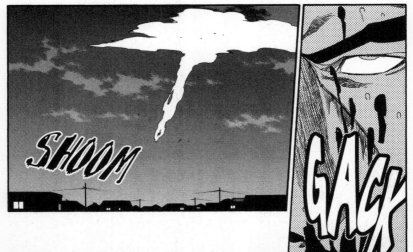

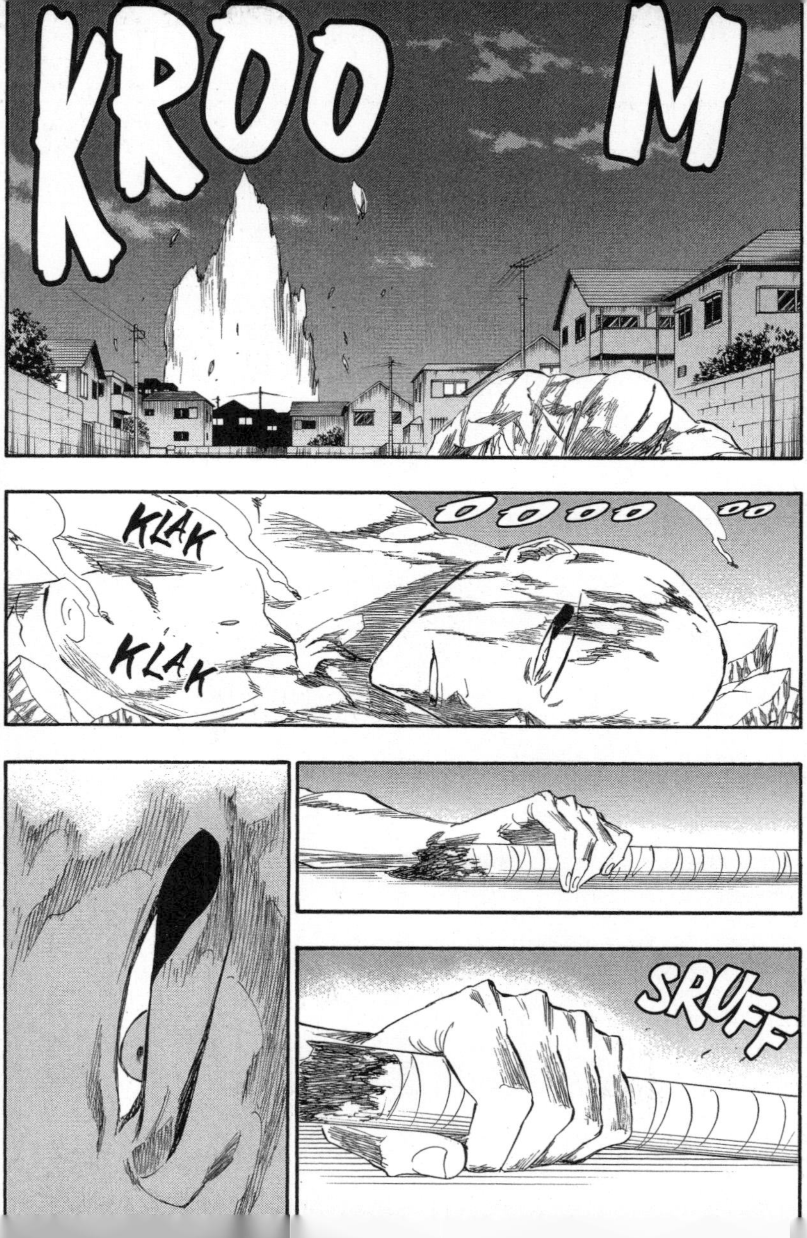
KROOM
KLAK
KLAK
OOOOOO
SRUFF

SRUFF

# 206.

¡Mala       Suerte!       5

# [LUCKY]

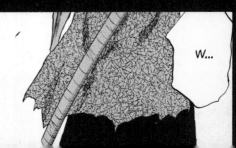

W-WAIT...

W...

READ THIS WAY

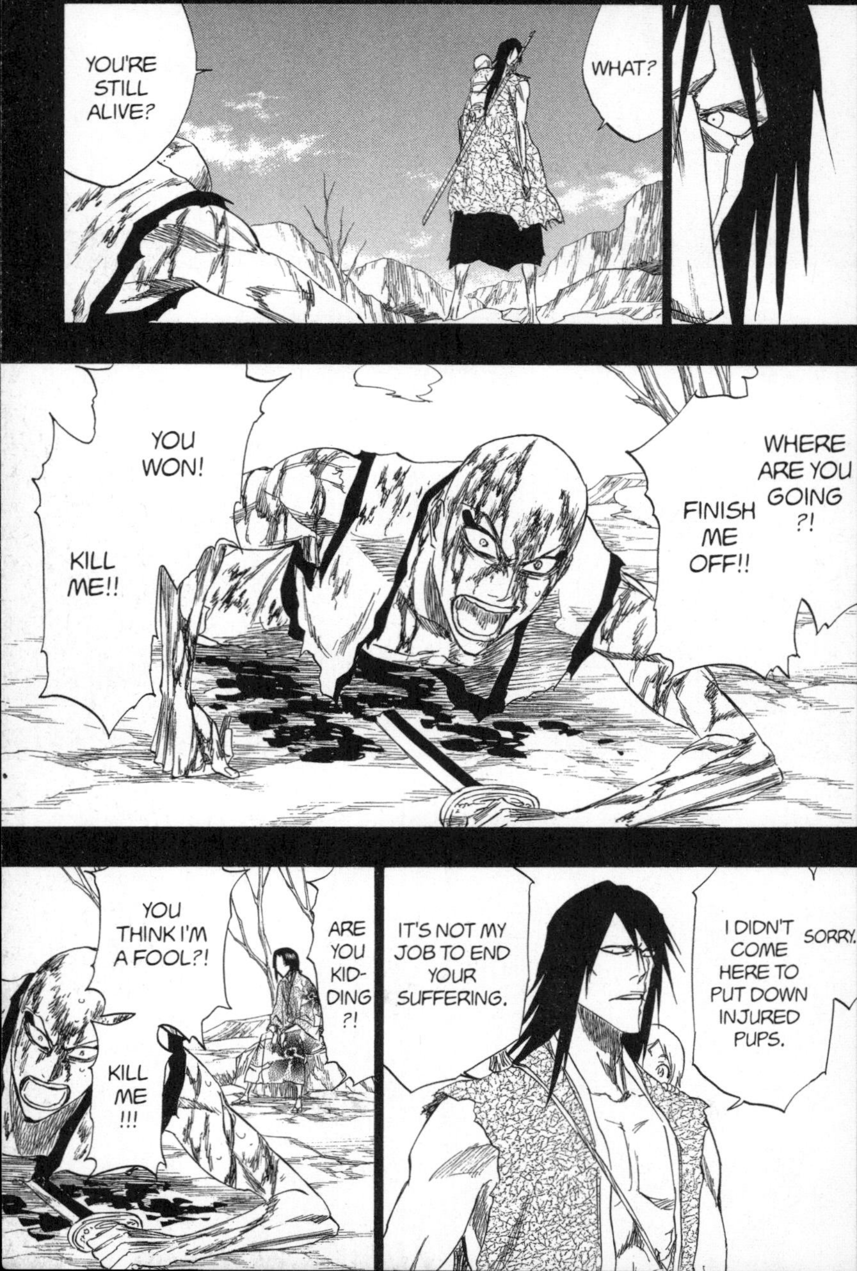
WHAT?
YOU'RE STILL ALIVE?
WHERE ARE YOU GOING ?!
FINISH ME OFF!!
YOU WON!
KILL ME!!
SORRY.
I DIDN'T COME HERE TO PUT DOWN INJURED PUPS.
IT'S NOT MY JOB TO END YOUR SUFFERING.
ARE YOU KID-DING ?!
YOU THINK I'M A FOOL?!
KILL ME !!!

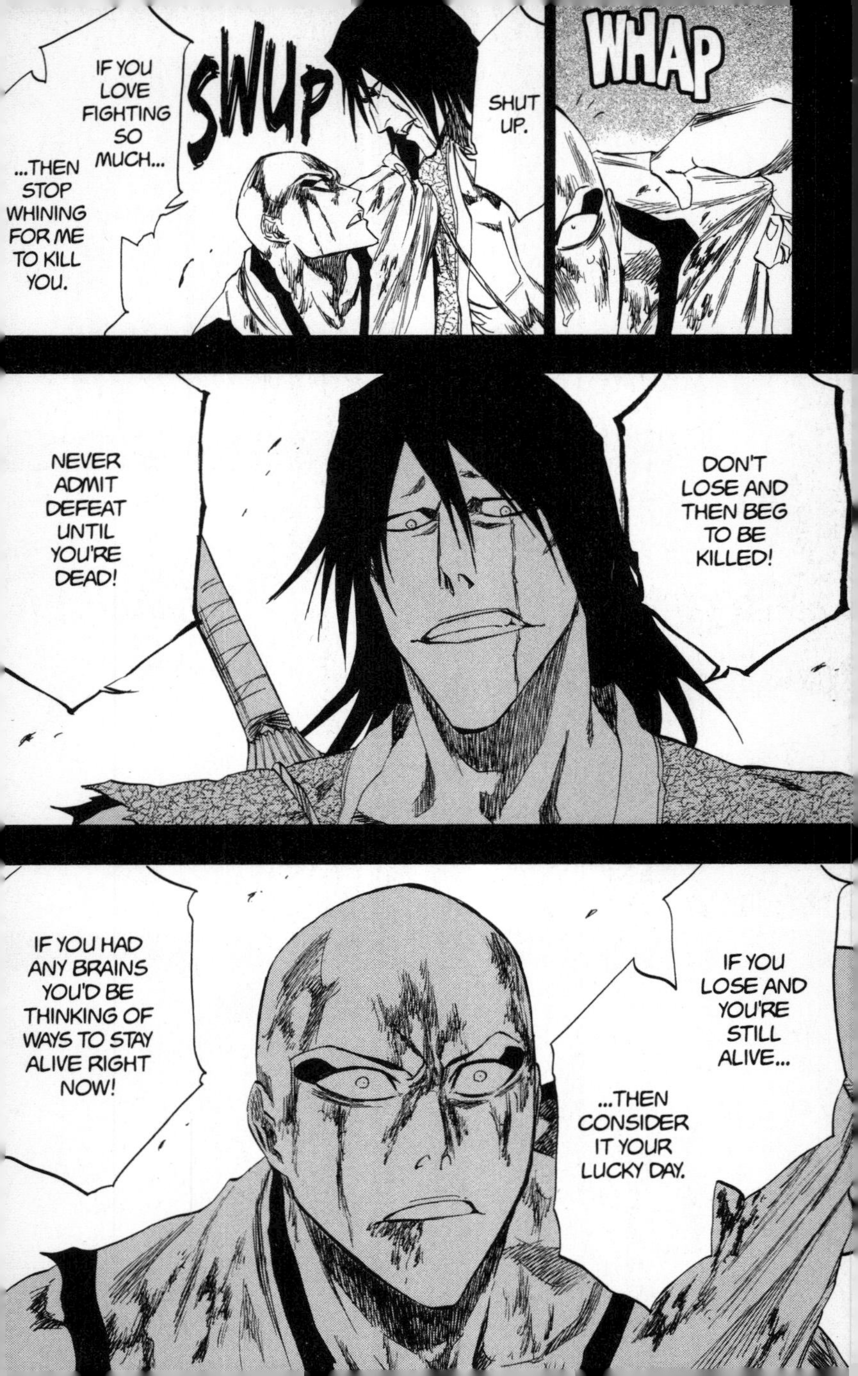
WHAP
SHUT UP.
SWUP
IF YOU LOVE FIGHTING SO MUCH...
...THEN STOP WHINING FOR ME TO KILL YOU.
DON'T LOSE AND THEN BEG TO BE KILLED!
NEVER ADMIT DEFEAT UNTIL YOU'RE DEAD!
IF YOU LOSE AND YOU'RE STILL ALIVE...
...THEN CONSIDER IT YOUR LUCKY DAY.
IF YOU HAD ANY BRAINS YOU'D BE THINKING OF WAYS TO STAY ALIVE RIGHT NOW!

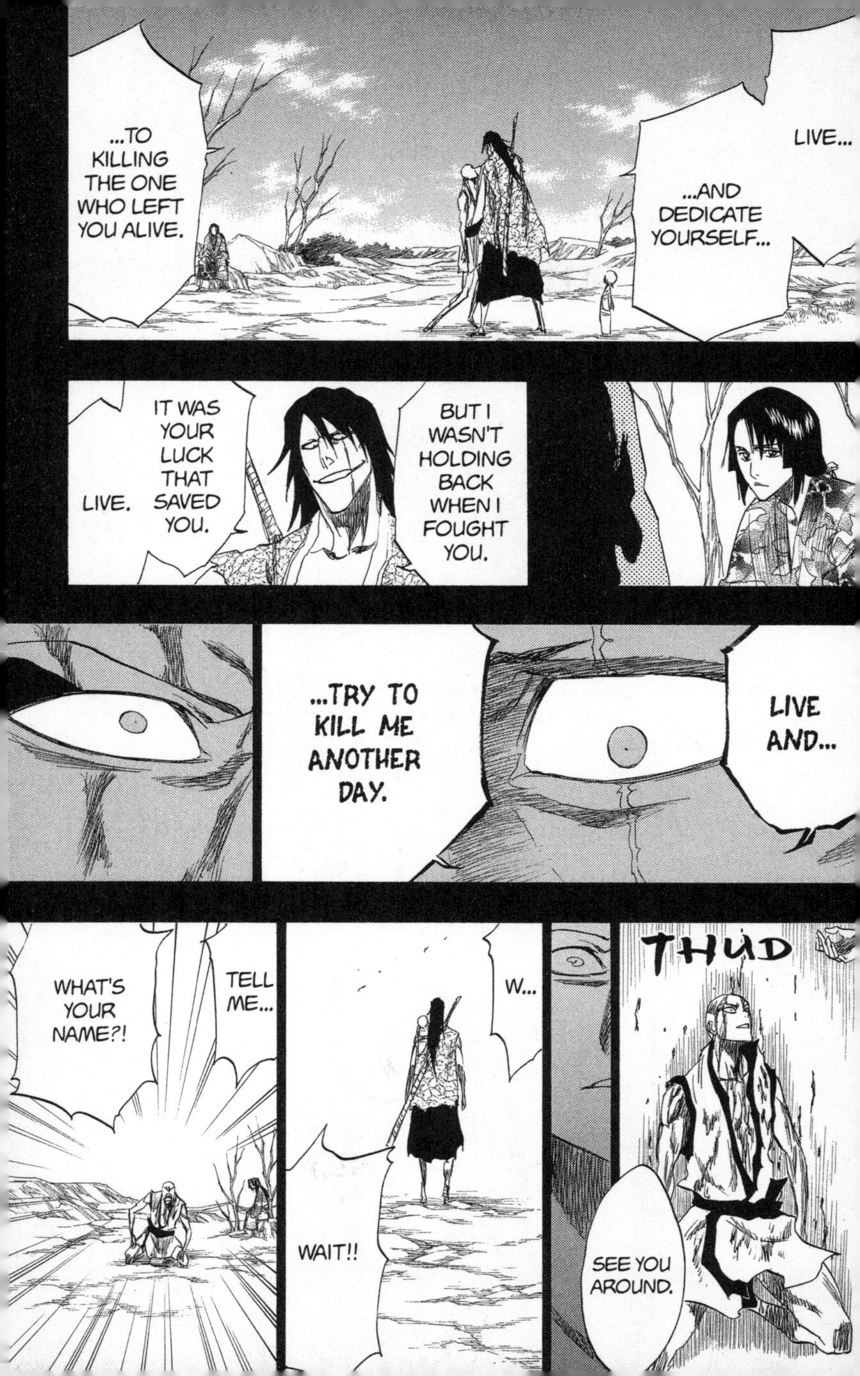
LIVE...
...AND DEDICATE YOURSELF...
...TO KILLING THE ONE WHO LEFT YOU ALIVE.
BUT I WASN'T HOLDING BACK WHEN I FOUGHT YOU.
IT WAS YOUR LUCK THAT SAVED YOU.
LIVE.
LIVE AND...
...TRY TO KILL ME ANOTHER DAY.
THUD
SEE YOU AROUND.
W...
WAIT!!
TELL ME...
WHAT'S YOUR NAME?!

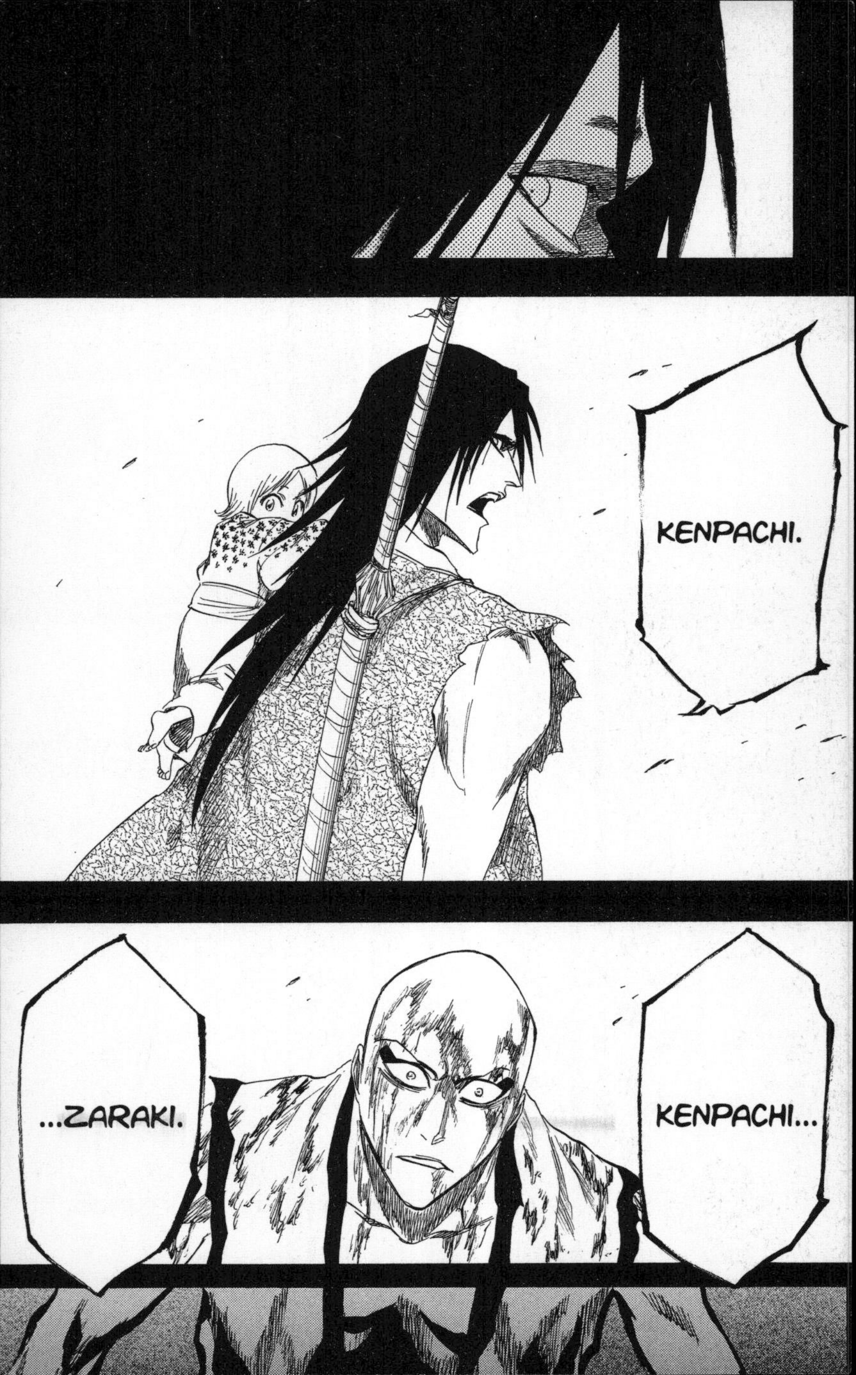
KENPACHI.
KENPACHI...
...ZARAKI.

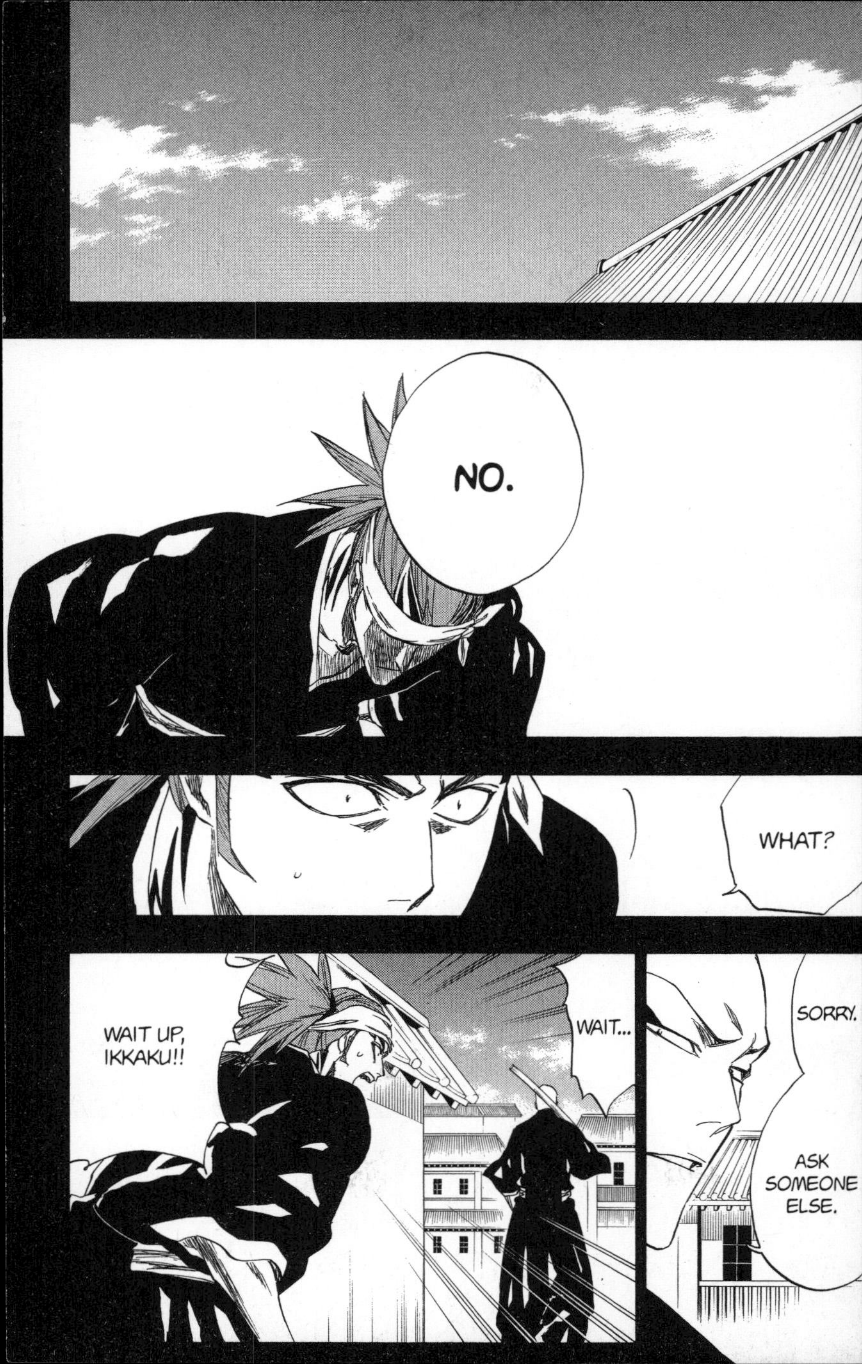
NO.
WHAT?
SORRY.
ASK SOMEONE ELSE.
WAIT...
WAIT UP, IKKAKU!!

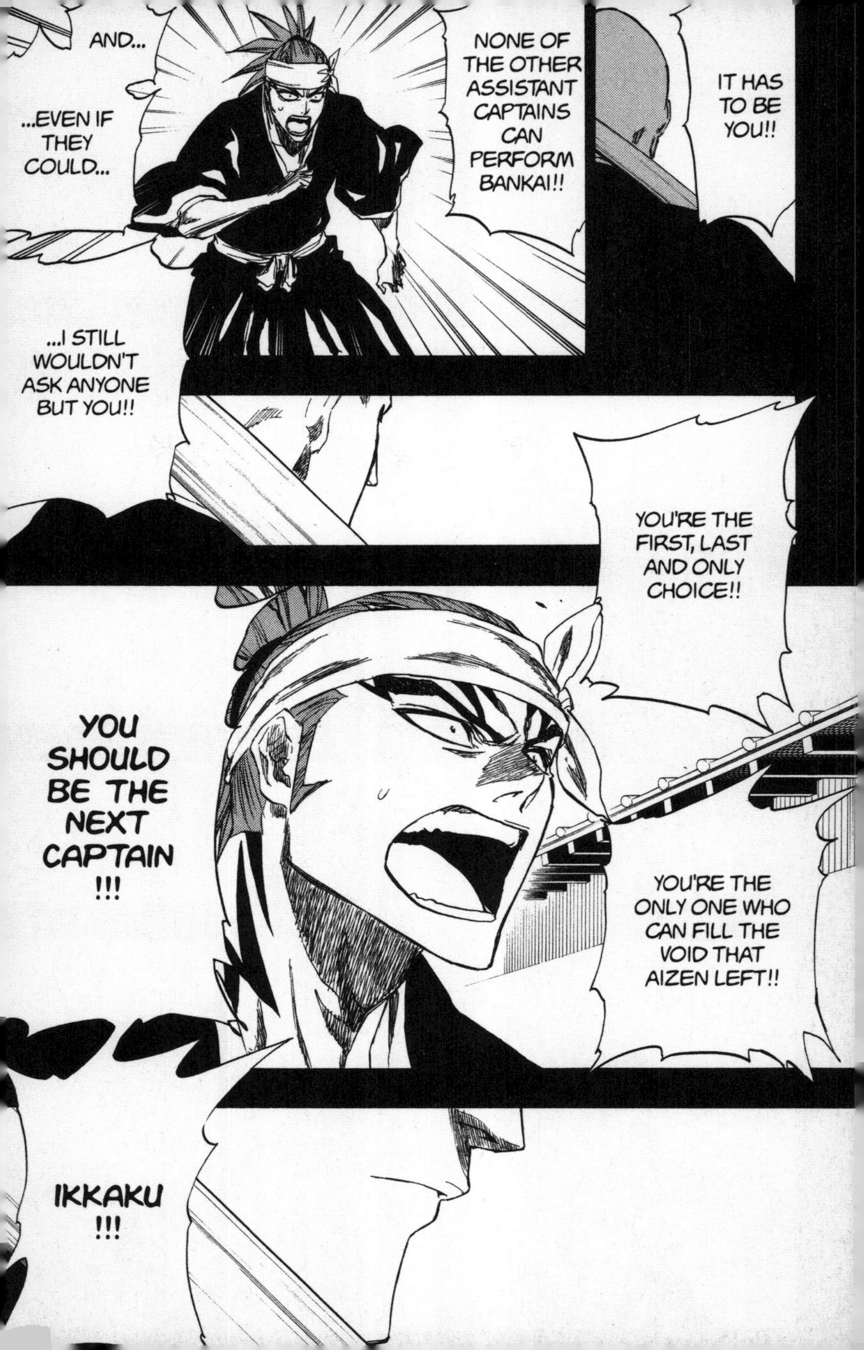
IT HAS TO BE YOU!!
NONE OF THE OTHER ASSISTANT CAPTAINS CAN PERFORM BANKAI!!
AND...
...EVEN IF THEY COULD...
...I STILL WOULDN'T ASK ANYONE BUT YOU!!
YOU'RE THE FIRST, LAST AND ONLY CHOICE!!
YOU'RE THE ONLY ONE WHO CAN FILL THE VOID THAT AIZEN LEFT!!
YOU SHOULD BE THE NEXT CAPTAIN!!!
IKKAKU!!!

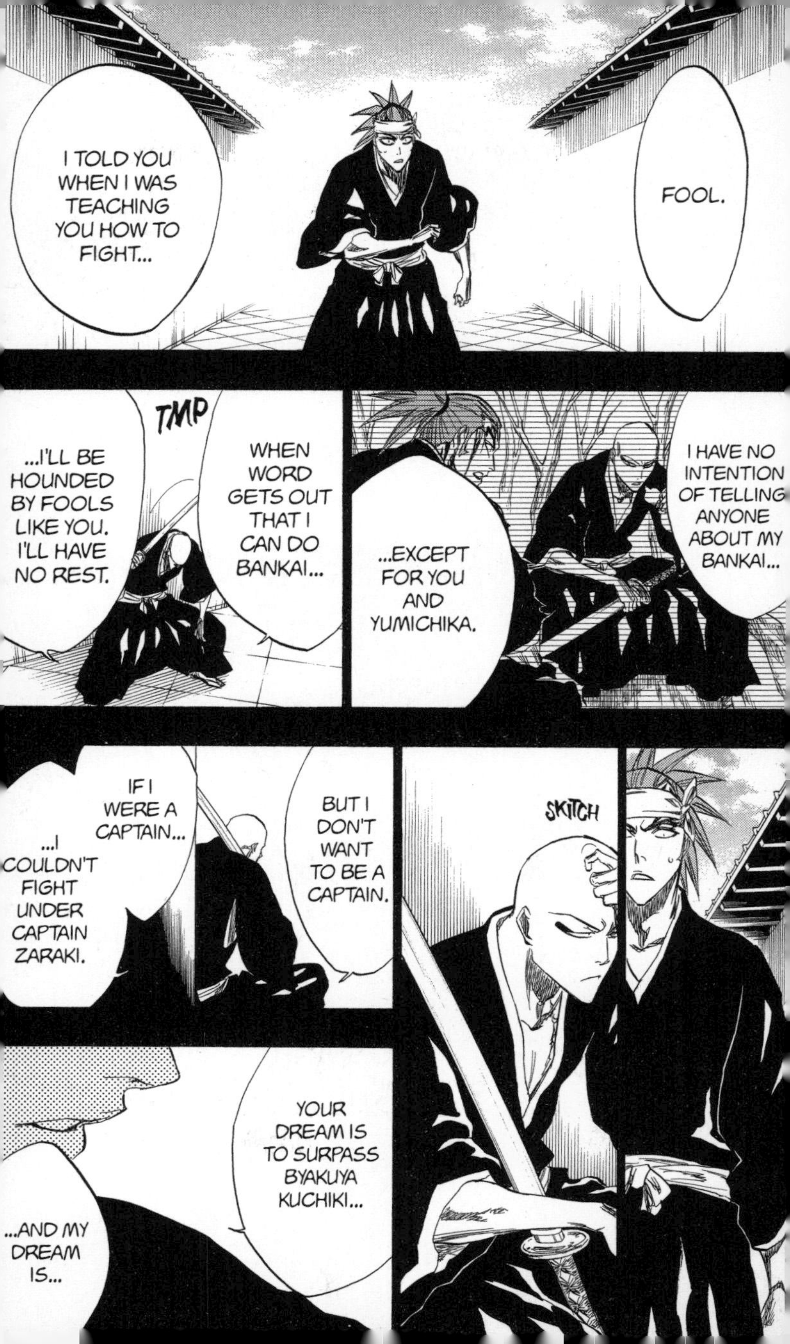
FOOL.
I TOLD YOU WHEN I WAS TEACHING YOU HOW TO FIGHT...
I HAVE NO INTENTION OF TELLING ANYONE ABOUT MY BANKAI...
...EXCEPT FOR YOU AND YUMICHIKA.
TMP
WHEN WORD GETS OUT THAT I CAN DO BANKAI...
...I'LL BE HOUNDED BY FOOLS LIKE YOU. I'LL HAVE NO REST.
SKITCH
BUT I DON'T WANT TO BE A CAPTAIN.
IF I WERE A CAPTAIN...
...I COULDN'T FIGHT UNDER CAPTAIN ZARAKI.
YOUR DREAM IS TO SURPASS BYAKUYA KUCHIKI...
...AND MY DREAM IS...

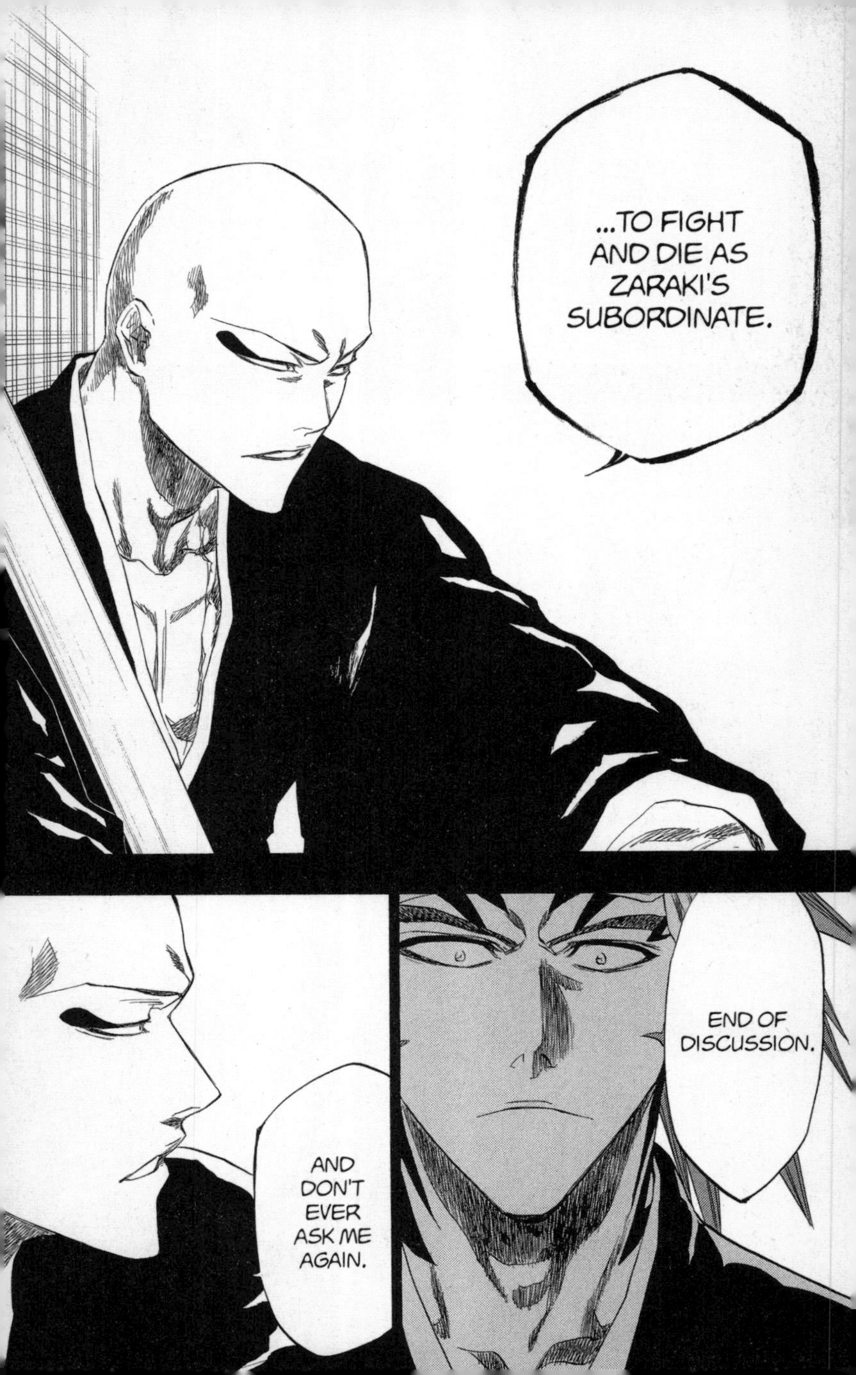
...TO FIGHT AND DIE AS ZARAKI'S SUBORDINATE.
END OF DISCUSSION.
AND DON'T EVER ASK ME AGAIN.

YES,
SIR!

HERG

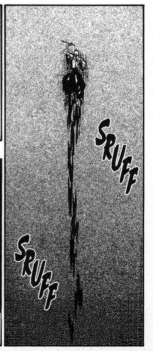

SRUFF

SRUFF

TMP

I
KNEW
IT.

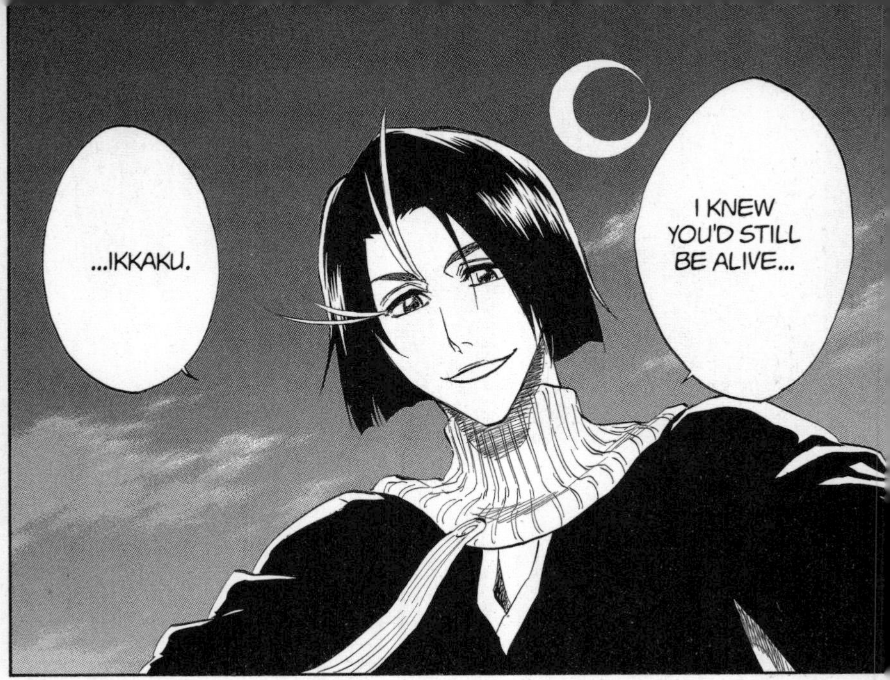
I KNEW YOU'D STILL BE ALIVE...
...IKKAKU.

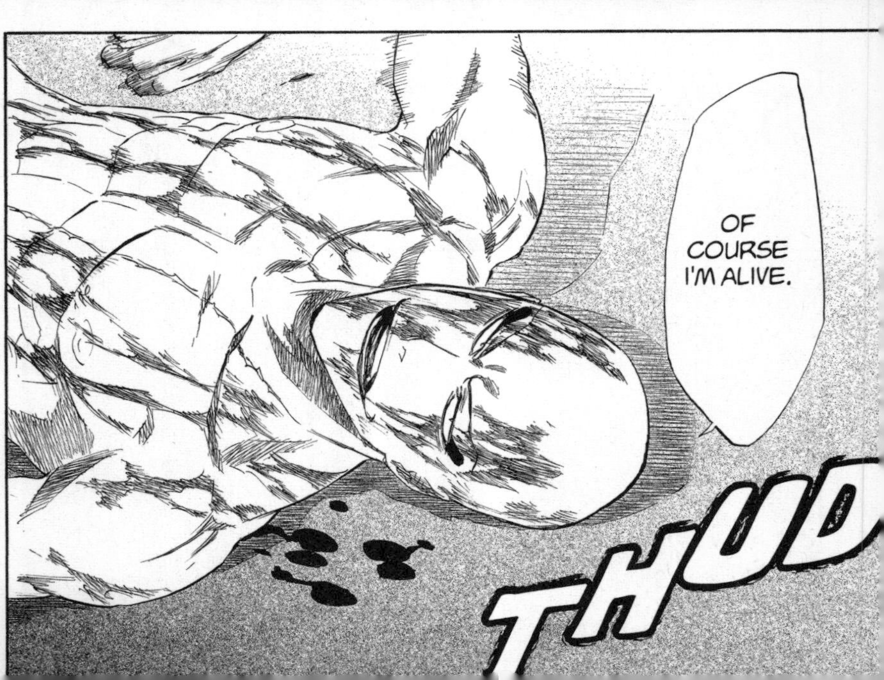
OF COURSE I'M ALIVE.
THUD

« READ THIS WAY «

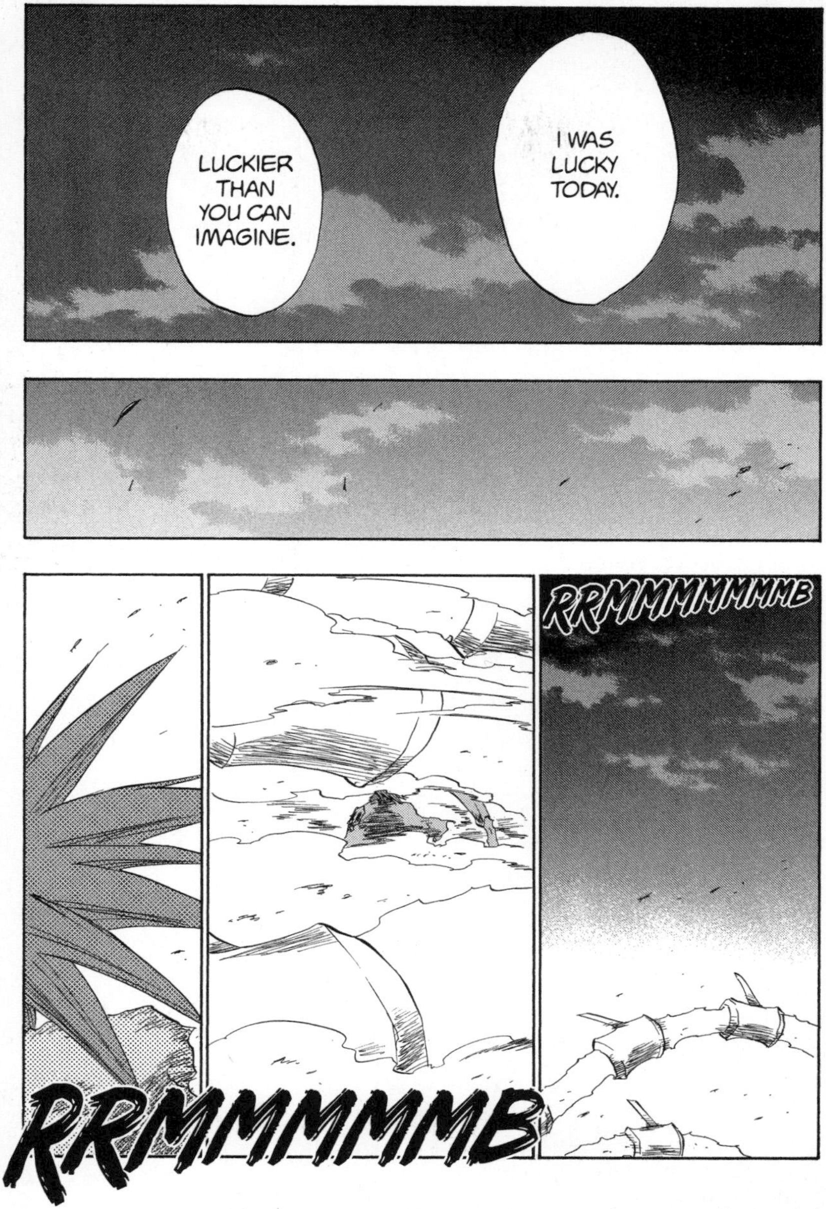
I WAS LUCKY TODAY.
LUCKIER THAN YOU CAN IMAGINE.
RRMMMMMMMMB
RRMMMMMMB

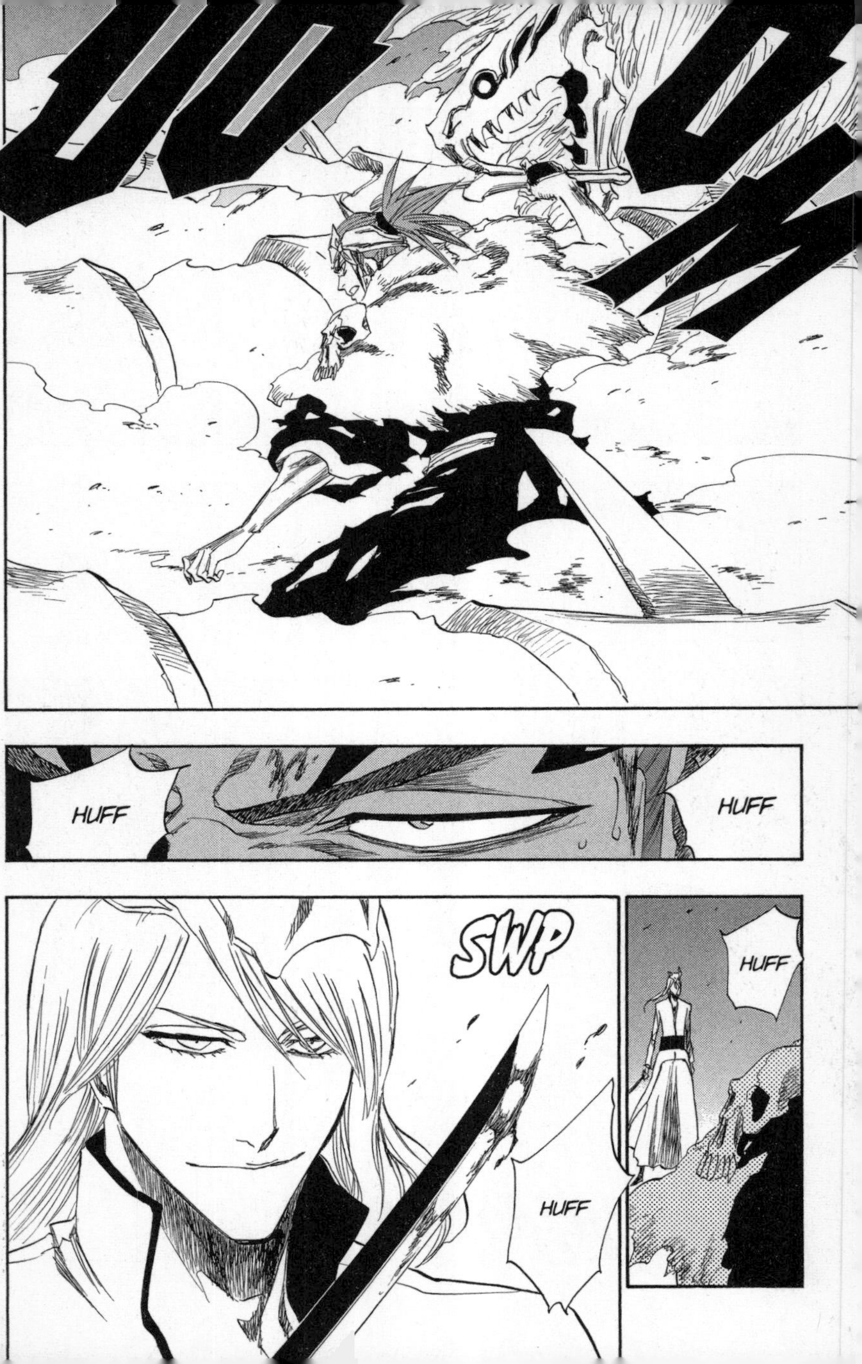
HUFF
HUFF
HUFF
SWP
HUFF

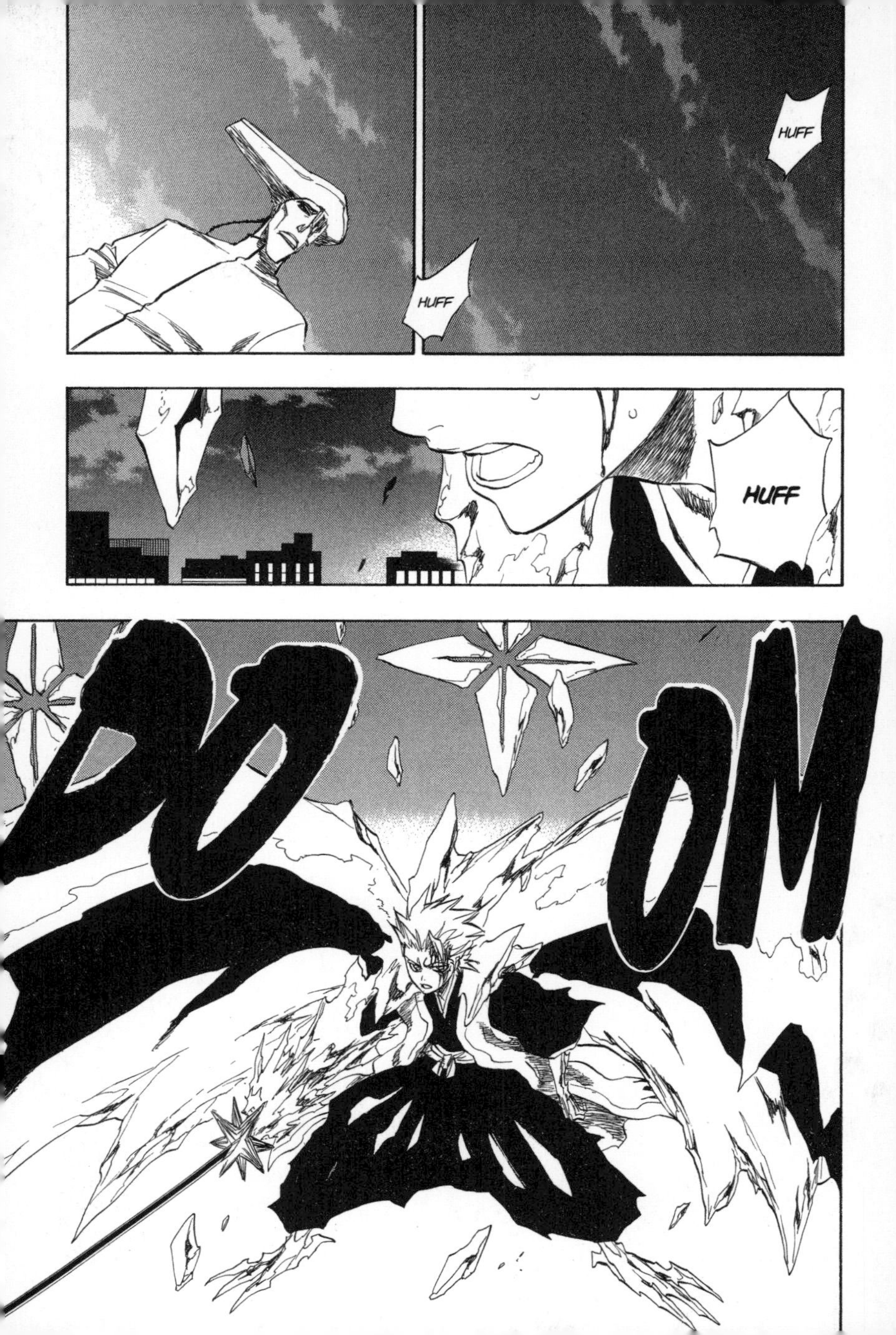
HUFF
HUFF
HUFF
DOOM

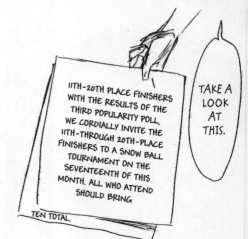

TAKE A LOOK AT THIS.
11TH-20TH PLACE FINISHERS
WITH THE RESULTS OF THE THIRD POPULARITY POLL, WE CORDIALLY INVITE THE 11TH-THROUGH 20TH-PLACE FINISHERS TO A SNOW BALL TOURNAMENT ON THE SEVENTEENTH OF THIS MONTH. ALL WHO ATTEND SHOULD BRING
TEN TOTAL.

## 207. Mode: Genocide

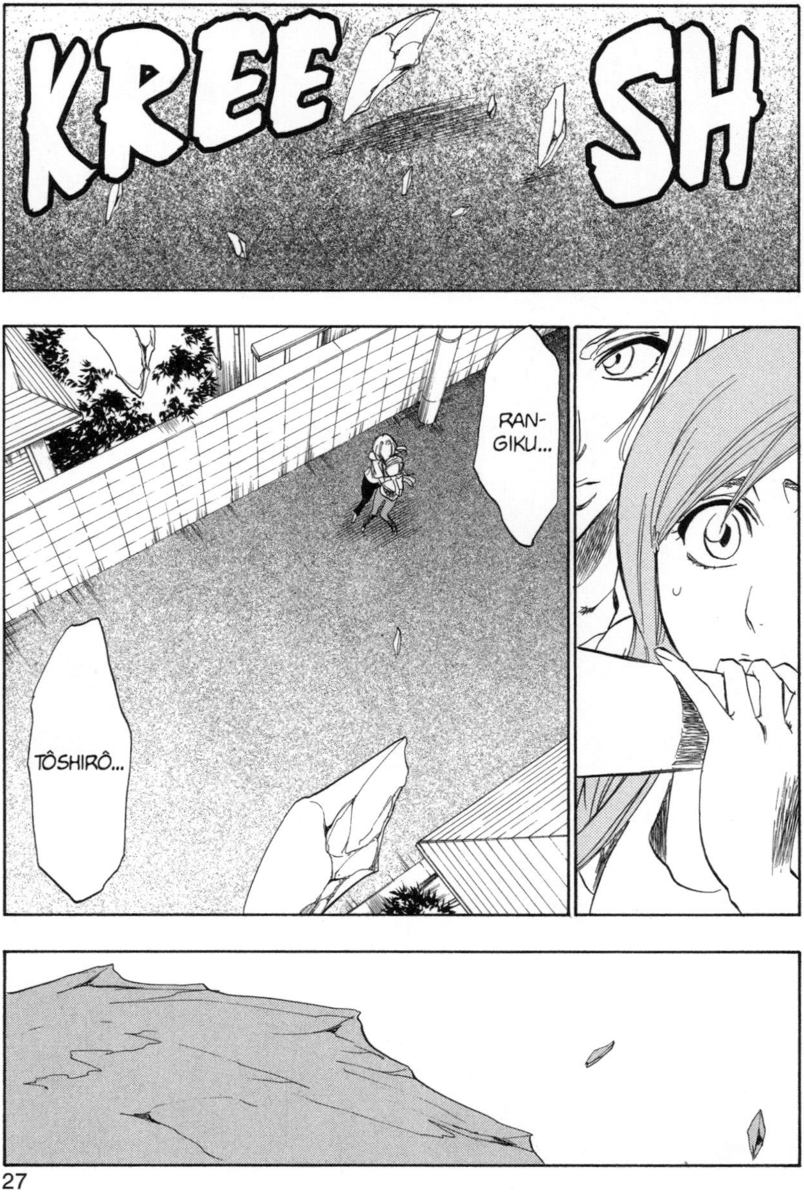
KREE SH
RAN-GIKU...
TÔSHIRÔ...

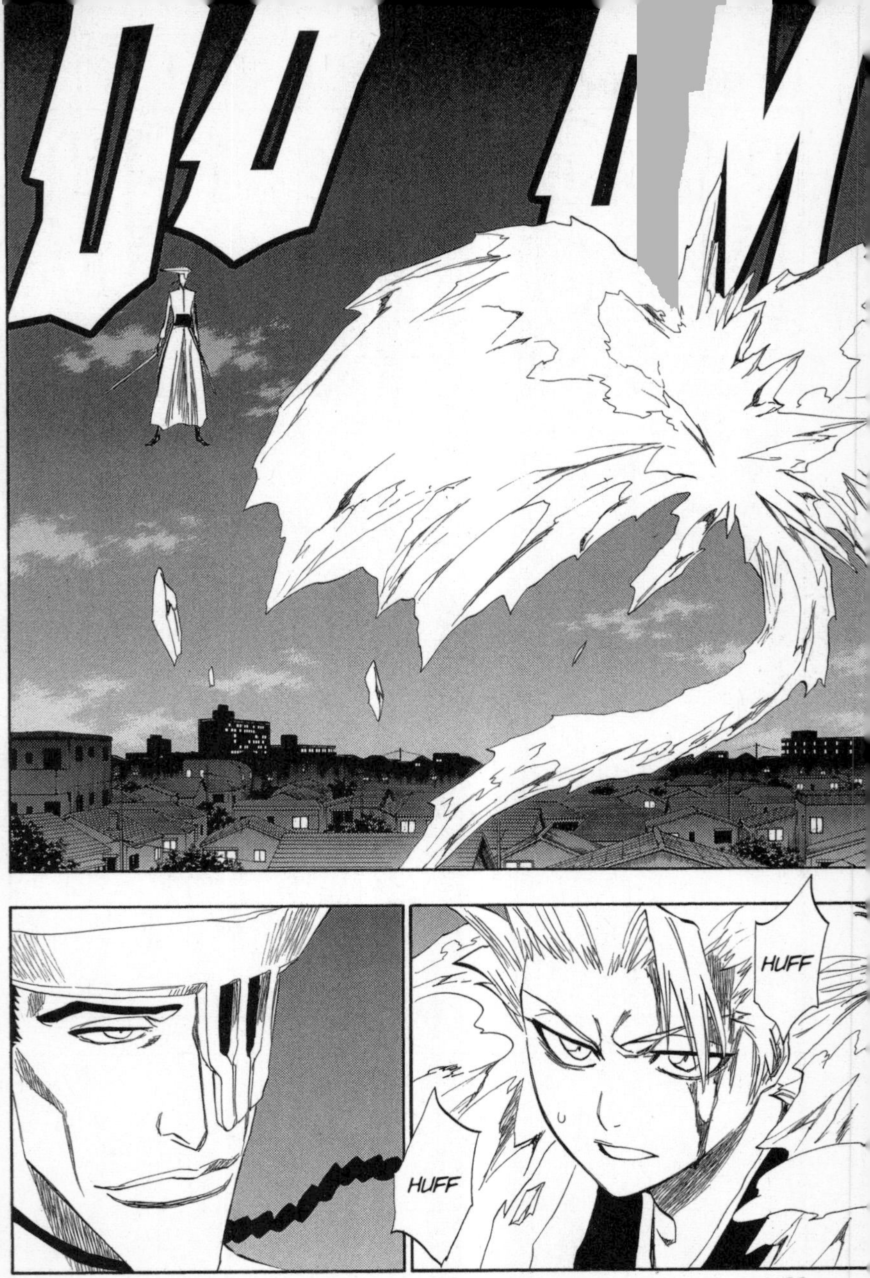
HUFF
HUFF

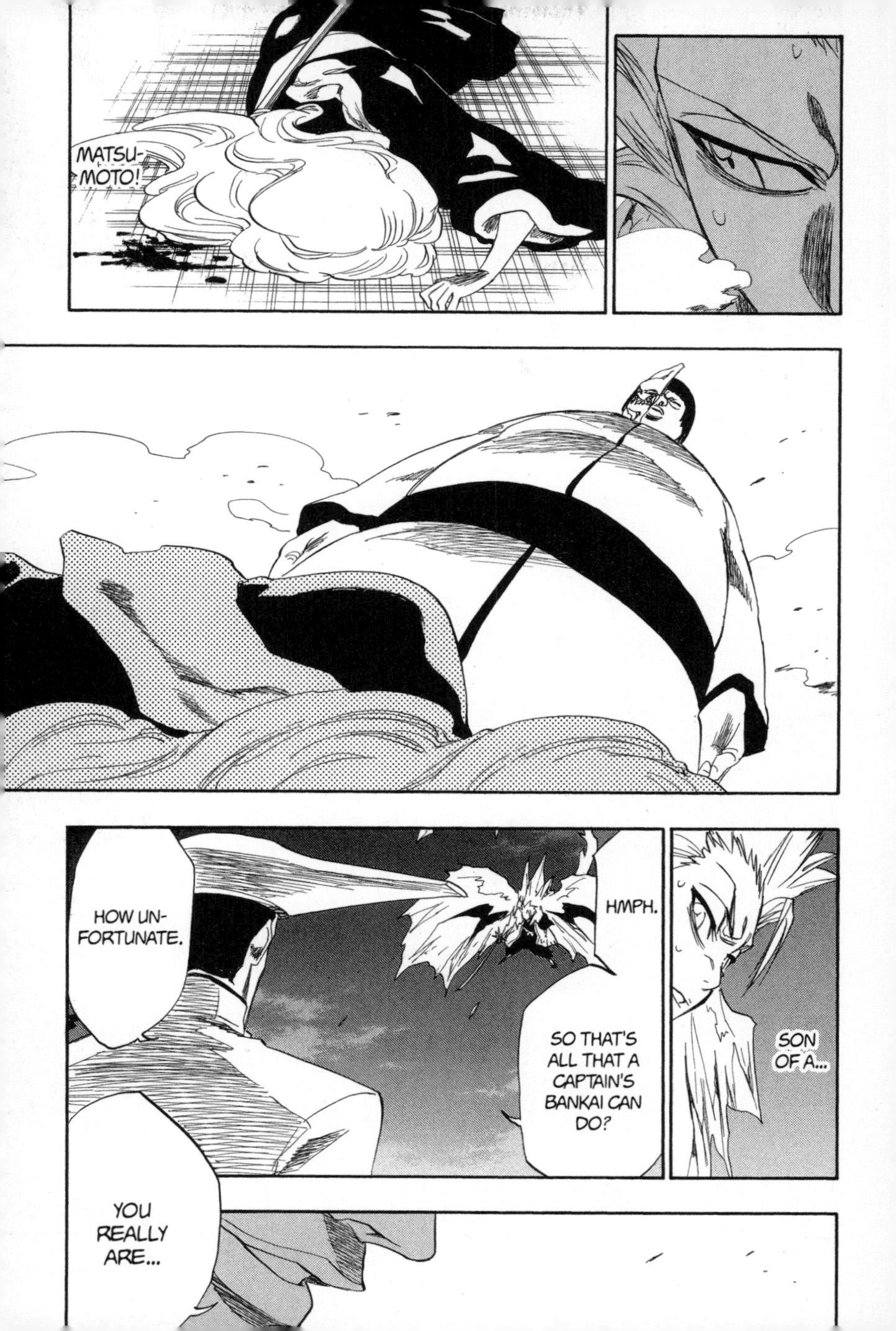
MATSU-MOTO!
SON OF A...
HMPH.
SO THAT'S ALL THAT A CAPTAIN'S BANKAI CAN DO?
HOW UN-FORTUNATE.
YOU REALLY ARE...

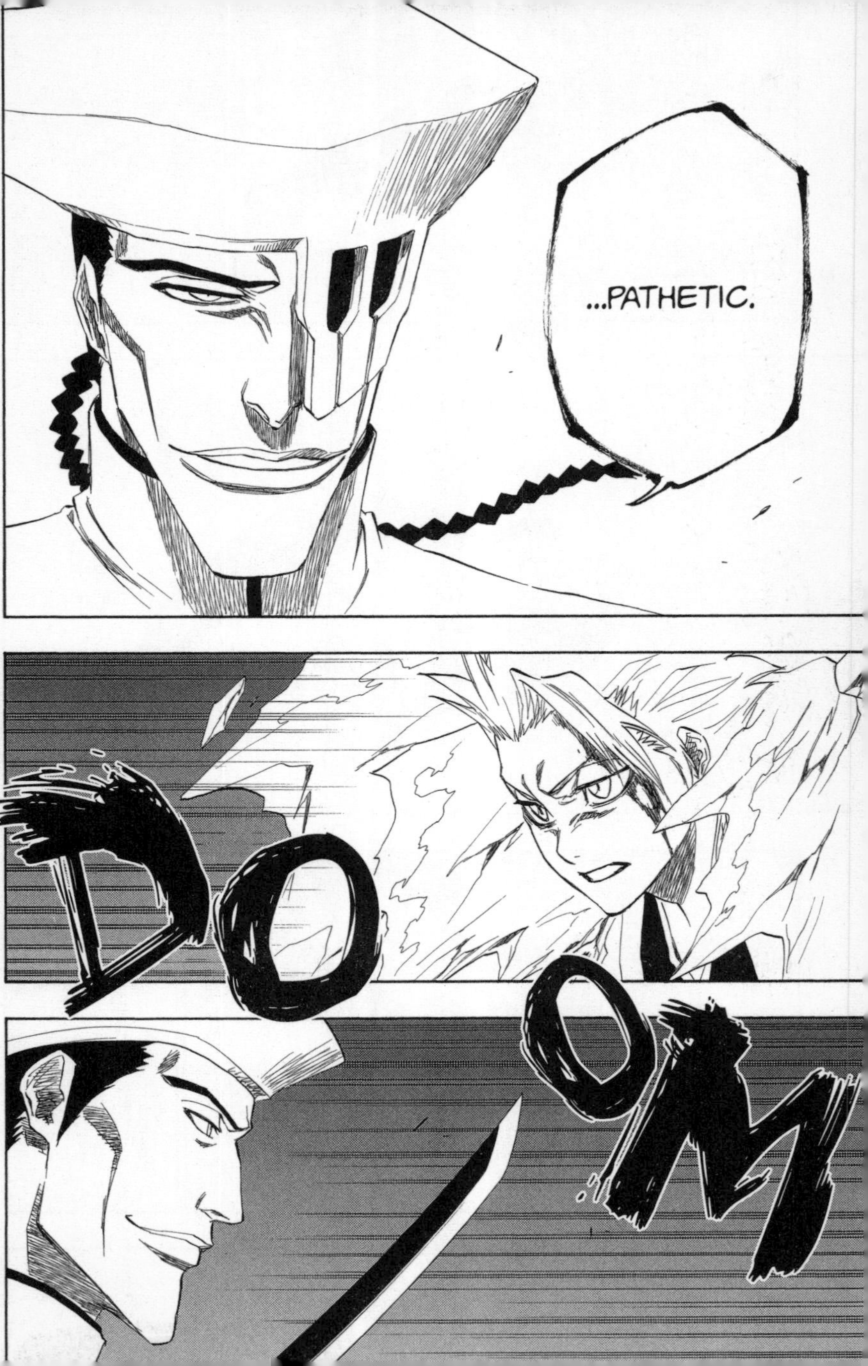
...PATHETIC.
DOOOM

**BLEACH 207. Mode: Genocide**

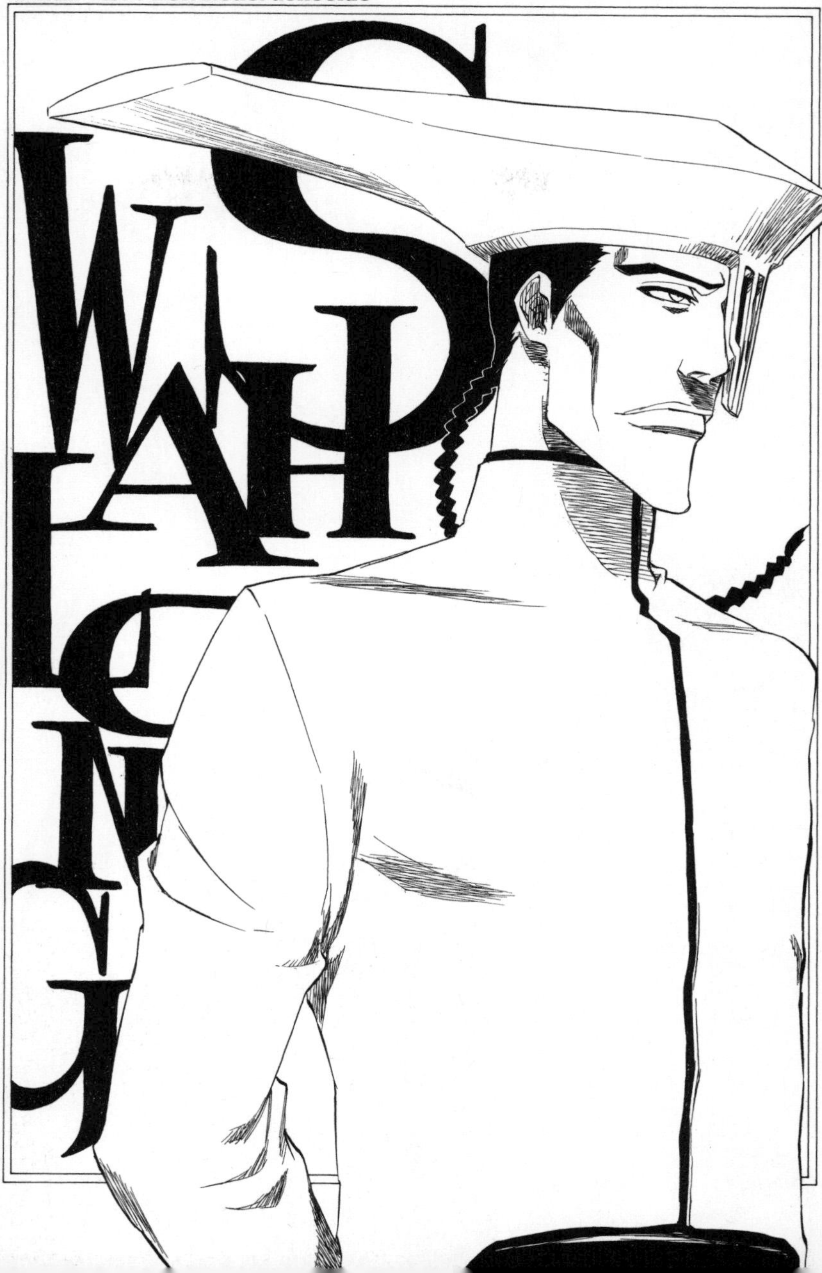

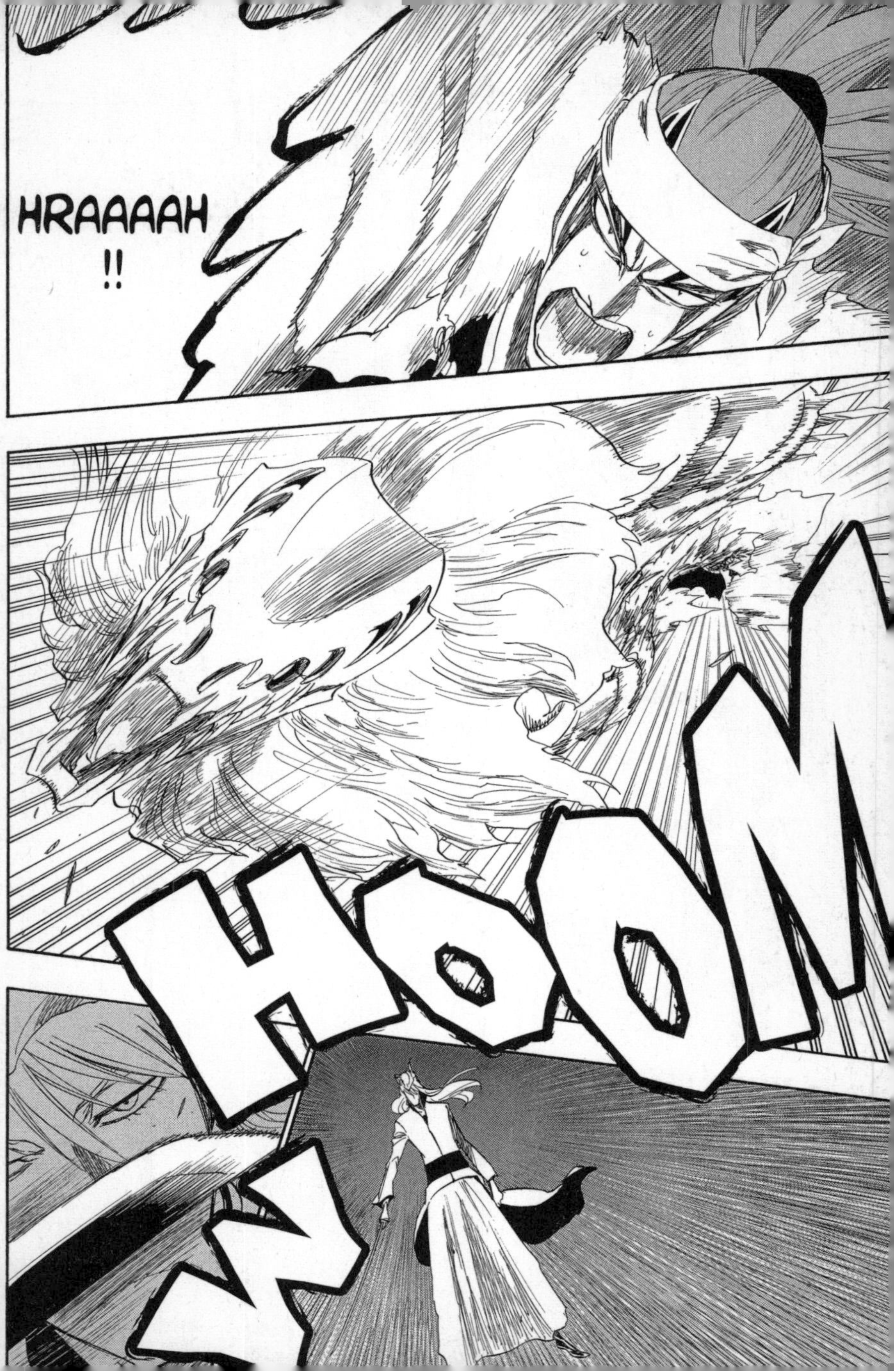
HRAAAAH !!
WHOOM

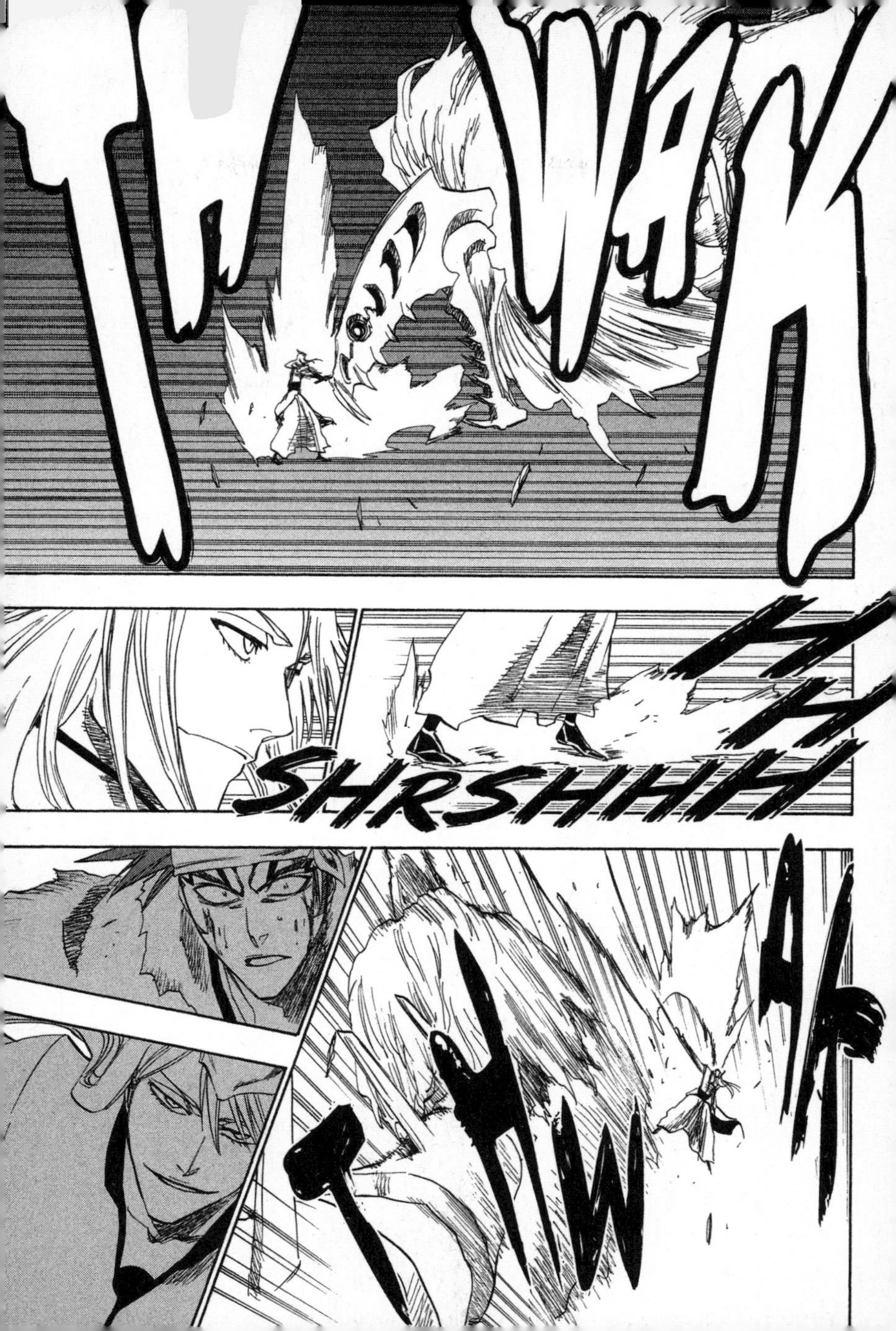
THWACK
SHRSHHH
THWAK

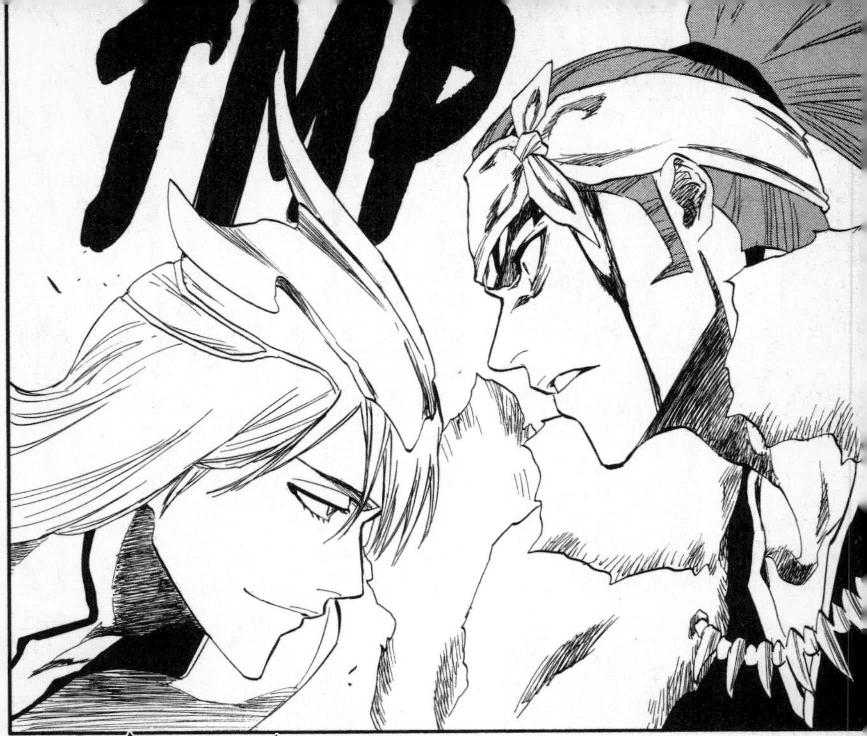
TMP
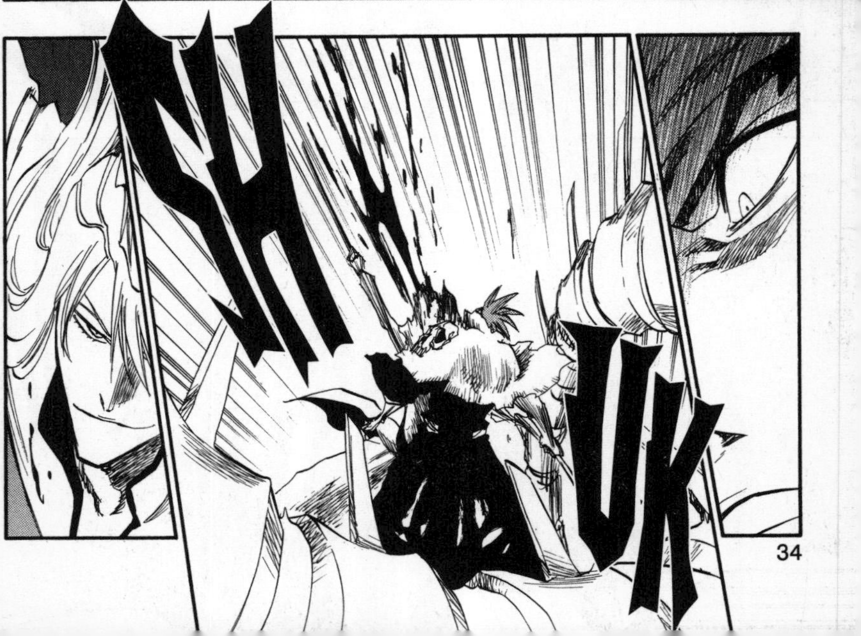
SHHUK

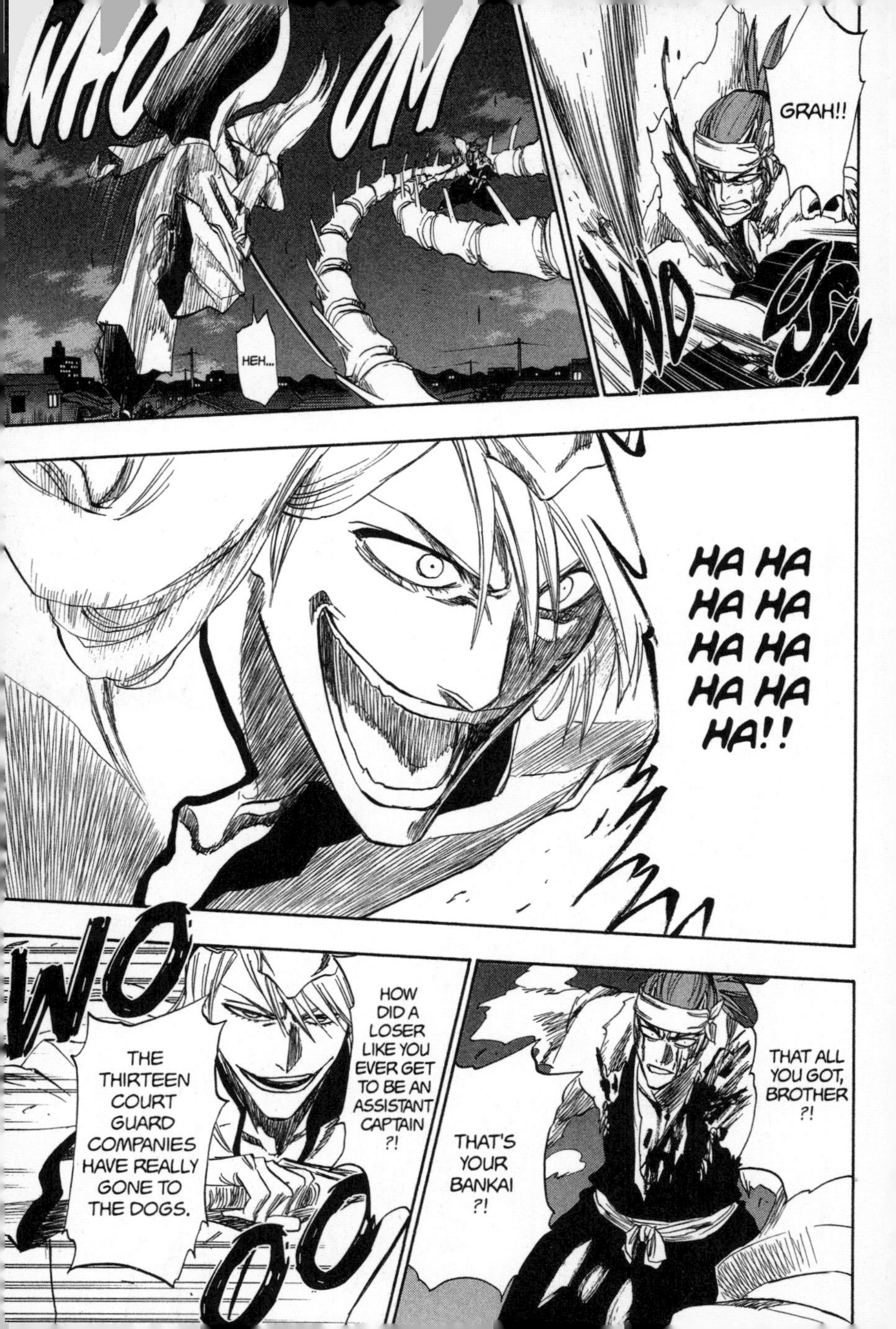
GRAH!!
WOOSH
HEH...
HA HA HA HA HA HA HA HA HA!!
THAT ALL YOU GOT, BROTHER?!
THAT'S YOUR BANKAI?!
HOW DID A LOSER LIKE YOU EVER GET TO BE AN ASSISTANT CAPTAIN?!
THE THIRTEEN COURT GUARD COMPANIES HAVE REALLY GONE TO THE DOGS.
WOOOO

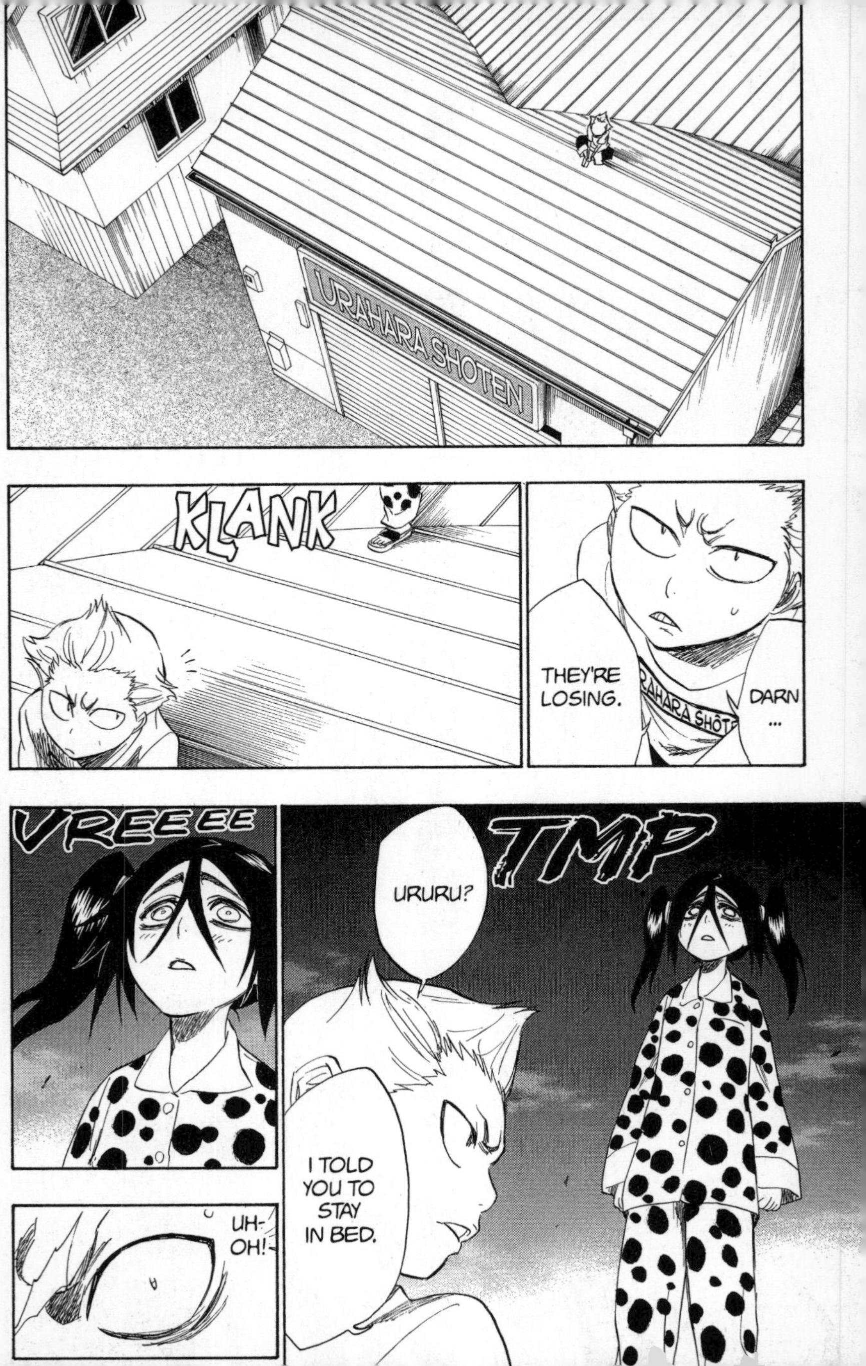
URAHARA SHOTEN
DARN ...
THEY'RE LOSING.
URAHARA SHOT
KLANK
TMP
URURU?
I TOLD YOU TO STAY IN BED.
VREEEEE
UH-OH!

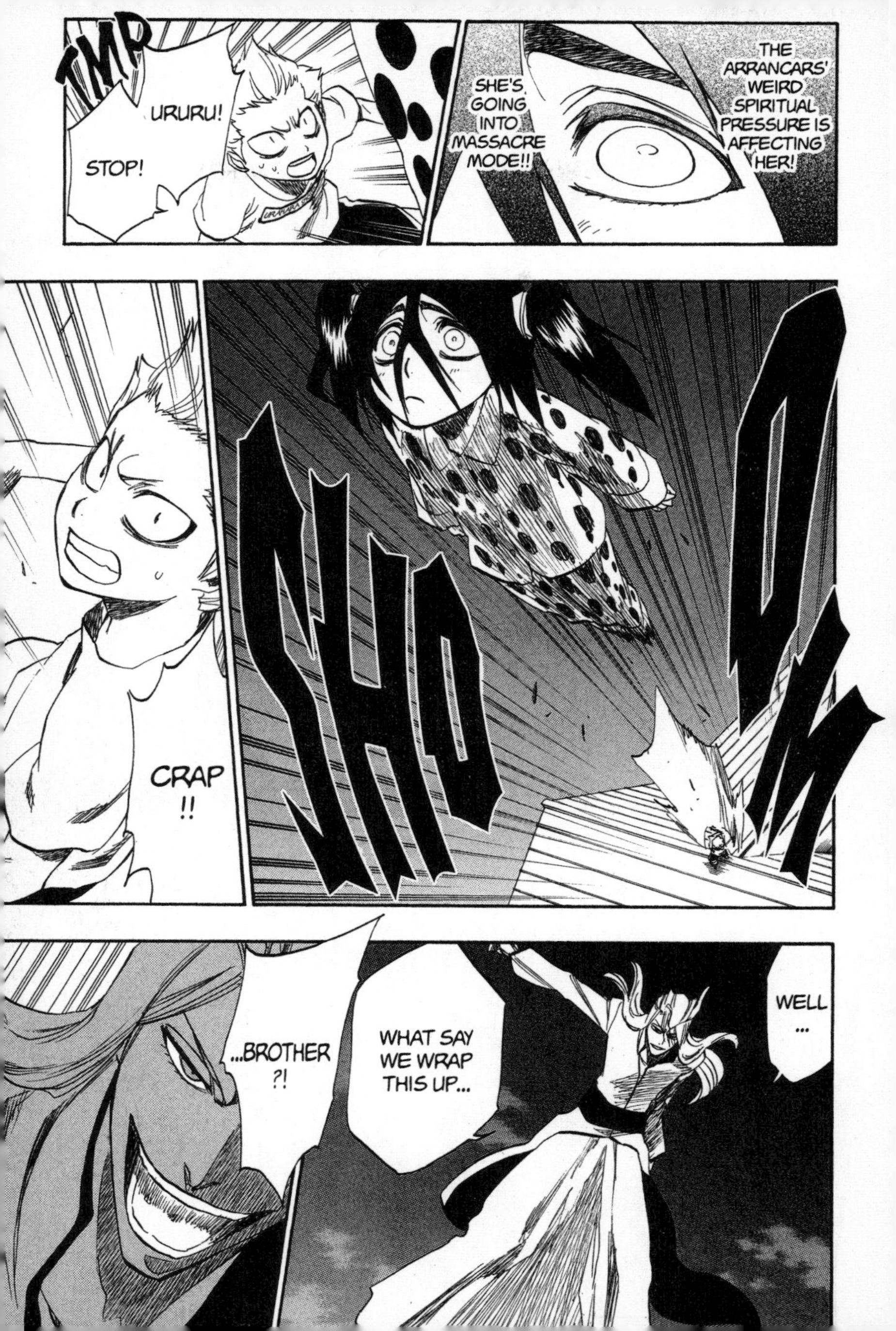
THE ARRANCARS' WEIRD SPIRITUAL PRESSURE IS AFFECTING HER!
SHE'S GOING INTO MASSACRE MODE!!
TMP
URURU!
STOP!
SHOOM
CRAP !!
WELL ...
WHAT SAY WE WRAP THIS UP...
...BROTHER ?!

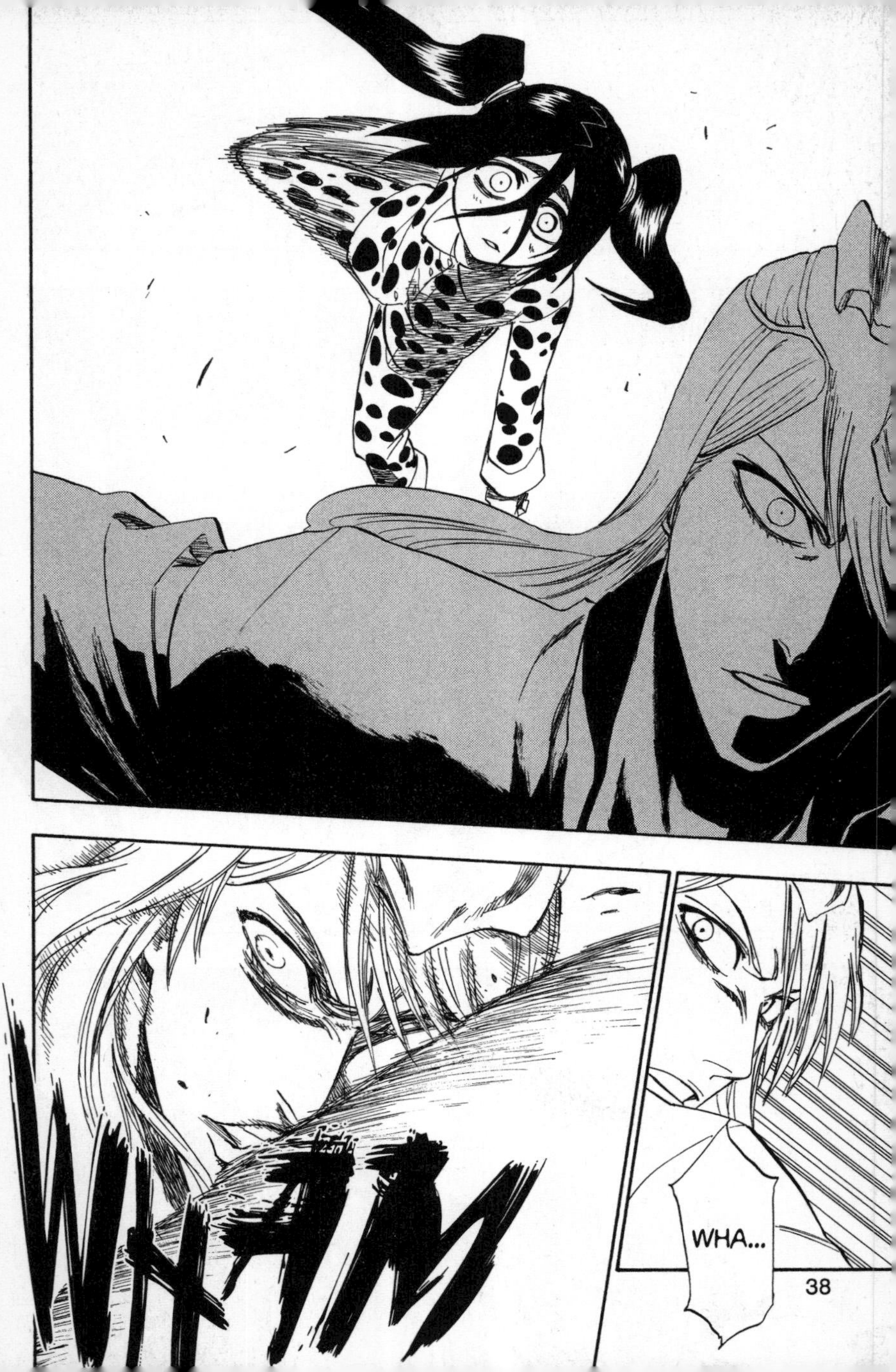
WHA...
WHAM

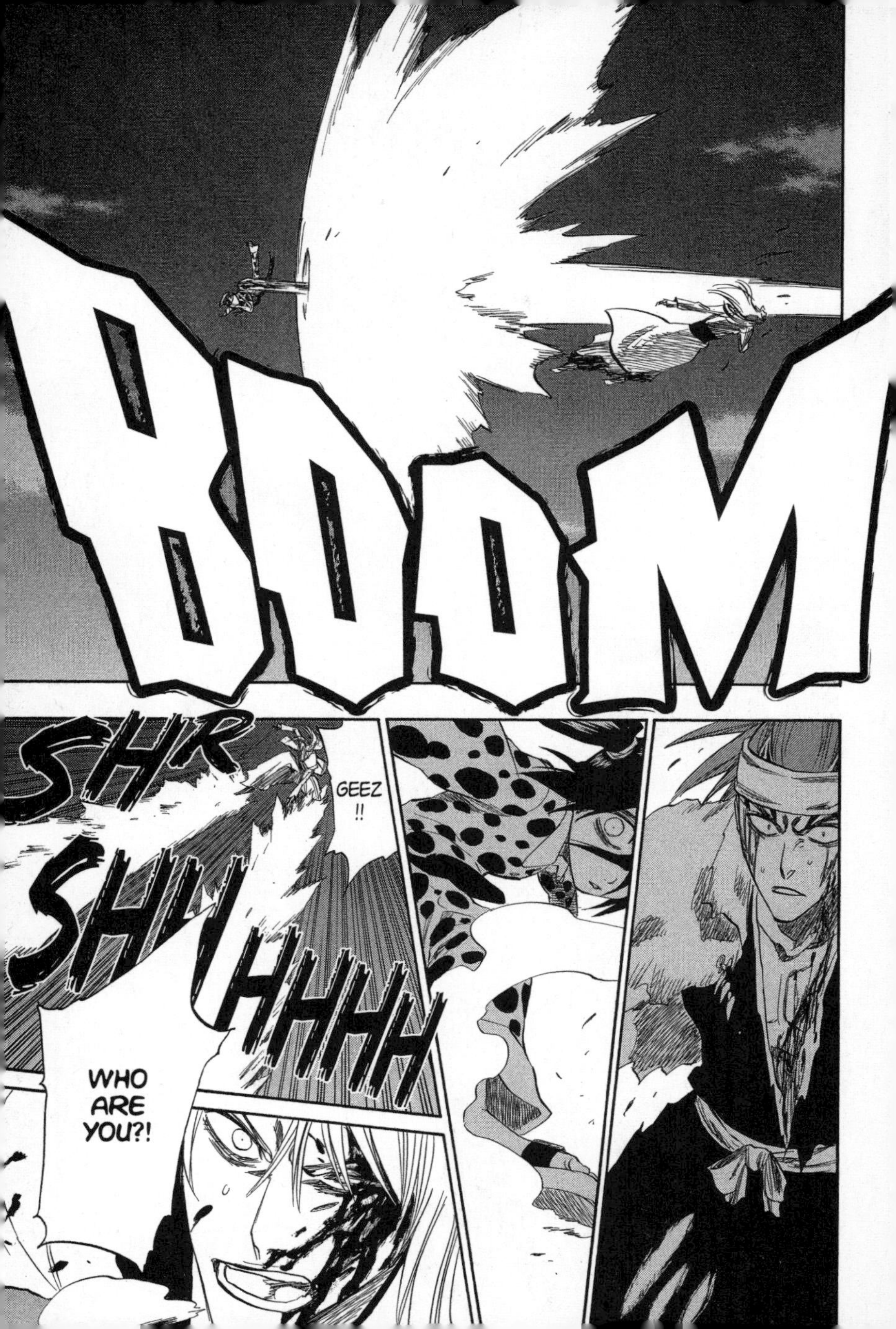
BOOM
GEEZ!!
WHO ARE YOU?!

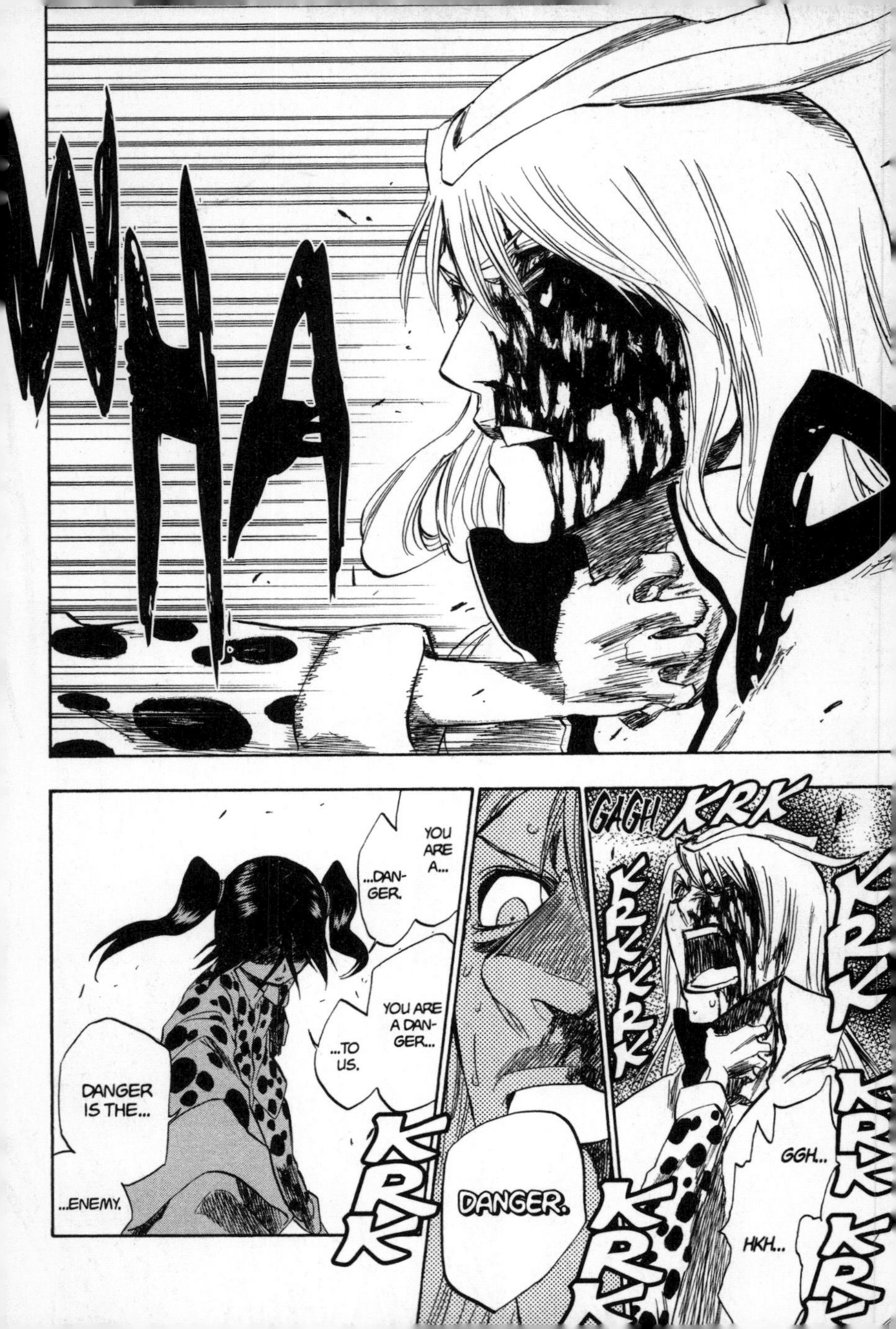
WHAP
GAGH KRK
KRKKRK
KRK KRK KRK KRK
GGH...
HKH...
YOU ARE A...
...DAN-GER.
YOU ARE A DAN-GER...
...TO US.
DANGER.
KRK
KRK
DANGER IS THE...
...ENEMY.

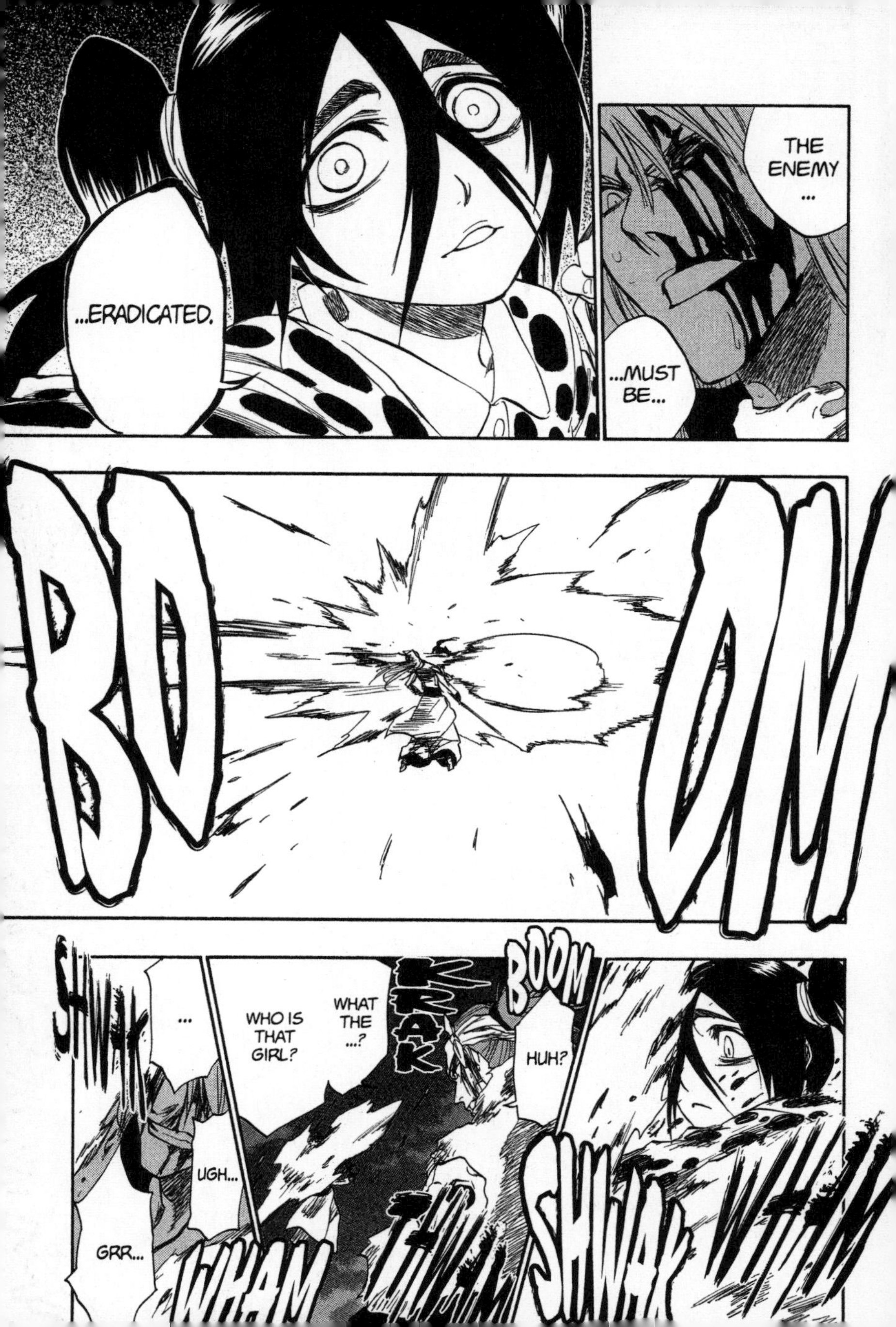
THE ENEMY ...
...MUST BE...
...ERADICATED.
BOOM
HUH?
BOOM
KRAK
WHAT THE ...?
WHO IS THAT GIRL?
...
SHWAK
UGH...
GRR...
SHWAK
WHAM

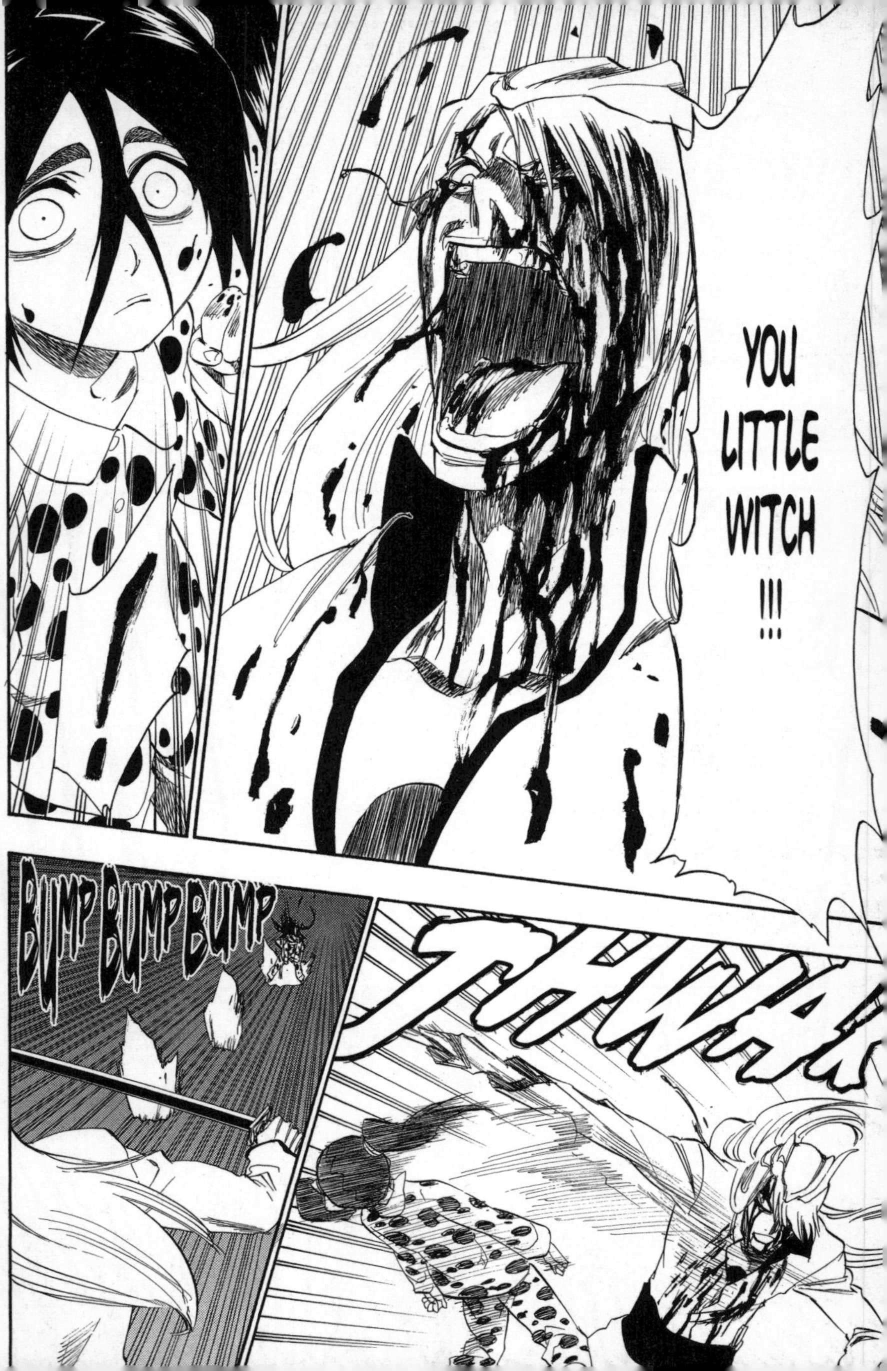
YOU LITTLE WITCH !!!
THWAK
BUMP BUMP BUMP

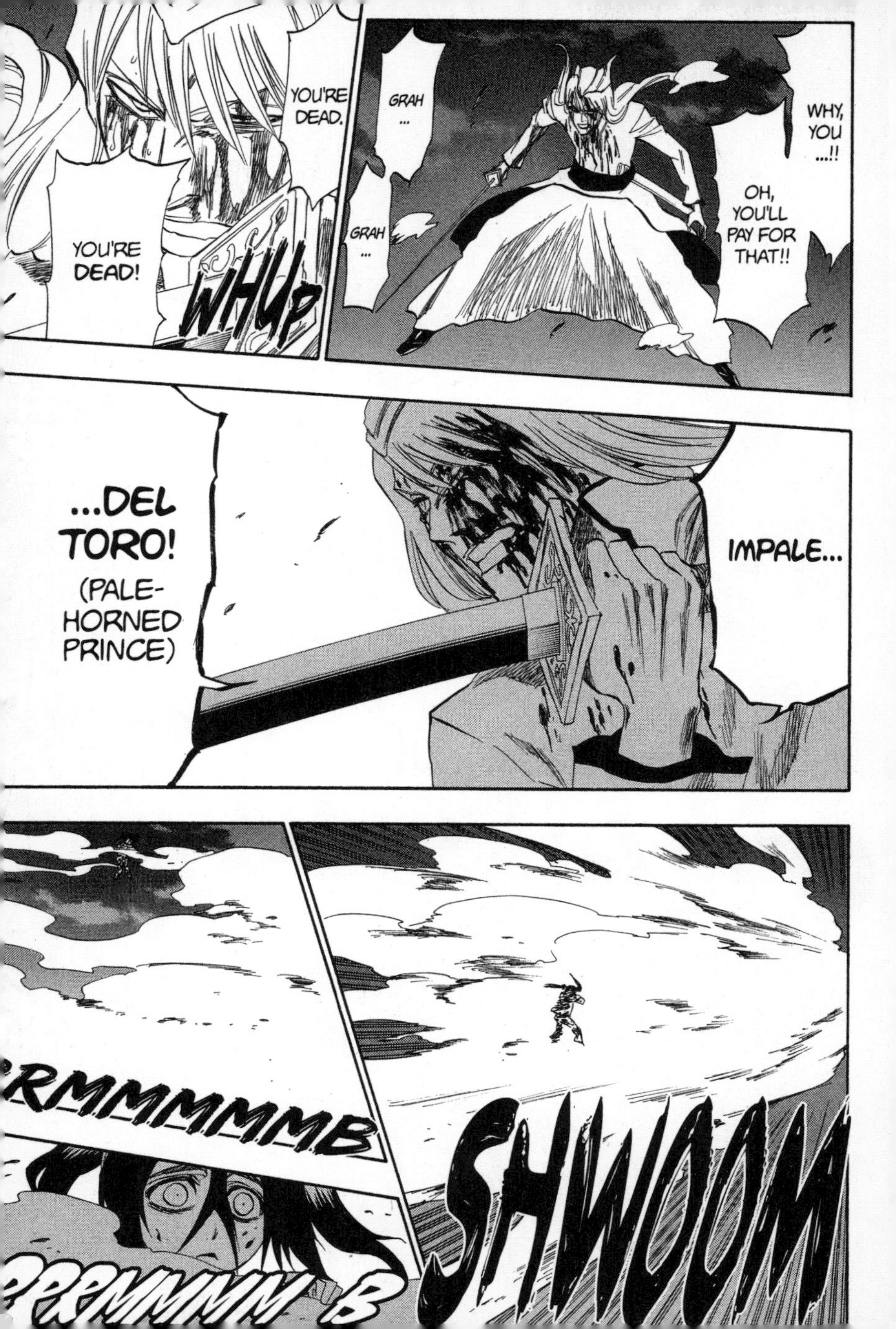
WHY, YOU ...!!
OH, YOU'LL PAY FOR THAT!!
GRAH ...
GRAH ...
YOU'RE DEAD.
YOU'RE DEAD!
WHUP
IMPALE...
...DEL TORO! (PALE-HORNED PRINCE)
SHWOOM
RMMMMMMMB
PPRMMMMM B

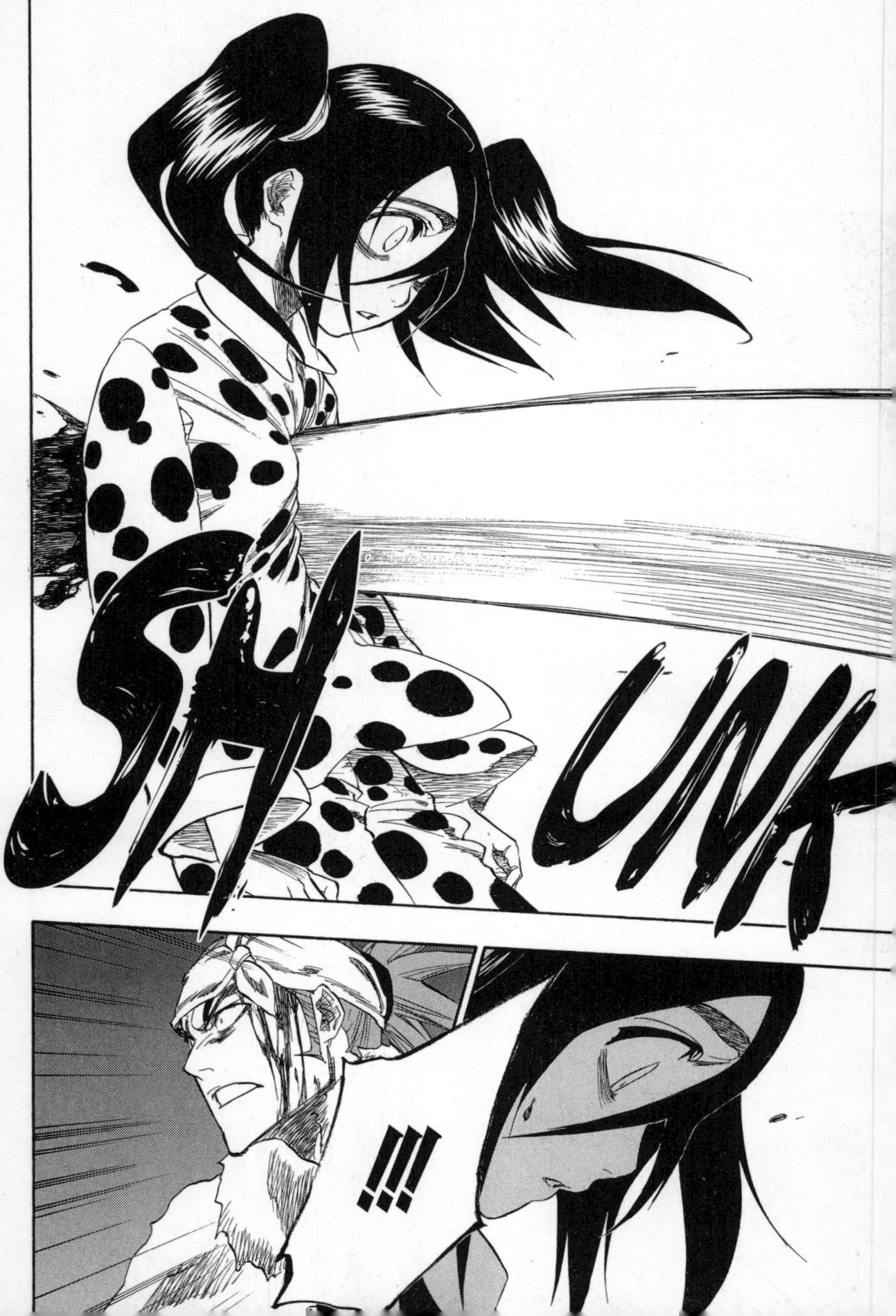
SHUNK
!!!

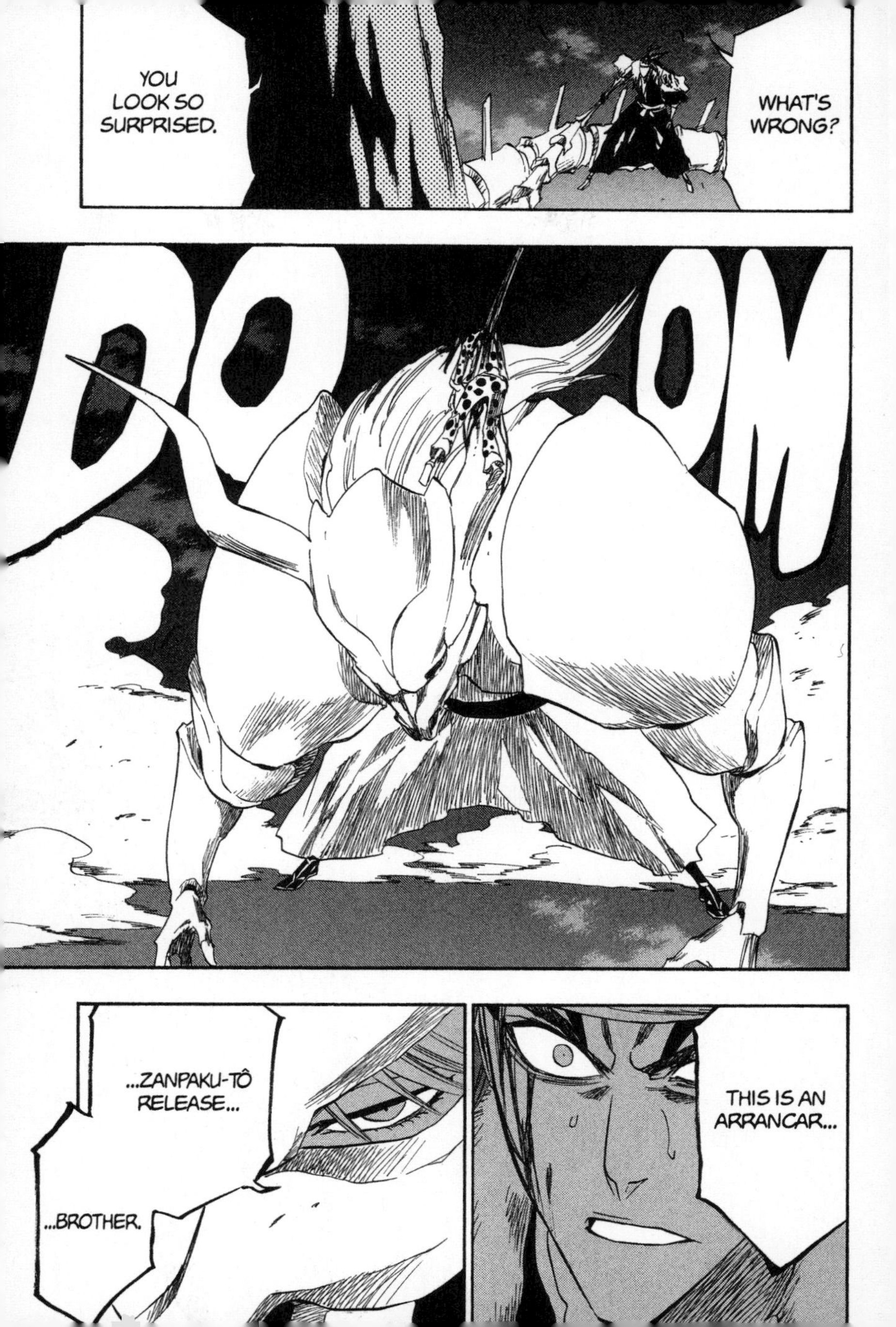
WHAT'S WRONG?
YOU LOOK SO SURPRISED.
DOOM
THIS IS AN ARRANCAR...
...ZANPAKU-TÔ RELEASE...
...BROTHER.

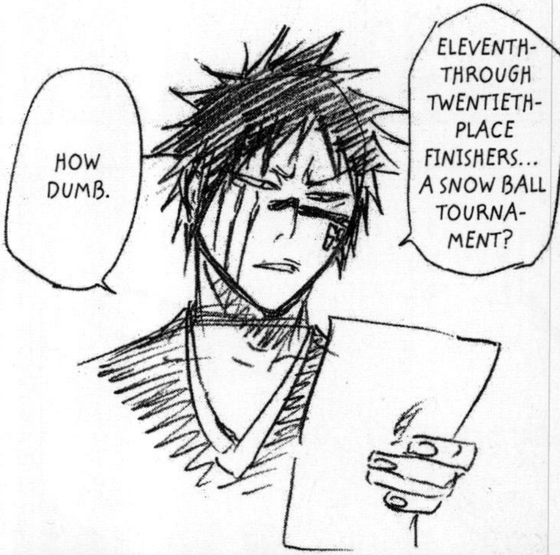
ELEVENTH- THROUGH TWENTIETH- PLACE FINISHERS... A SNOW BALL TOURNA- MENT?
HOW DUMB.

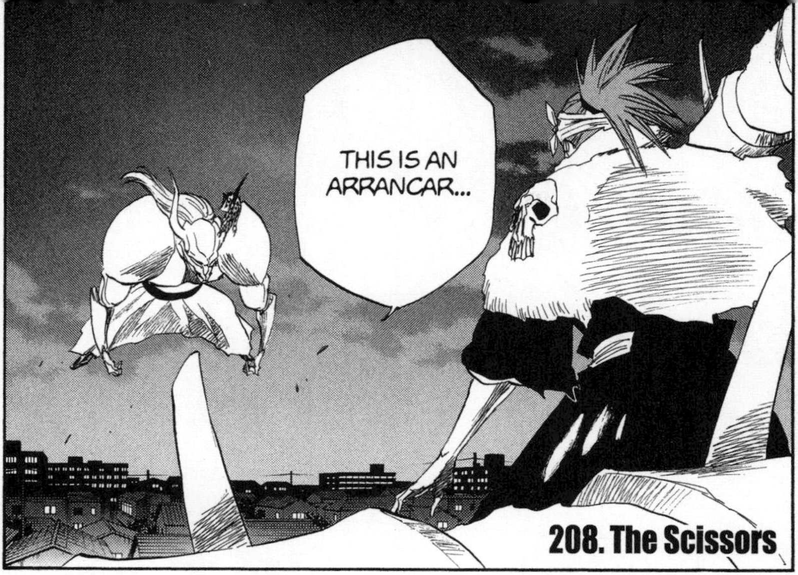
THIS IS AN ARRANCAR...

## 208. The Scissors

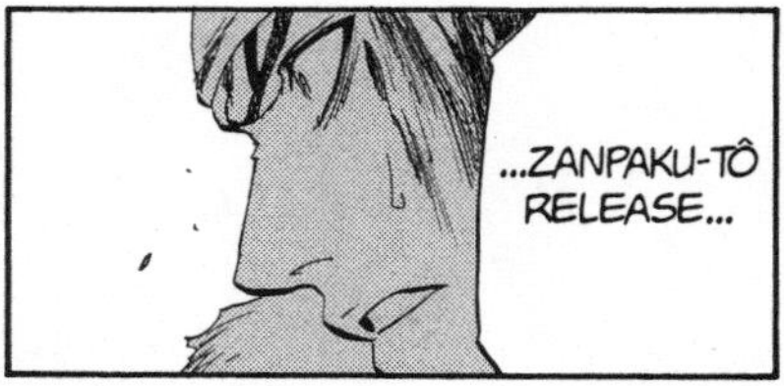
...ZANPAKU-TÔ RELEASE...

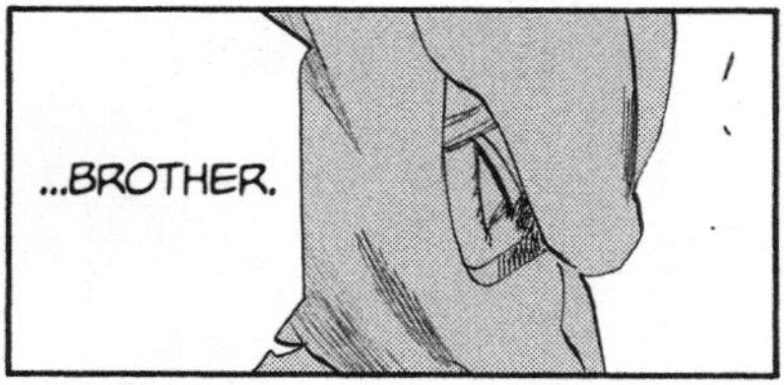
...BROTHER.

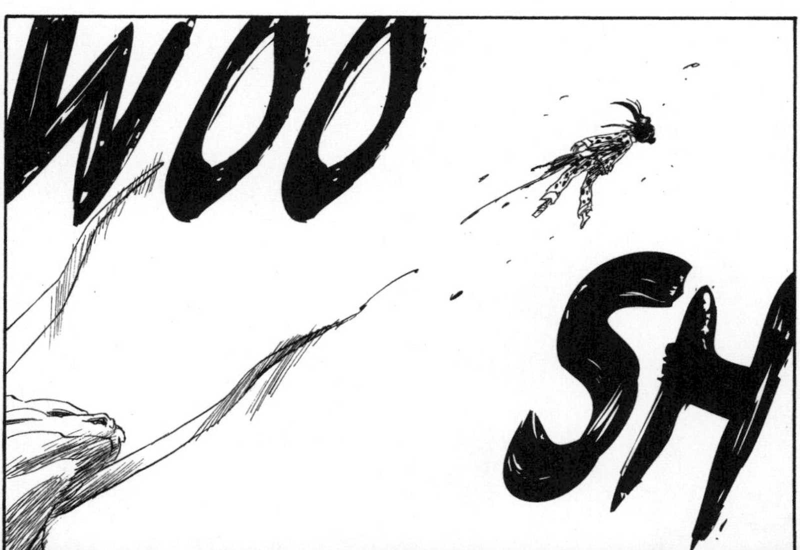
WOO
SH

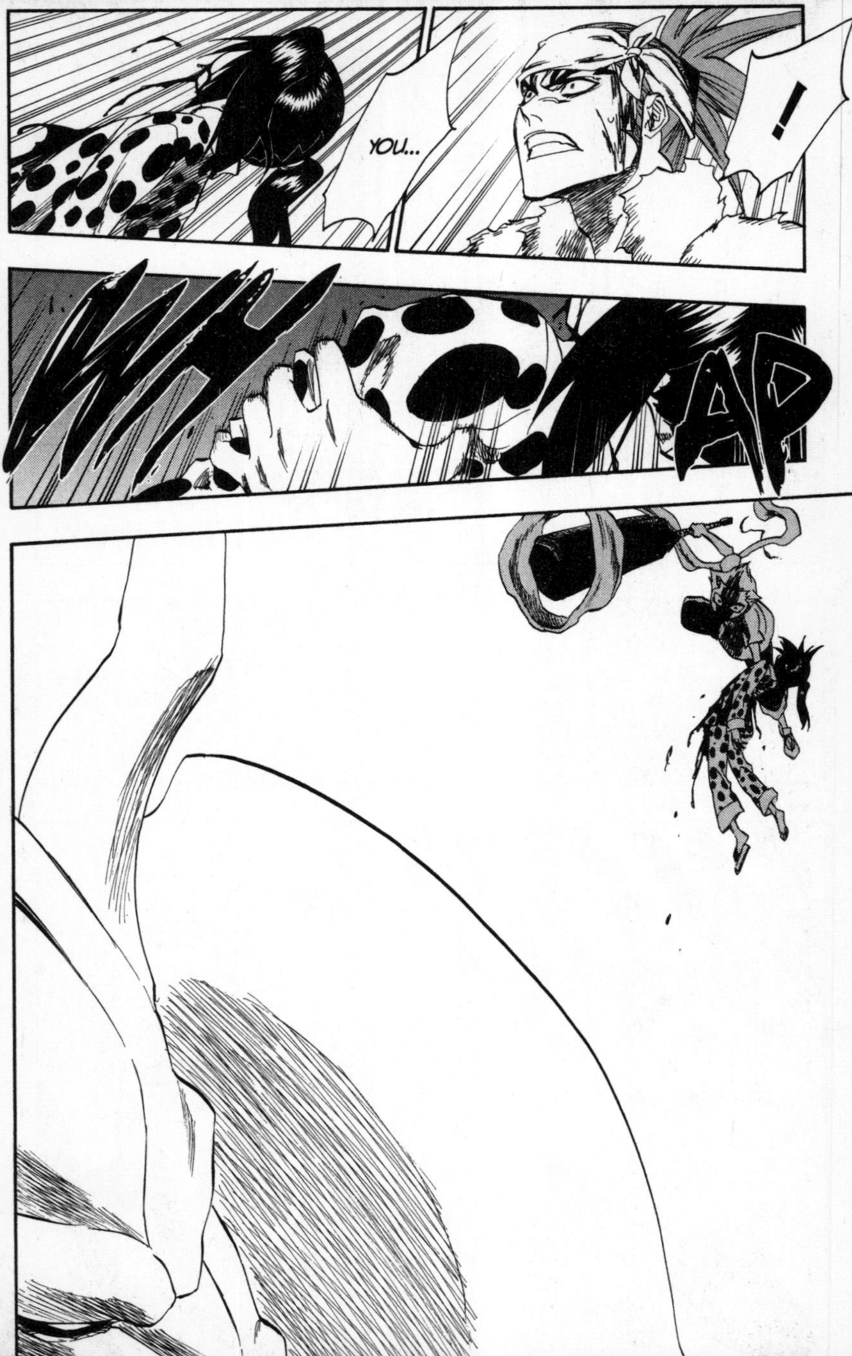
!
YOU...
WHAP

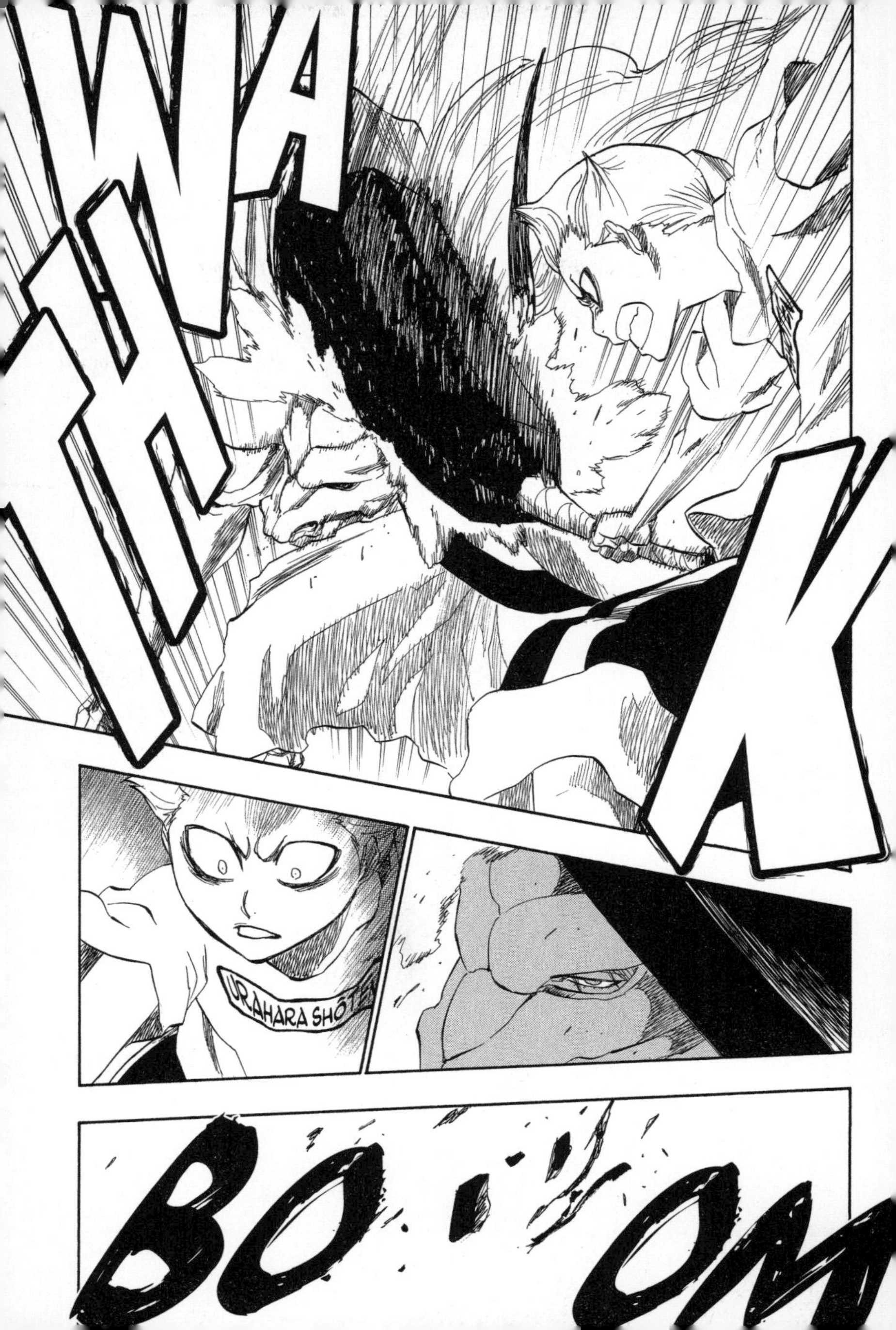
WHAK
URAHARA SHŌTEN
BOOM

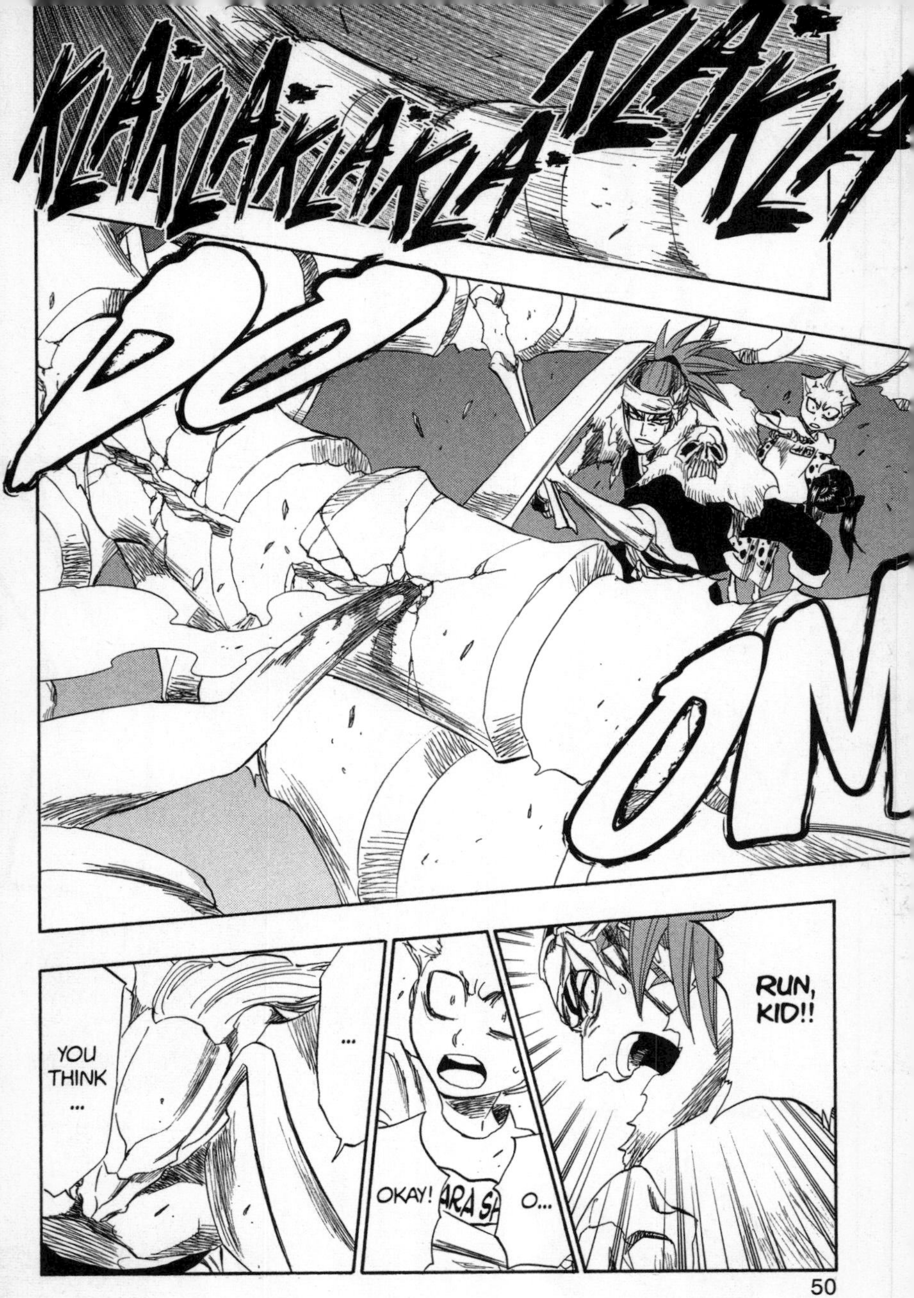
KLAKLA
KLAKLAKLAKLAKLA
DO
OM
RUN, KID!!
O...
...
OKAY!
YOU THINK ...

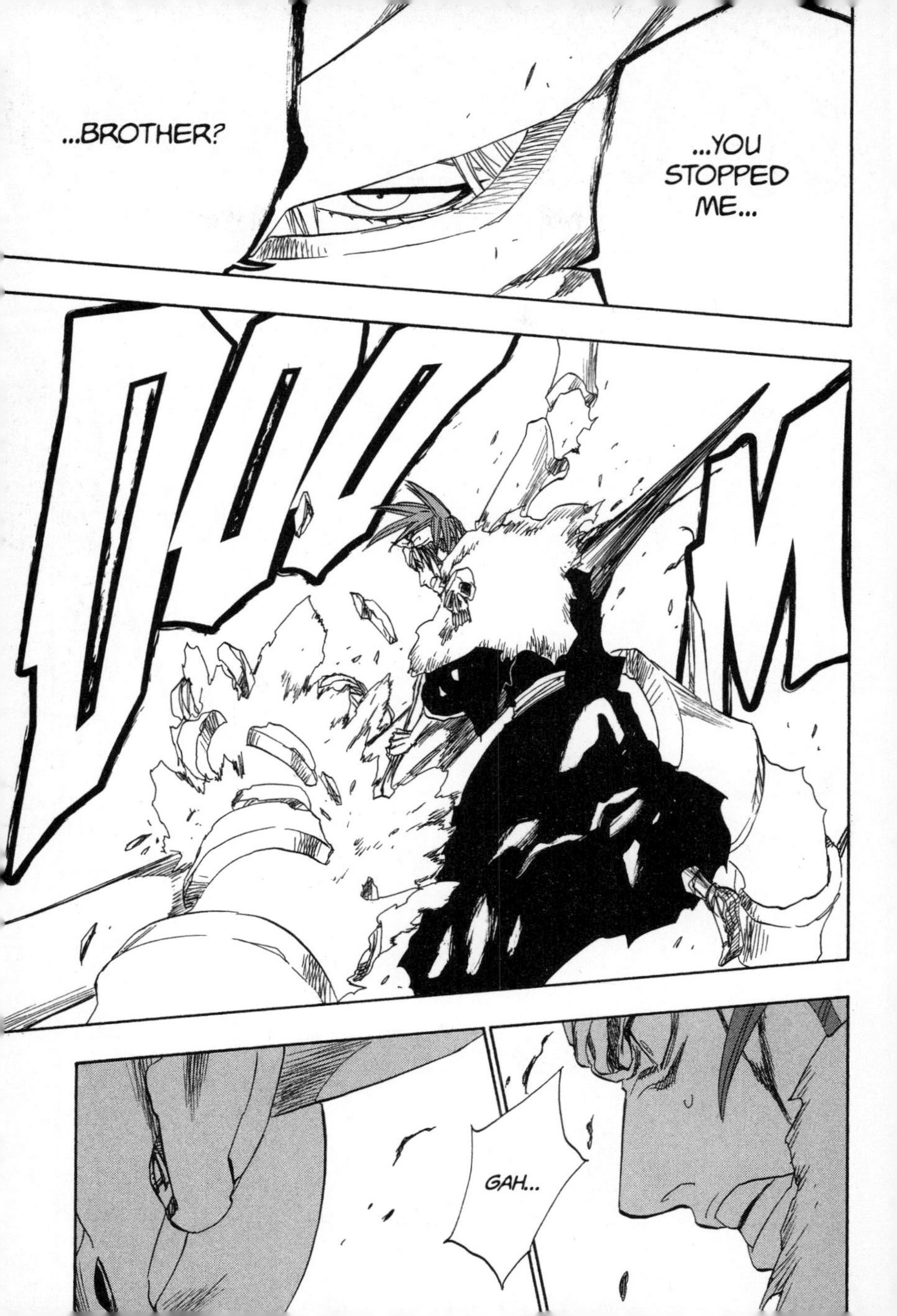
...YOU STOPPED ME...
...BROTHER?
DOOM
GAH...

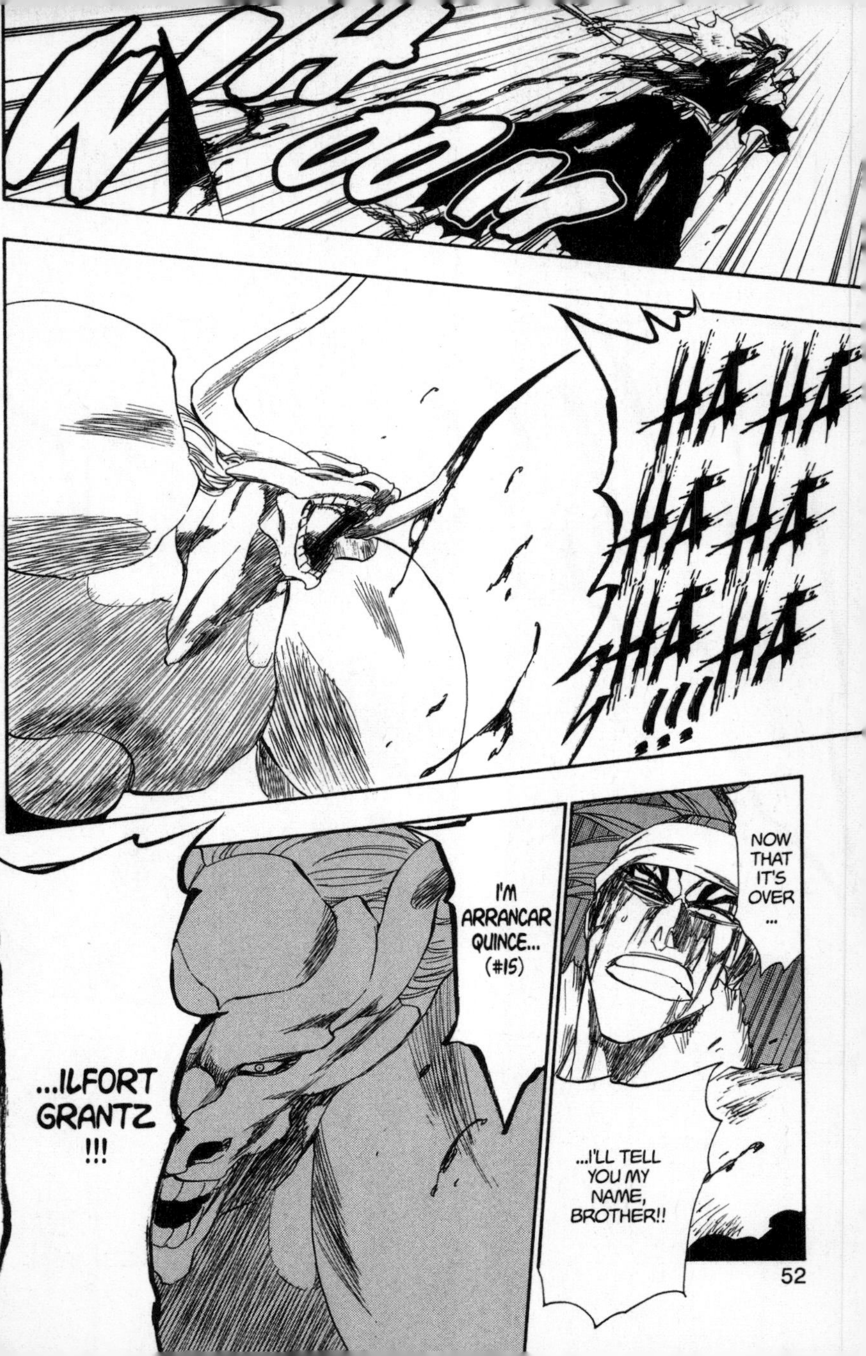
WHOOM
HAHA HAHA HAHA HAHA!!!
NOW THAT IT'S OVER...
...I'LL TELL YOU MY NAME, BROTHER!!
I'M ARRANCAR QUINCE... (#15)
...ILFORT GRANTZ!!!

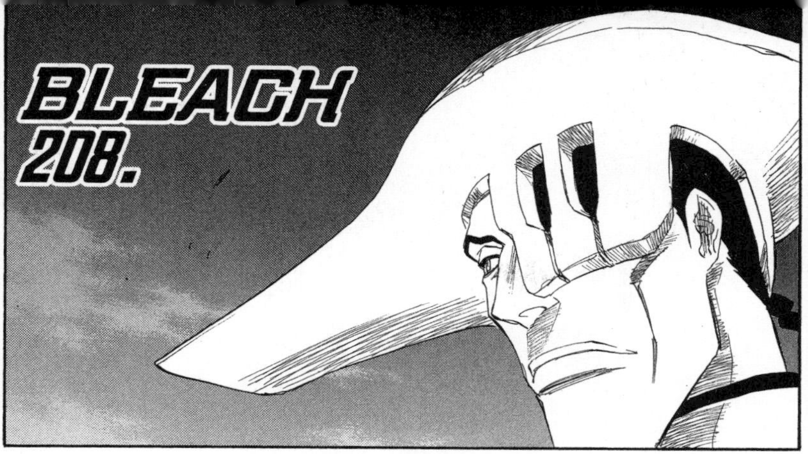
BLEACH
208.

## The Scissors

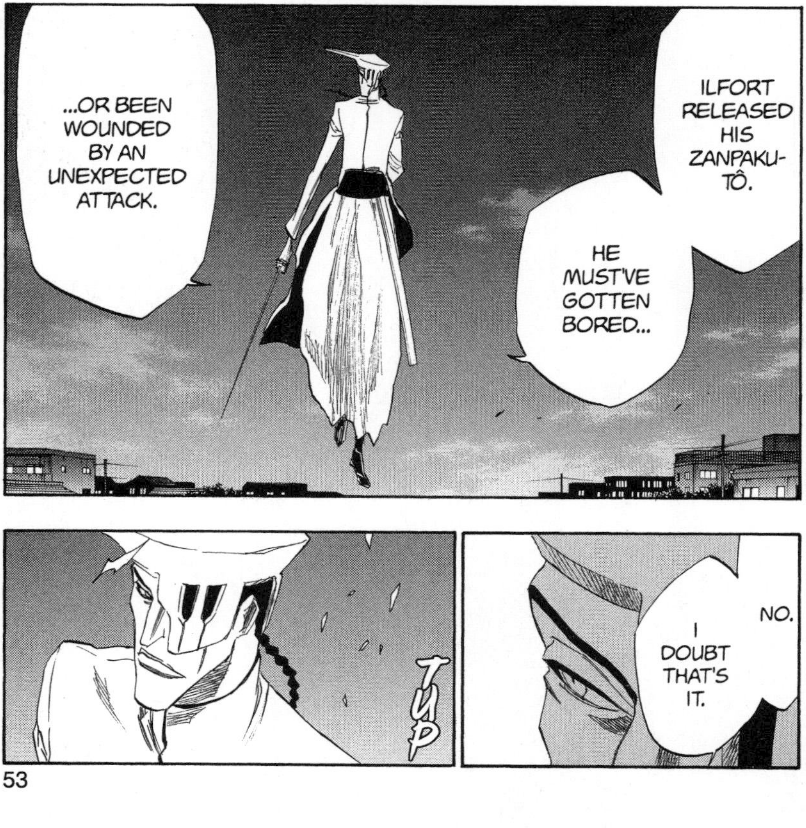
ILFORT RELEASED HIS ZANPAKU-TÔ.
HE MUST'VE GOTTEN BORED...
...OR BEEN WOUNDED BY AN UNEXPECTED ATTACK.
NO.
I DOUBT THAT'S IT.
TUP

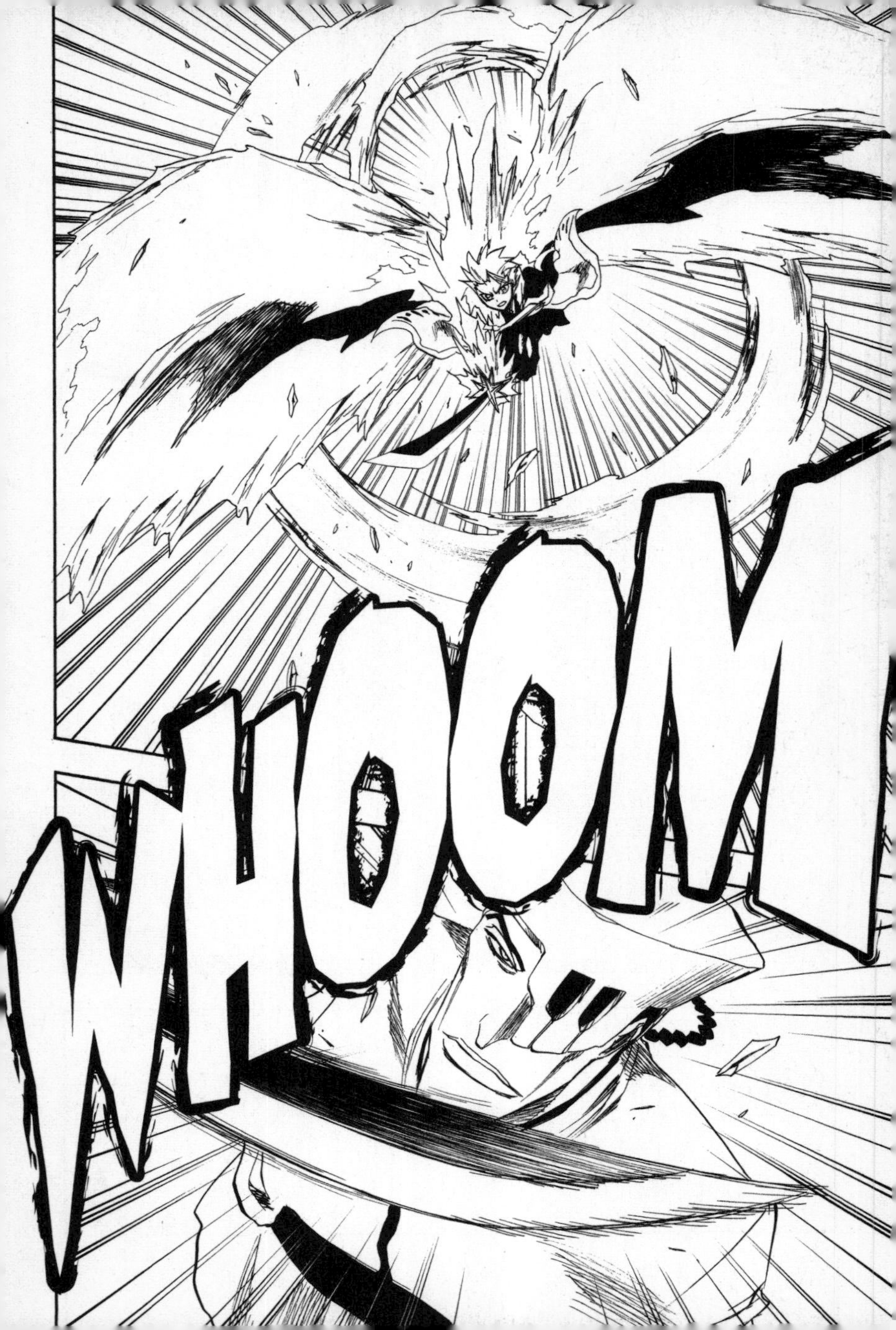
WHOOM

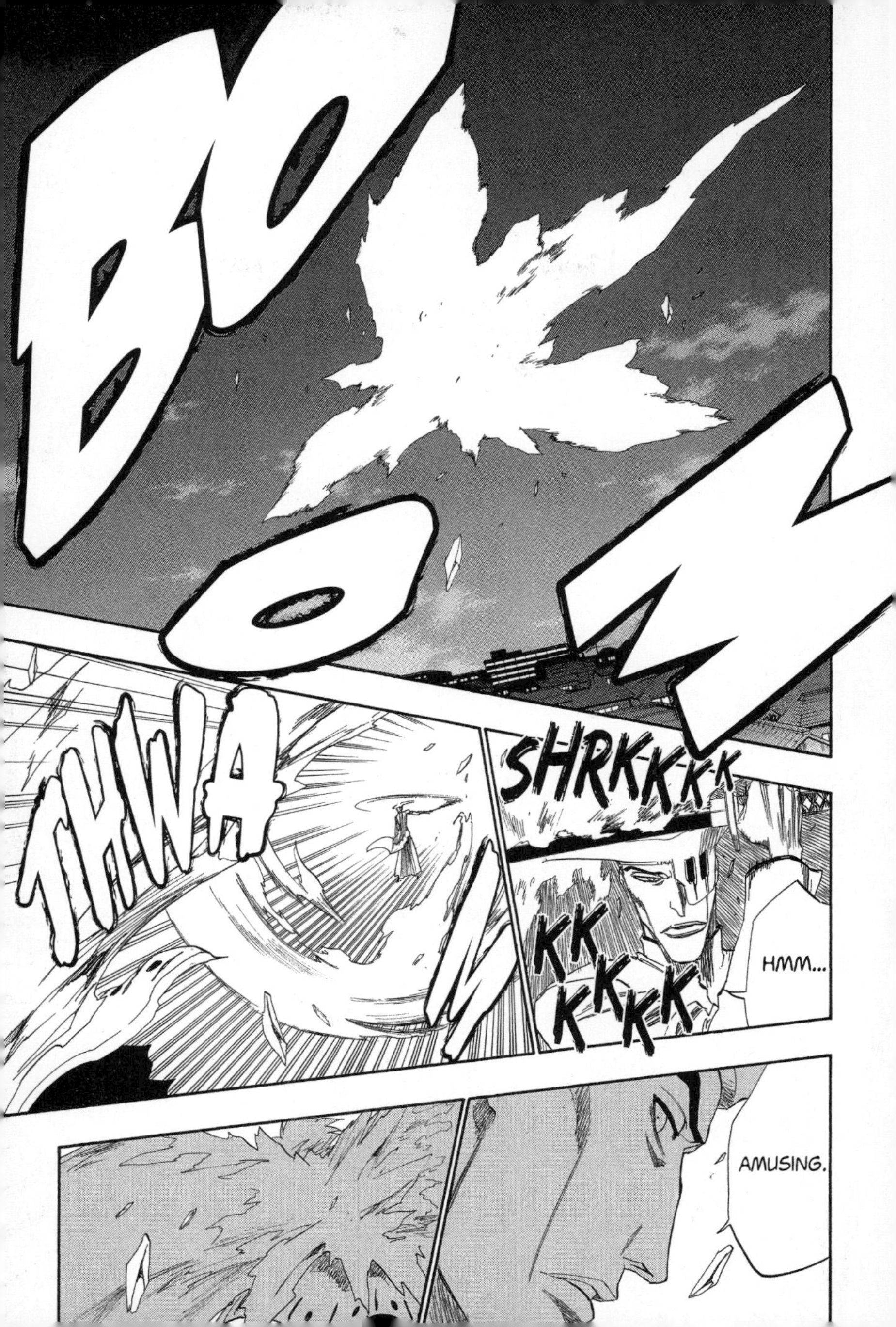
BOOM
SHRK-K-K-K
KK
KKKK
HMM...
THWA
AMUSING.

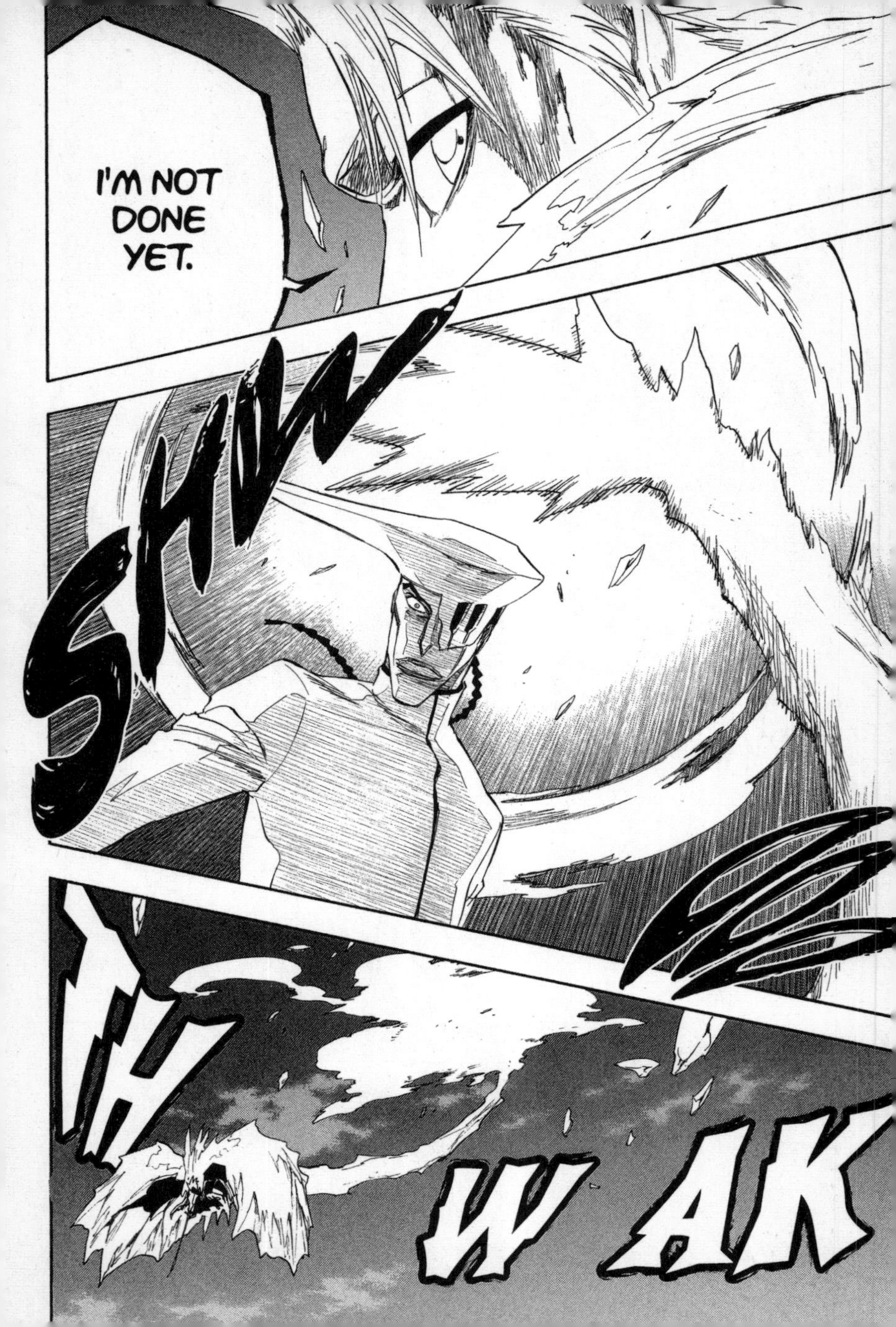
I'M NOT DONE YET.
SHW
THWAK

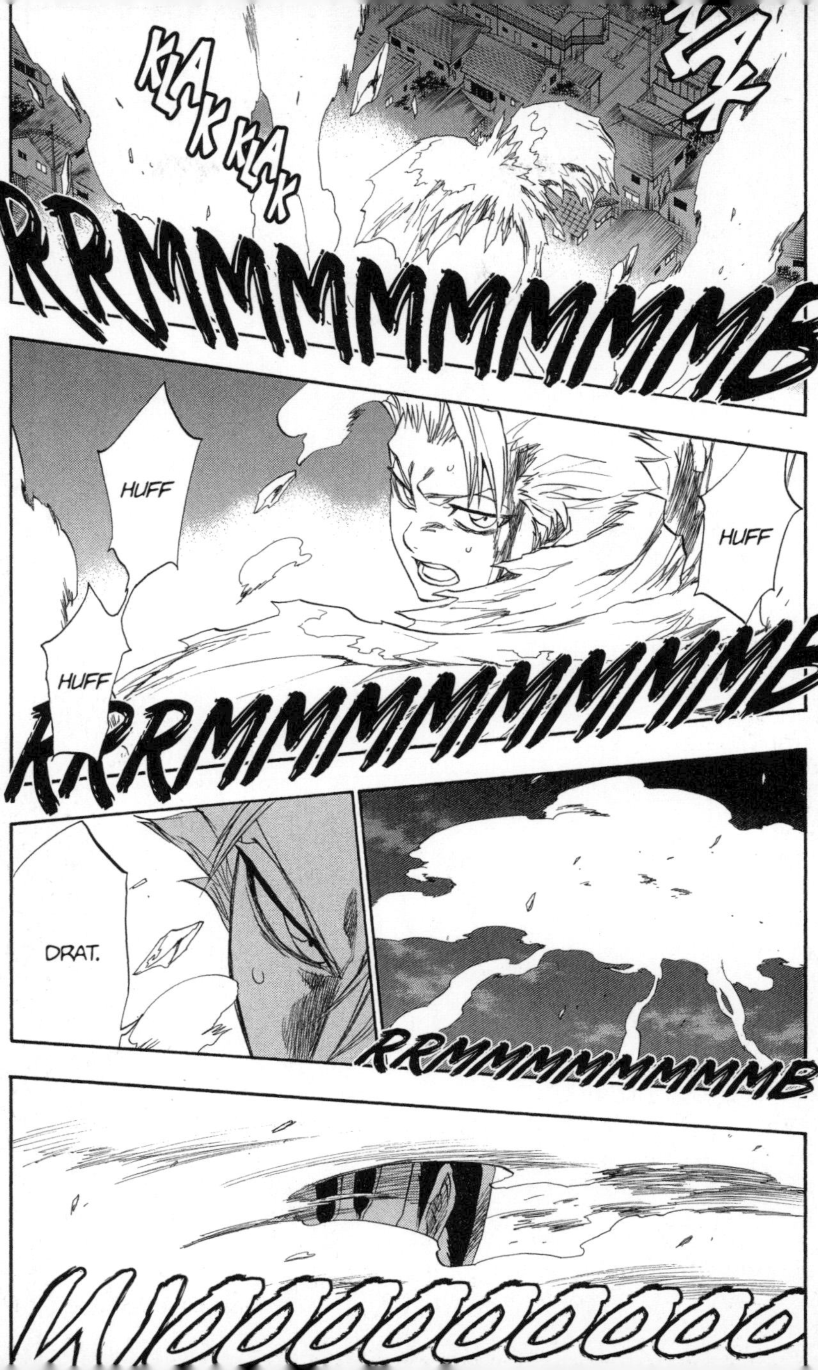

KLAK
KLAK KLAK
RRMMMMMMMMMB
HUFF
HUFF
HUFF
RRRMMMMMMMMMMB
DRAT.
RRMMMMMMMMMB
WHOOOOOOOOOO

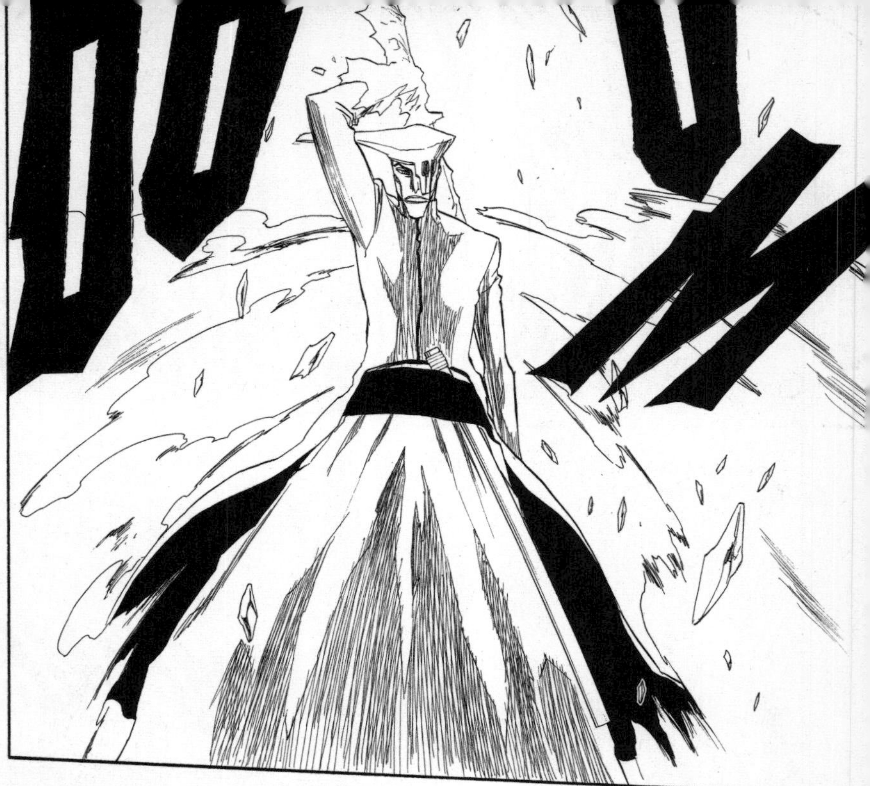
DOOM
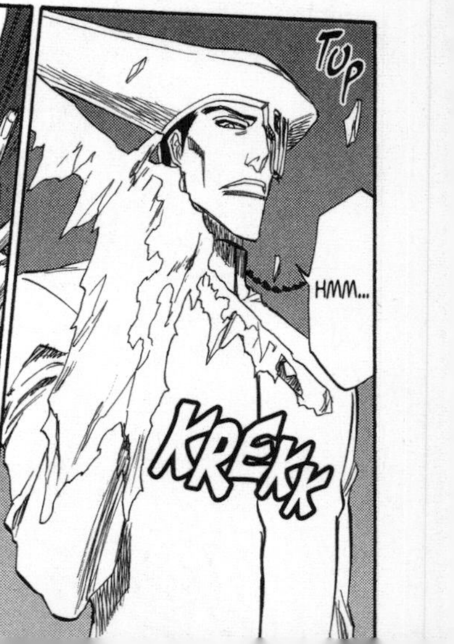
TUP
HMM...
KREKK
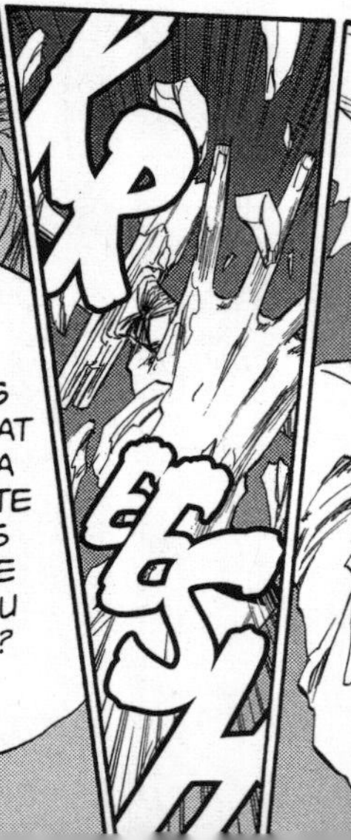
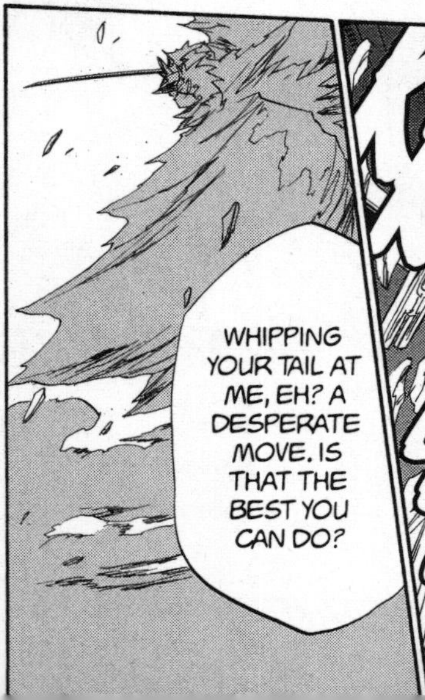
WHIPPING YOUR TAIL AT ME, EH? A DESPERATE MOVE. IS THAT THE BEST YOU CAN DO?

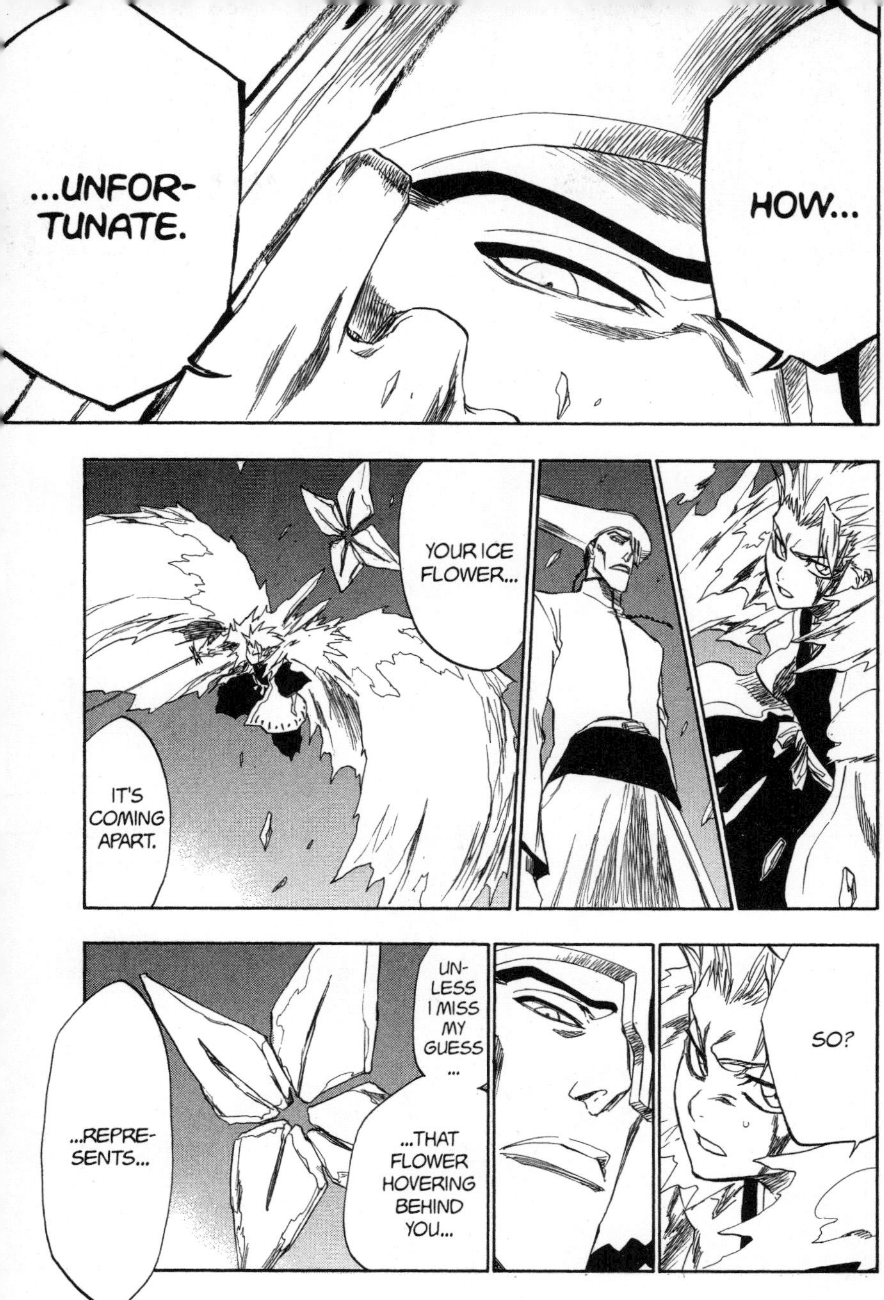
HOW...
...UNFOR-TUNATE.
YOUR ICE FLOWER...
IT'S COMING APART.
SO?
UN-LESS I MISS MY GUESS...
...THAT FLOWER HOVERING BEHIND YOU...
...REPRE-SENTS...

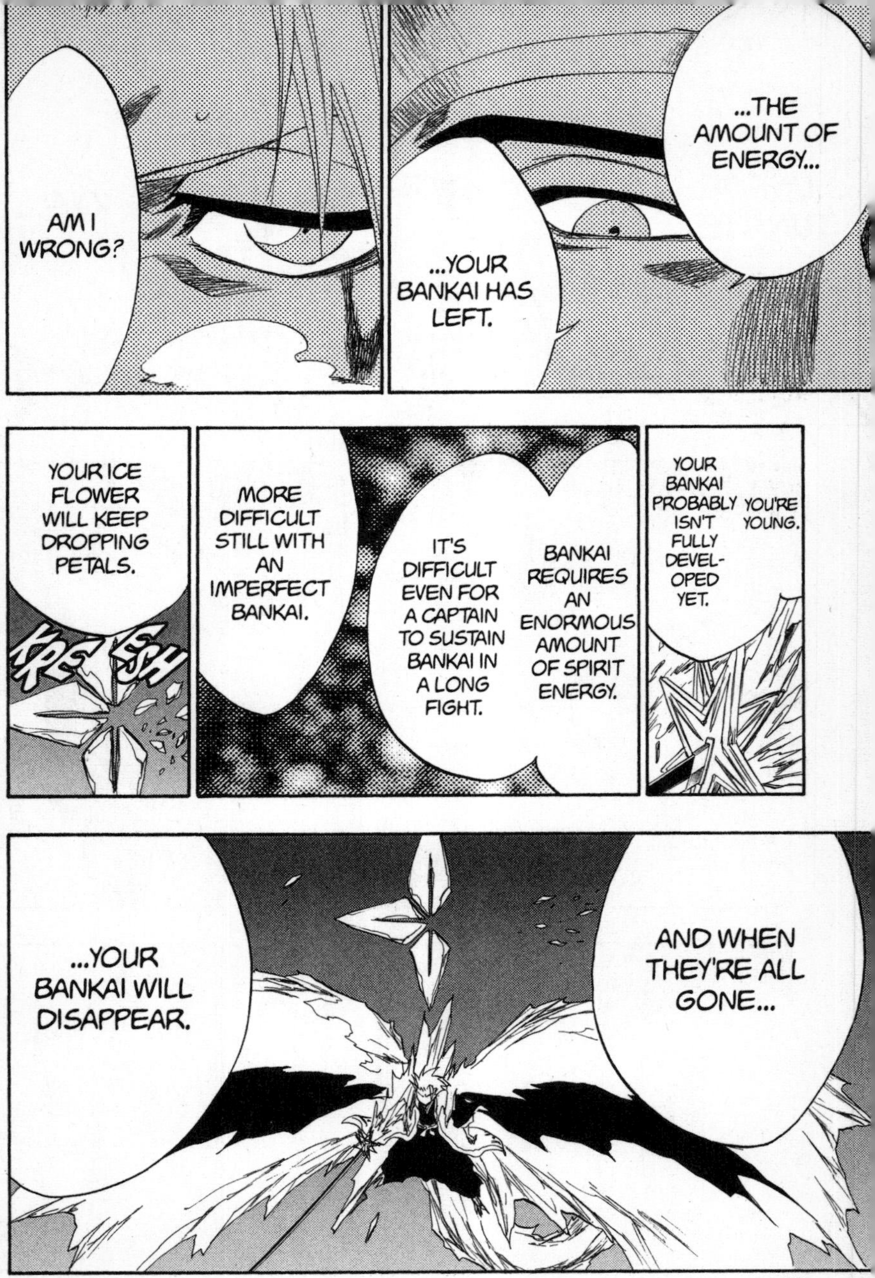
...THE AMOUNT OF ENERGY...
...YOUR BANKAI HAS LEFT.
AM I WRONG?
YOU'RE YOUNG.
YOUR BANKAI PROBABLY ISN'T FULLY DEVEL-OPED YET.
BANKAI REQUIRES AN ENORMOUS AMOUNT OF SPIRIT ENERGY.
IT'S DIFFICULT EVEN FOR A CAPTAIN TO SUSTAIN BANKAI IN A LONG FIGHT.
MORE DIFFICULT STILL WITH AN IMPERFECT BANKAI.
YOUR ICE FLOWER WILL KEEP DROPPING PETALS.
AND WHEN THEY'RE ALL GONE...
...YOUR BANKAI WILL DISAPPEAR.

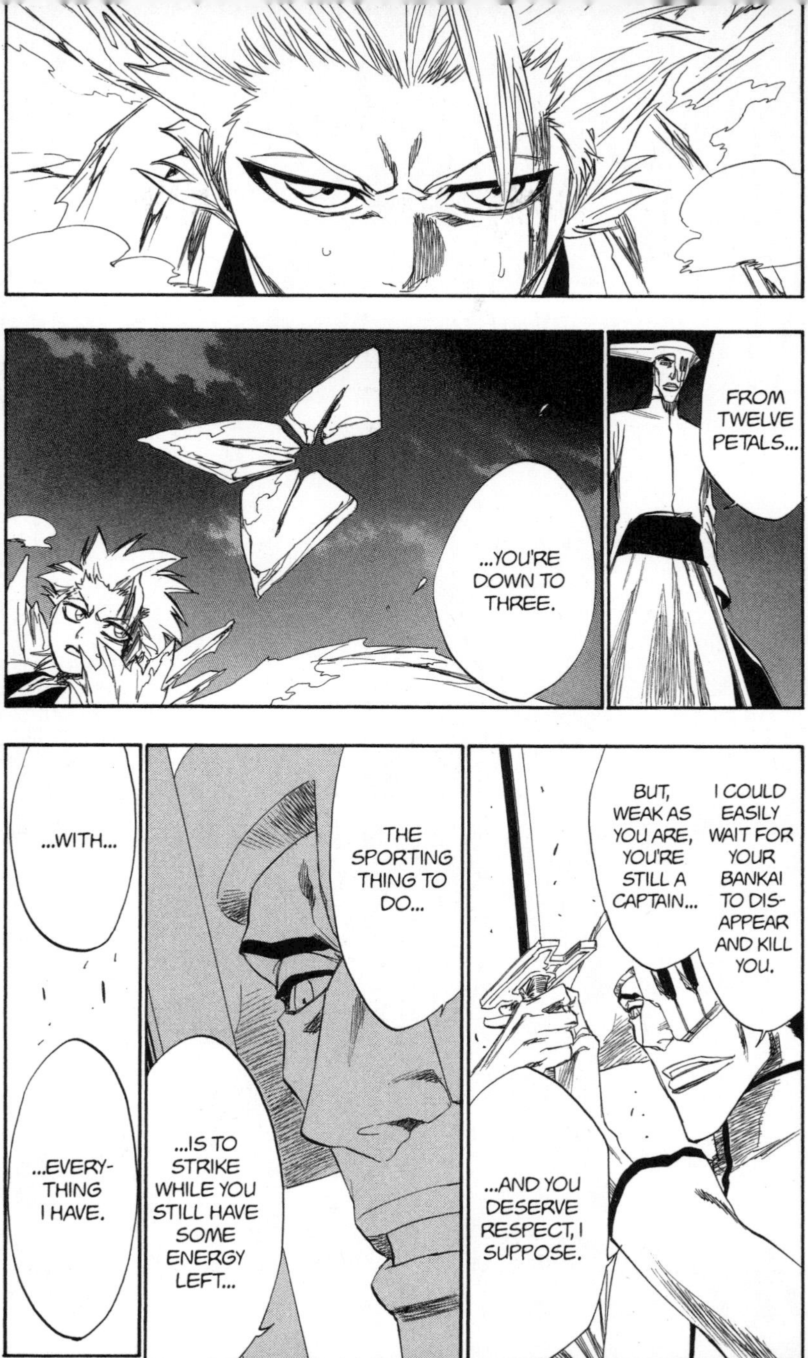
FROM TWELVE PETALS...
...YOU'RE DOWN TO THREE.
I COULD EASILY WAIT FOR YOUR BANKAI TO DISAPPEAR AND KILL YOU.
BUT, WEAK AS YOU ARE, YOU'RE STILL A CAPTAIN...
...AND YOU DESERVE RESPECT, I SUPPOSE.
THE SPORTING THING TO DO...
...IS TO STRIKE WHILE YOU STILL HAVE SOME ENERGY LEFT...
...WITH...
...EVERYTHING I HAVE.

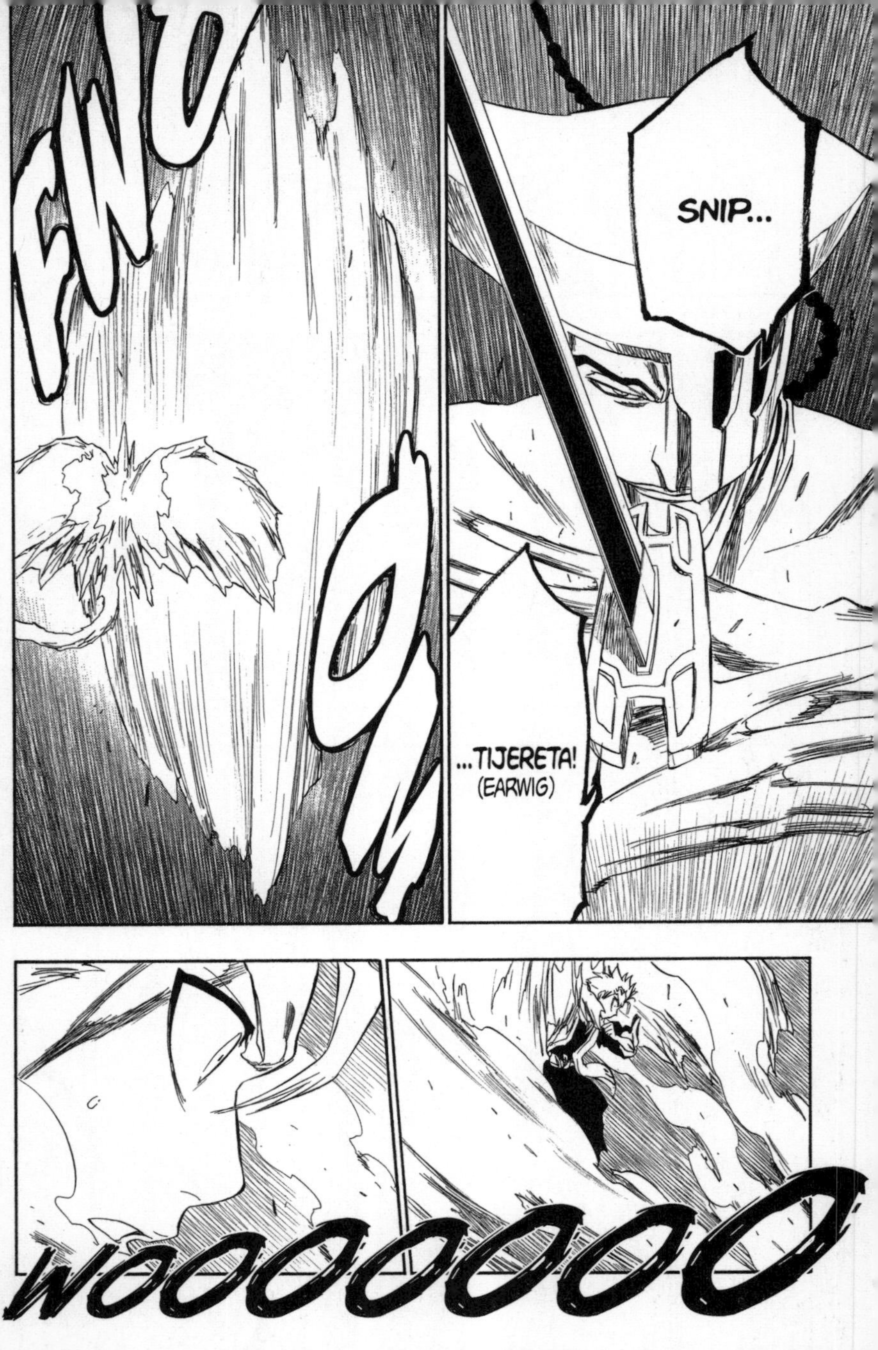
SNIP...
...TIJERETA!
(EARWIG)
WOOOOOOOO

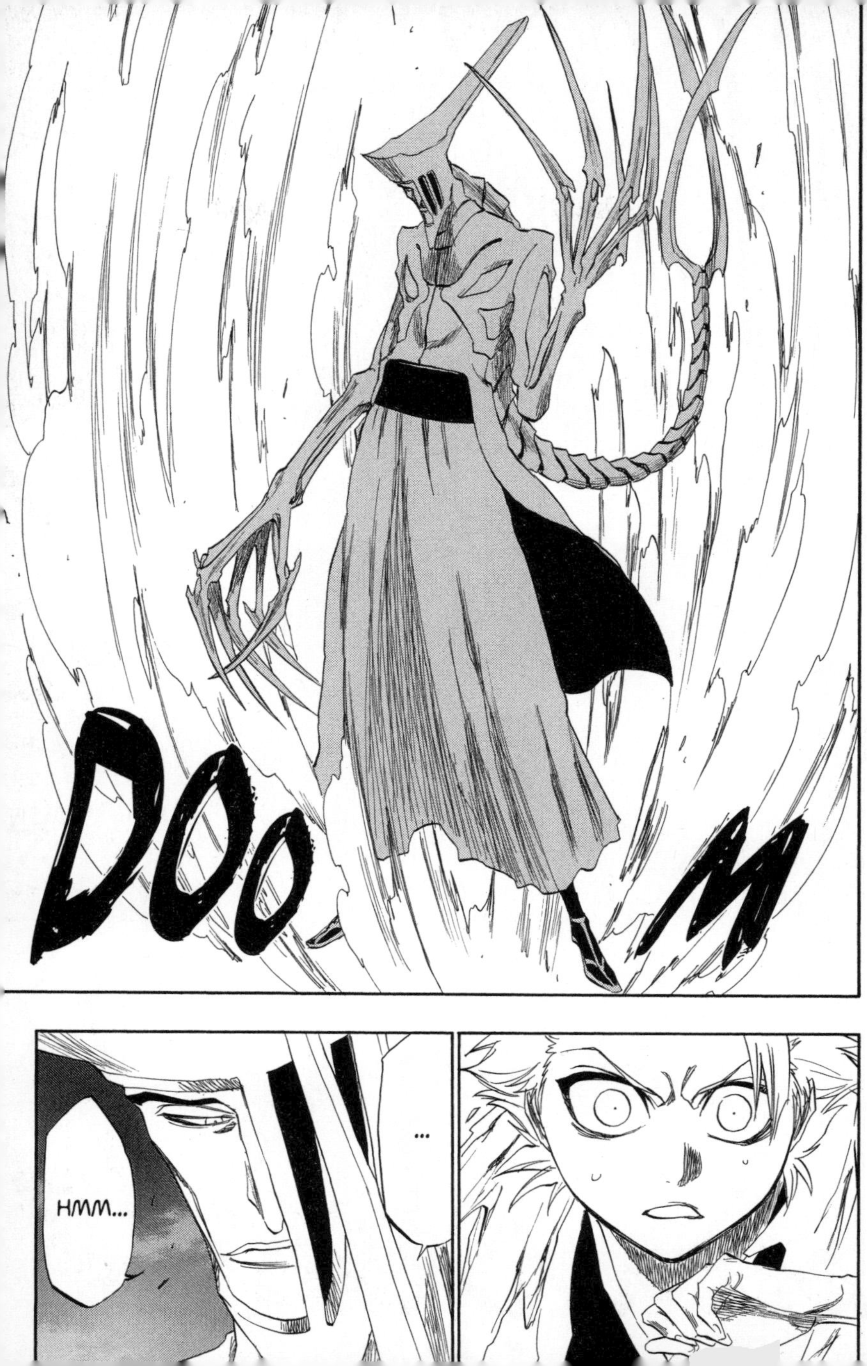
DOOOM
...
HMM...

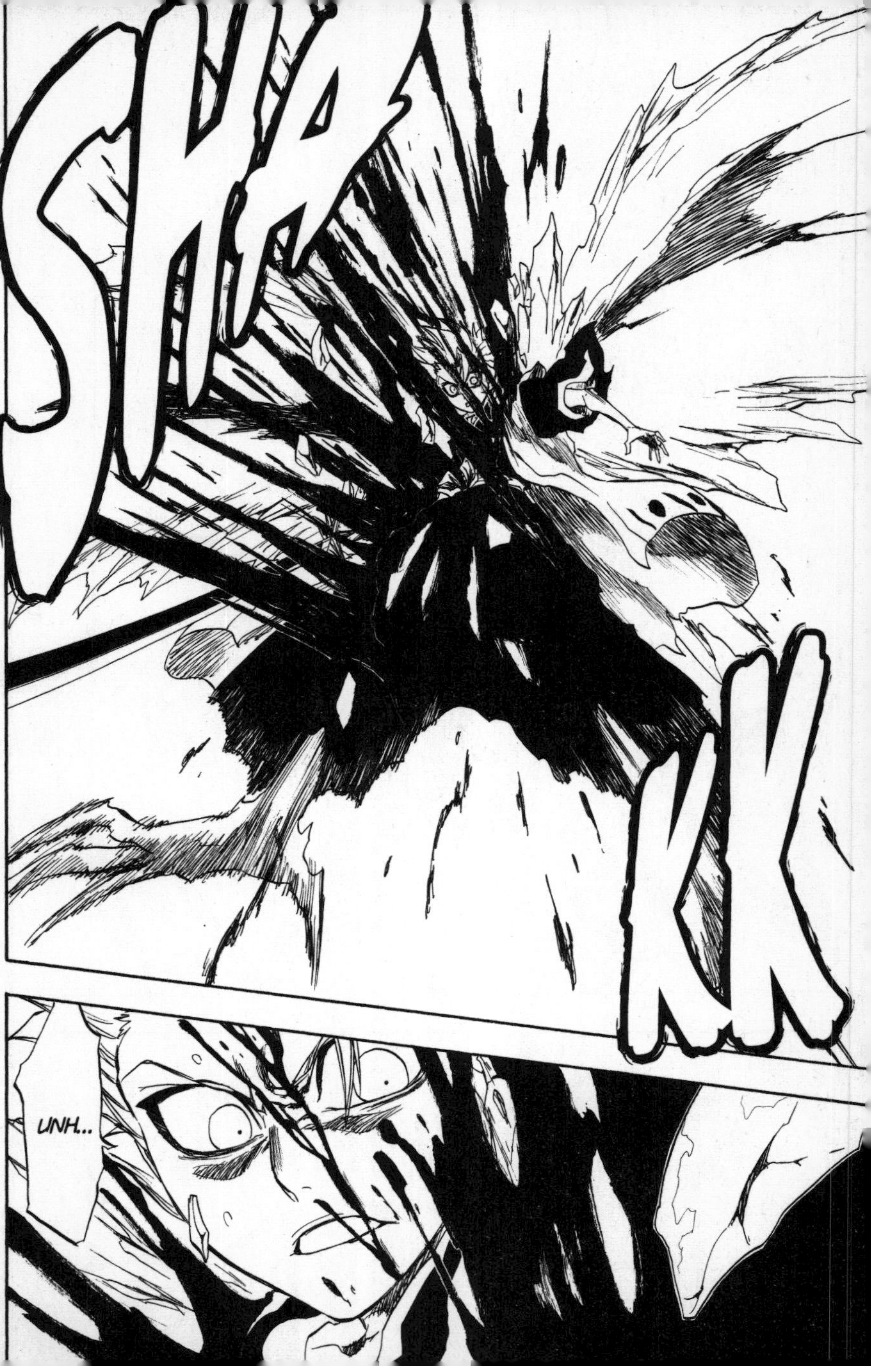
SHA
KK
UNH...

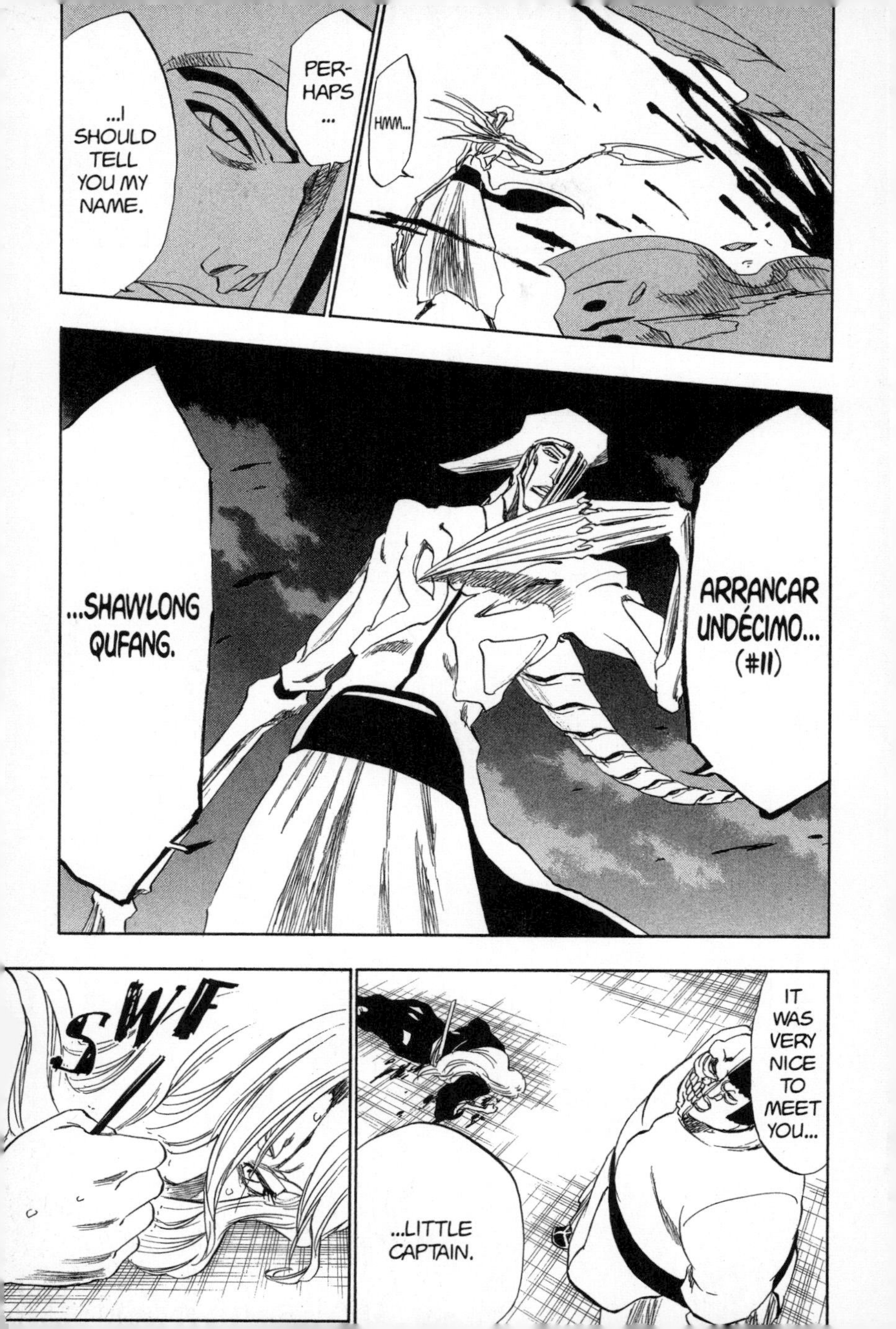
HMM...
PER-HAPS...
...I SHOULD TELL YOU MY NAME.
ARRANCAR UNDÉCIMO... (#11)
...SHAWLONG QUFANG.
IT WAS VERY NICE TO MEET YOU...
...LITTLE CAPTAIN.
SWF

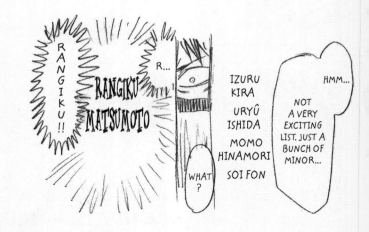

HMM...
NOT A VERY EXCITING LIST. JUST A BUNCH OF MINOR...
IZURU KIRA
URYÛ ISHIDA
MOMO HINAMORI
SOI FON
WHAT ?
R...
RANGIKU MATSUMOTO
RANGIKU!!

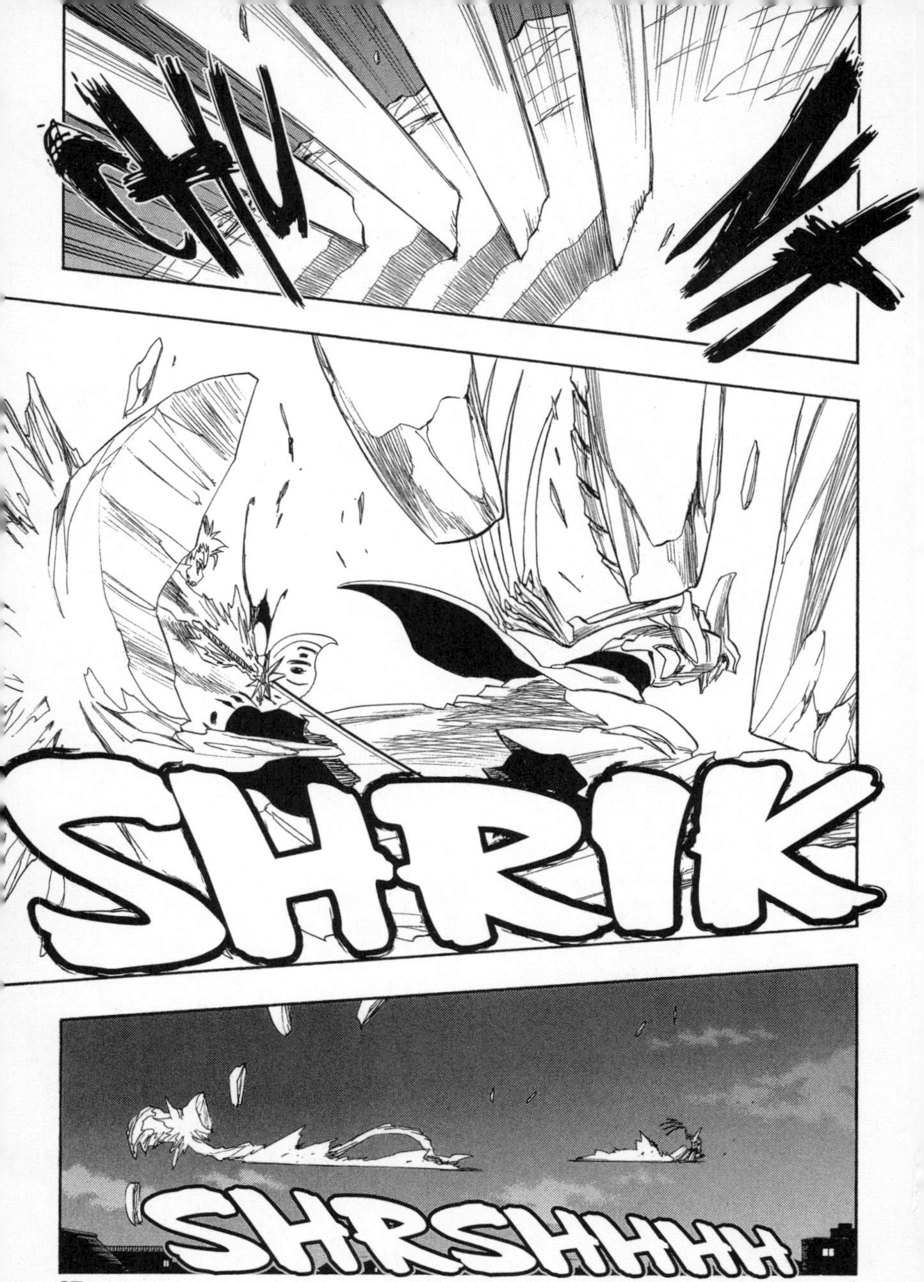
CHU
NK
SHRIK
SHRSHHHH



BLEACH 209. Lift the Limit

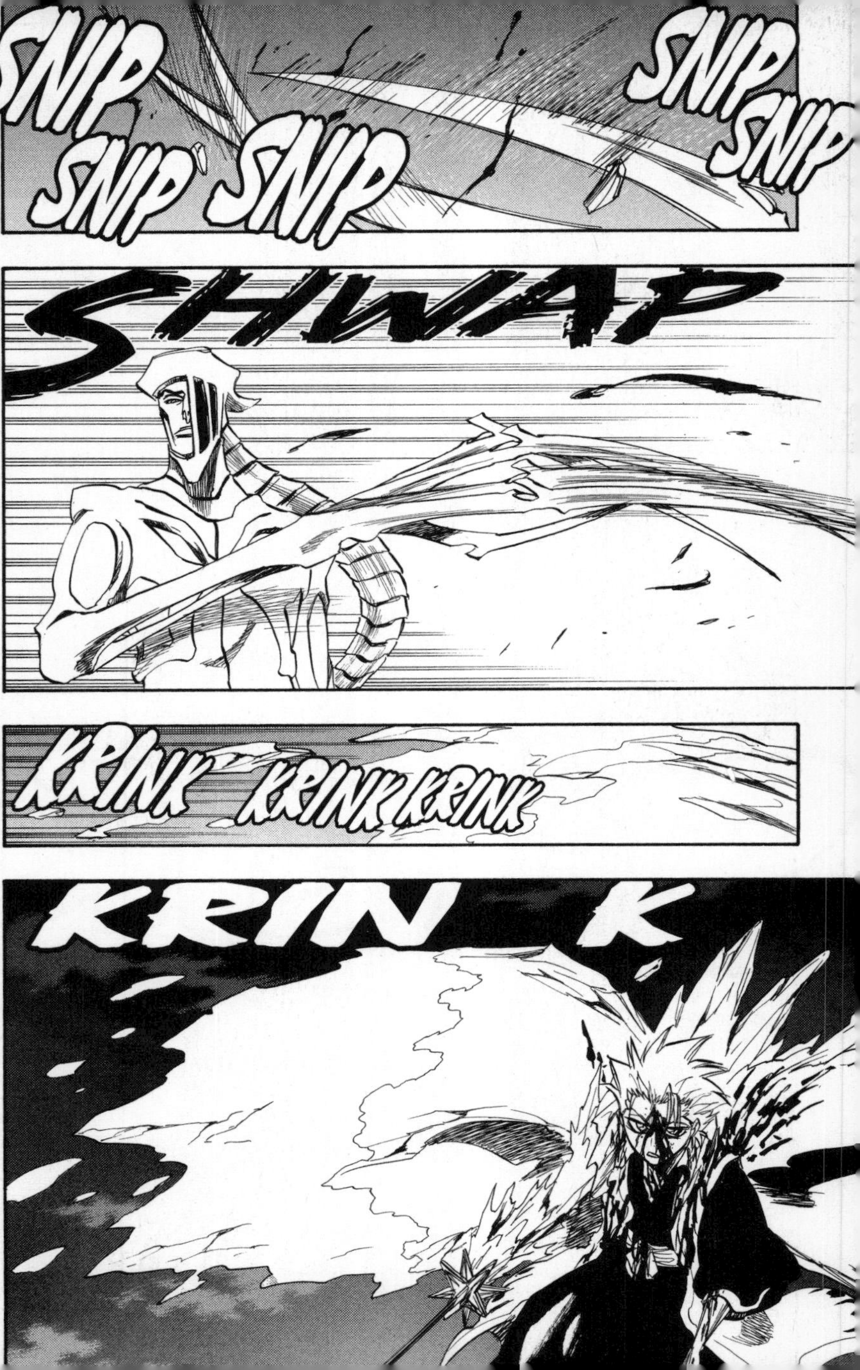
SNIP SNIP
SNIP
SNIP SNIP
SHWAP
KRINK KRINK
KRINK
KRIN K

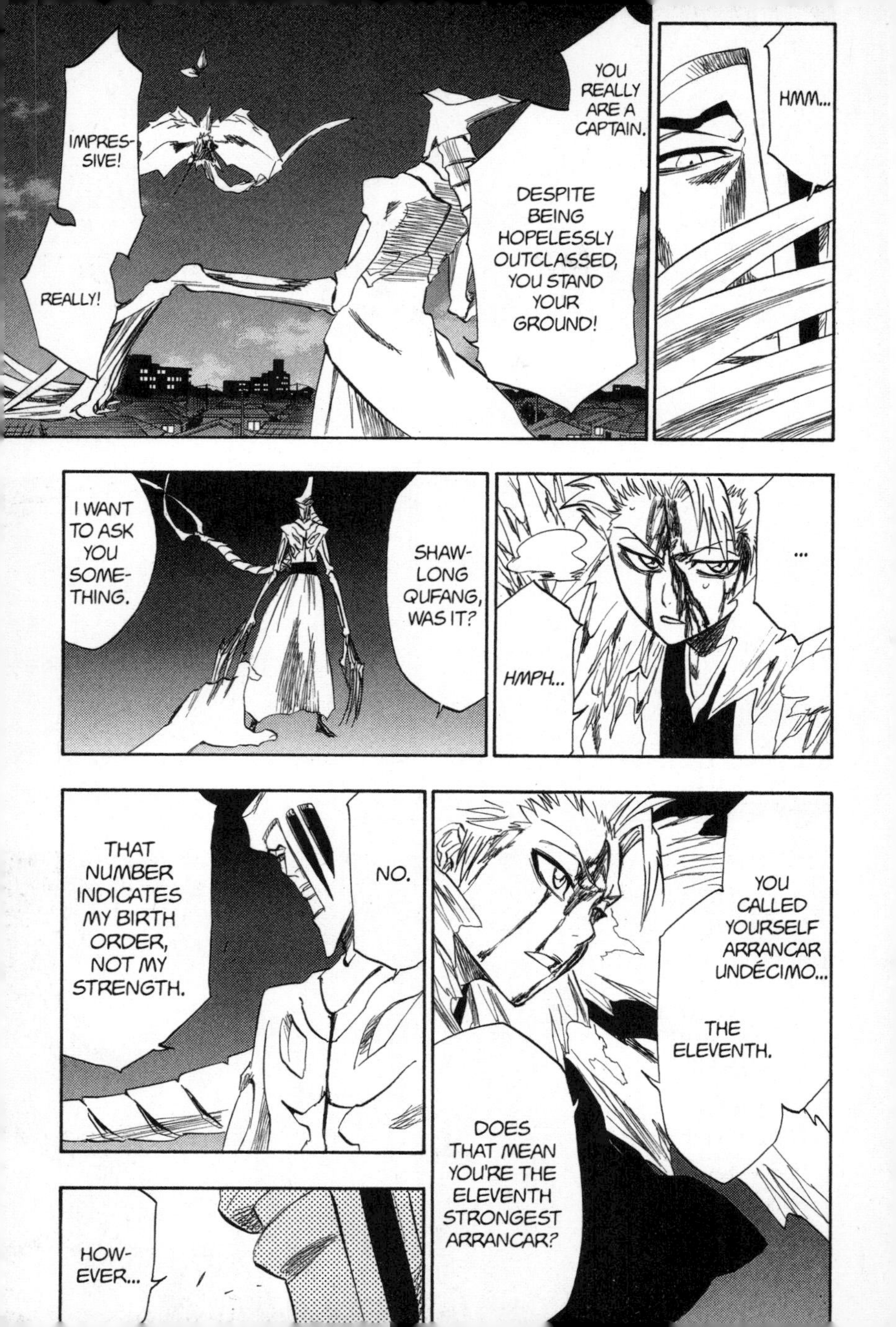
HMM...
YOU REALLY ARE A CAPTAIN.
DESPITE BEING HOPELESSLY OUTCLASSED, YOU STAND YOUR GROUND!
IMPRESSIVE!
REALLY!
...
HMPH...
SHAW-LONG QUFANG, WAS IT?
I WANT TO ASK YOU SOMETHING.
YOU CALLED YOURSELF ARRANCAR UNDÉCIMO...
THE ELEVENTH.
DOES THAT MEAN YOU'RE THE ELEVENTH STRONGEST ARRANCAR?
NO.
THAT NUMBER INDICATES MY BIRTH ORDER, NOT MY STRENGTH.
HOW-EVER...

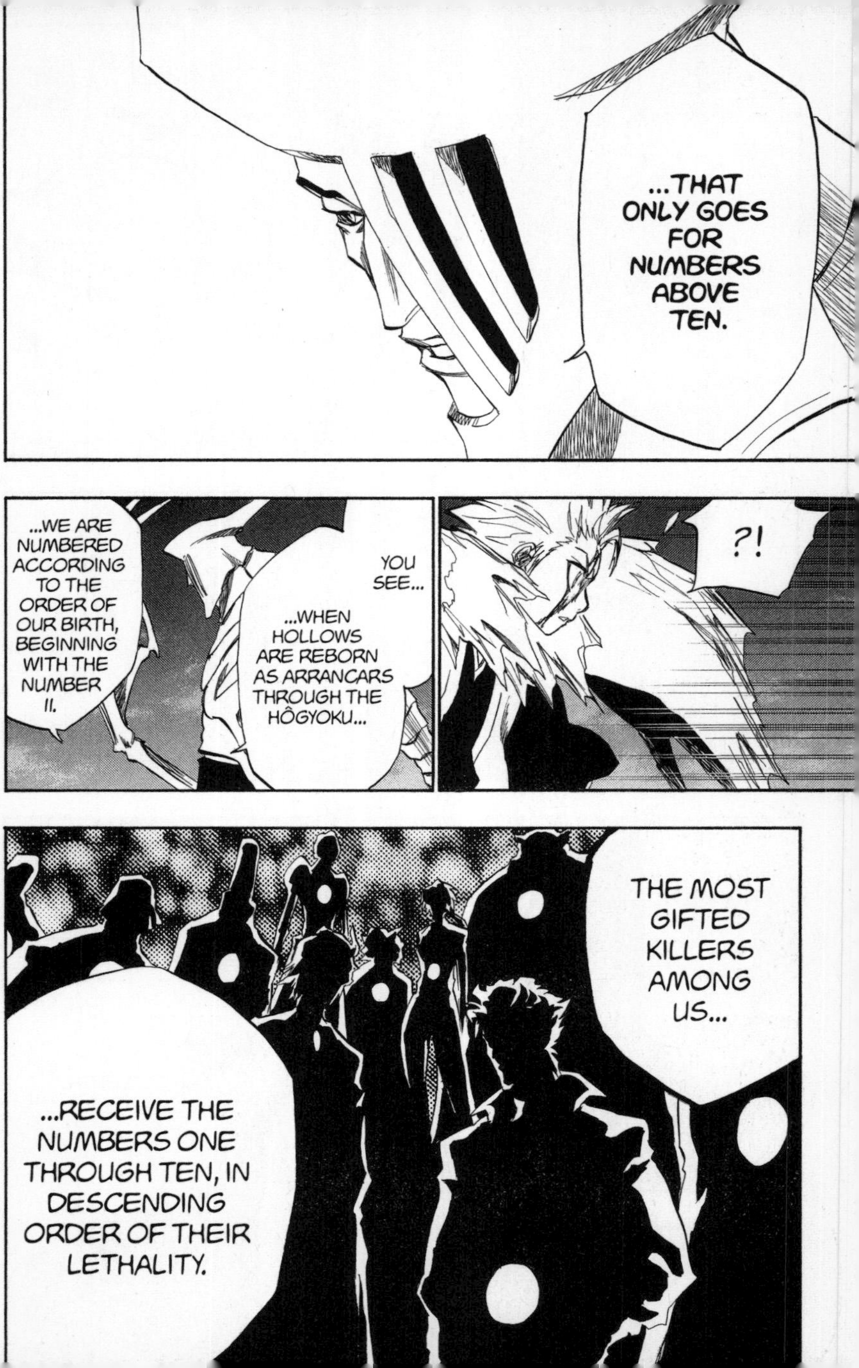
...THAT ONLY GOES FOR NUMBERS ABOVE TEN.
?!
YOU SEE...
...WHEN HOLLOWS ARE REBORN AS ARRANCARS THROUGH THE HÔGYOKU...
...WE ARE NUMBERED ACCORDING TO THE ORDER OF OUR BIRTH, BEGINNING WITH THE NUMBER 11.
THE MOST GIFTED KILLERS AMONG US...
...RECEIVE THE NUMBERS ONE THROUGH TEN, IN DESCENDING ORDER OF THEIR LETHALITY.

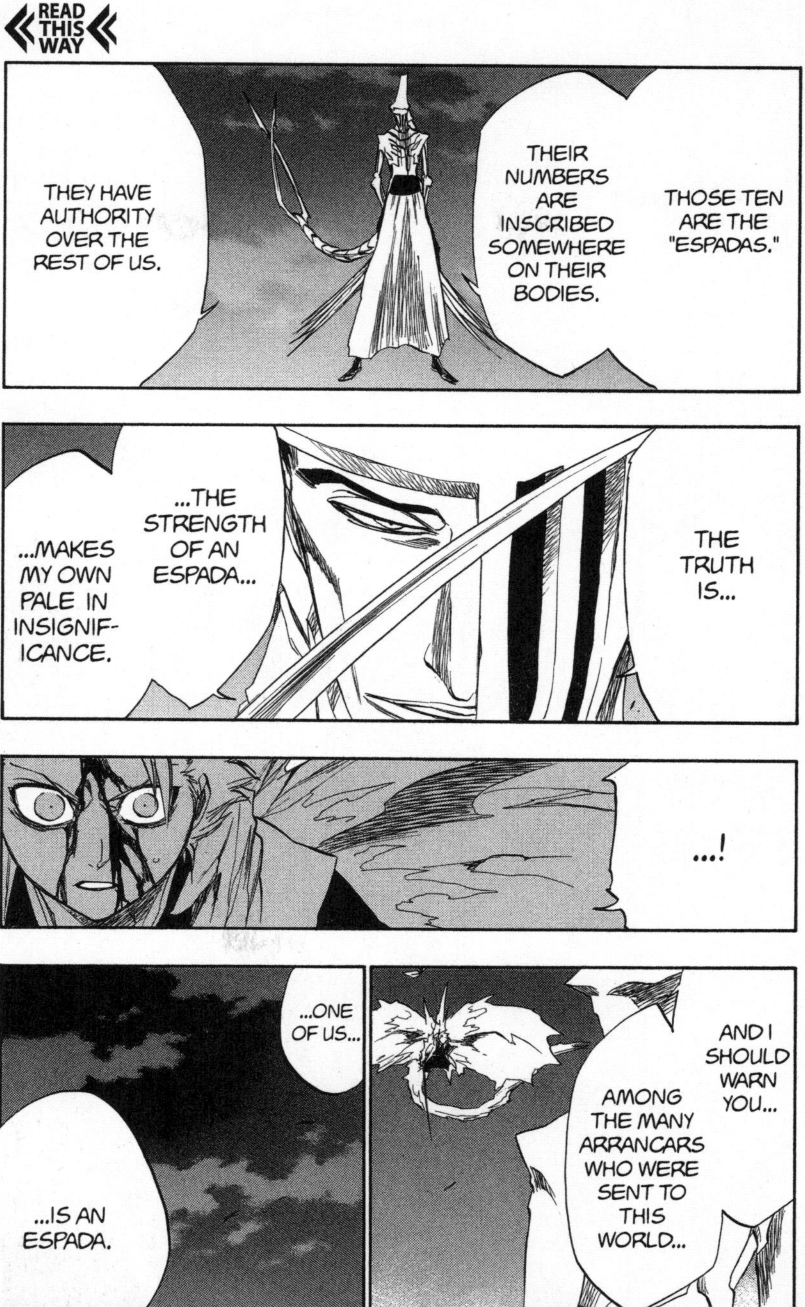
READ THIS WAY
THOSE TEN ARE THE "ESPADAS."
THEIR NUMBERS ARE INSCRIBED SOMEWHERE ON THEIR BODIES.
THEY HAVE AUTHORITY OVER THE REST OF US.
THE TRUTH IS...
...THE STRENGTH OF AN ESPADA...
...MAKES MY OWN PALE IN INSIGNIF-ICANCE.
...!
AND I SHOULD WARN YOU...
AMONG THE MANY ARRANCARS WHO WERE SENT TO THIS WORLD...
...ONE OF US...
...IS AN ESPADA.

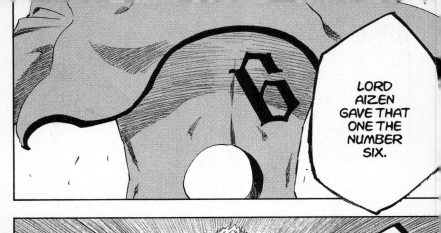

LORD AIZEN GAVE THAT ONE THE NUMBER SIX.

THE ESPADA SEXTA...

...GRIMMJOW JEAGERJAQUES.

READ THIS WAY

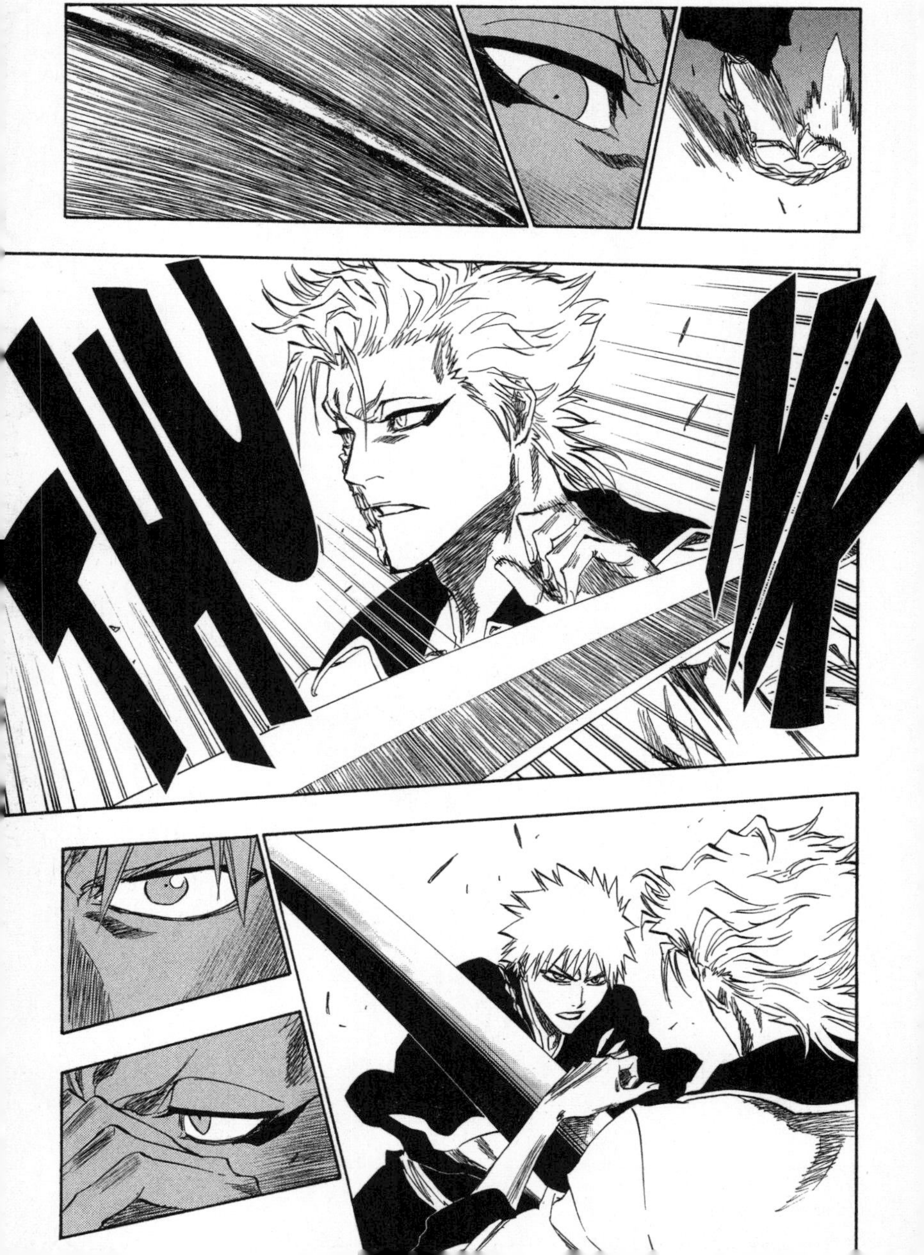
THUNK

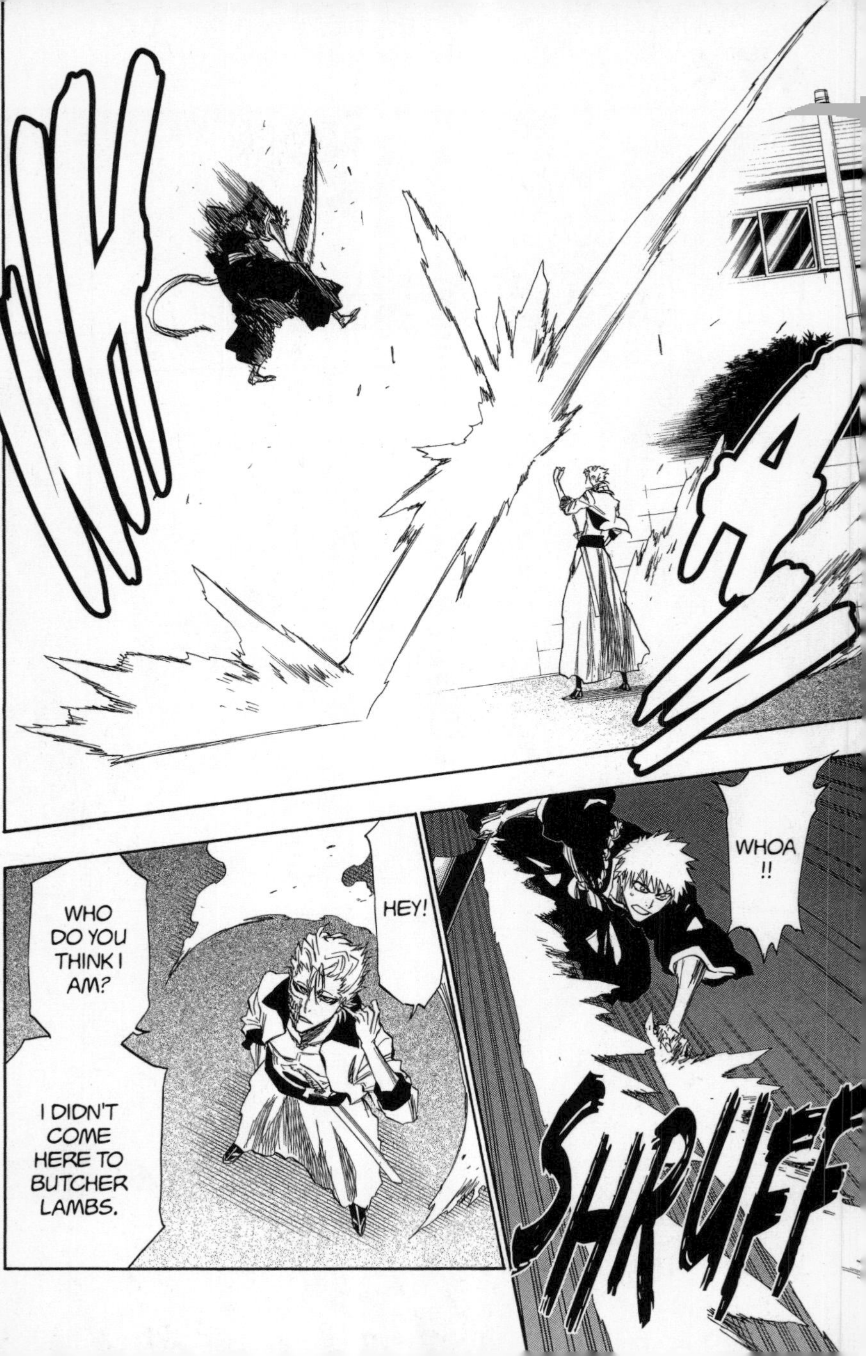
WHOA !!
HEY!
WHO DO YOU THINK I AM?
I DIDN'T COME HERE TO BUTCHER LAMBS.

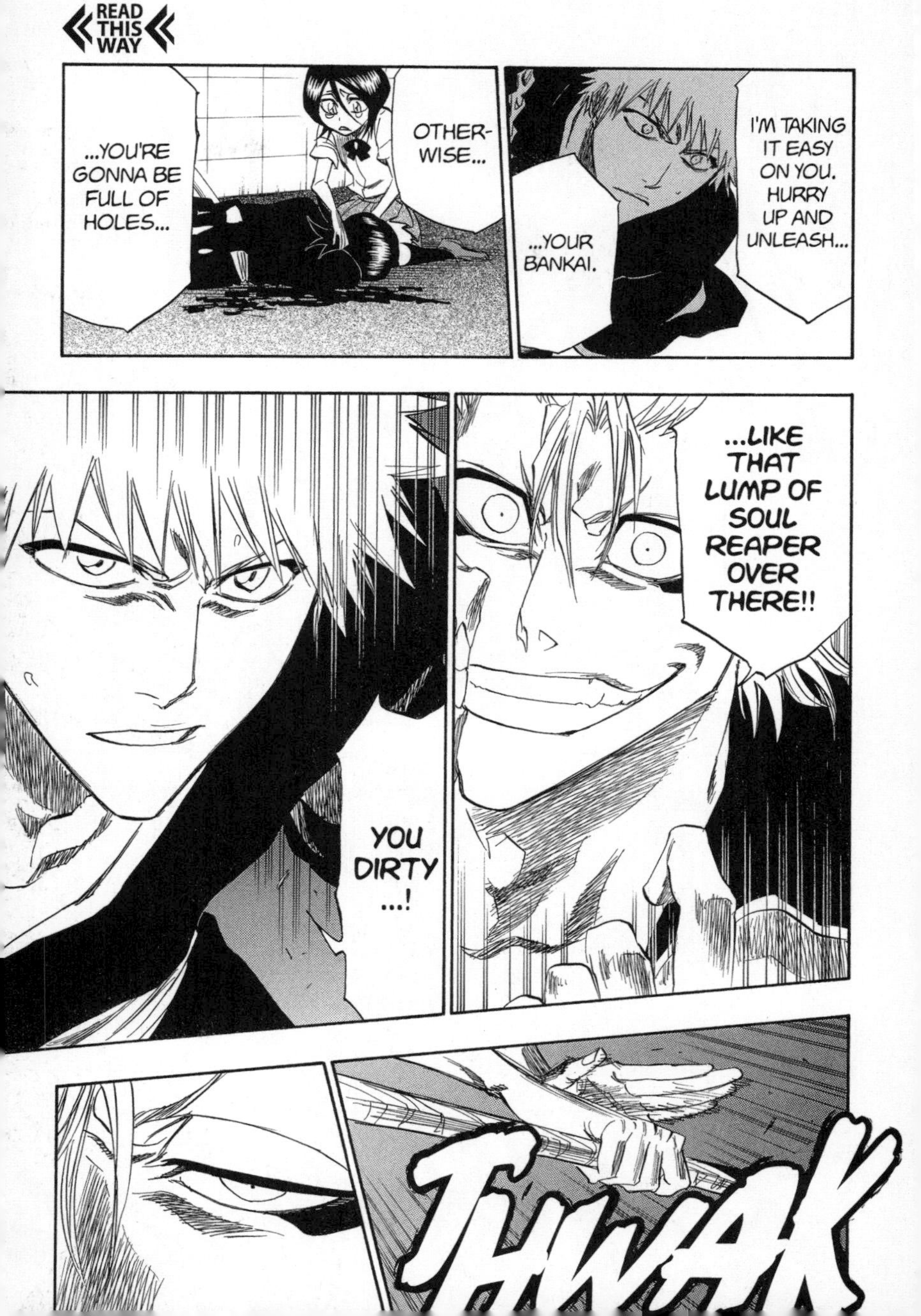
READ THIS WAY
I'M TAKING IT EASY ON YOU. HURRY UP AND UNLEASH...
...YOUR BANKAI.
OTHER-WISE...
...YOU'RE GONNA BE FULL OF HOLES...
...LIKE THAT LUMP OF SOUL REAPER OVER THERE!!
YOU DIRTY ...!
THWAK

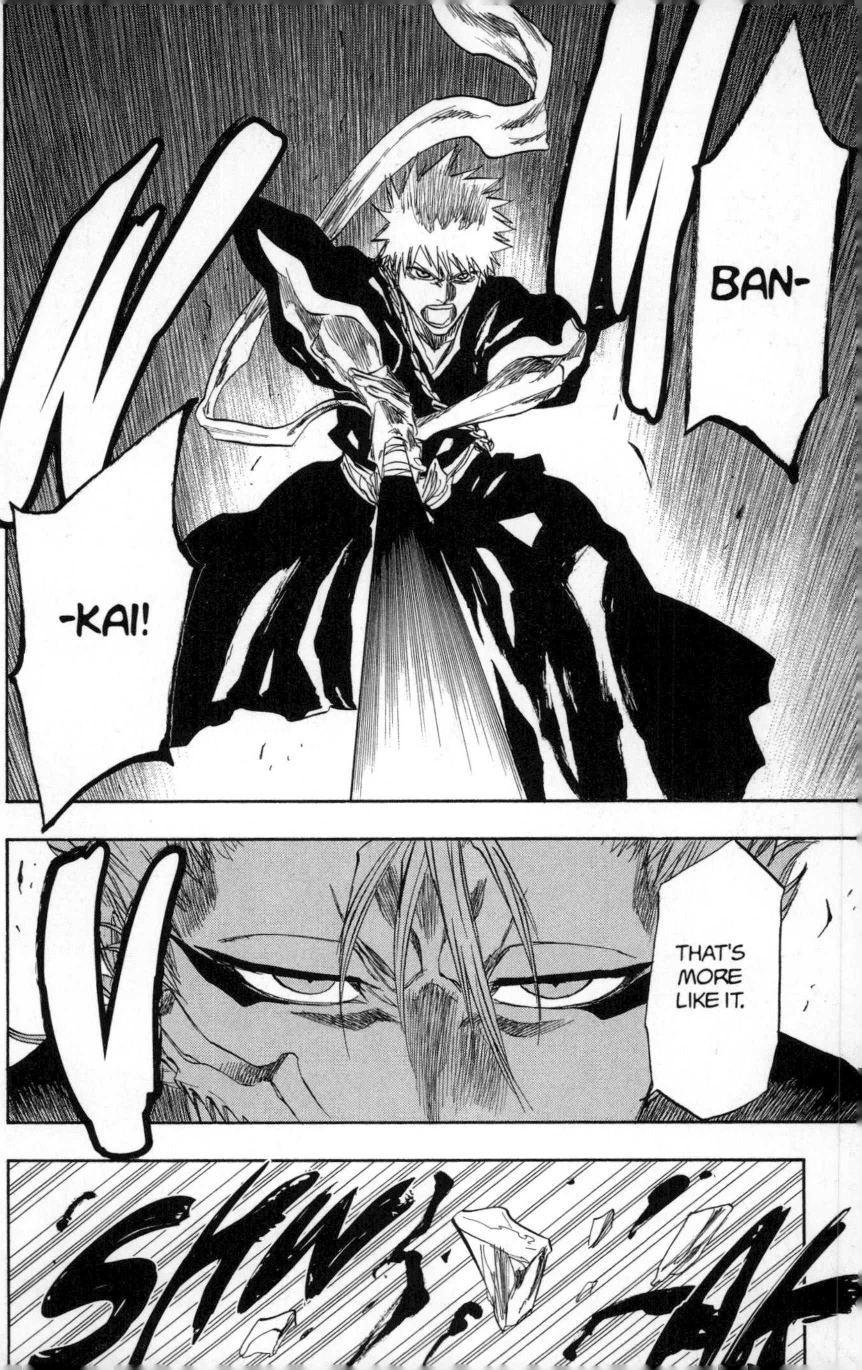
BAN-
-KAI!
THAT'S MORE LIKE IT.

...MATSU-MOTO!

I CAN'T KEEP THIS UP MUCH LONGER...

COME ON!...

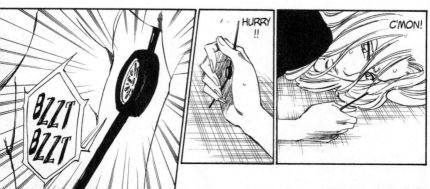

BZZT BZZT

HURRY!!

C'MON!

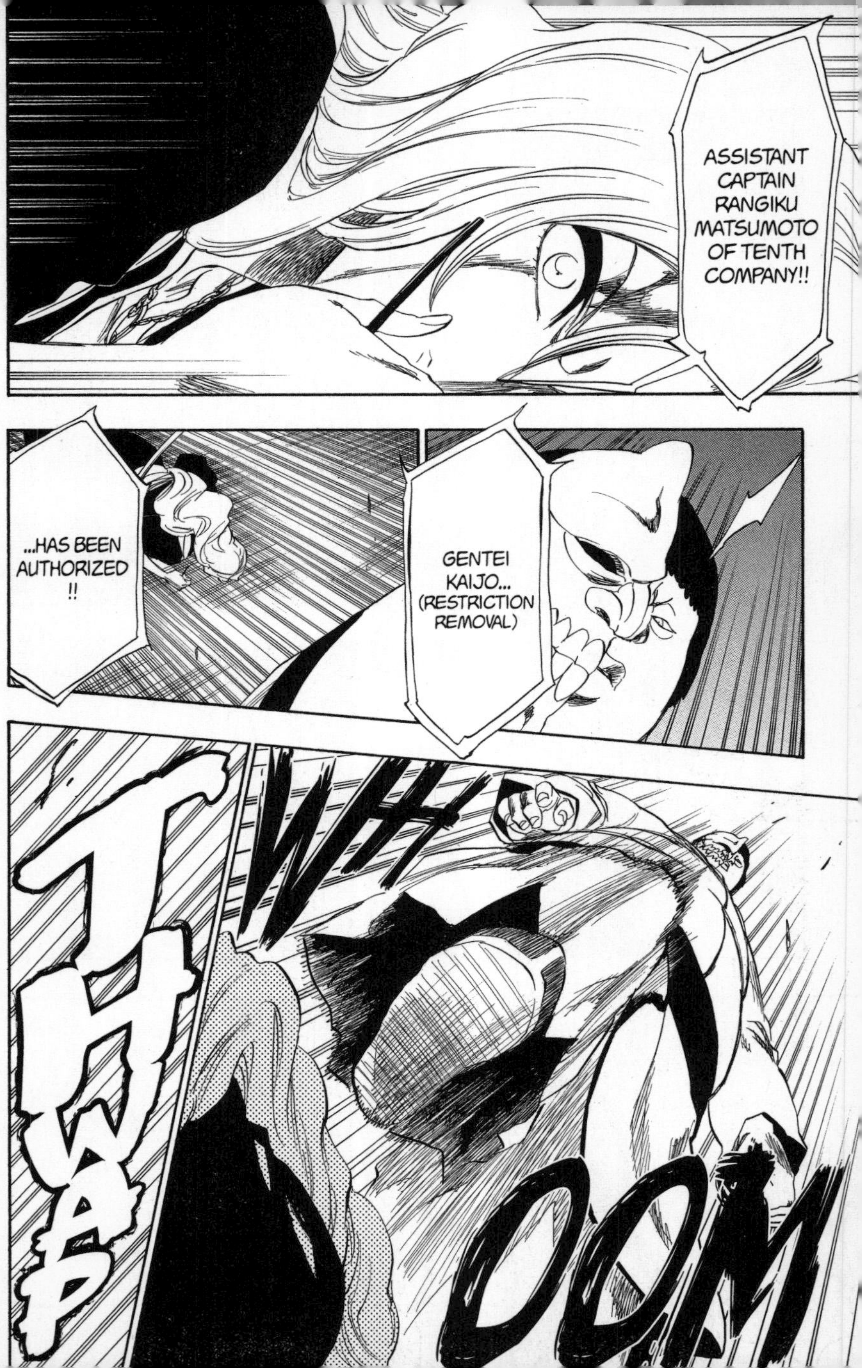
ASSISTANT CAPTAIN RANGIKU MATSUMOTO OF TENTH COMPANY!!
GENTEI KAIJO... (RESTRICTION REMOVAL)
...HAS BEEN AUTHORIZED !!
WHOOM
THWAP

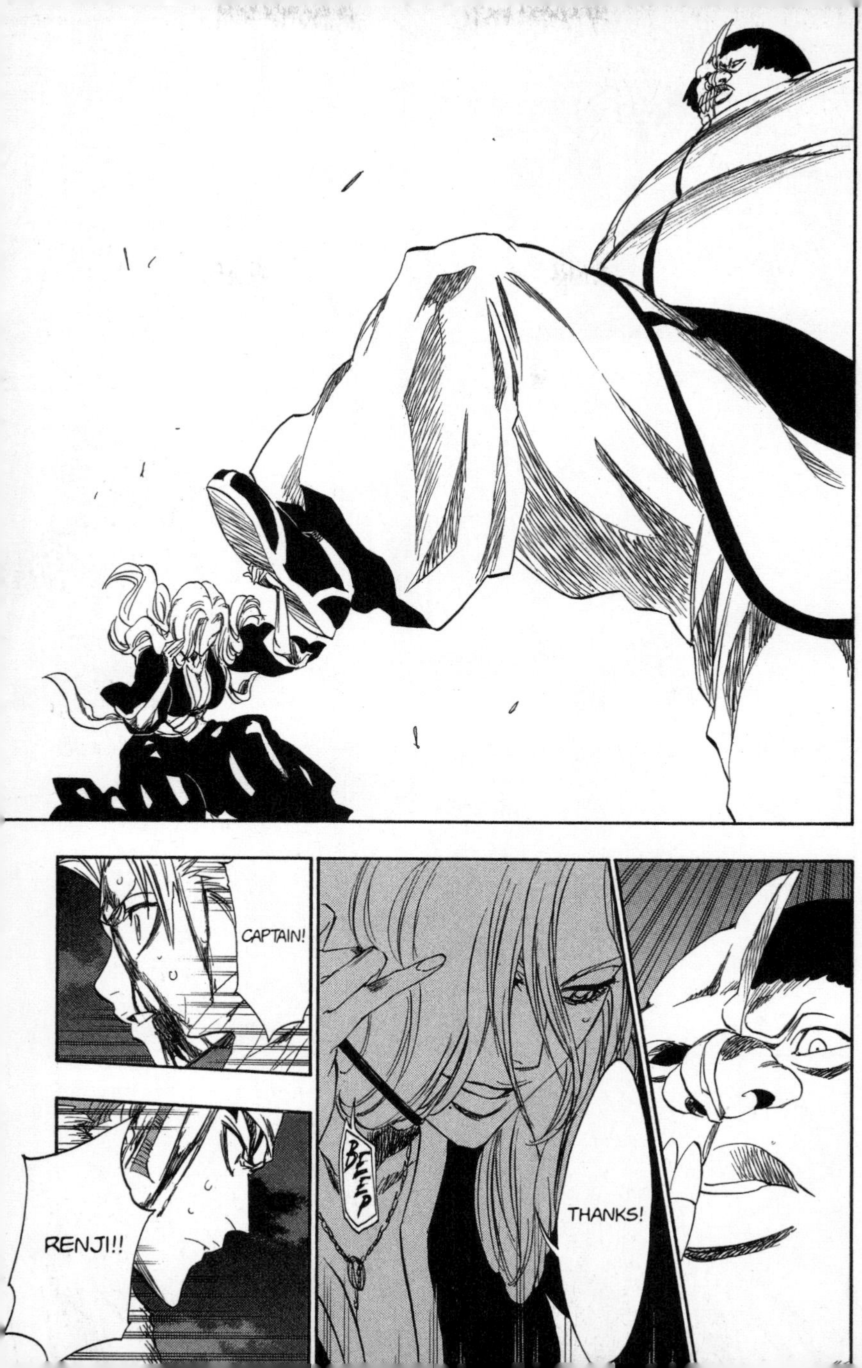
BEEP
THANKS!
CAPTAIN!
RENJI!!

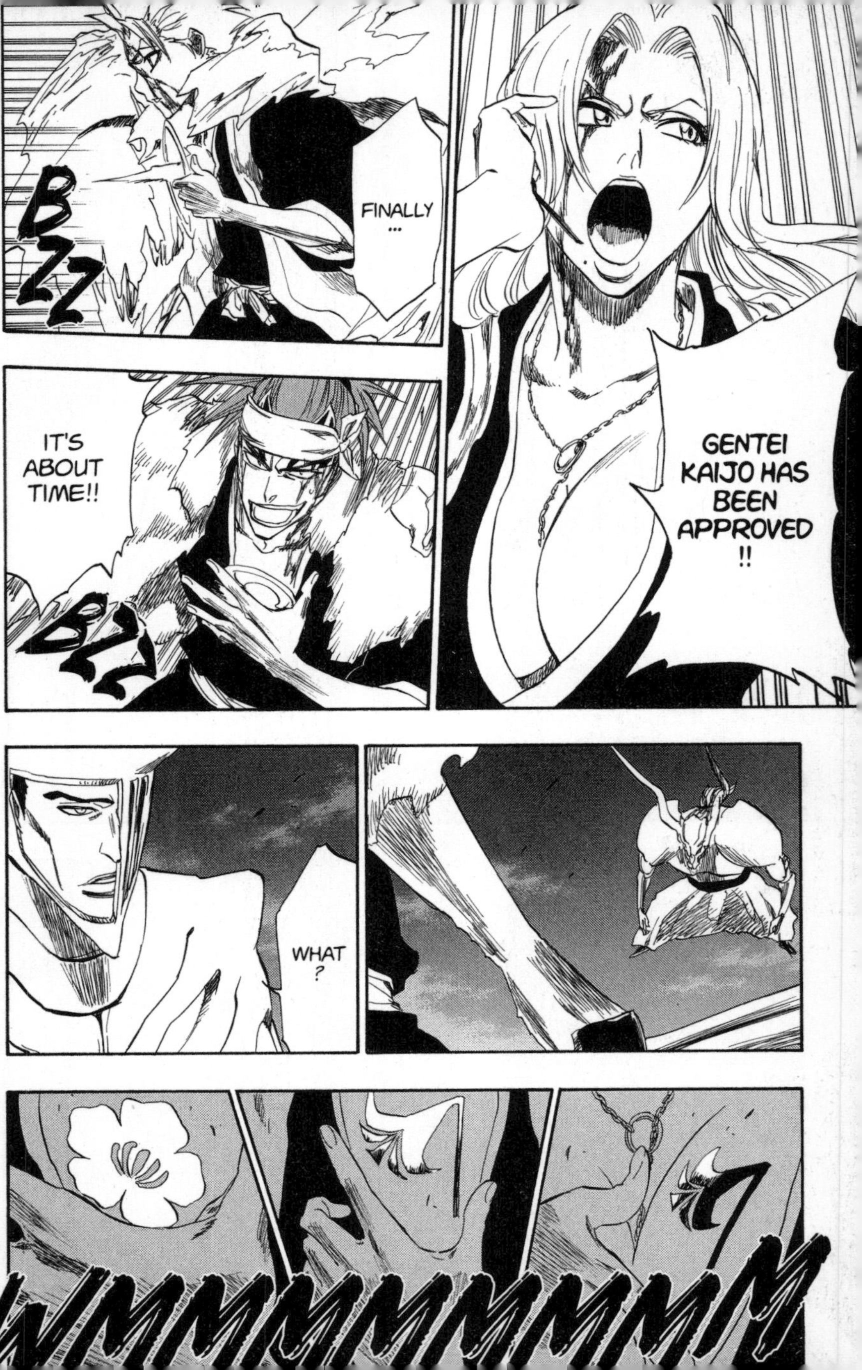
GENTEI KAIJO HAS BEEN APPROVED !!
BZZ
FINALLY ...
BZZ
IT'S ABOUT TIME!!
WHAT ?
WMMMMMMMMM

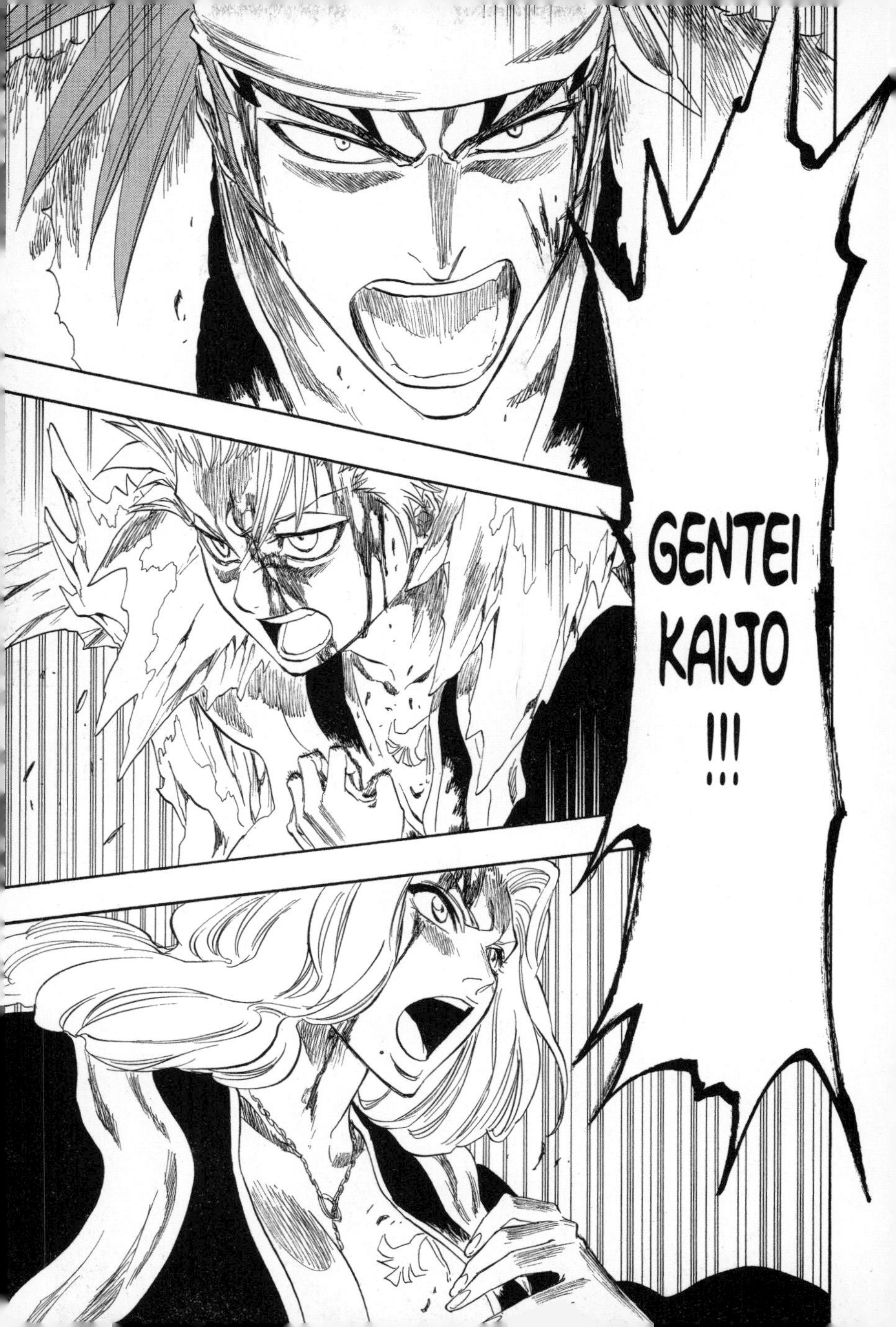
GENTEI KAIJO !!!

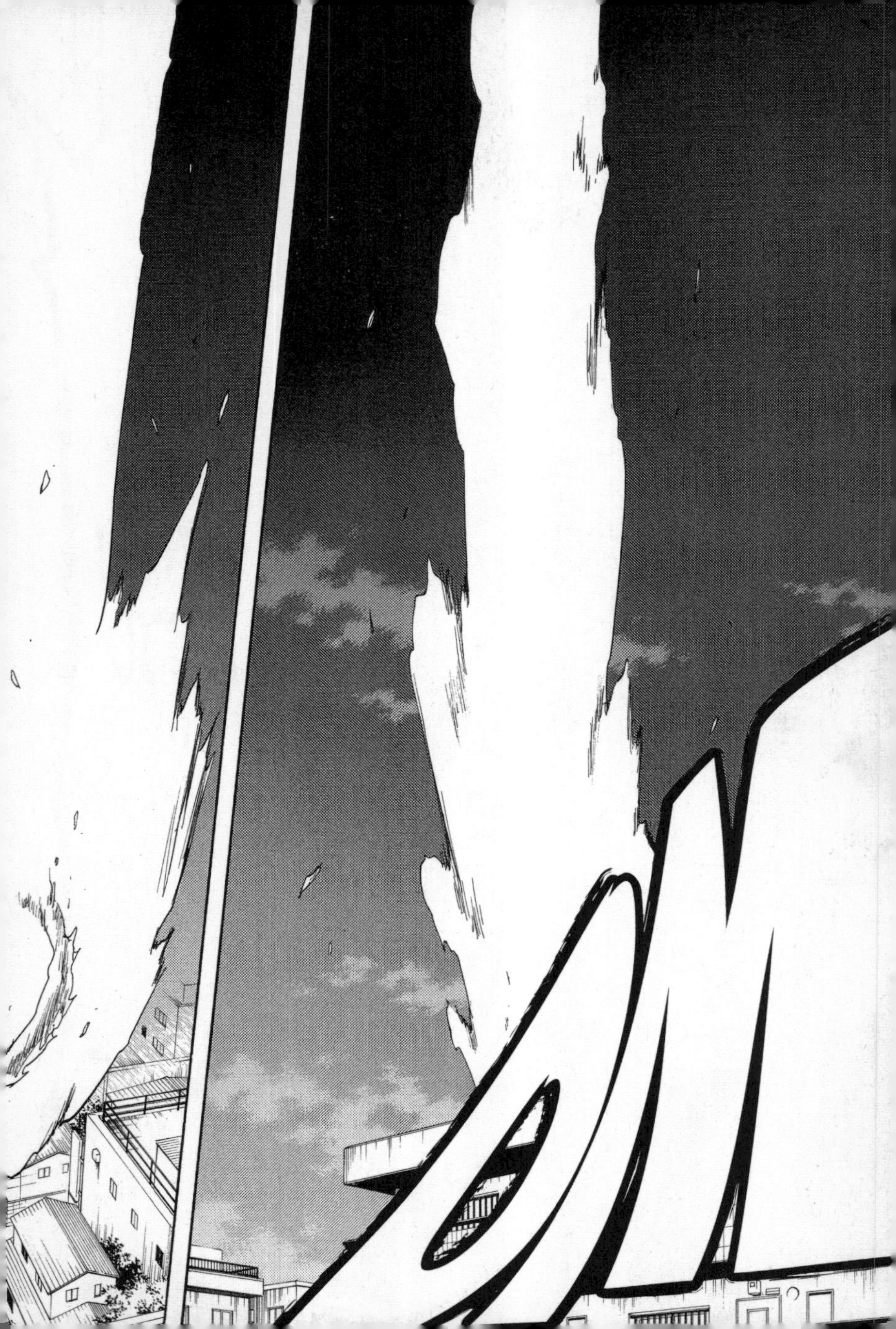

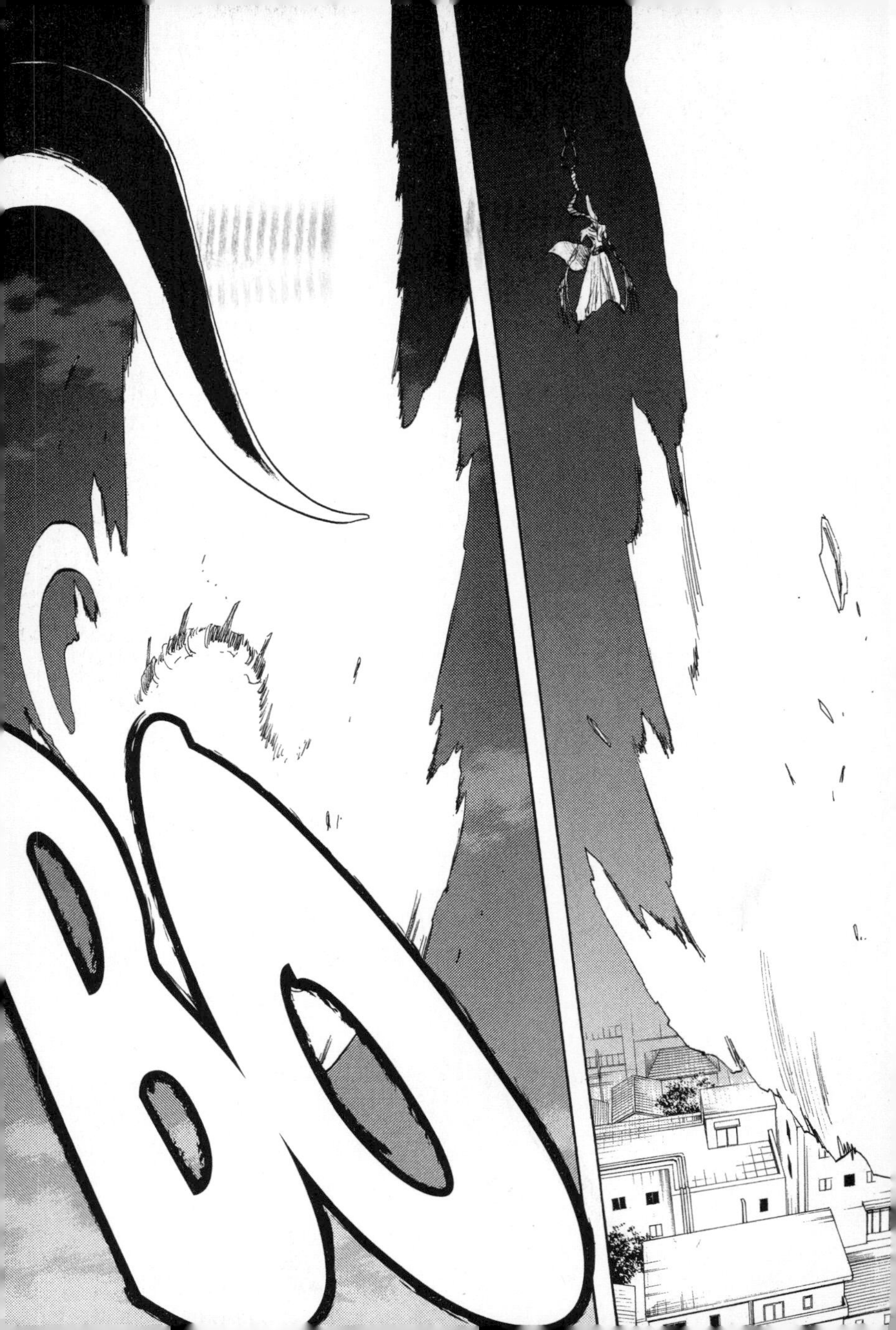

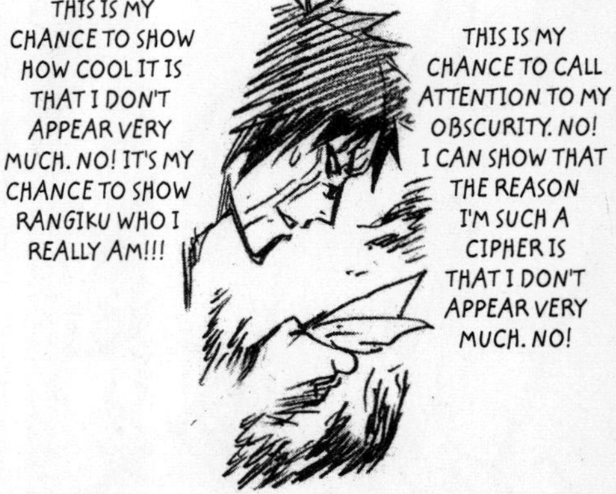
THIS IS MY CHANCE TO CALL ATTENTION TO MY OBSCURITY. NO! I CAN SHOW THAT THE REASON I'M SUCH A CIPHER IS THAT I DON'T APPEAR VERY MUCH. NO!
THIS IS MY CHANCE TO SHOW HOW COOL IT IS THAT I DON'T APPEAR VERY MUCH. NO! IT'S MY CHANCE TO SHOW RANGIKU WHO I REALLY AM!!!

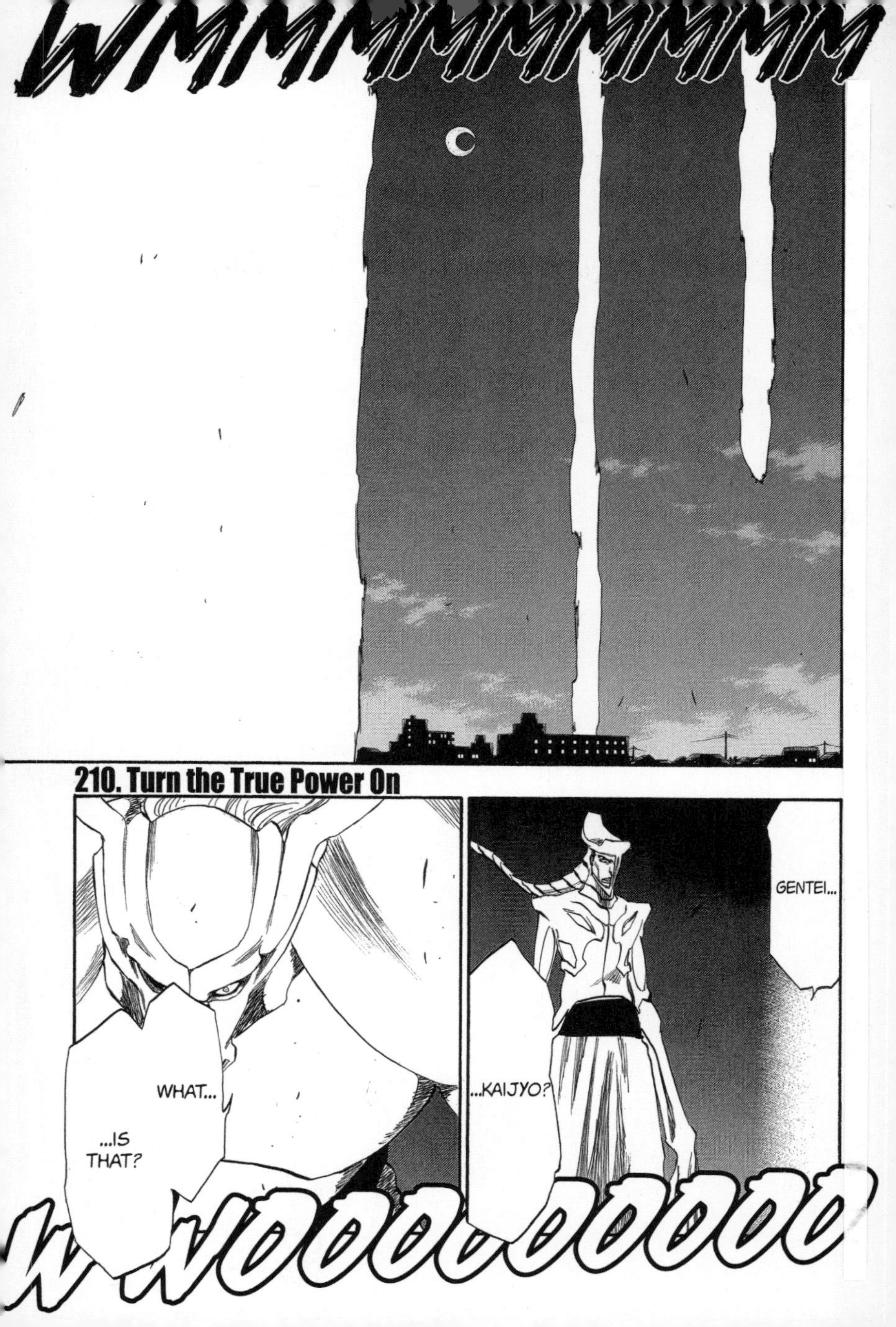
WMMMMMMMMMM
210. Turn the True Power On
GENTEI...
...KAIJYO?
WHAT...
...IS THAT?
WNOOOOOOOOOO

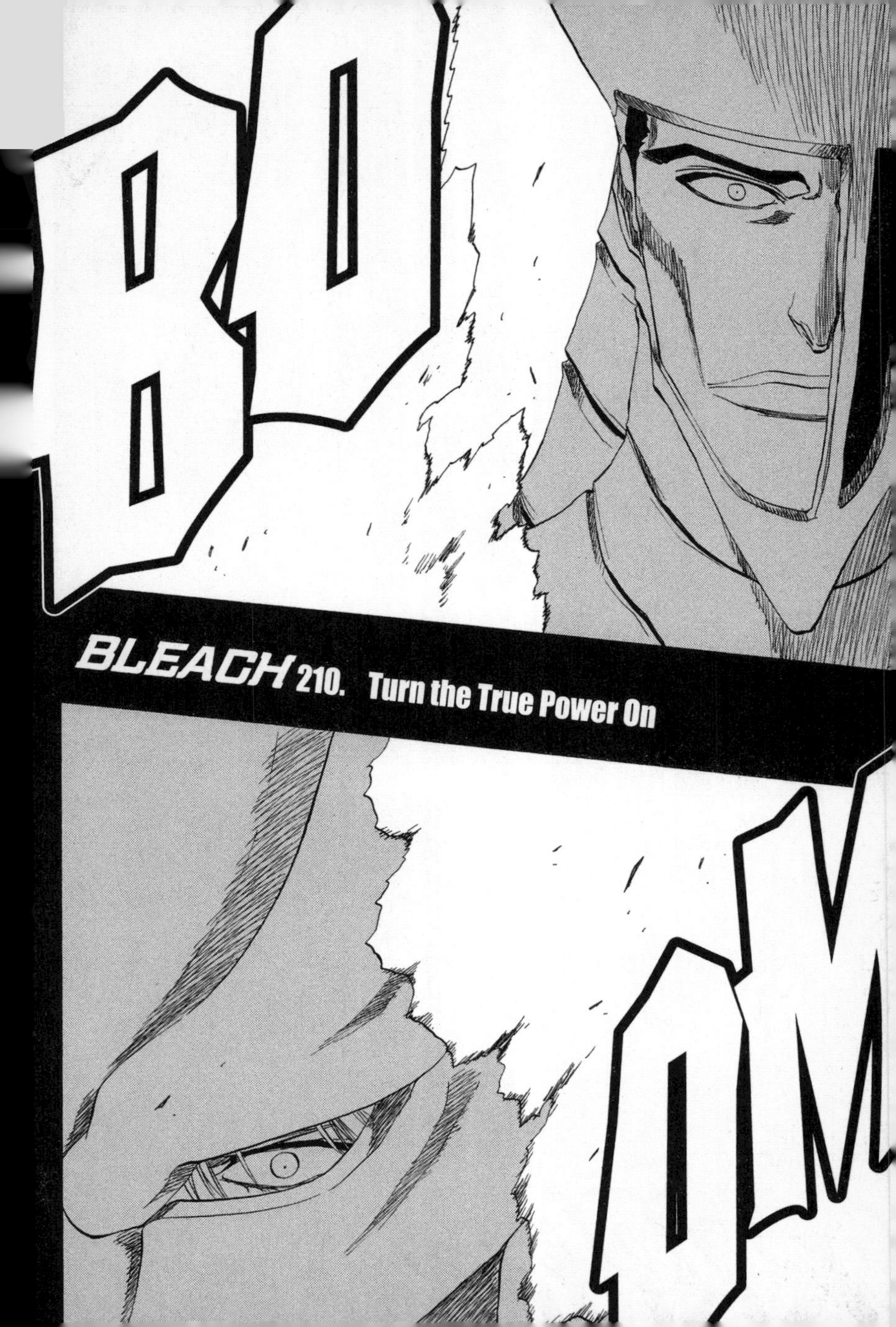
BA
BLEACH 210. Turn the True Power On
OM

READ THIS WAY

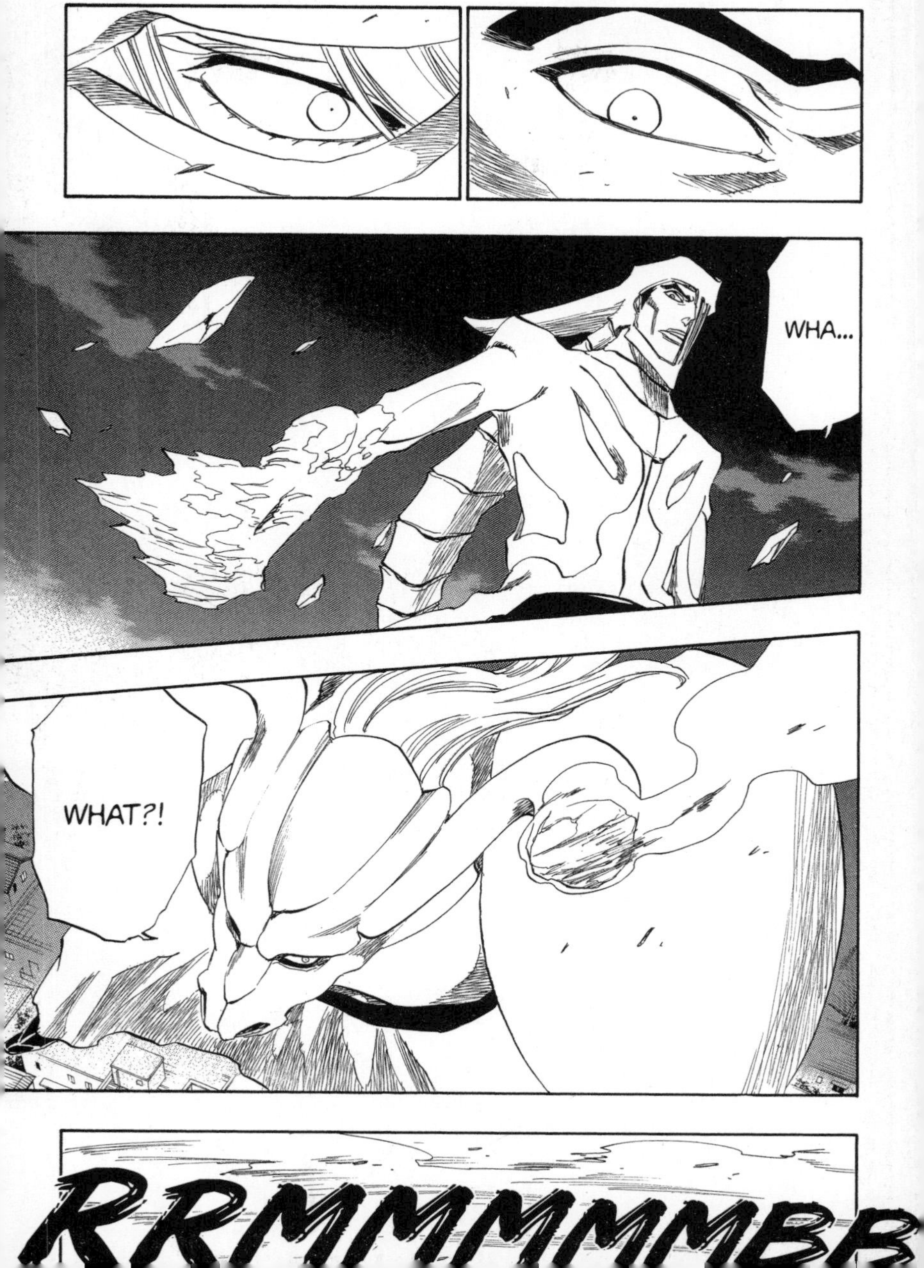
WHA...
WHAT?!
RRMMMMMMBR

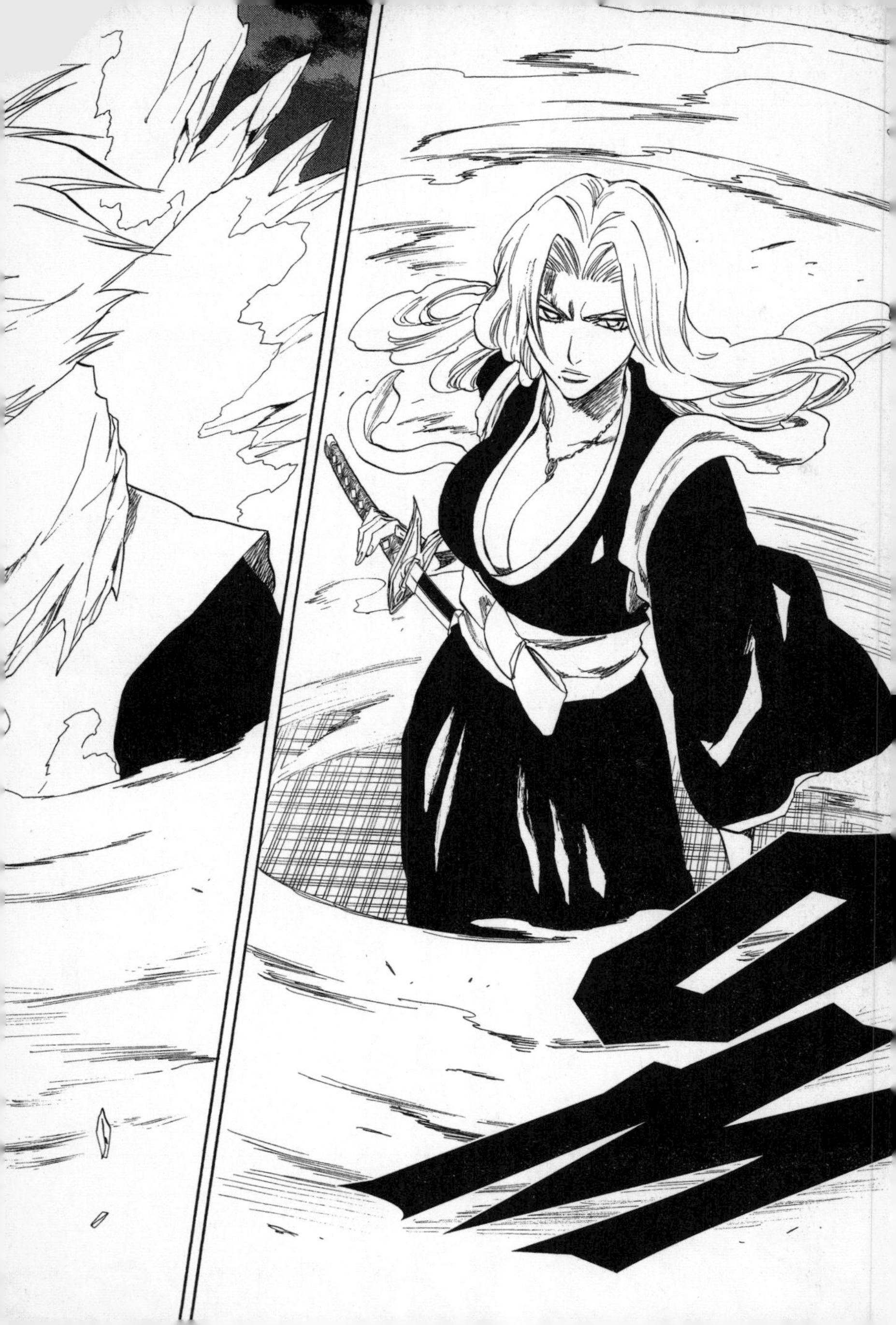

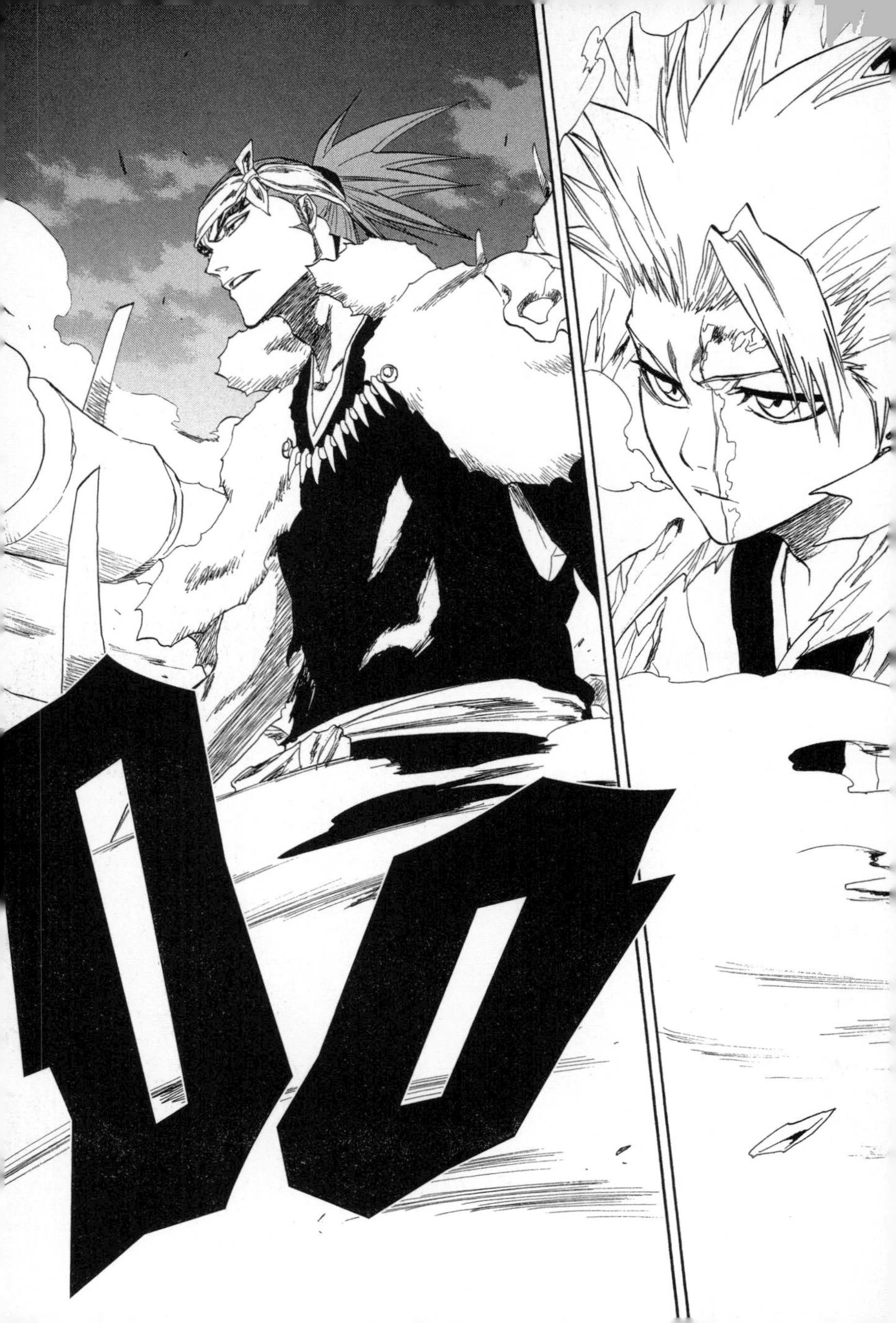

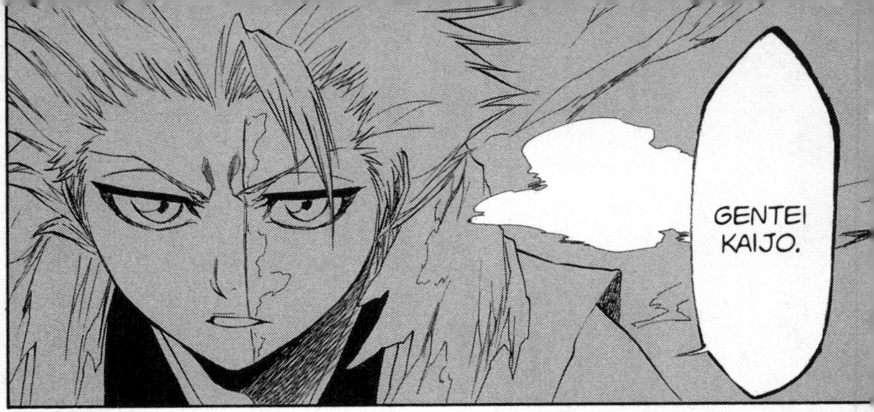
GENTEI KAIJO.

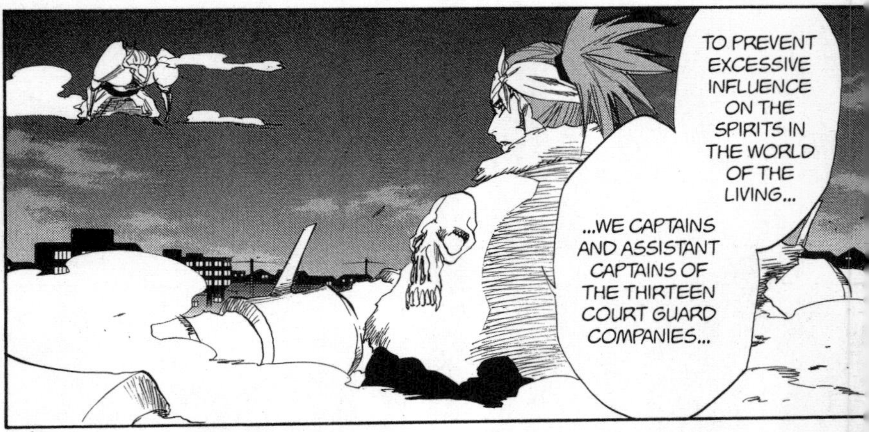
TO PREVENT EXCESSIVE INFLUENCE ON THE SPIRITS IN THE WORLD OF THE LIVING...
...WE CAPTAINS AND ASSISTANT CAPTAINS OF THE THIRTEEN COURT GUARD COMPANIES...

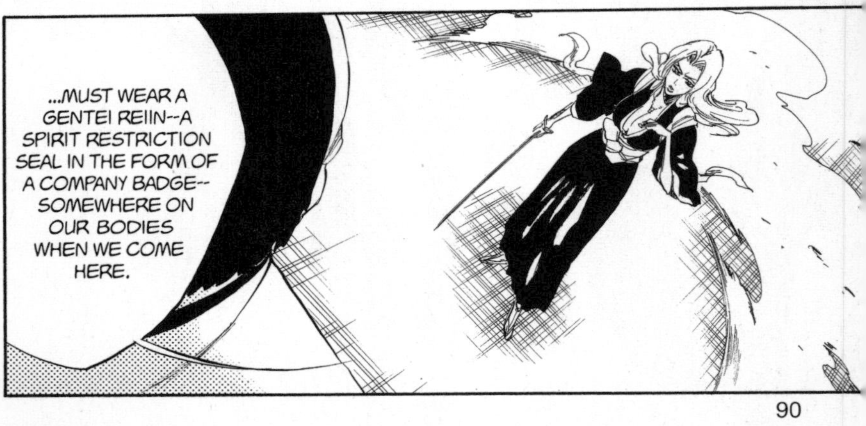
...MUST WEAR A GENTEI REIIN--A SPIRIT RESTRICTION SEAL IN THE FORM OF A COMPANY BADGE--SOMEWHERE ON OUR BODIES WHEN WE COME HERE.

READ THIS WAY

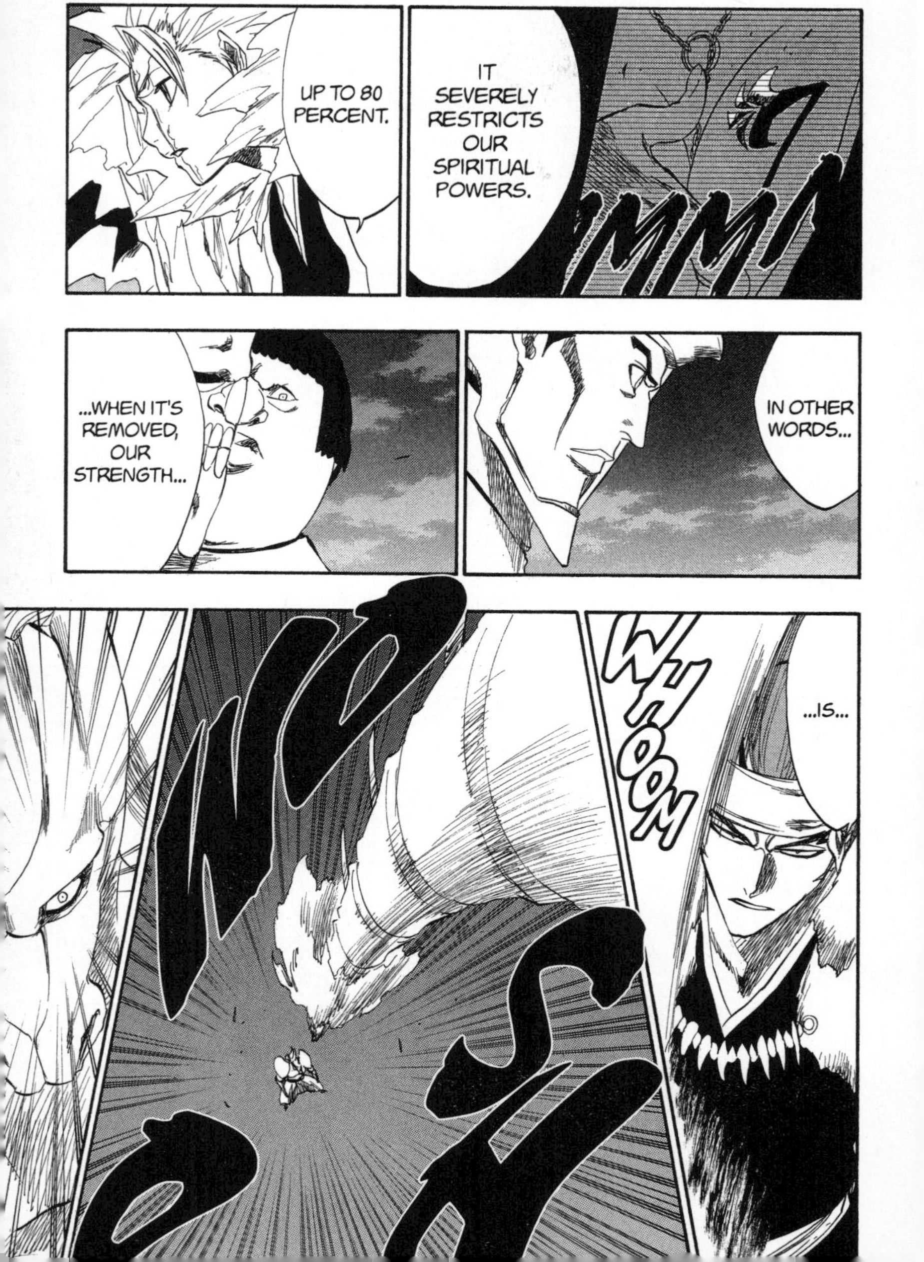
IT SEVERELY RESTRICTS OUR SPIRITUAL POWERS.
UP TO 80 PERCENT.
IN OTHER WORDS...
...WHEN IT'S REMOVED, OUR STRENGTH...
...IS...
WHOOM

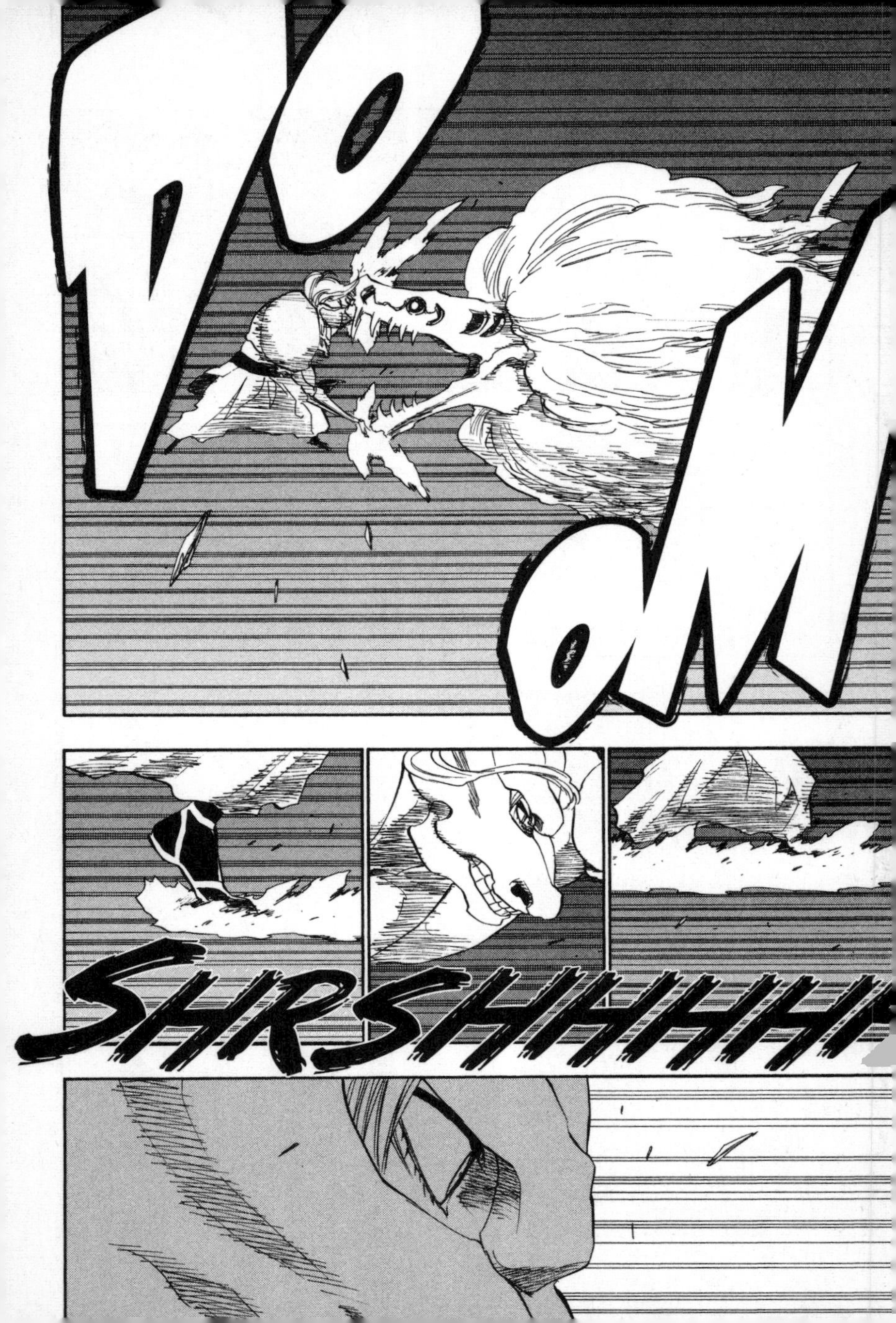
VOOM
SHRSHHHH

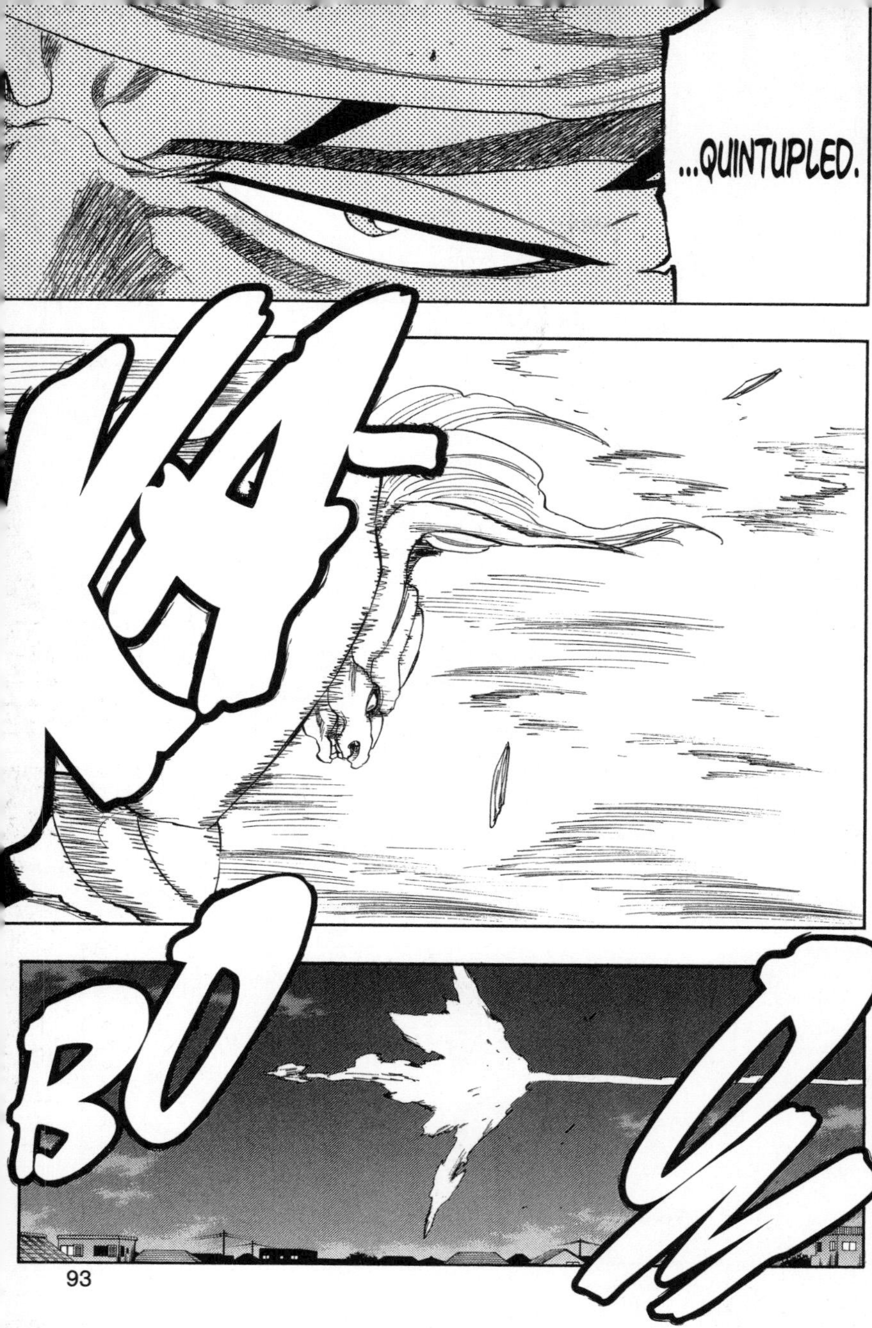
...QUINTUPLED.
KA
BOOM

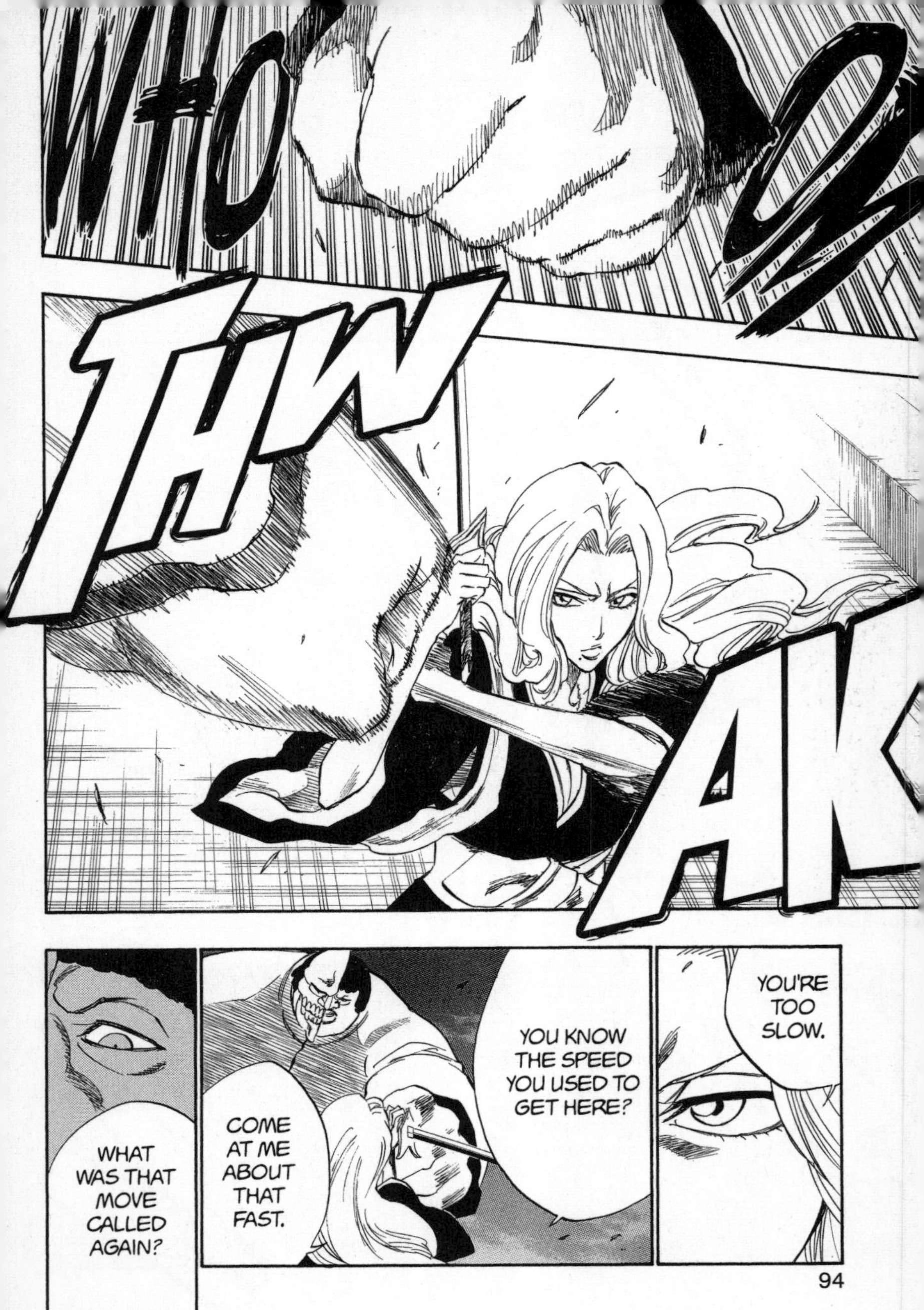
WHO
THWAK
YOU'RE TOO SLOW.
YOU KNOW THE SPEED YOU USED TO GET HERE?
COME AT ME ABOUT THAT FAST.
WHAT WAS THAT MOVE CALLED AGAIN?

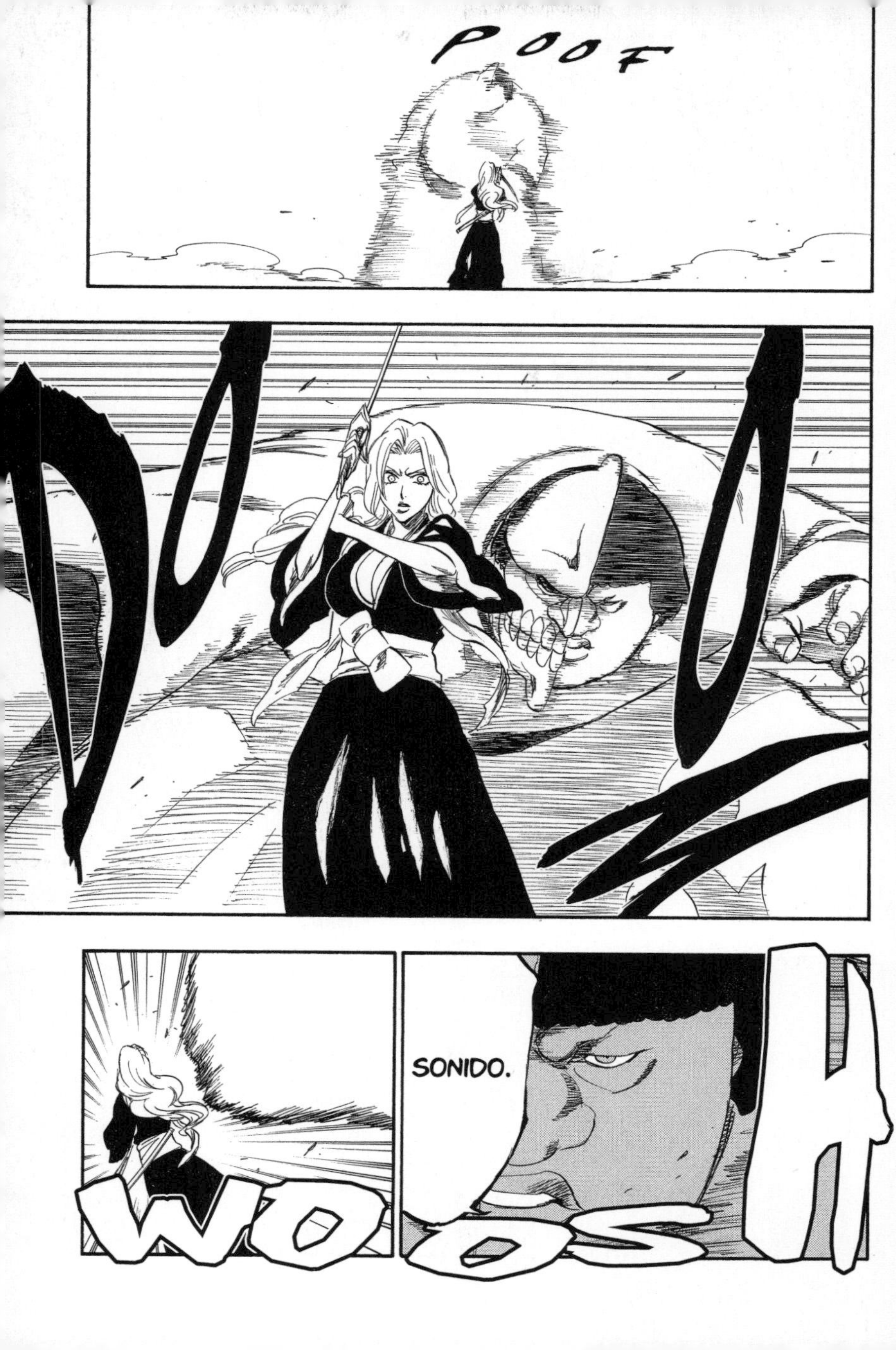
POOF
DOOM
SONIDO.
WOOSH

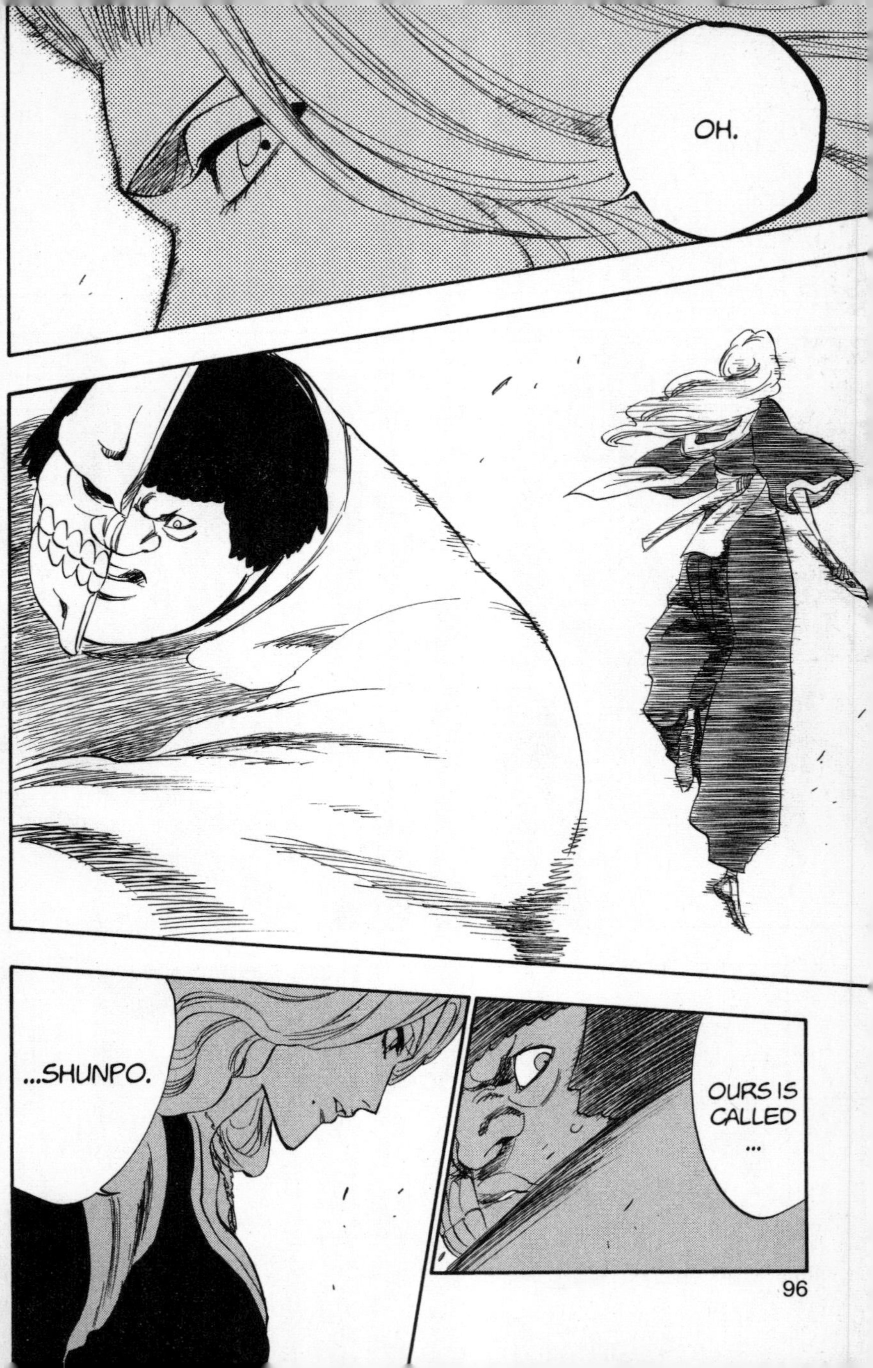
OH.
OURS IS CALLED ...
...SHUNPO.

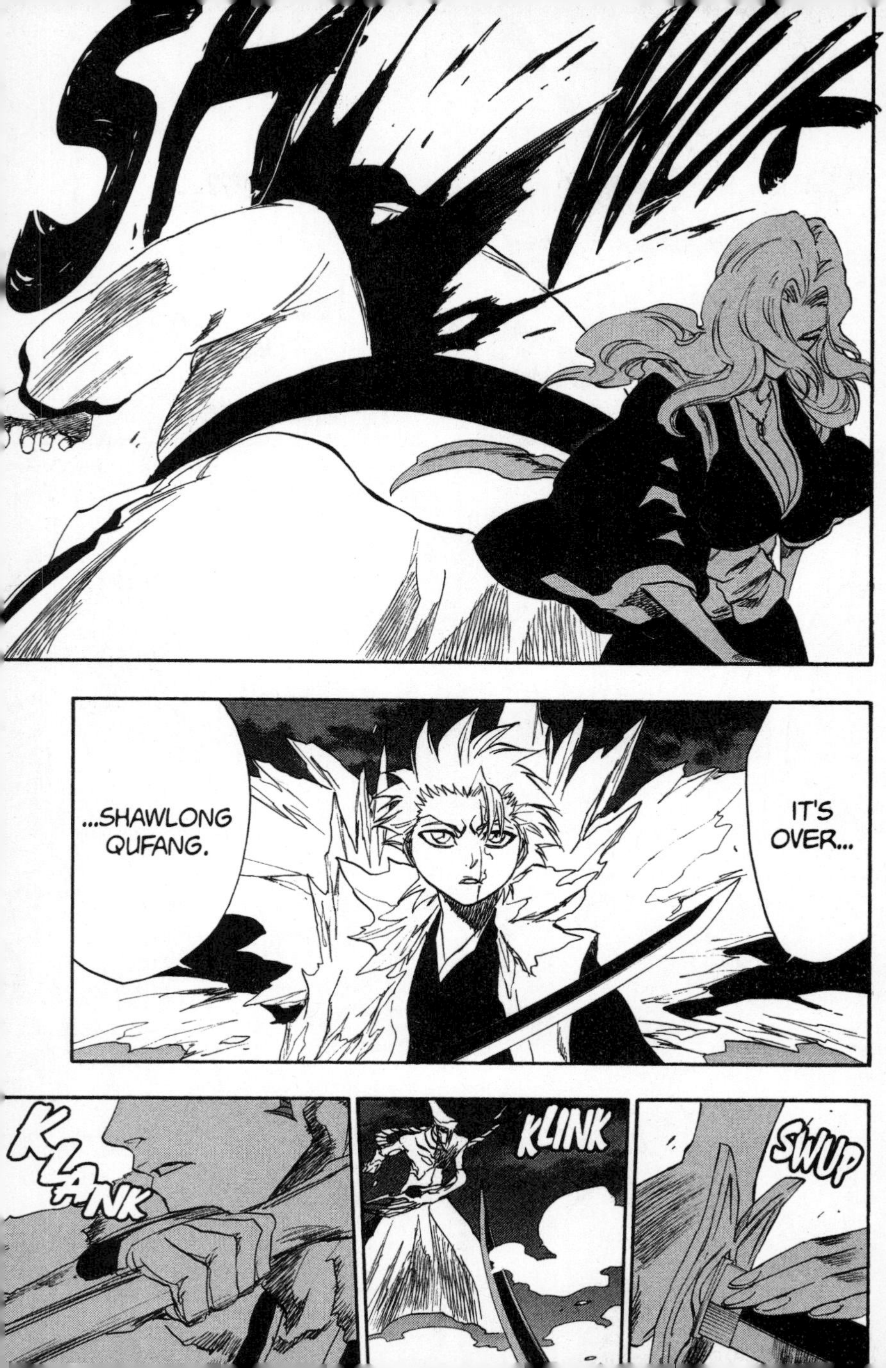
IT'S OVER...
...SHAWLONG QUFANG.
SWUP
KLINK
KLANK

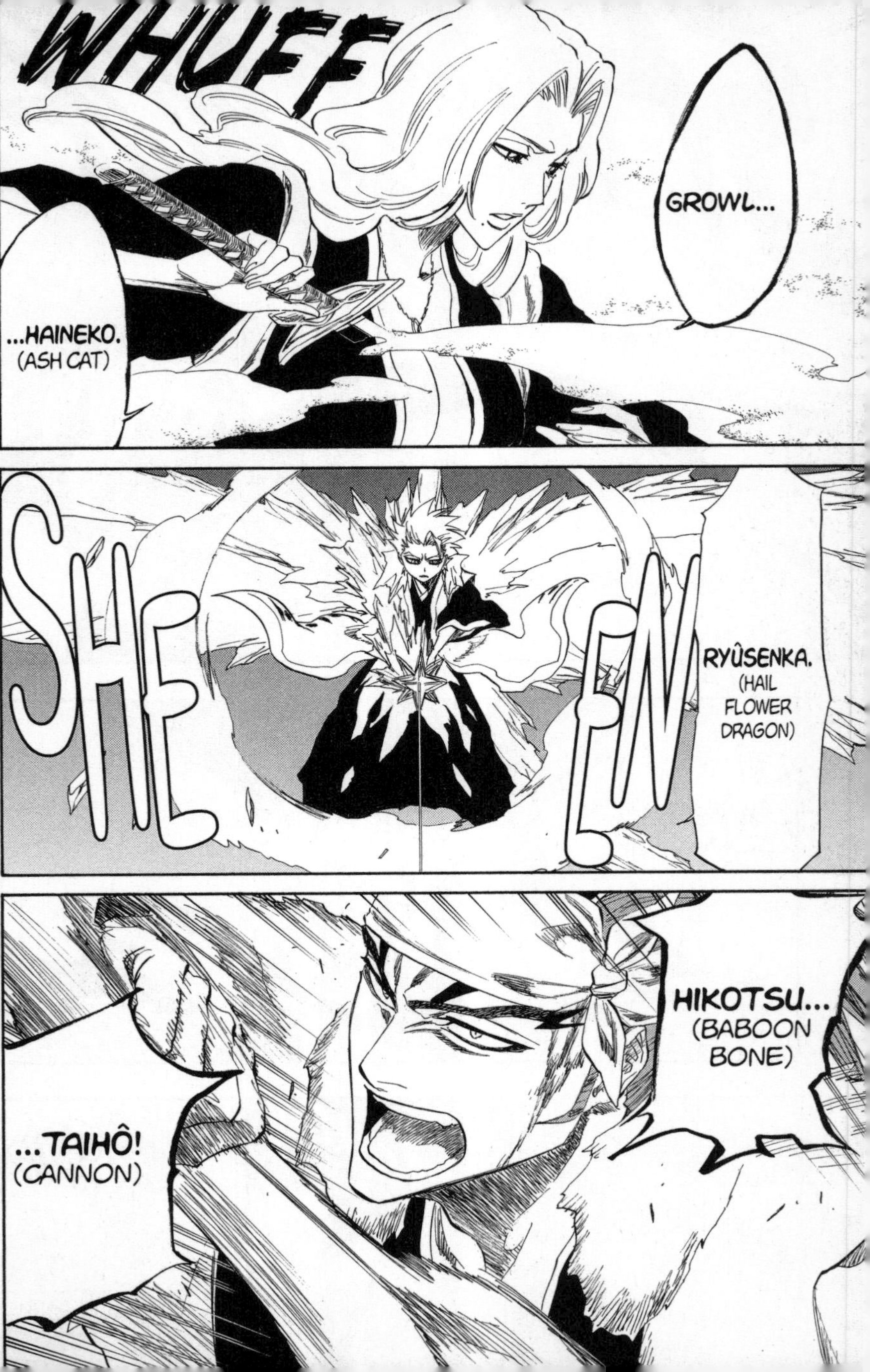
WHUFF
GROWL...
...HAINEKO.
(ASH CAT)
RYÛSENKA.
(HAIL FLOWER DRAGON)
SHEEN
HIKOTSU...
(BABOON BONE)
...TAIHÔ!
(CANNON)

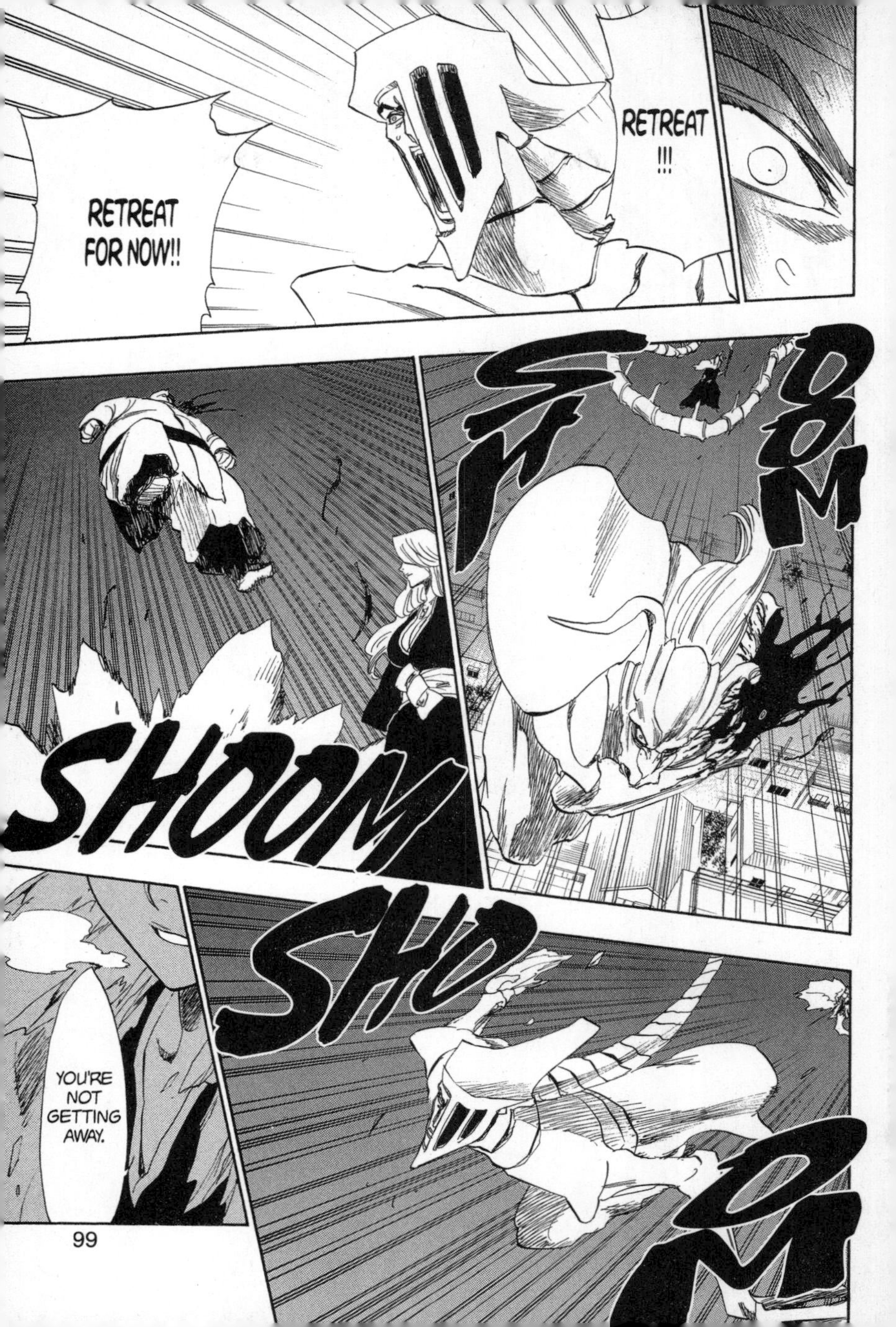
RETREAT !!!
RETREAT FOR NOW!!
SHOOM
SHOOM
SHOOOM
YOU'RE NOT GETTING AWAY.

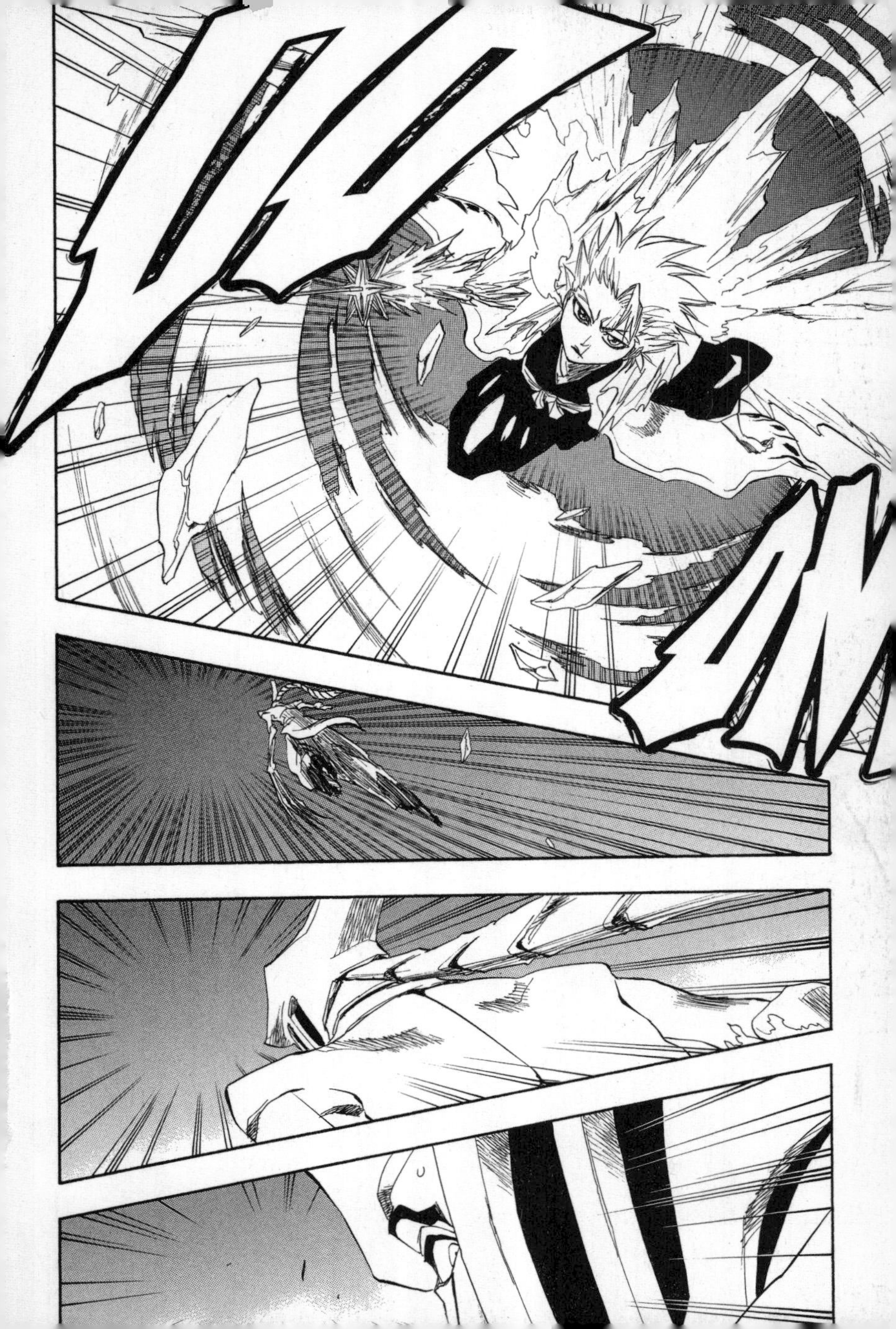

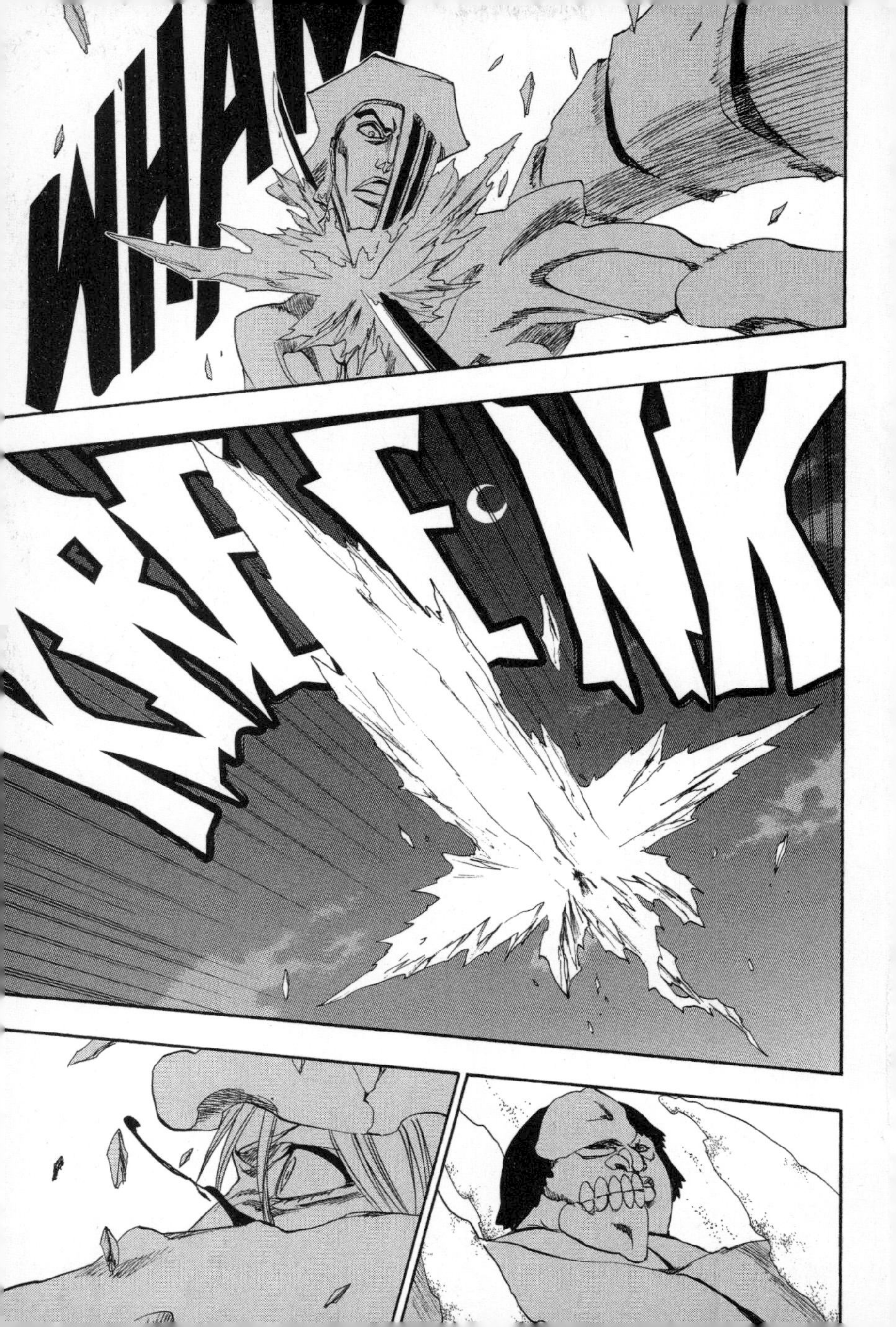
WHAM
KRAANK

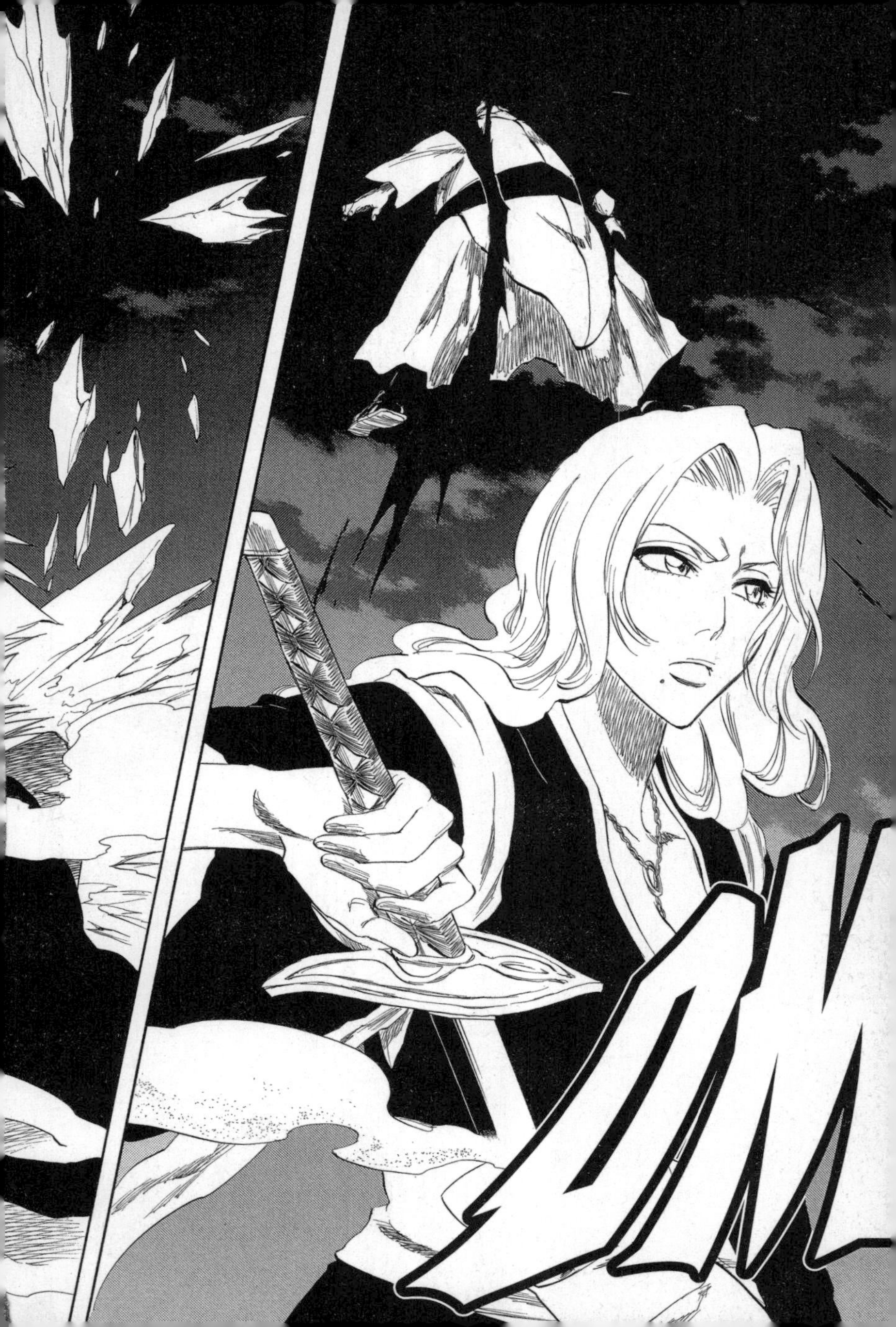

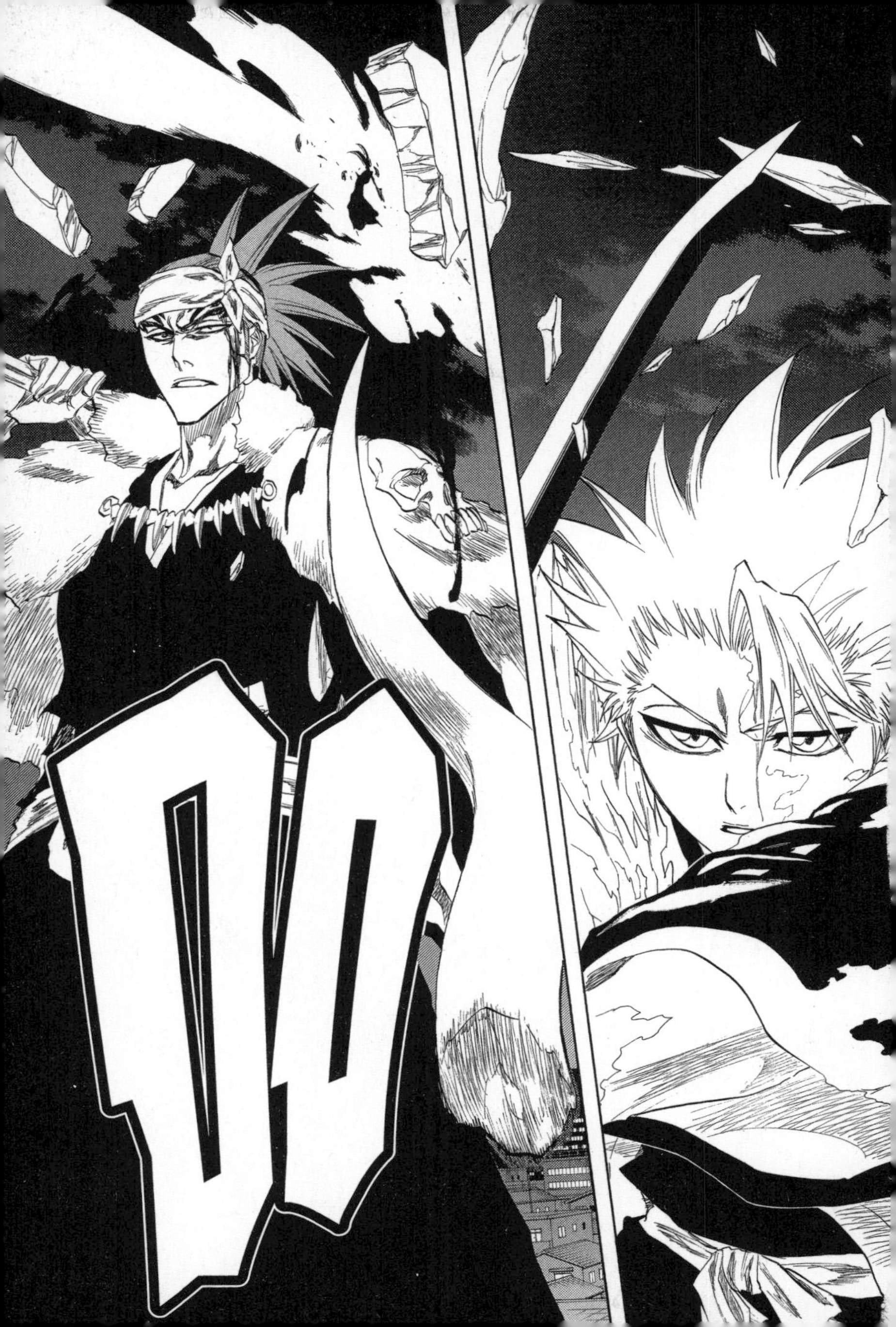
DO

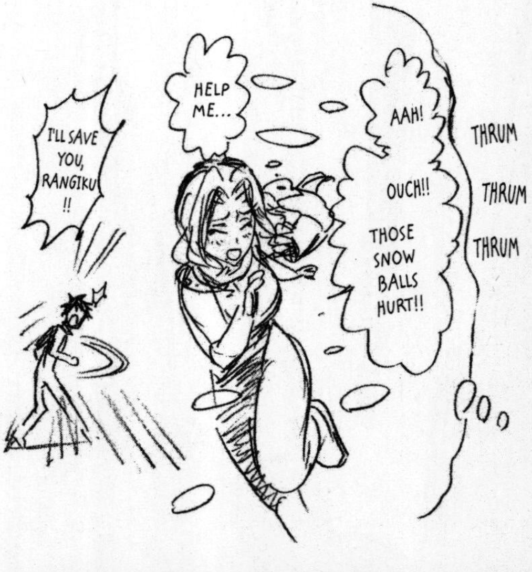
THRUM
THRUM
THRUM
AAH!
OUCH!!
THOSE SNOW BALLS HURT!!
HELP ME...
I'LL SAVE YOU, RANGIKU!!

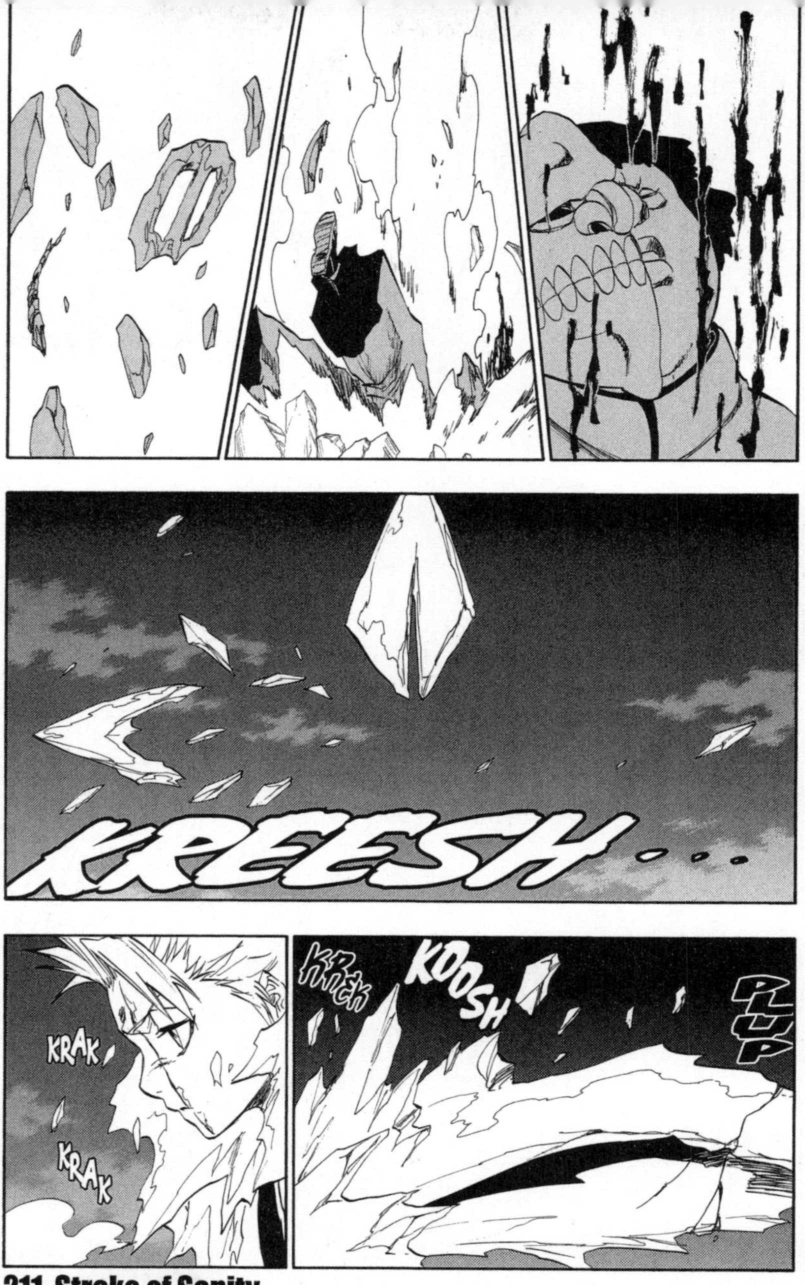
KREESH...
PLUP
KOOSH
KRAK
KRAK

## 211. Stroke of Sanity

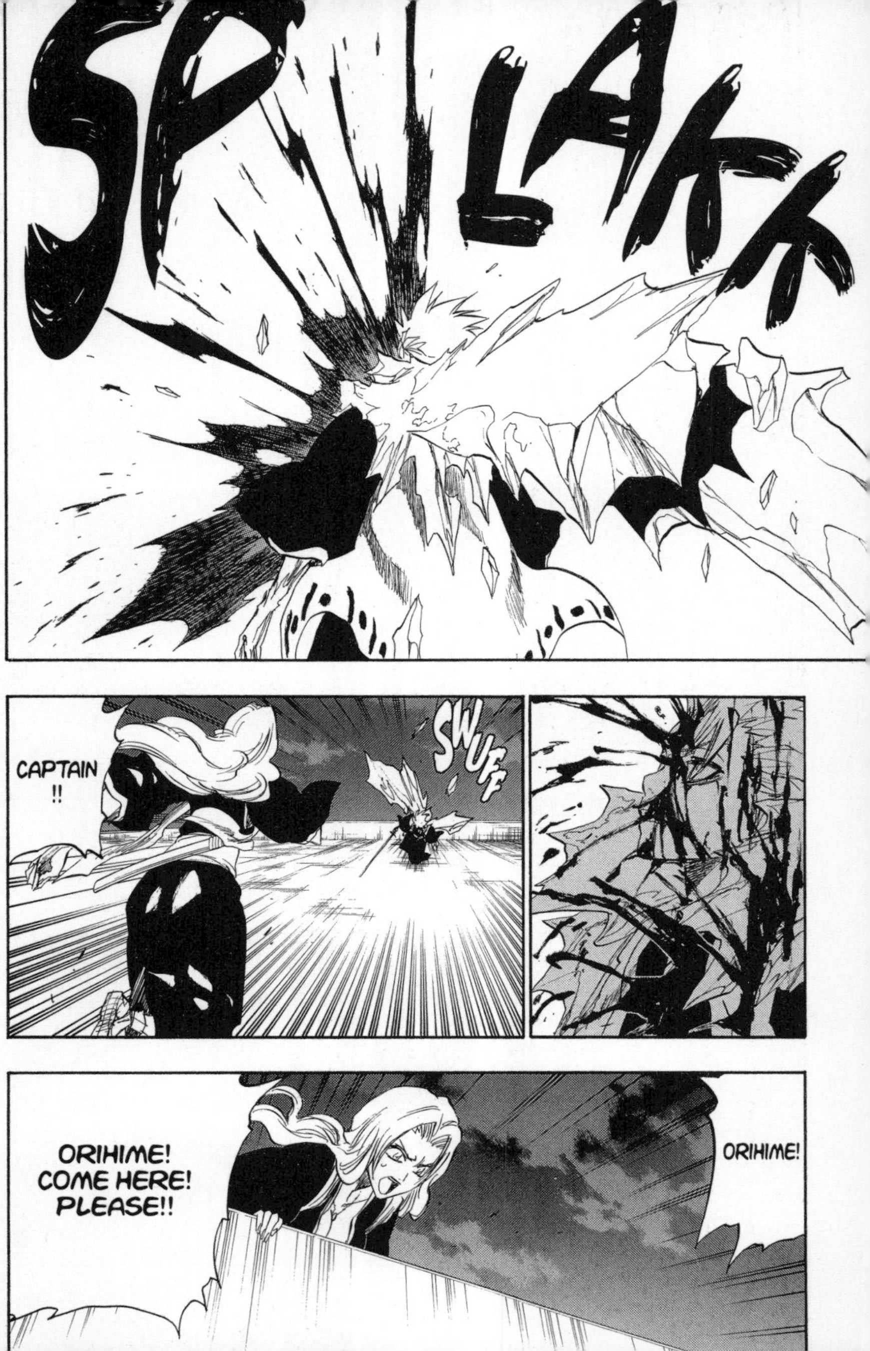
SPLAKK
SWUFF
CAPTAIN !!
ORIHIME!
ORIHIME! COME HERE! PLEASE!!

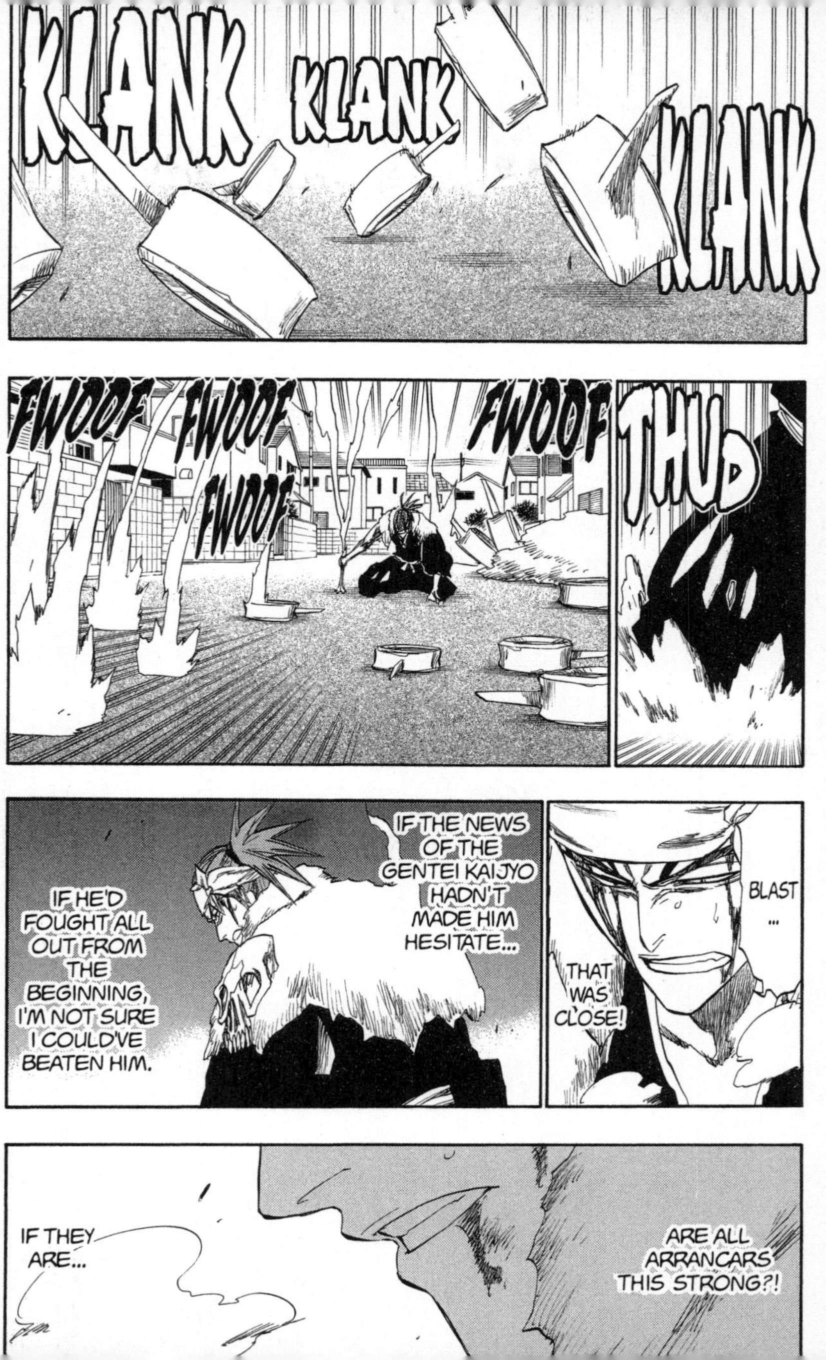
KLANK
KLANK
KLANK
THUD
FWOOF
FWOOF
FWOOF
FWOOF
BLAST...
THAT WAS CLOSE!
IF THE NEWS OF THE GENTEI KAIJYO HADN'T MADE HIM HESITATE...
IF HE'D FOUGHT ALL OUT FROM THE BEGINNING, I'M NOT SURE I COULD'VE BEATEN HIM.
ARE ALL ARRANCARS THIS STRONG?!
IF THEY ARE...

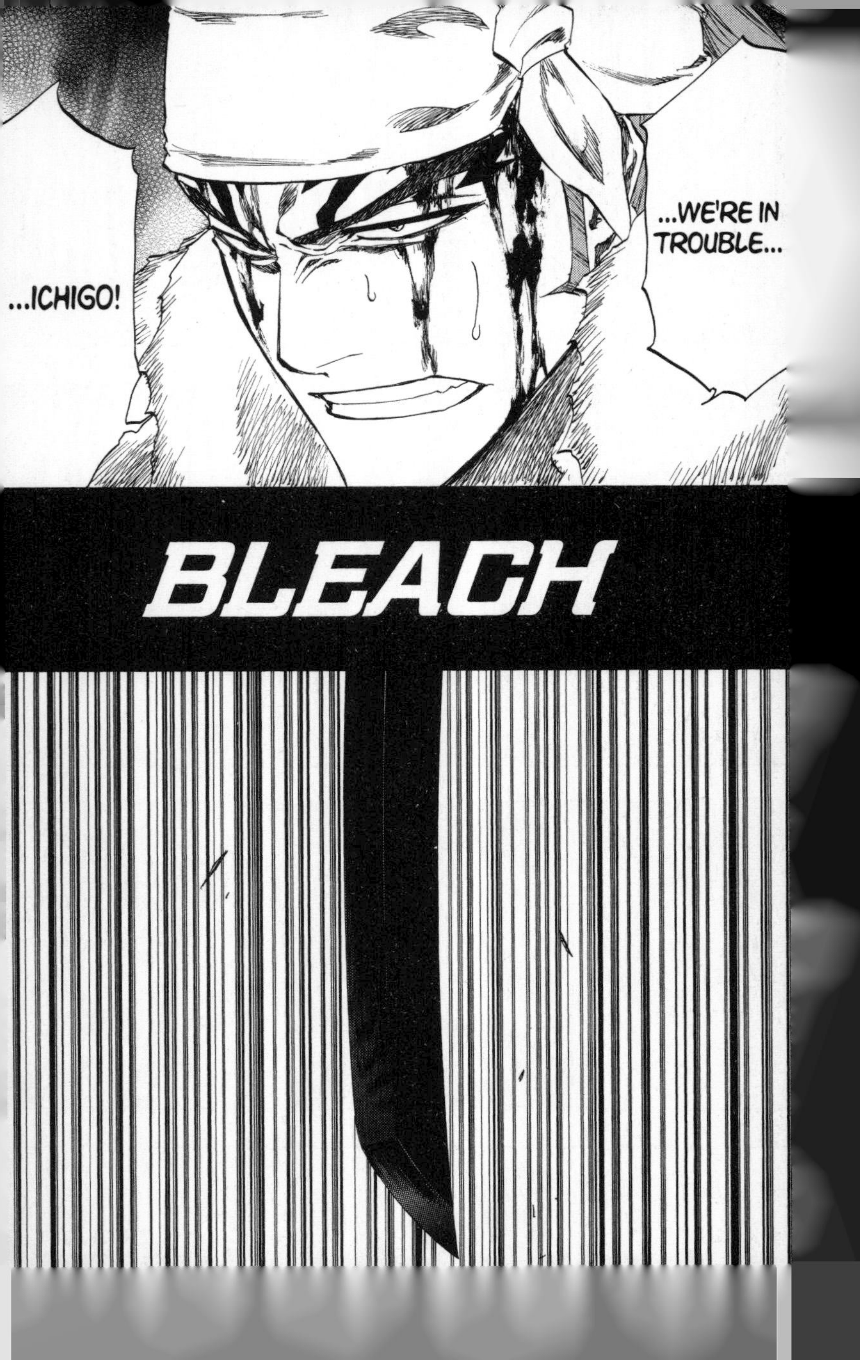
...WE'RE IN TROUBLE...
...ICHIGO!
BLEACH

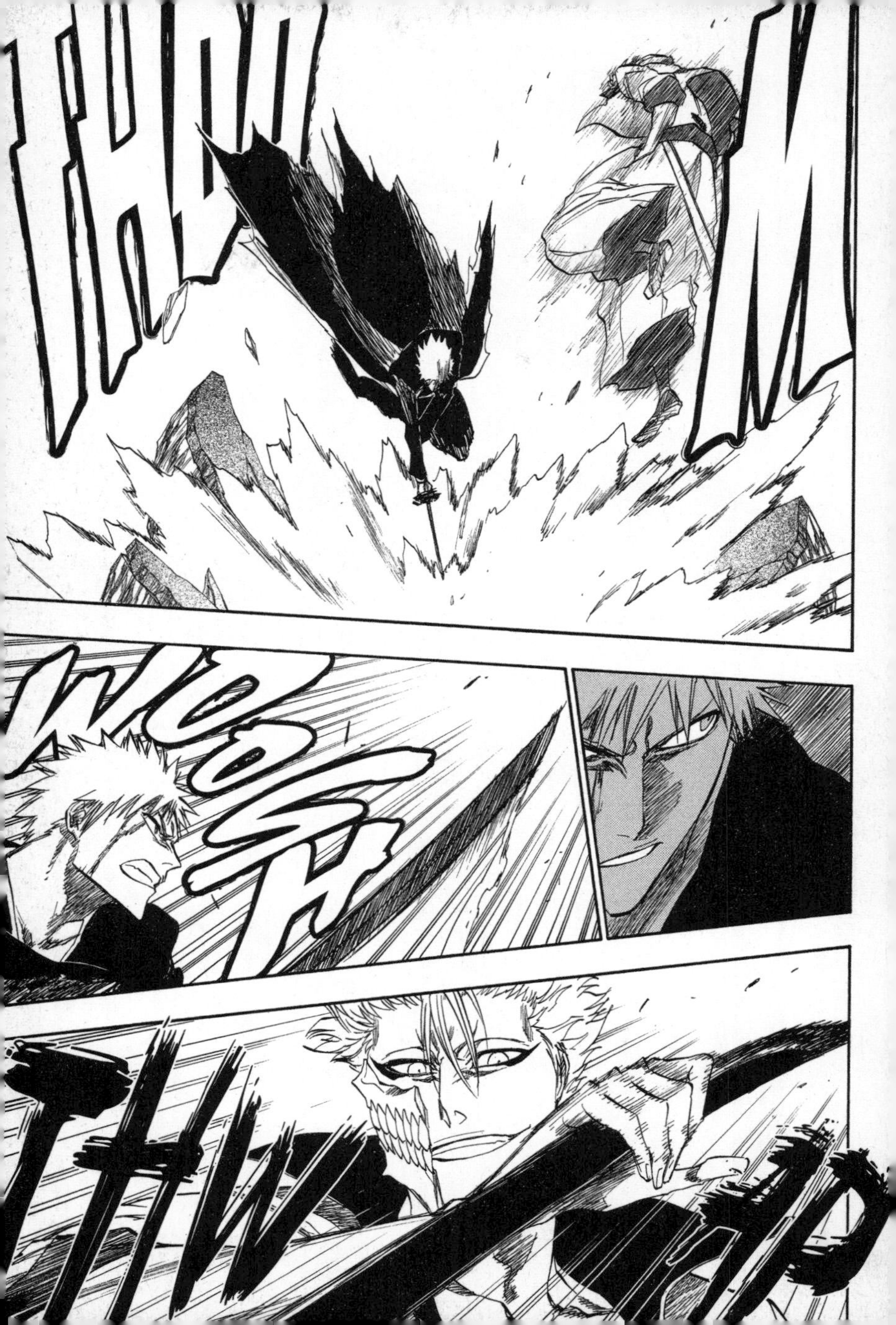
WHOOSH
THWAP

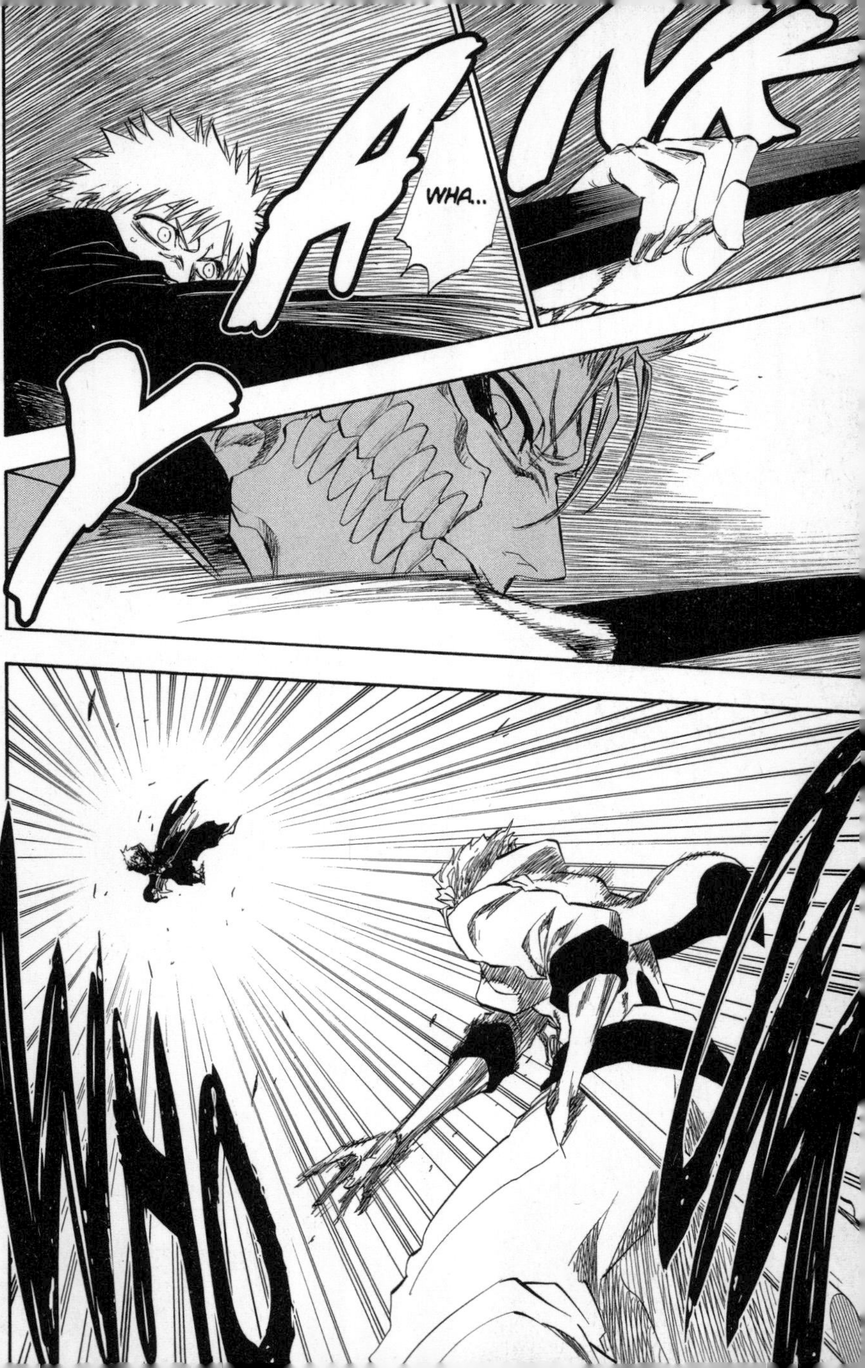
YANK
WHA...

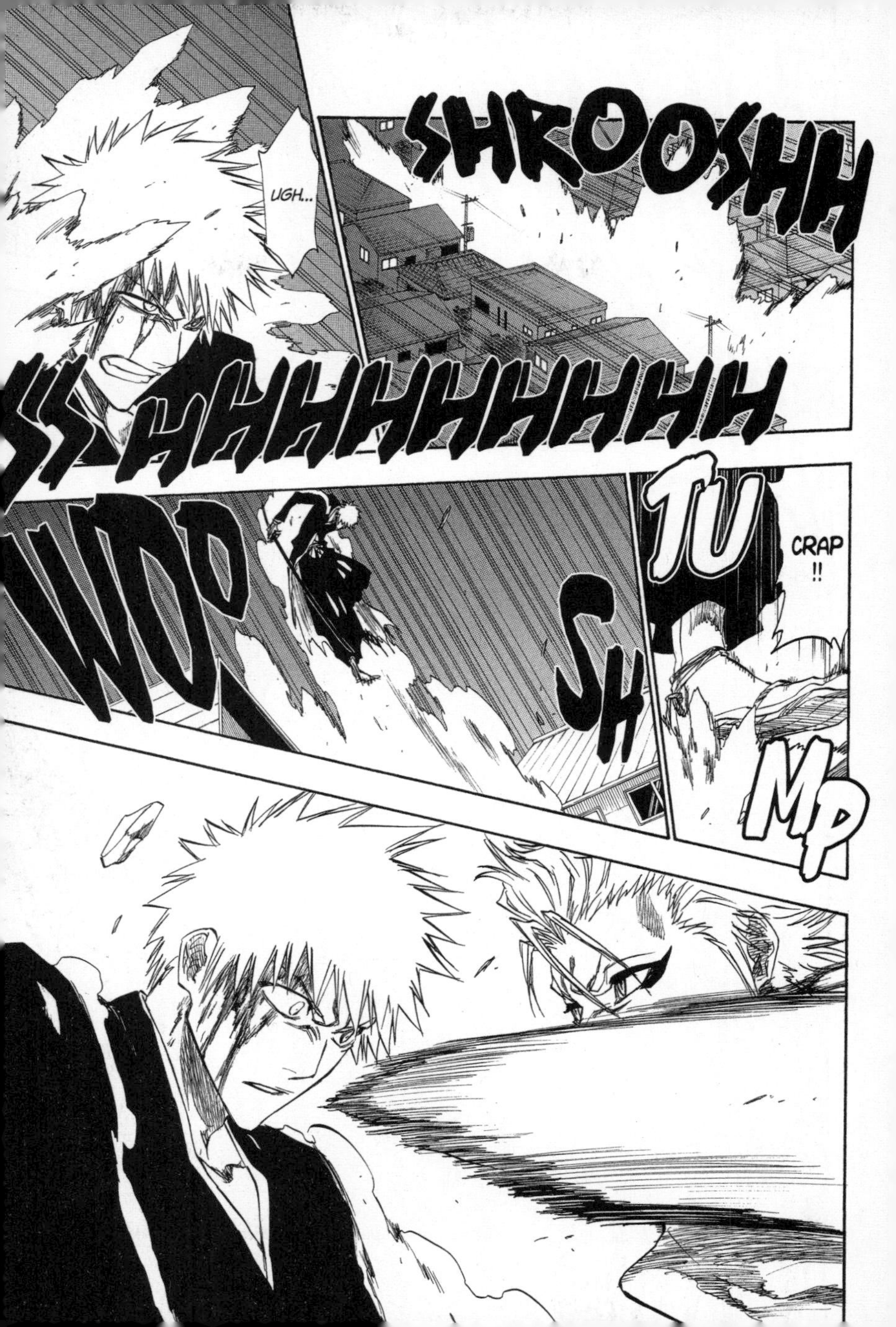
SHROOSHH
UGH...
SSHHHHHHHHHHHH
TU
MP
CRAP !!
SH
WOP

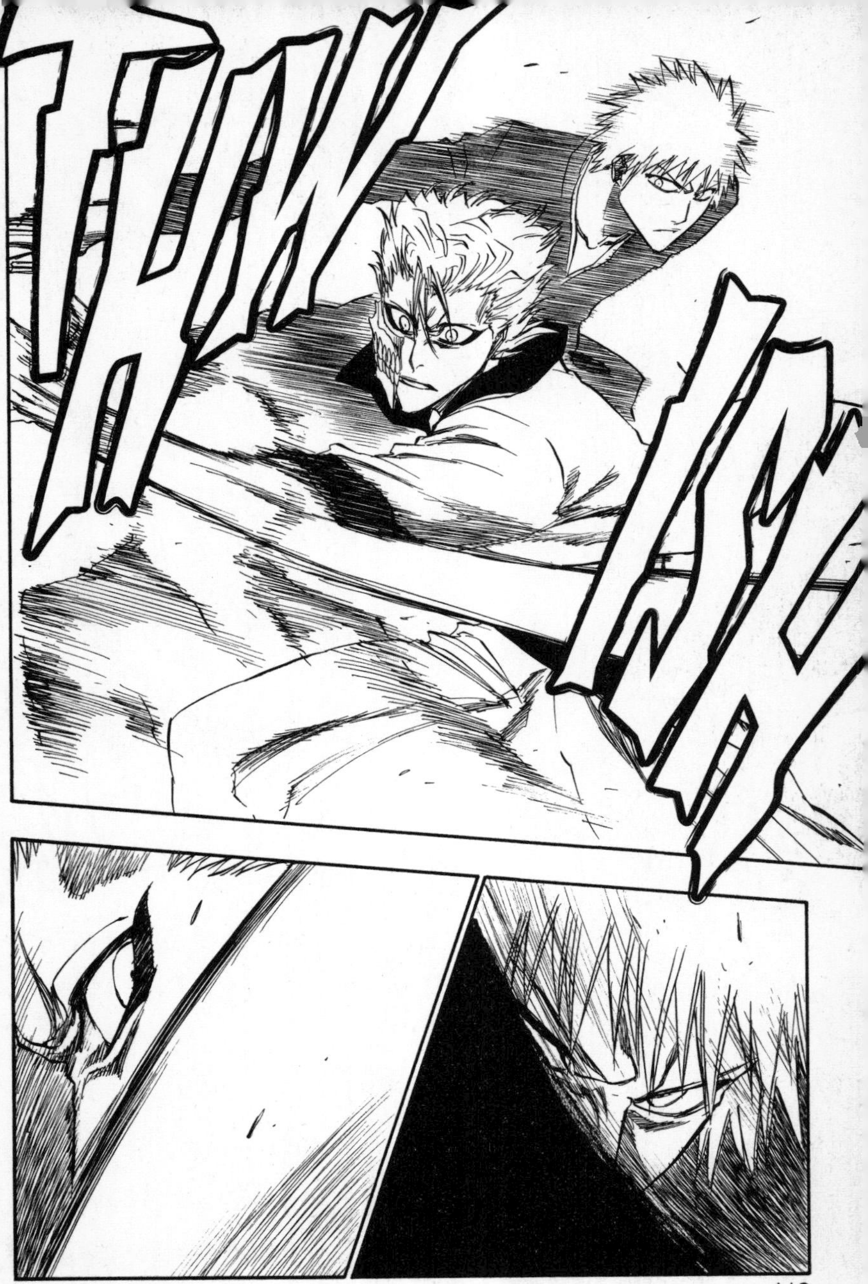

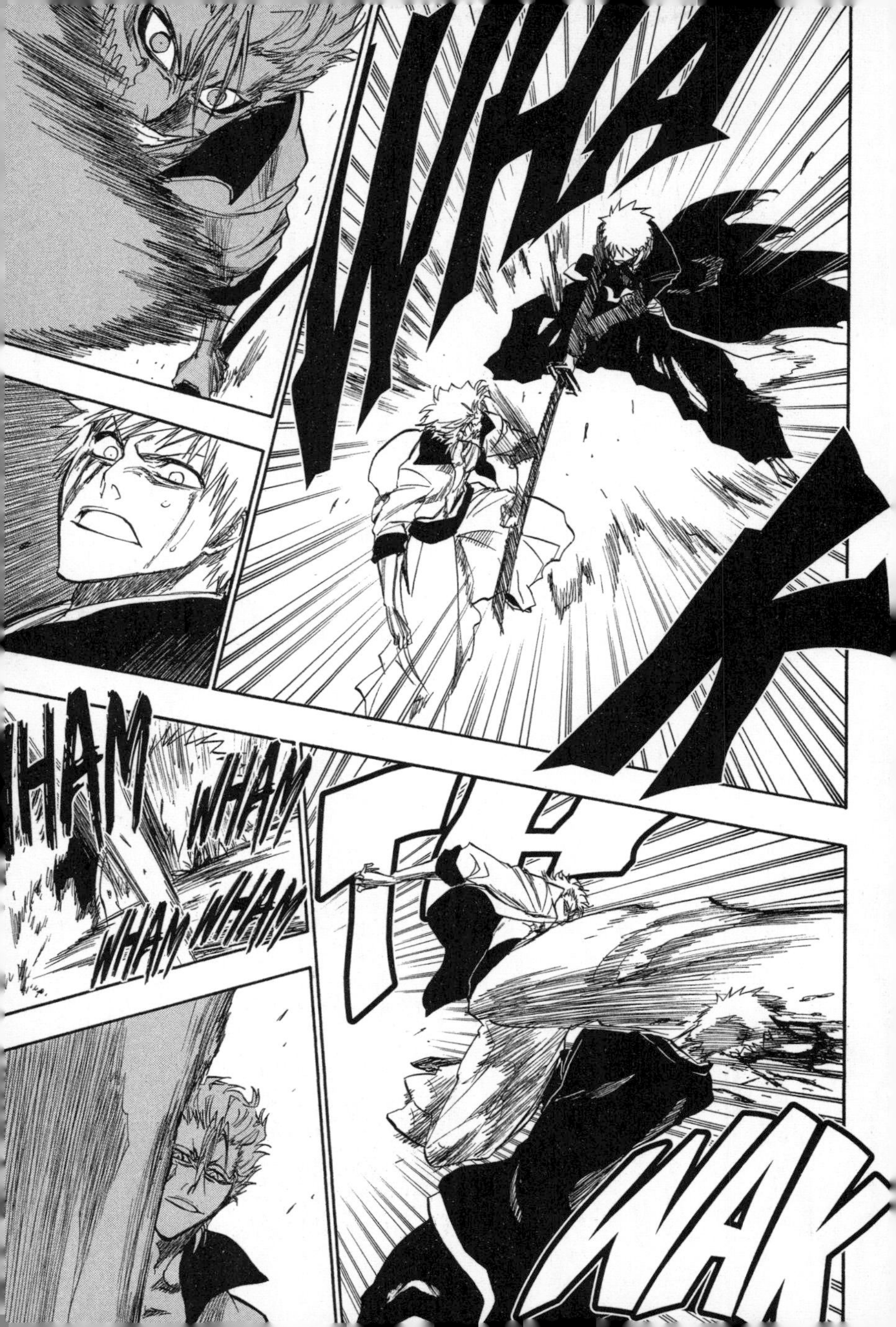
WHACK
WHAM
WHAM
WHAM
WHAM
WHAK

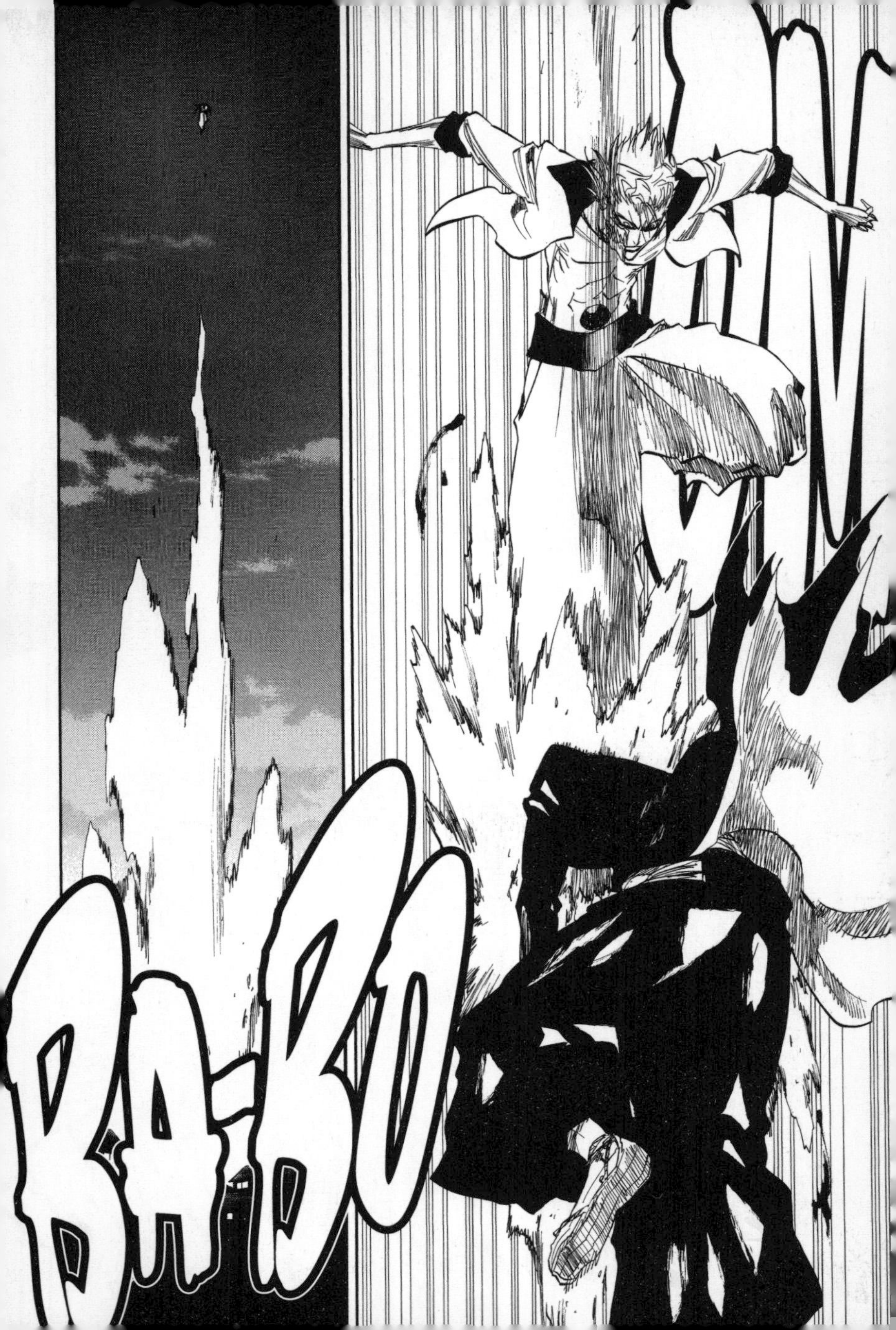

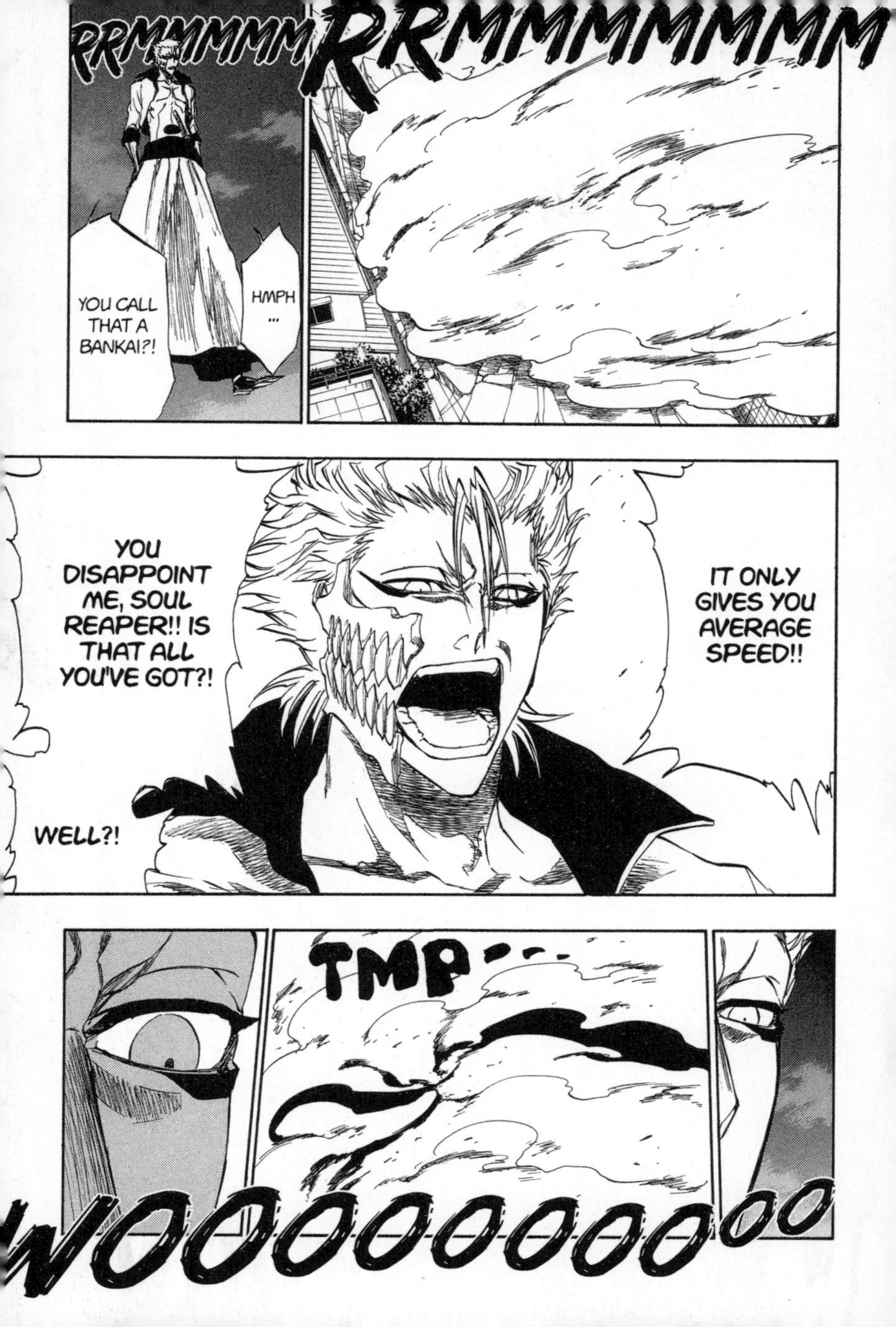
RRMMMMMMMM
RRMMMMMM
HMPH ...
YOU CALL THAT A BANKAI?!
IT ONLY GIVES YOU AVERAGE SPEED!!
YOU DISAPPOINT ME, SOUL REAPER!! IS THAT ALL YOU'VE GOT?!
WELL?!
TMP...
WOOOOOOOOOOOO

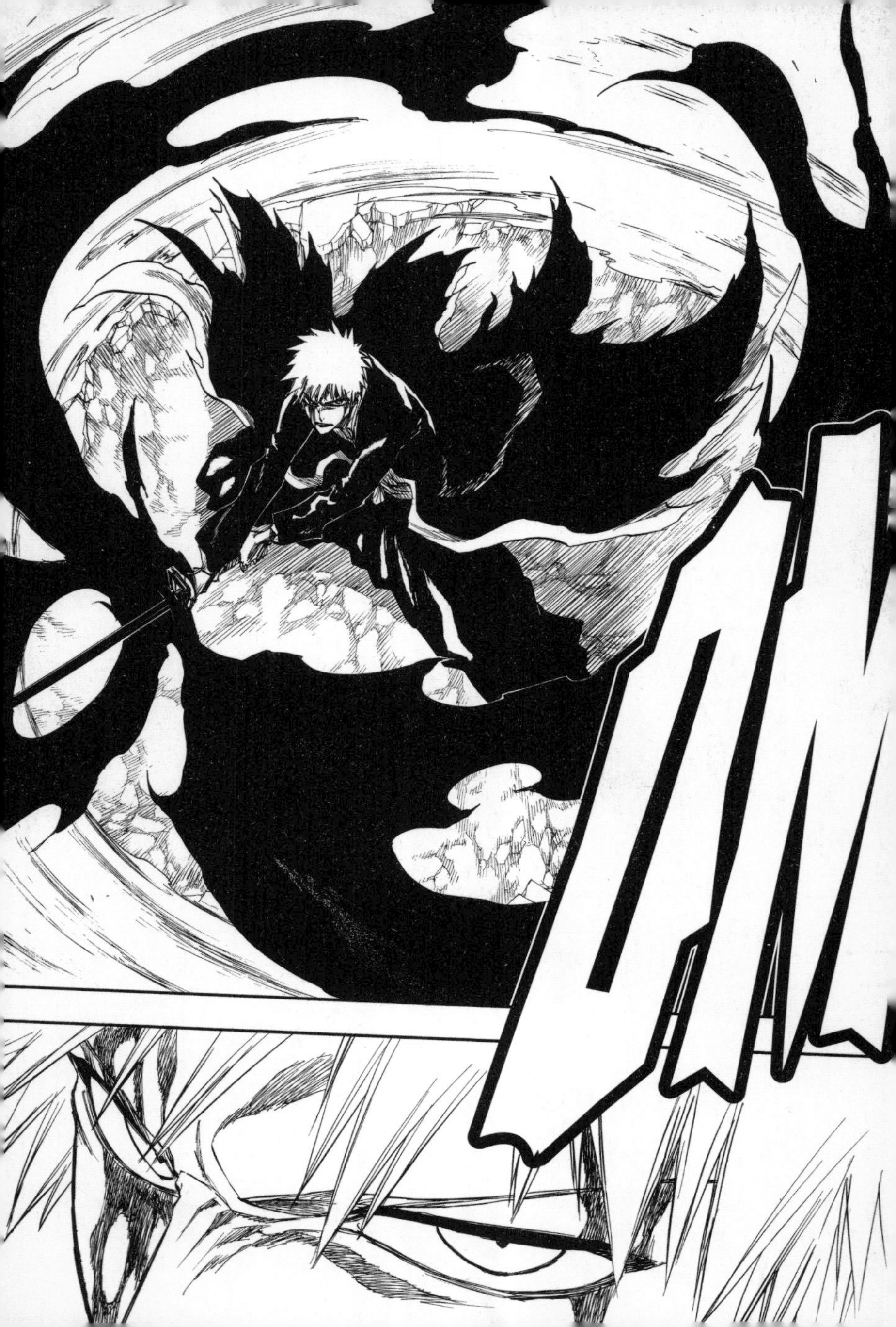

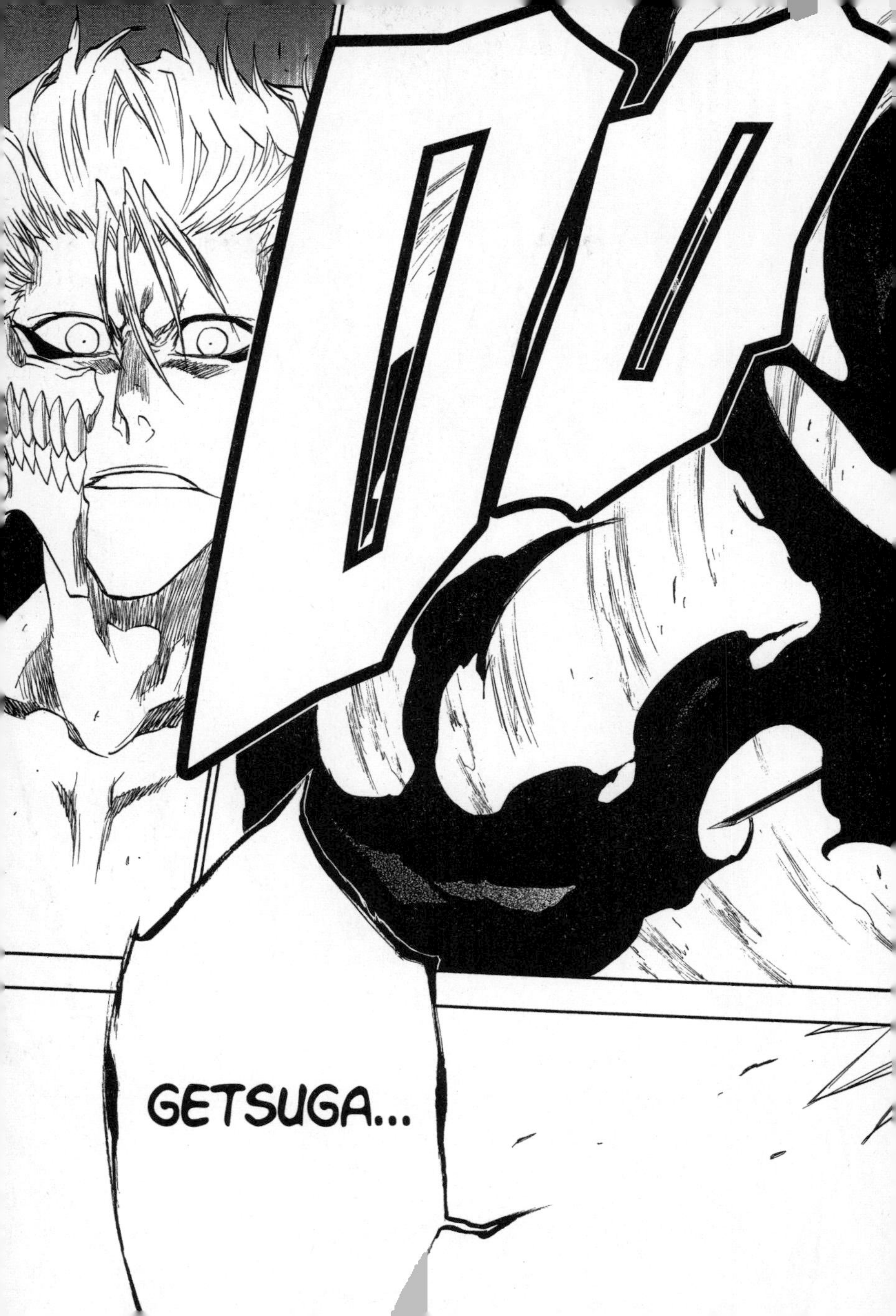
GETSUGA...

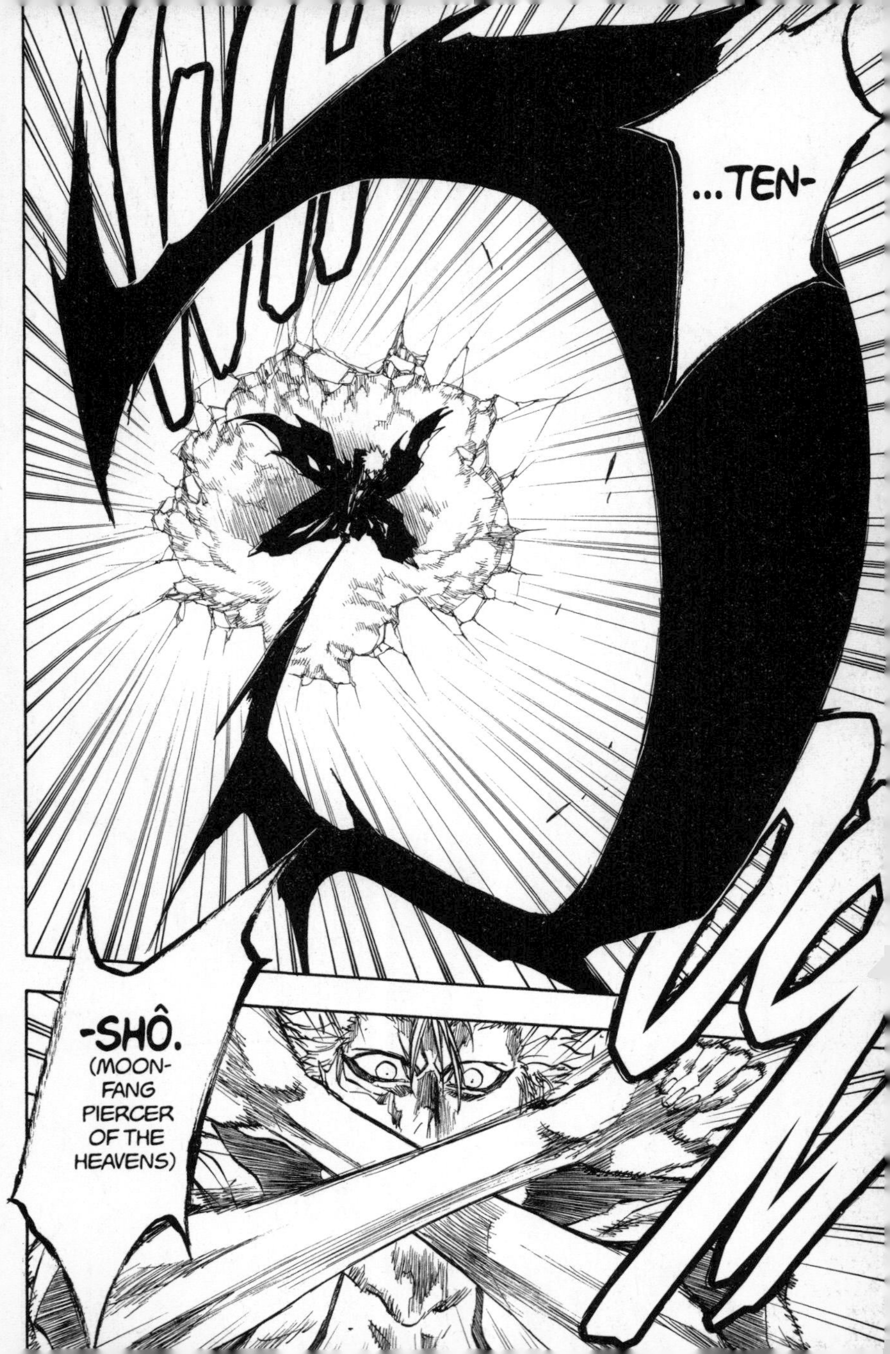
...TEN-
-SHÔ.
(MOON-FANG PIERCER OF THE HEAVENS)

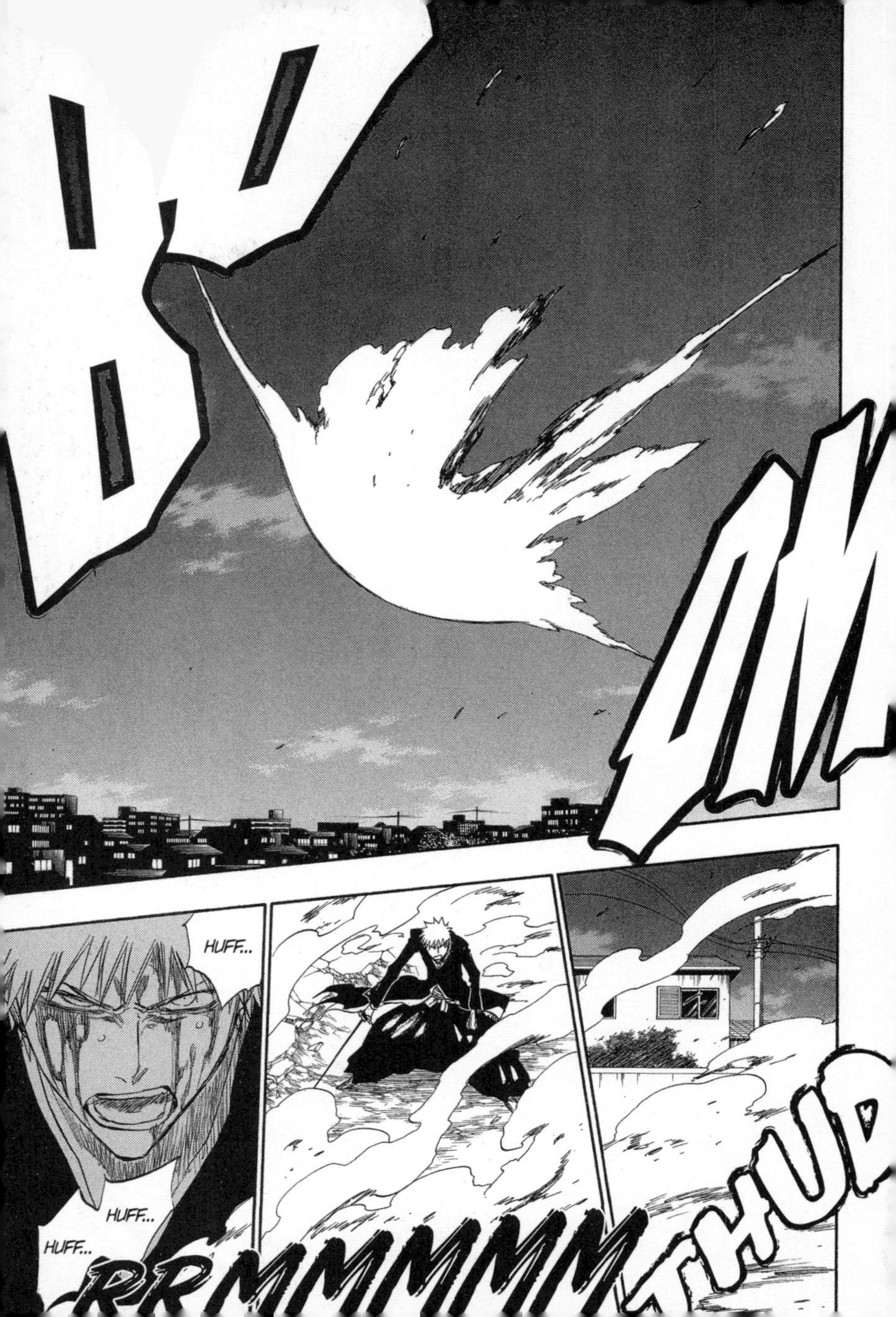
THUD
HUFF...
HUFF...
HUFF...
RRMMMMMM

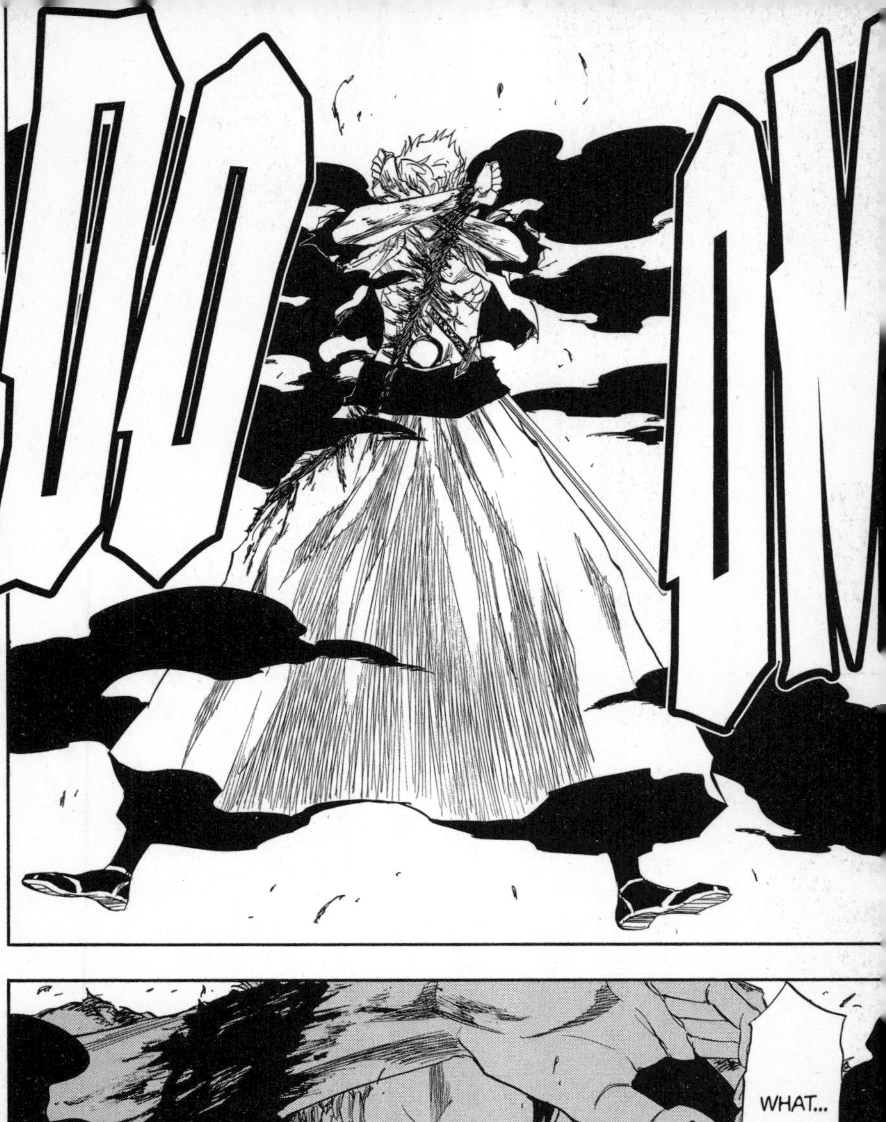

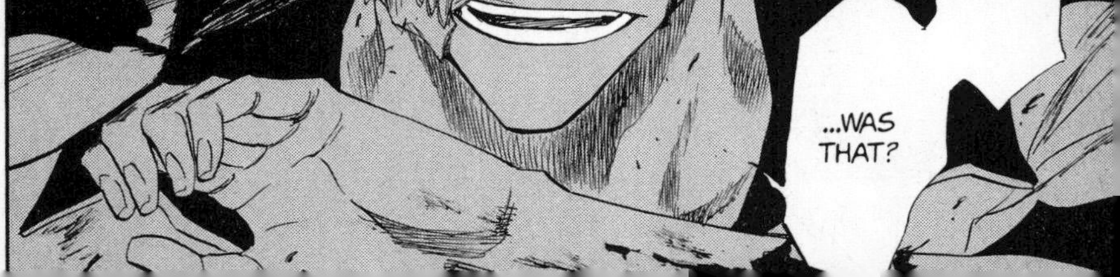
WHAT...
...WAS THAT?

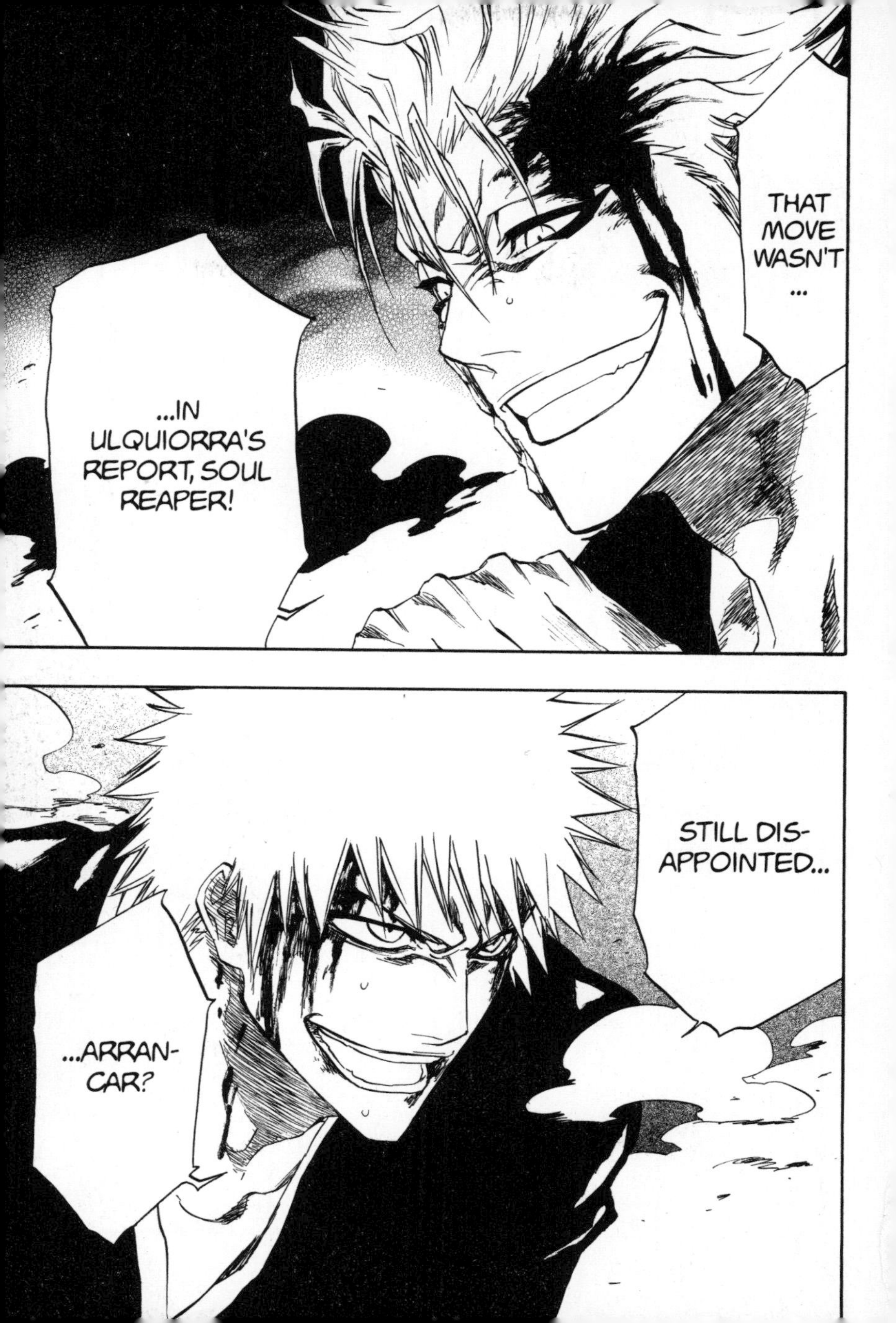
THAT MOVE WASN'T ...
...IN ULQUIORRA'S REPORT, SOUL REAPER!
STILL DIS-APPOINTED...
...ARRAN-CAR?

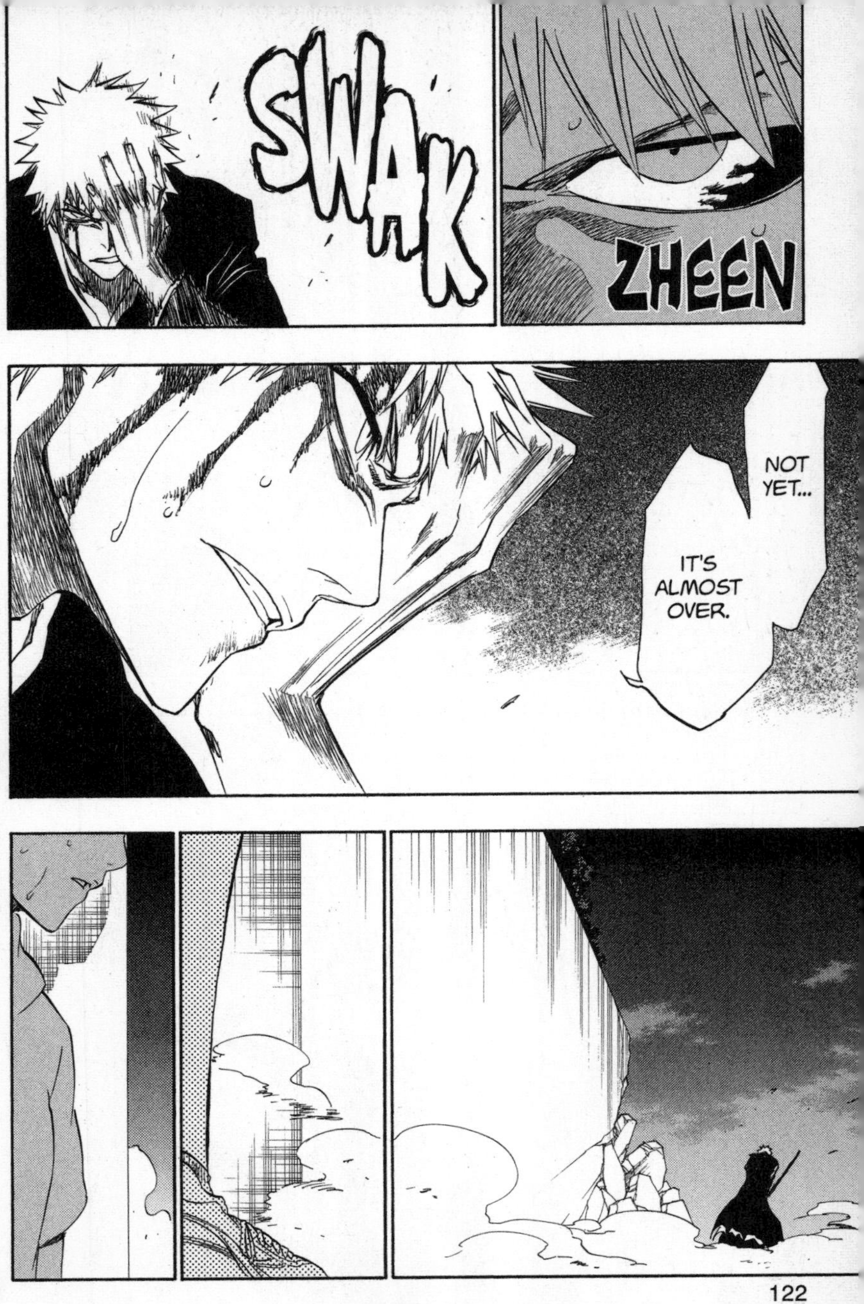
ZHEEN
SWAK
NOT YET...
IT'S ALMOST OVER.

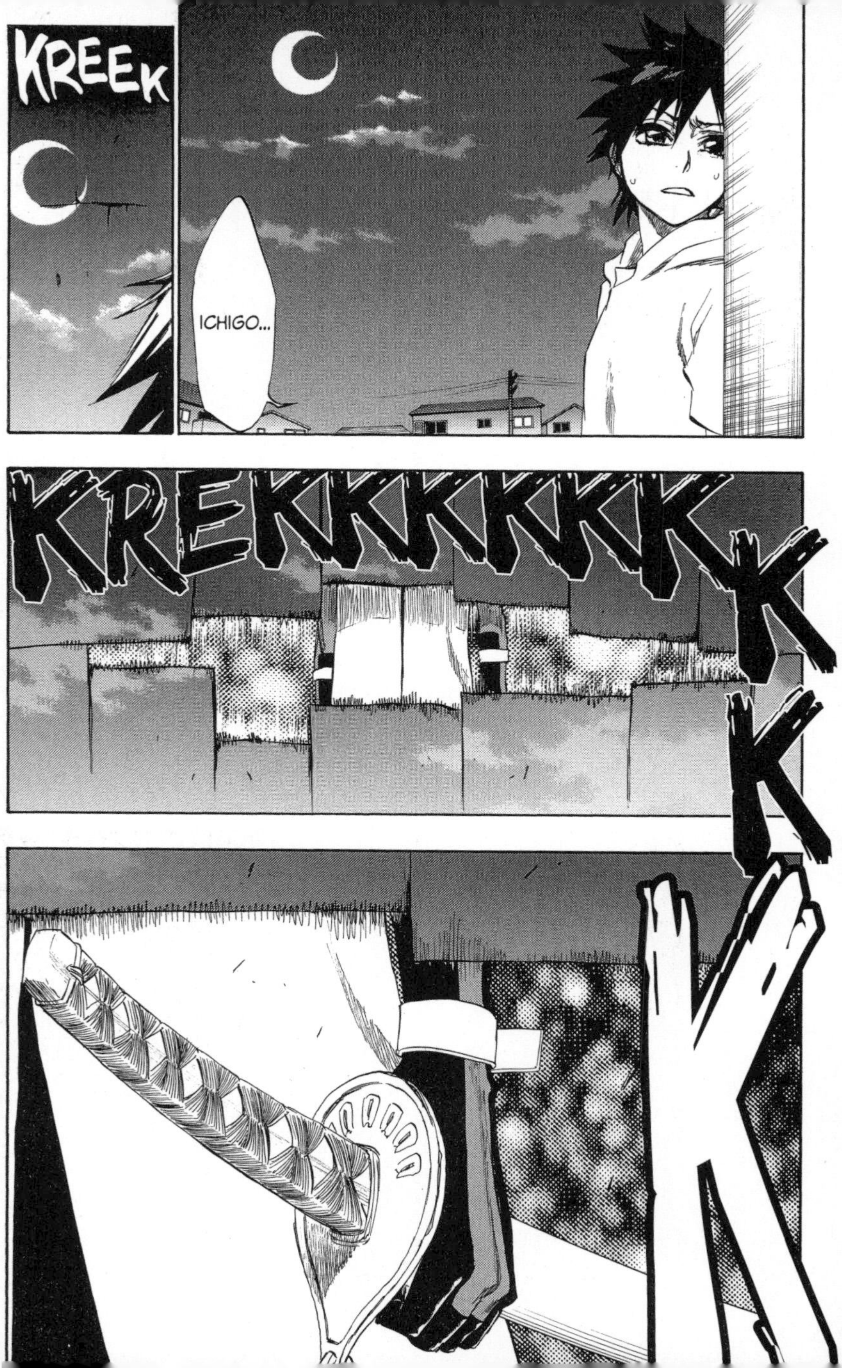
KREEK
ICHIGO...
KREKKKKKKKK
K
K

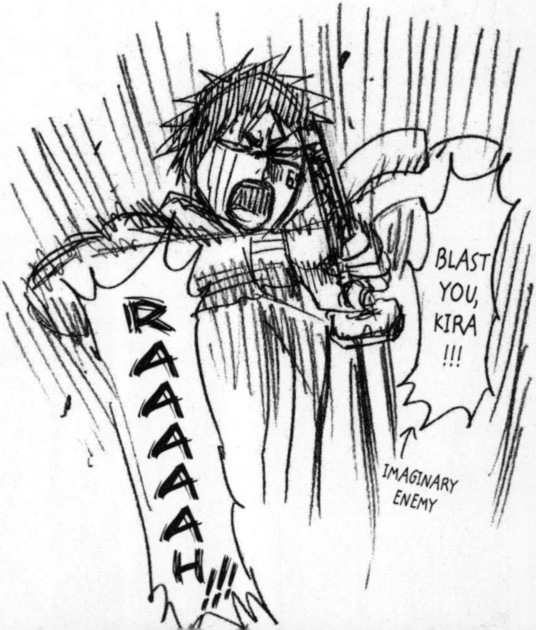
BLAST YOU, KIRA !!!
RAAAAAH!!!
IMAGINARY ENEMY

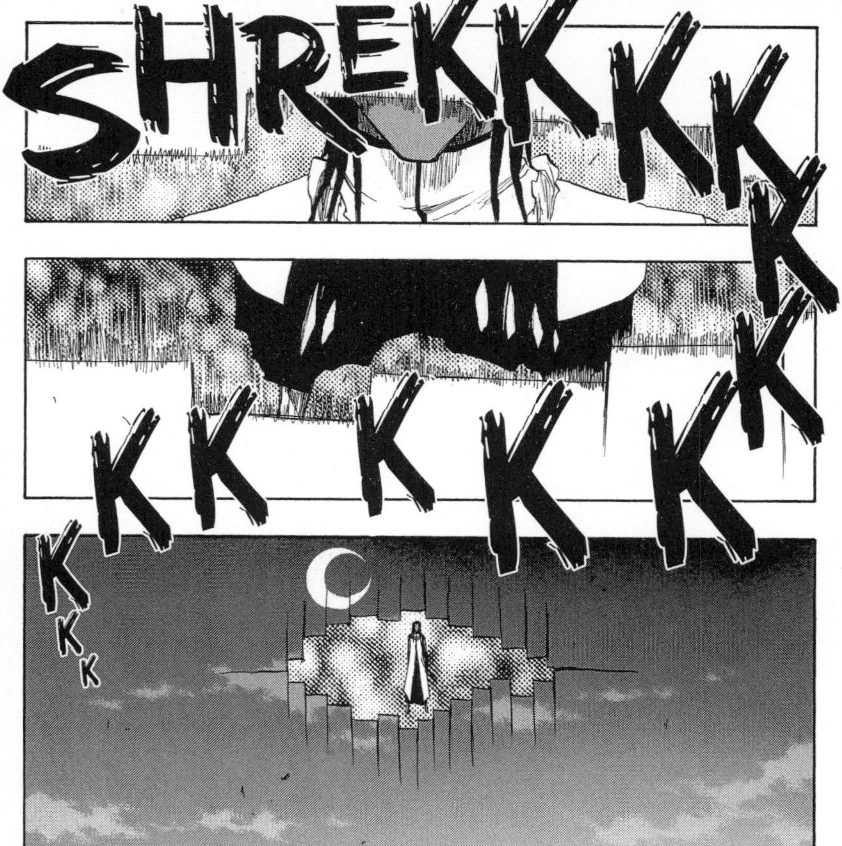
SHREKKKKK
KK
KKKKKK
KKK

## 212. You Don't Hear My Name Anymore

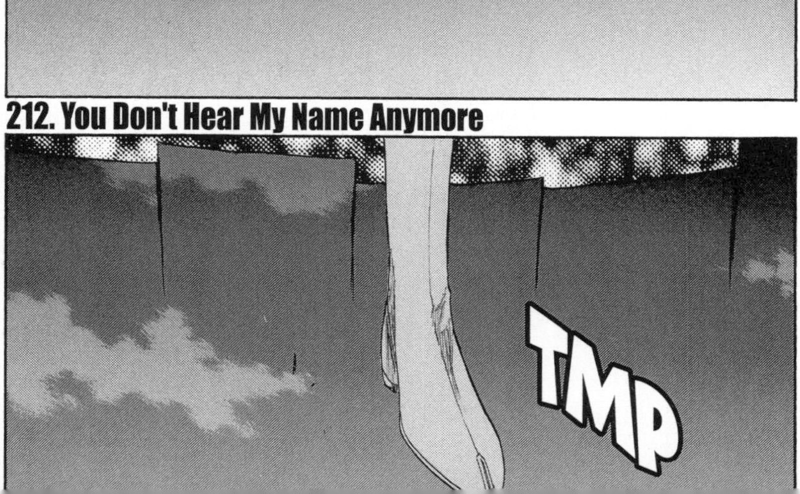
TMP

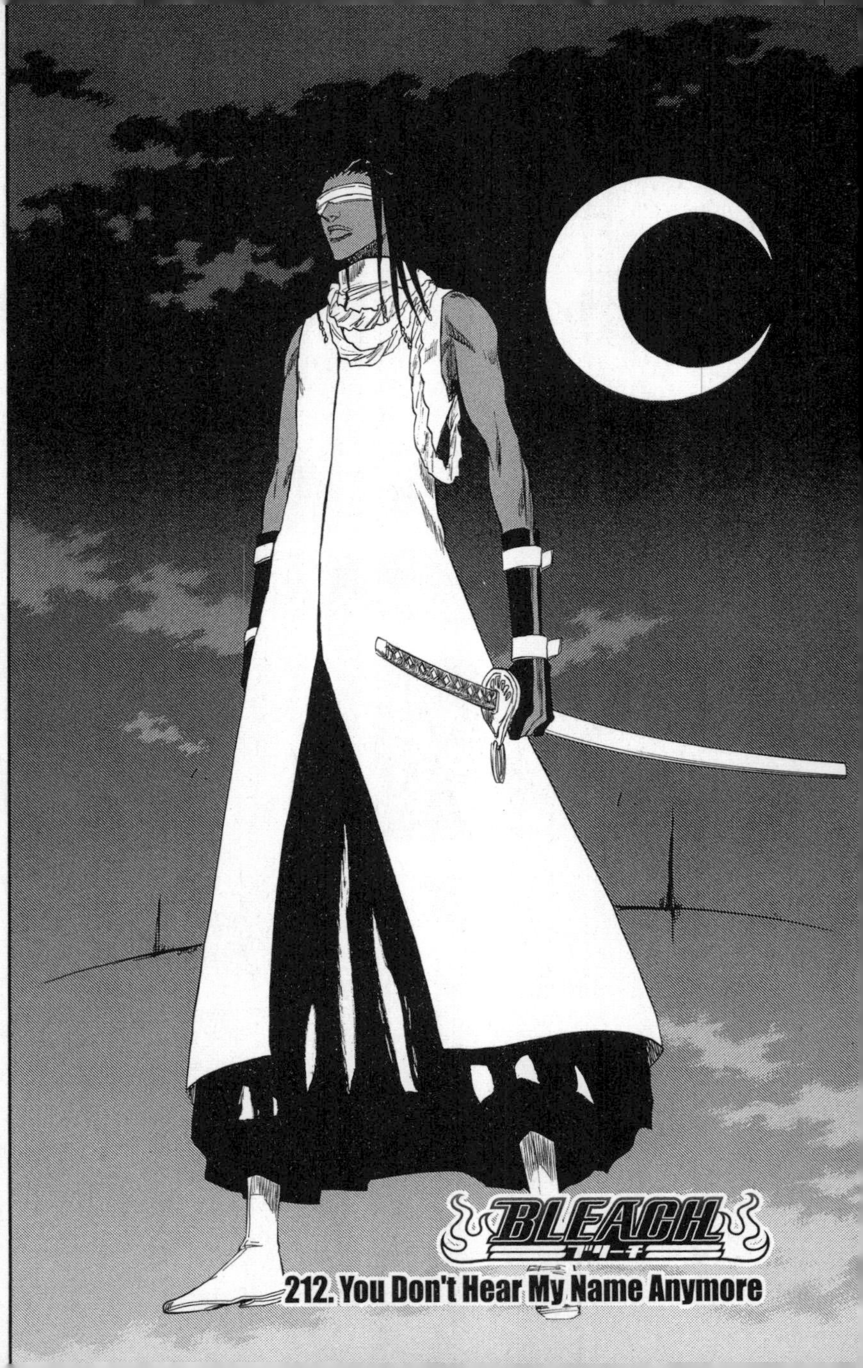
BLEACH
ブリーチ
212. You Don't Hear My Name Anymore

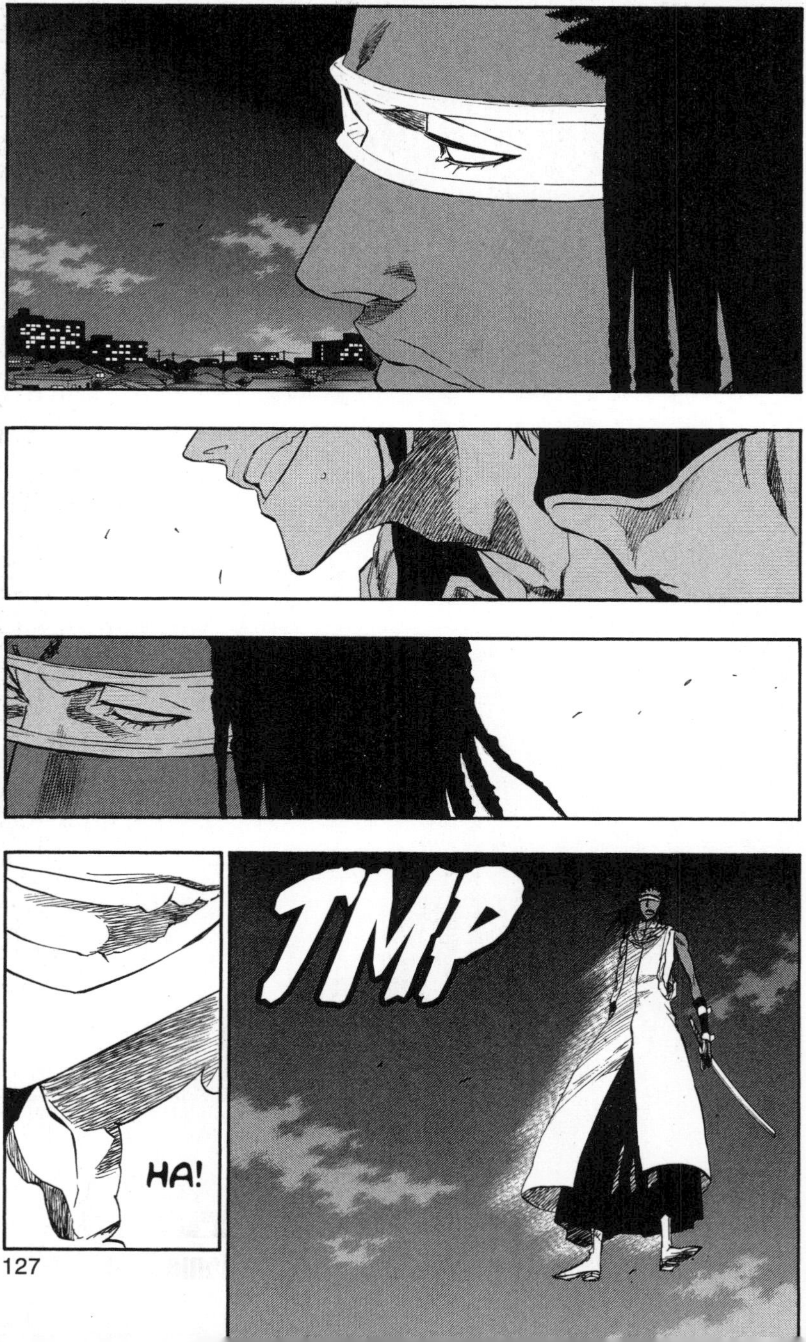
TMP
HA!

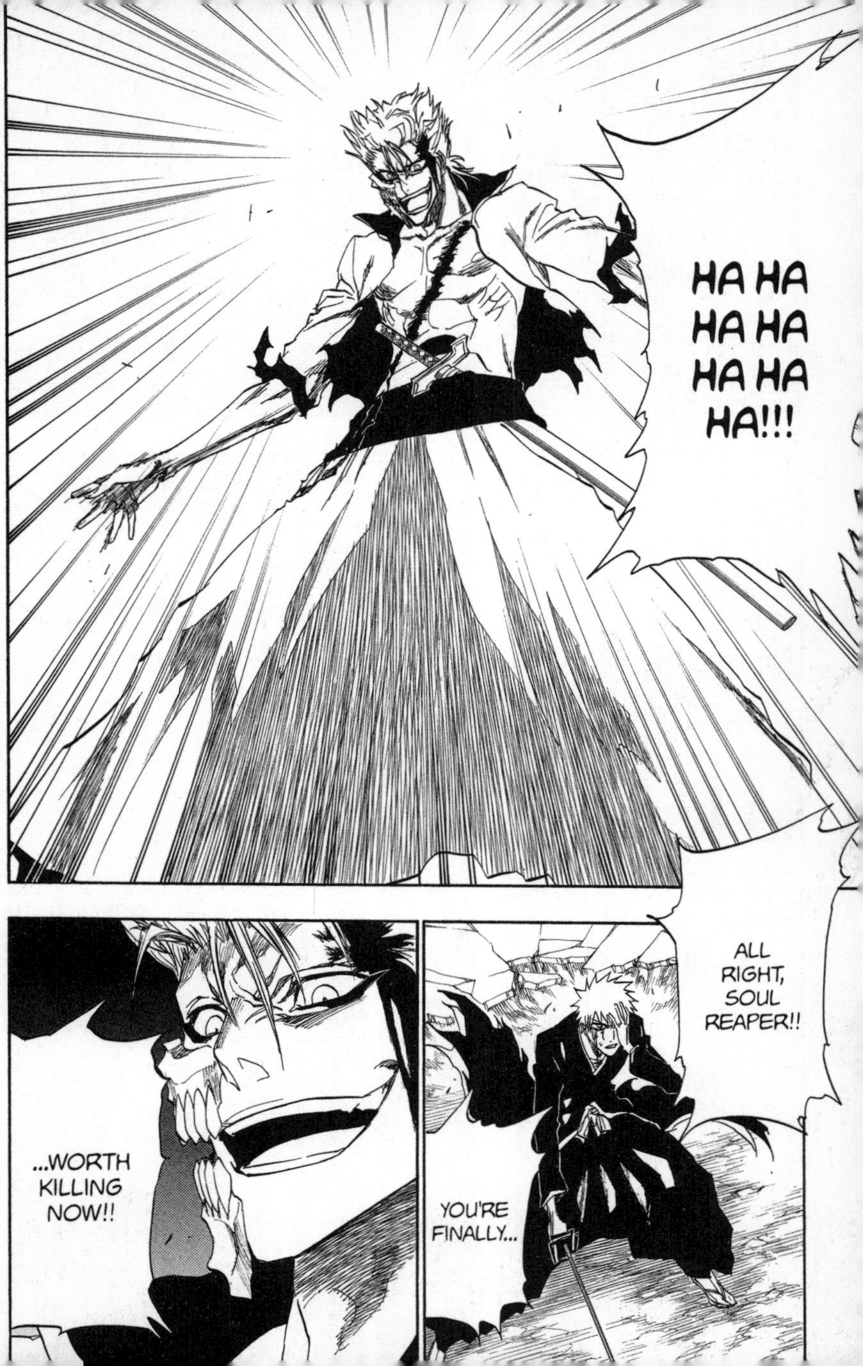
HA HA HA HA HA HA HA!!!
ALL RIGHT, SOUL REAPER!!
YOU'RE FINALLY...
...WORTH KILLING NOW!!

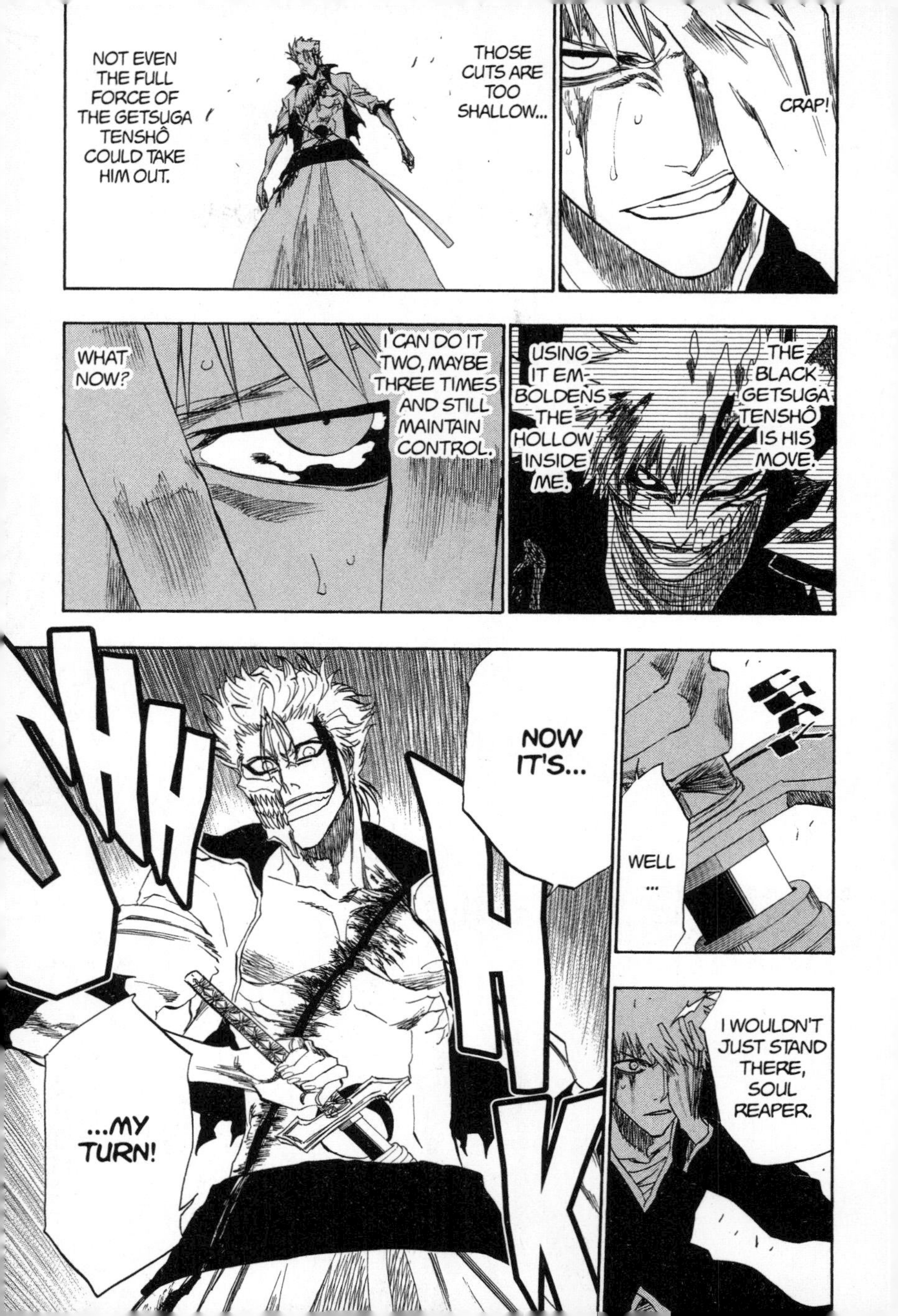
THOSE CUTS ARE TOO SHALLOW...
CRAP!
NOT EVEN THE FULL FORCE OF THE GETSUGA TENSHÔ COULD TAKE HIM OUT.
THE BLACK GETSUGA TENSHÔ IS HIS MOVE.
USING IT EMBOLDENS THE HOLLOW INSIDE ME.
I CAN DO IT TWO, MAYBE THREE TIMES AND STILL MAINTAIN CONTROL.
WHAT NOW?
WELL...
I WOULDN'T JUST STAND THERE, SOUL REAPER.
NOW IT'S...
...MY TURN!

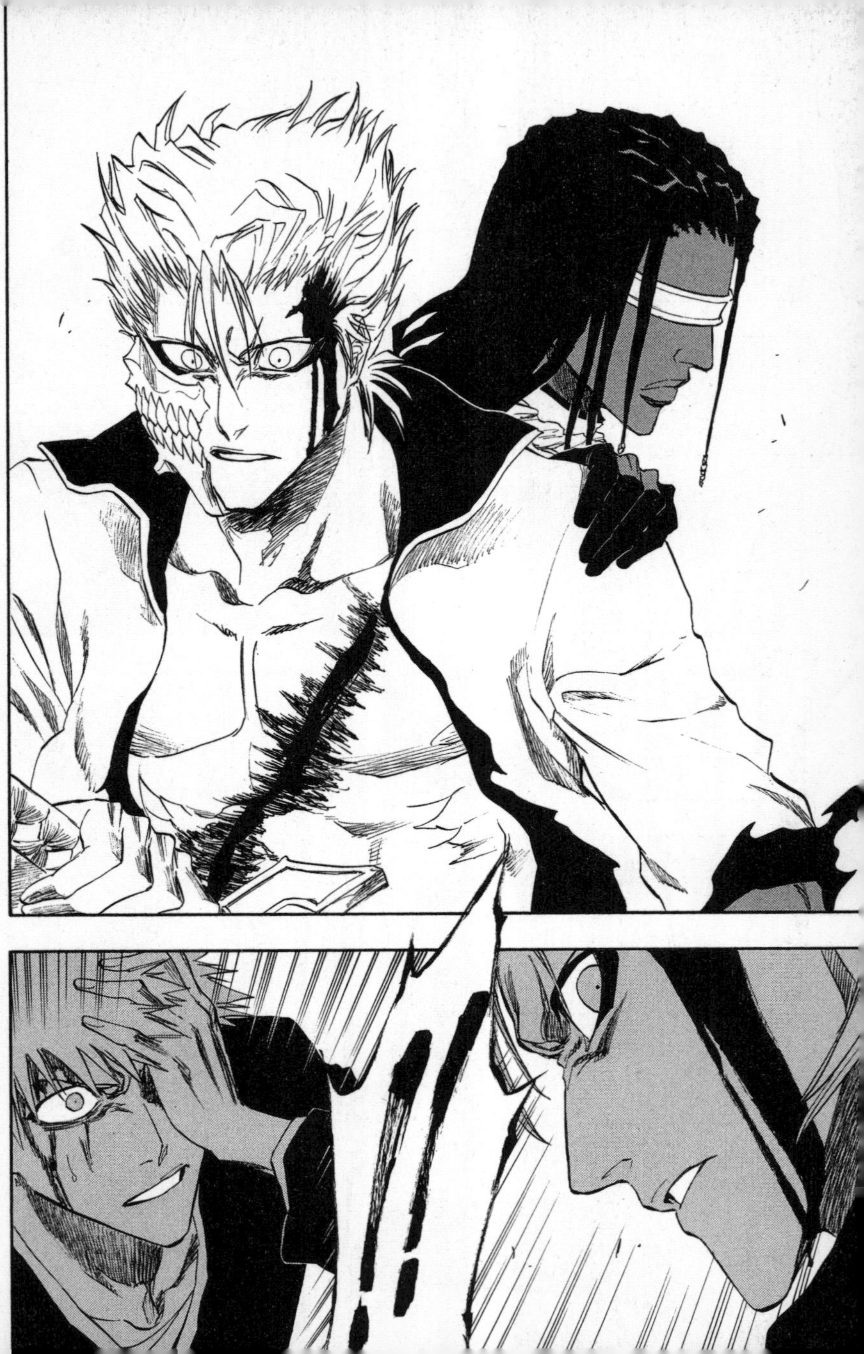

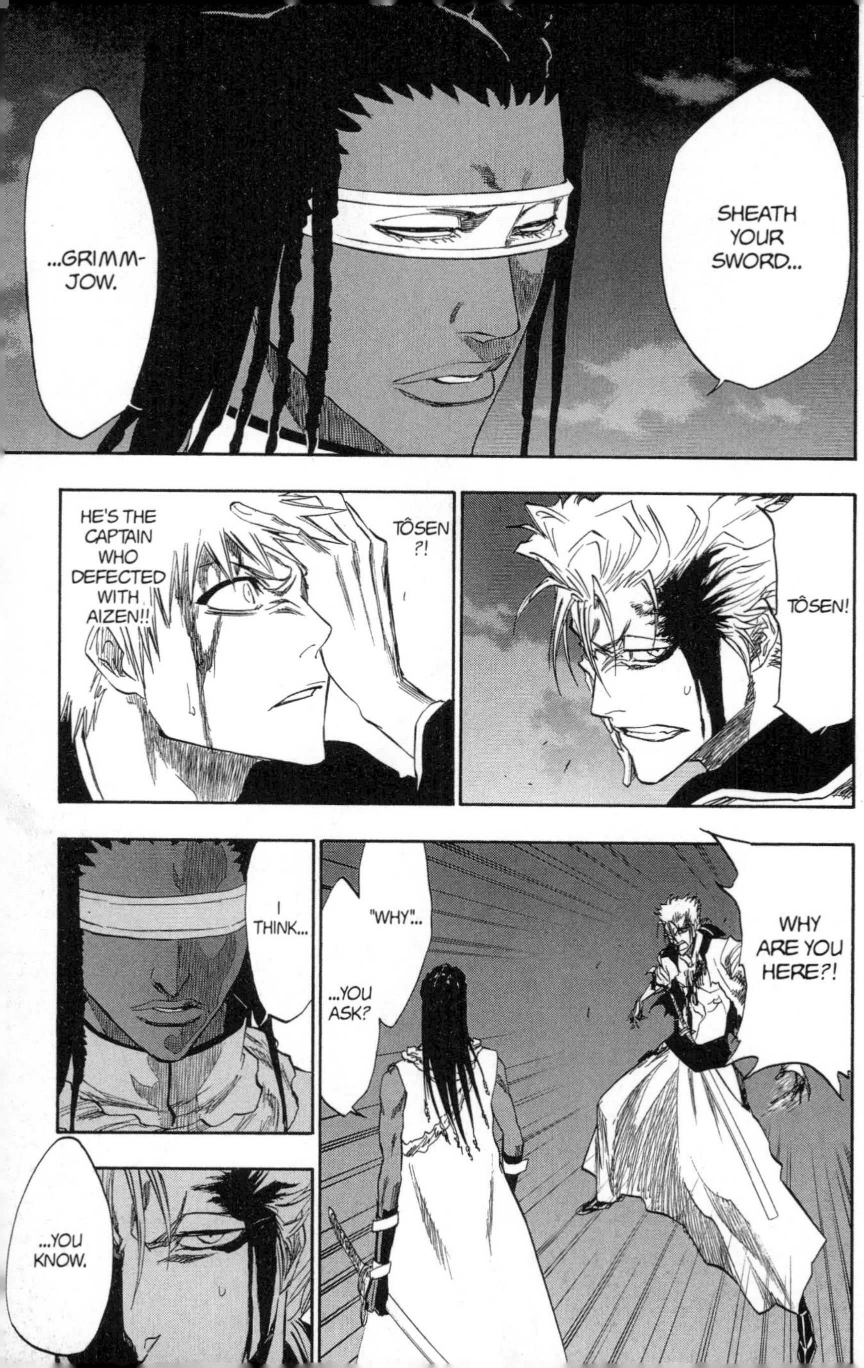
SHEATH YOUR SWORD...
...GRIMM-JOW.
TÔSEN!
TÔSEN?!
HE'S THE CAPTAIN WHO DEFECTED WITH AIZEN!!
WHY ARE YOU HERE?!
"WHY"...
...YOU ASK?
I THINK...
...YOU KNOW.

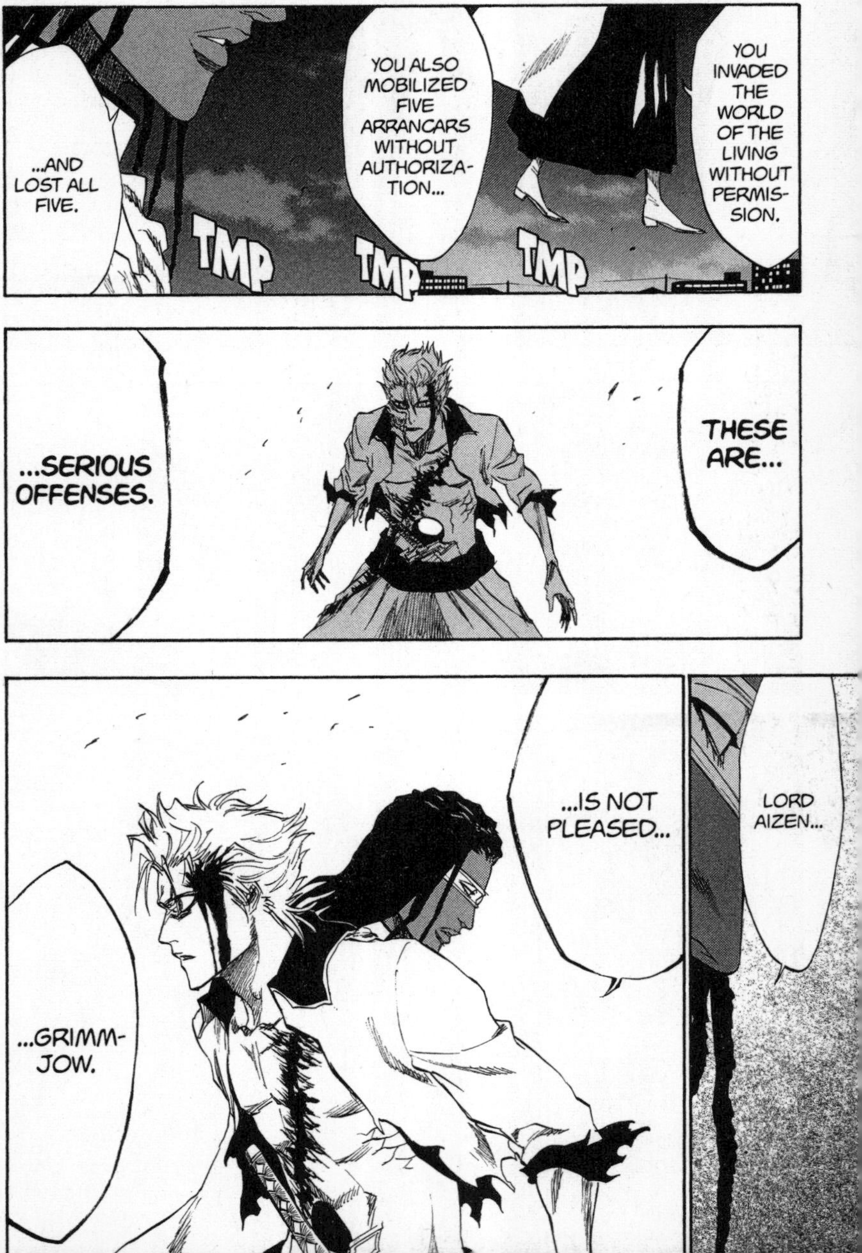
YOU INVADED THE WORLD OF THE LIVING WITHOUT PERMIS-SION.
YOU ALSO MOBILIZED FIVE ARRANCARS WITHOUT AUTHORIZA-TION...
TMP
TMP
TMP
...AND LOST ALL FIVE.
THESE ARE...
...SERIOUS OFFENSES.
LORD AIZEN...
...IS NOT PLEASED...
...GRIMM-JOW.

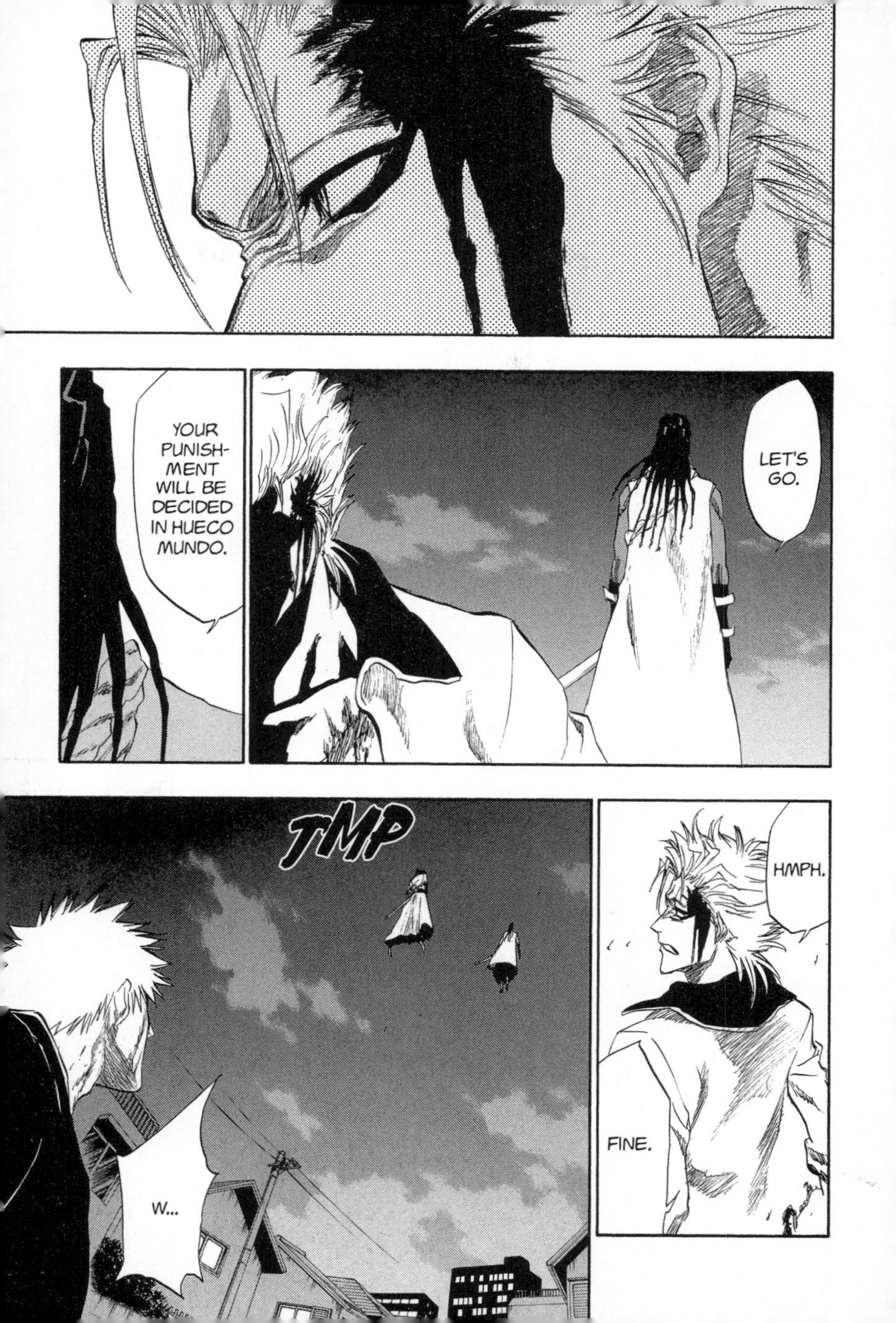
LET'S GO.
YOUR PUNISHMENT WILL BE DECIDED IN HUECO MUNDO.
HMPH.
FINE.
TMP
W...

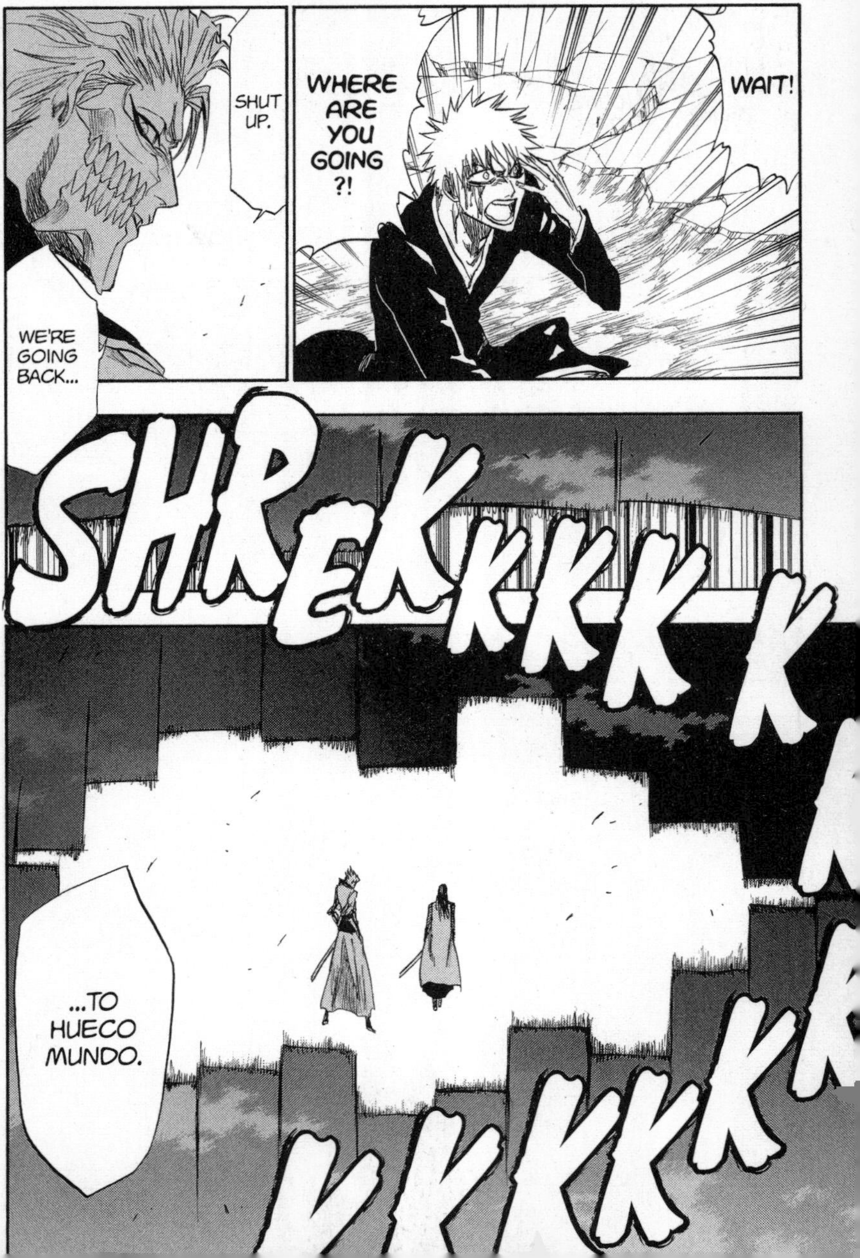
WAIT!
WHERE ARE YOU GOING ?!
SHUT UP.
WE'RE GOING BACK...
SHREKKKKKKKKKK
...TO HUECO MUNDO.

READ THIS WAY

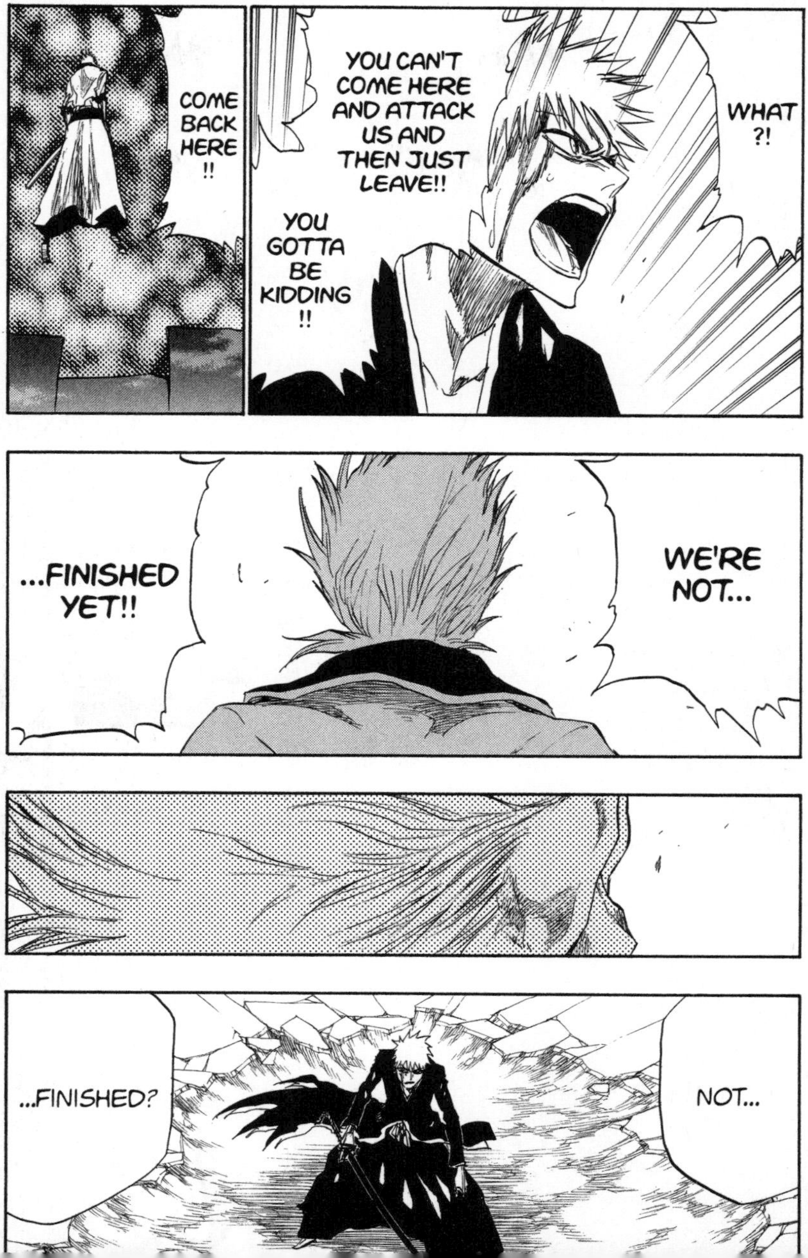
WHAT?!
YOU CAN'T COME HERE AND ATTACK US AND THEN JUST LEAVE!!
YOU GOTTA BE KIDDING!!
COME BACK HERE!!
WE'RE NOT...
...FINISHED YET!!
NOT...
...FINISHED?

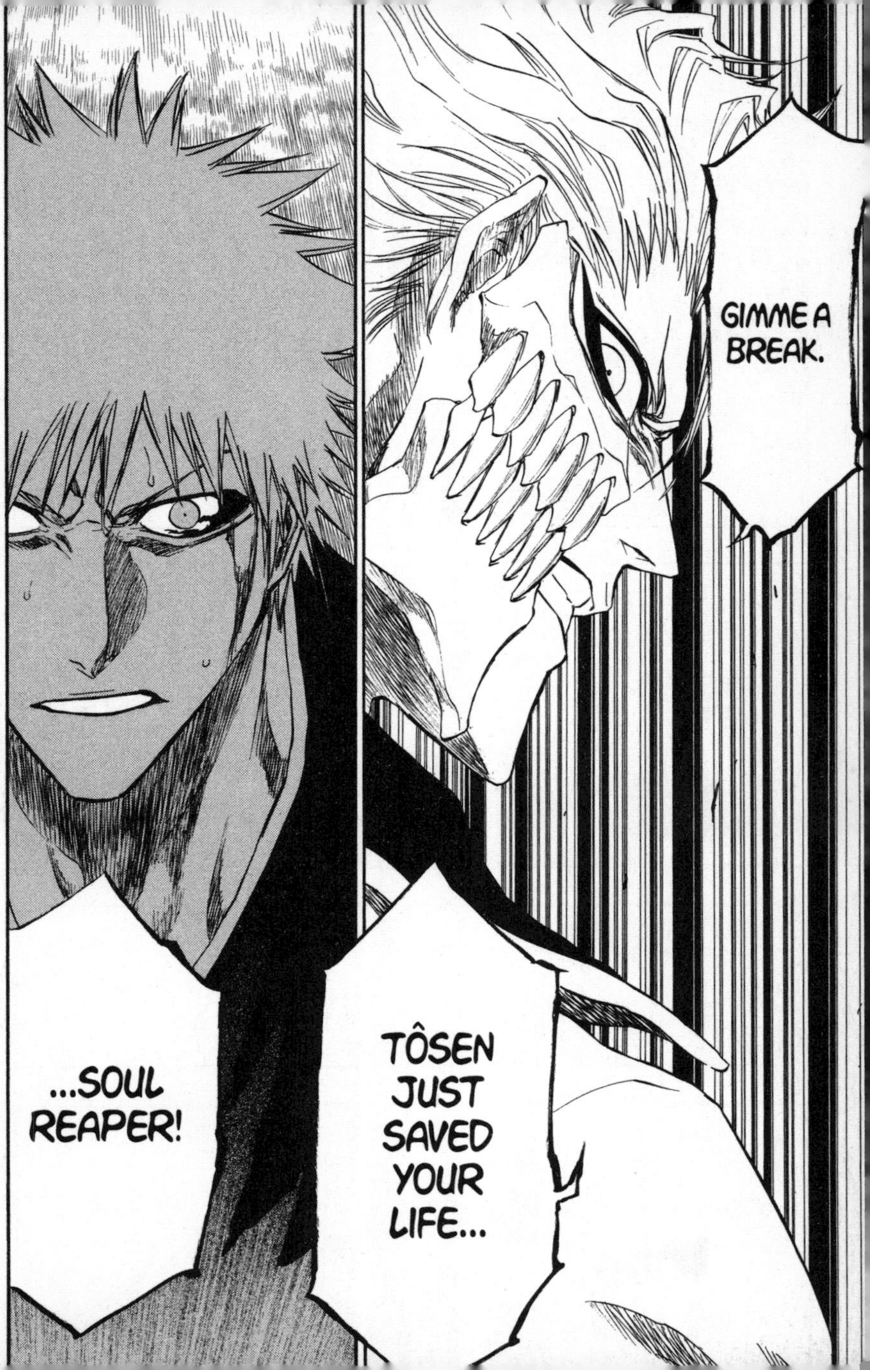
GIMME A BREAK.
TÔSEN JUST SAVED YOUR LIFE...
...SOUL REAPER!

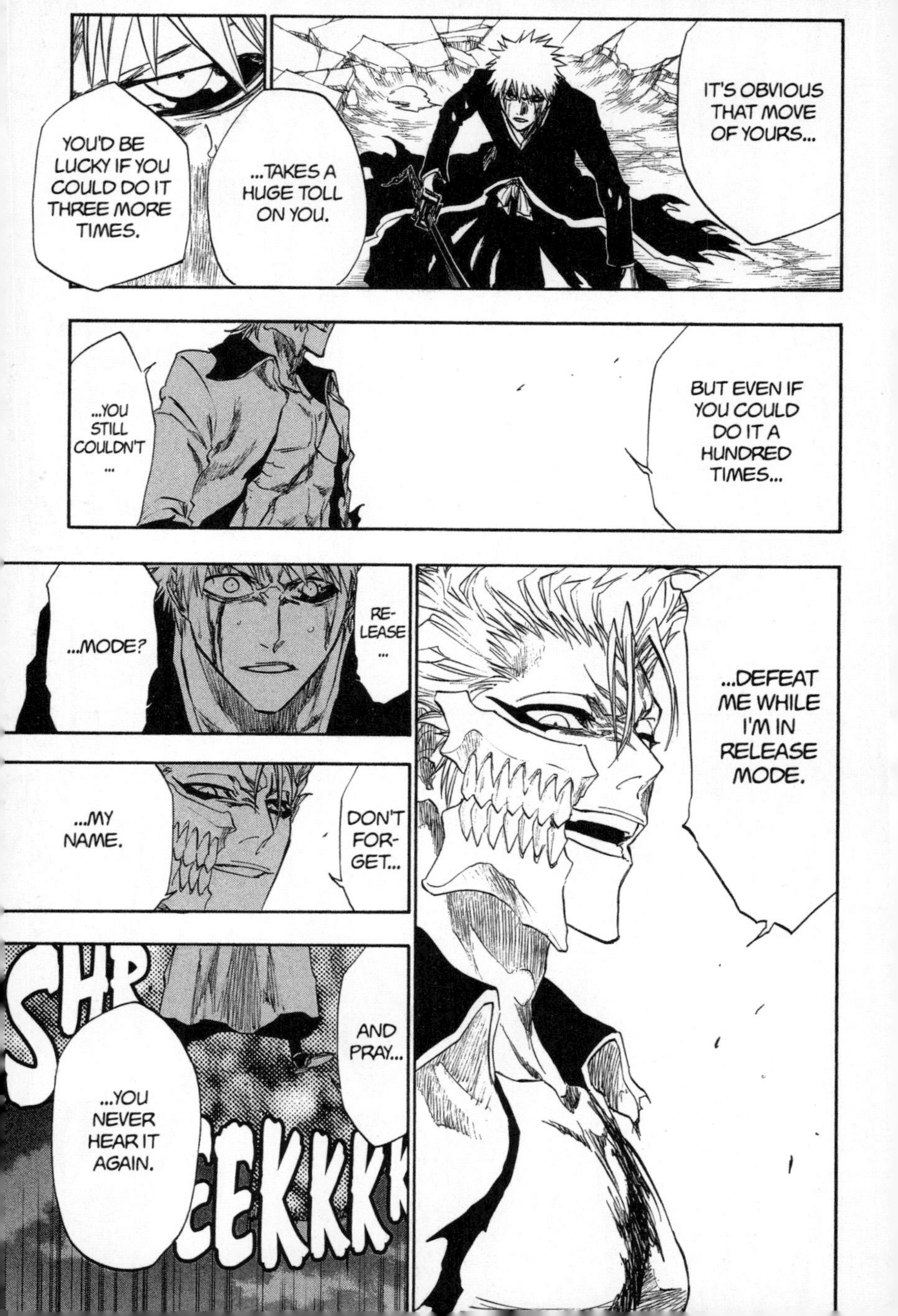
IT'S OBVIOUS THAT MOVE OF YOURS...
...TAKES A HUGE TOLL ON YOU.
YOU'D BE LUCKY IF YOU COULD DO IT THREE MORE TIMES.
BUT EVEN IF YOU COULD DO IT A HUNDRED TIMES...
...YOU STILL COULDN'T ...
...DEFEAT ME WHILE I'M IN RELEASE MODE.
RE-LEASE ...
...MODE?
DON'T FOR-GET...
...MY NAME.
AND PRAY...
...YOU NEVER HEAR IT AGAIN.

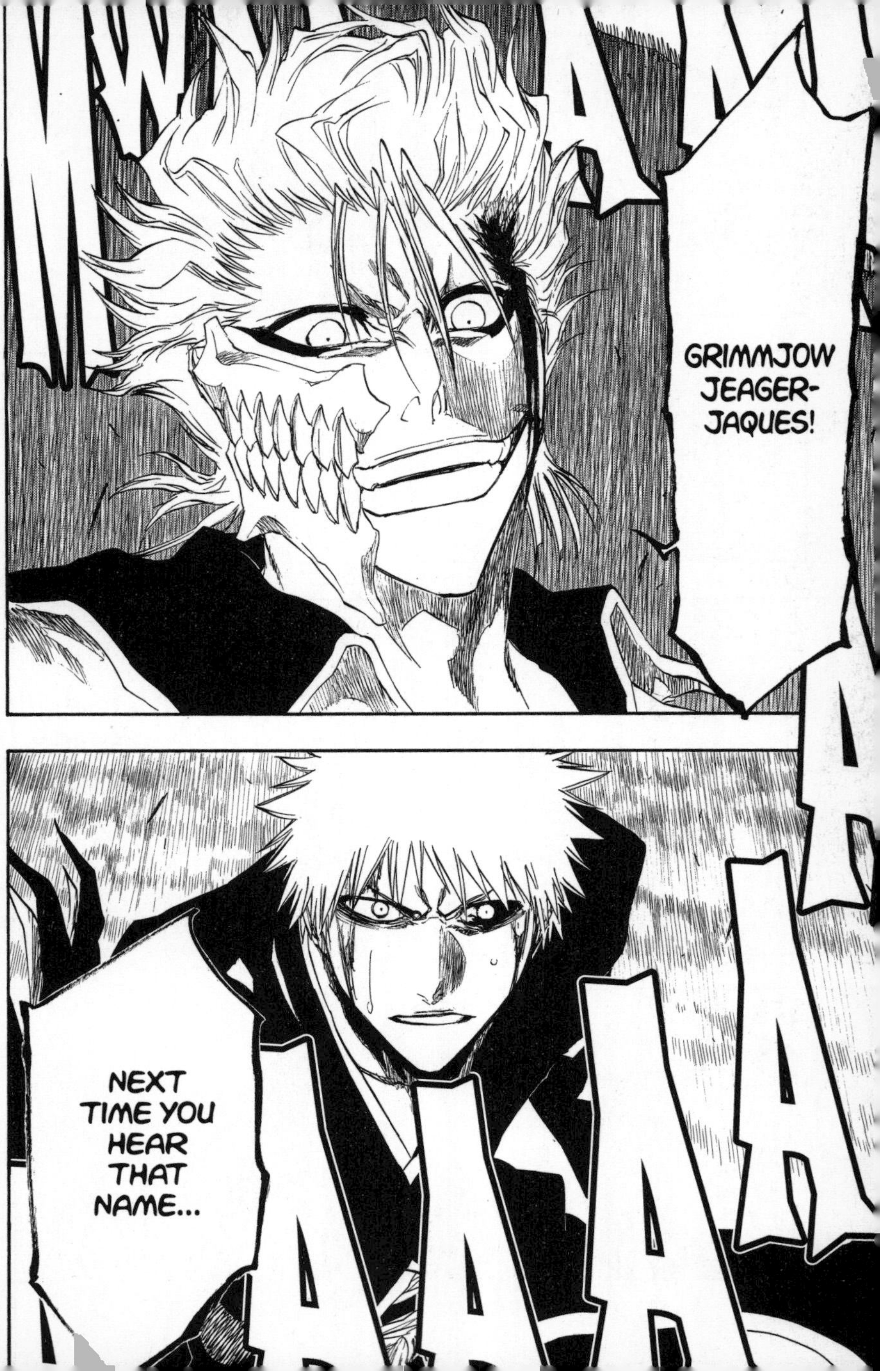
GRIMMJOW JEAGER-JAQUES!
NEXT TIME YOU HEAR THAT NAME...

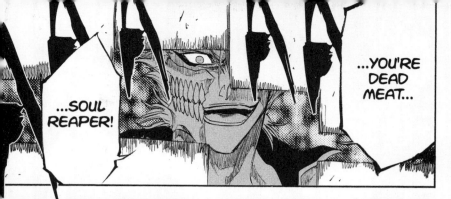

...SOUL REAPER!

...YOU'RE DEAD MEAT...

TMP

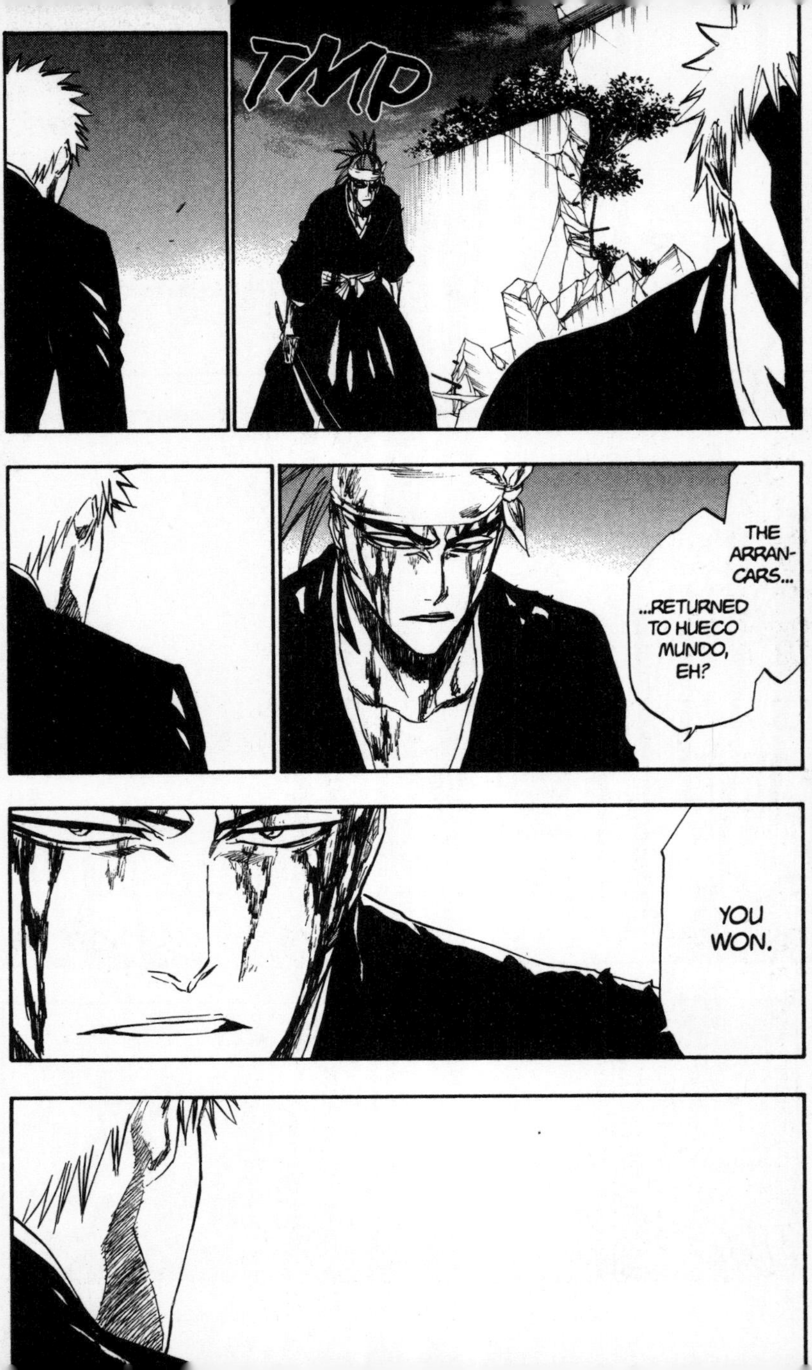
TMP
THE ARRANCARS...
...RETURNED TO HUECO MUNDO, EH?
YOU WON.

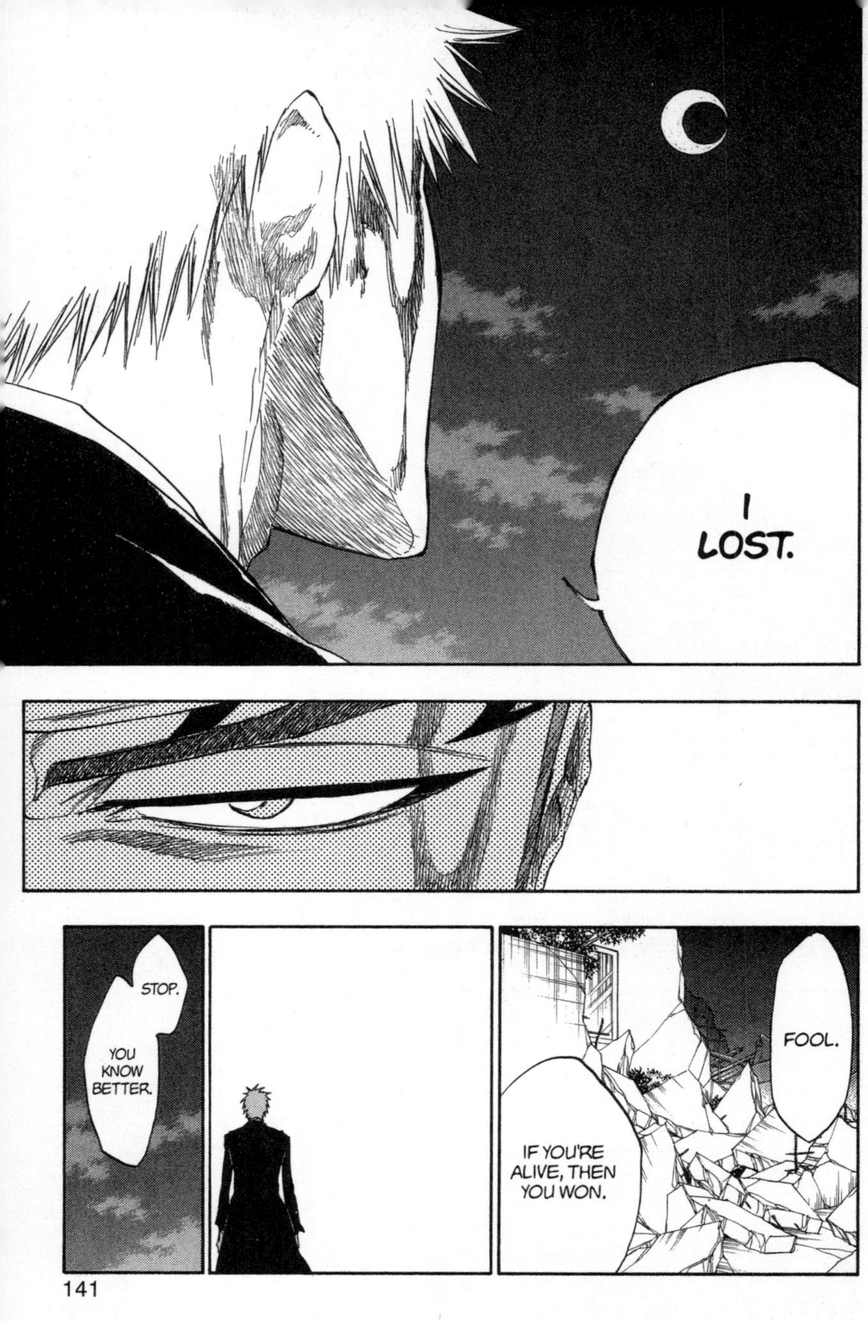
I LOST.
FOOL.
IF YOU'RE ALIVE, THEN YOU WON.
STOP.
YOU KNOW BETTER.

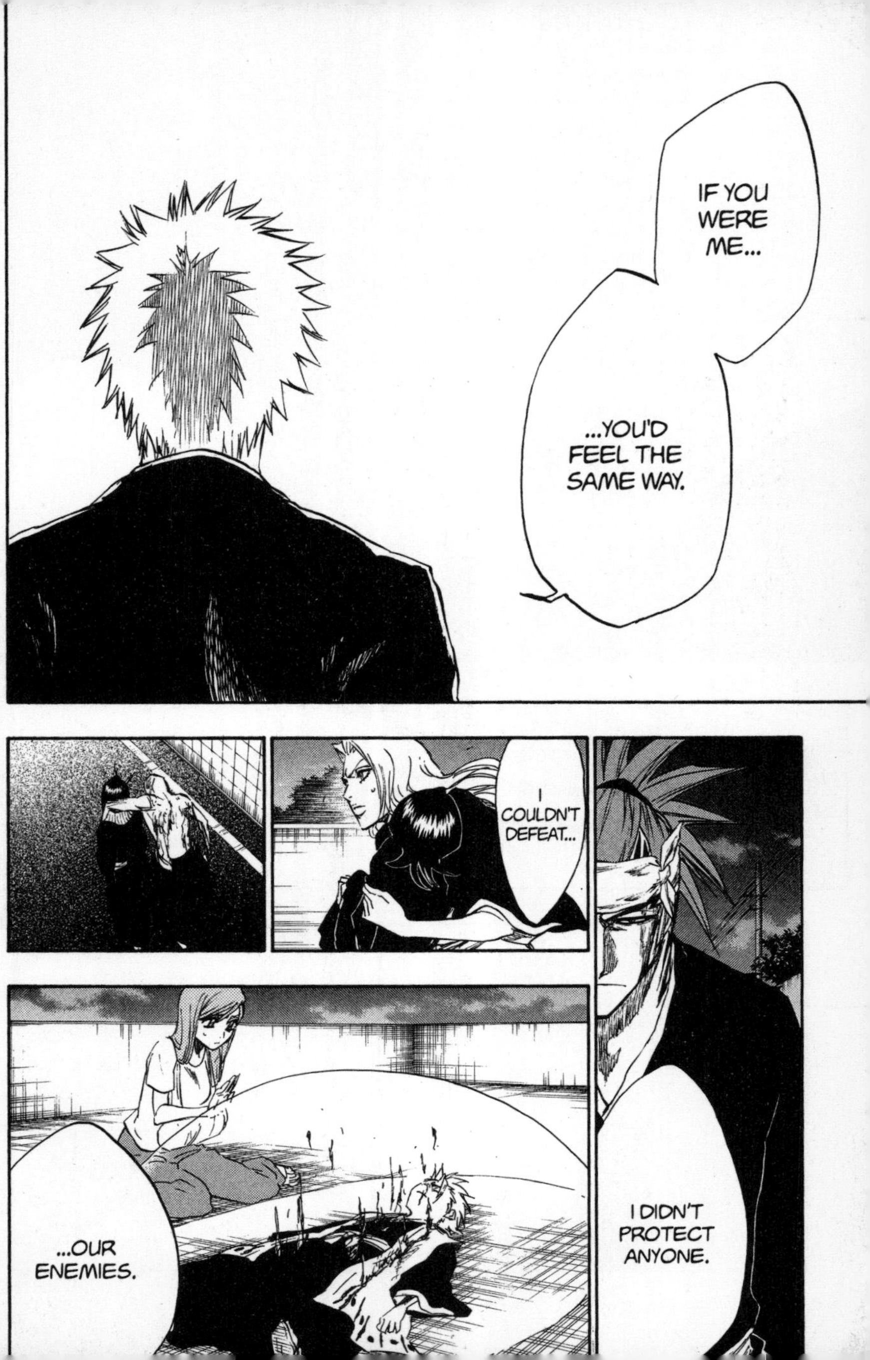
IF YOU WERE ME...
...YOU'D FEEL THE SAME WAY.
I DIDN'T PROTECT ANYONE.
I COULDN'T DEFEAT...
...OUR ENEMIES.

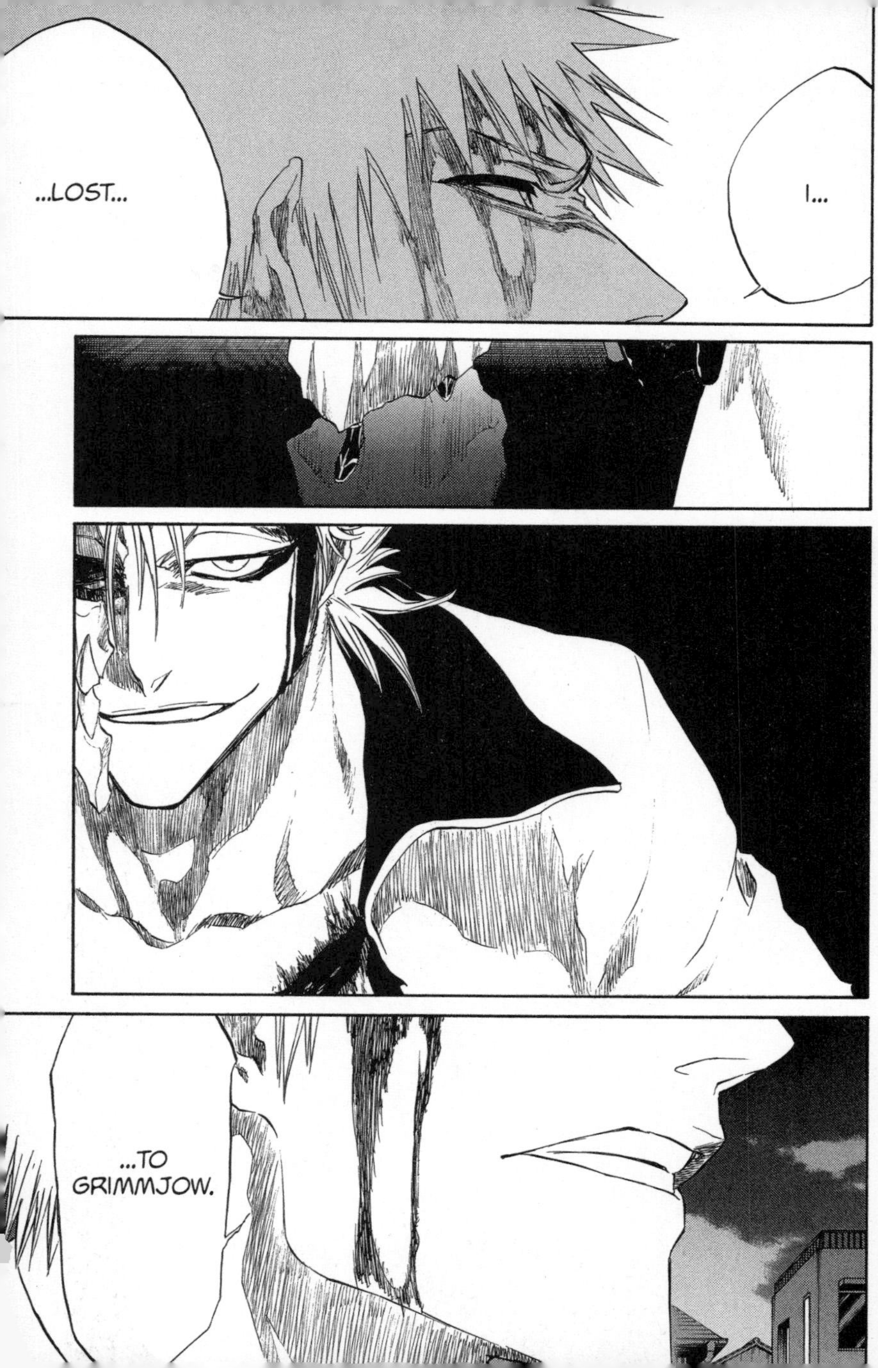
I...
...LOST...
...TO GRIMMJOW.

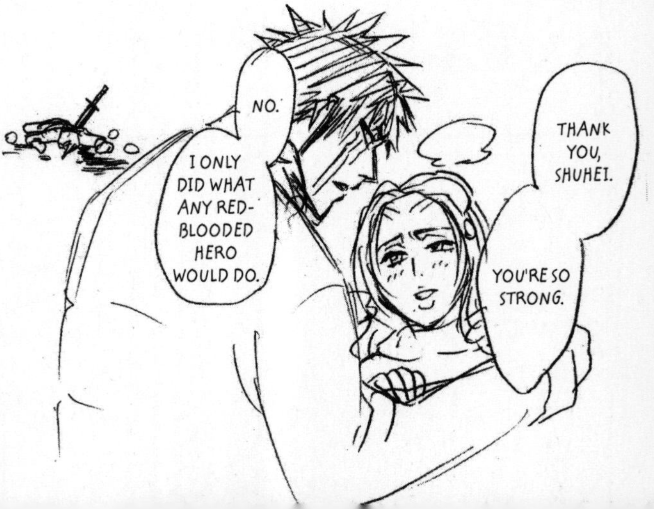
THANK YOU, SHUHEI.
YOU'RE SO STRONG.
NO.
I ONLY DID WHAT ANY RED-BLOODED HERO WOULD DO.

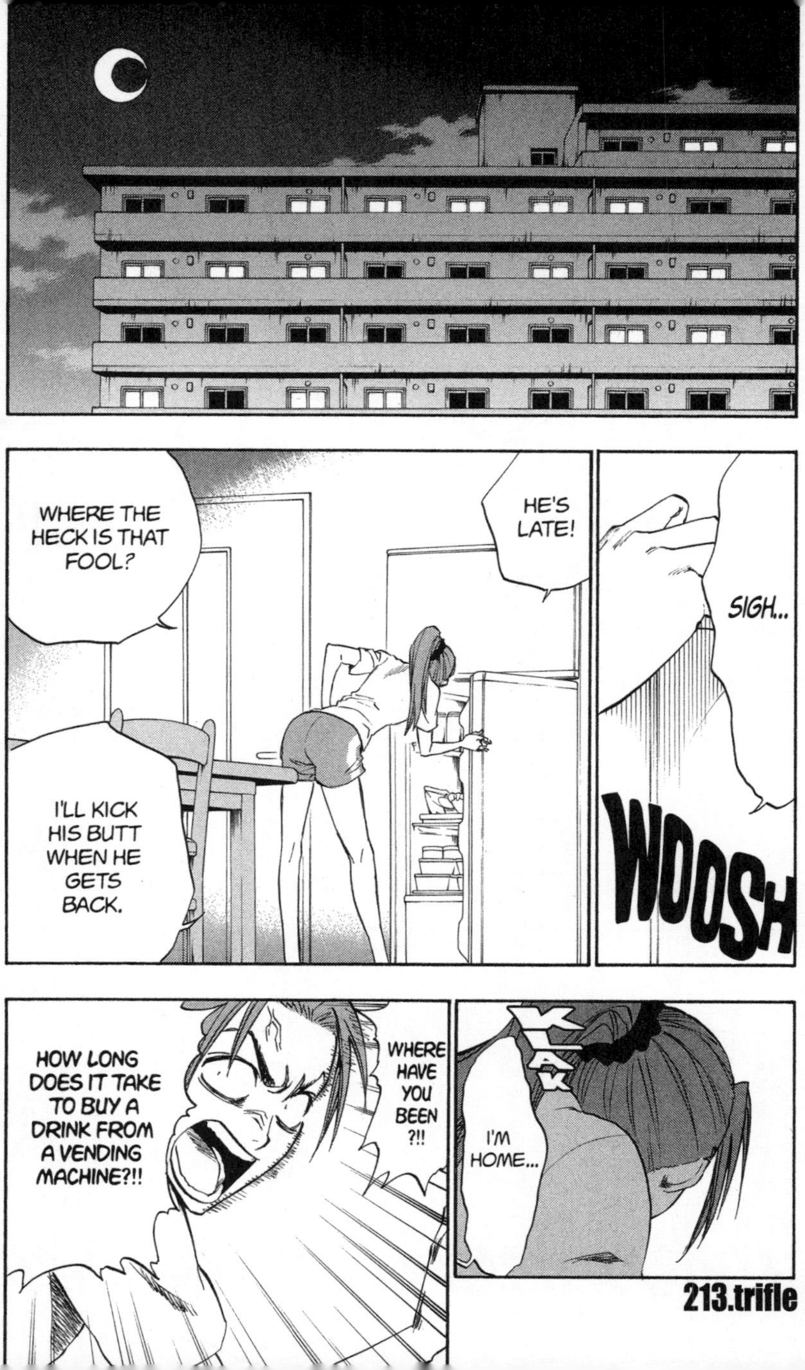
SIGH...
WOOSH
HE'S LATE!
WHERE THE HECK IS THAT FOOL?
I'LL KICK HIS BUTT WHEN HE GETS BACK.
KLAK
I'M HOME...
WHERE HAVE YOU BEEN?!!
HOW LONG DOES IT TAKE TO BUY A DRINK FROM A VENDING MACHINE?!!

## 213.trifle

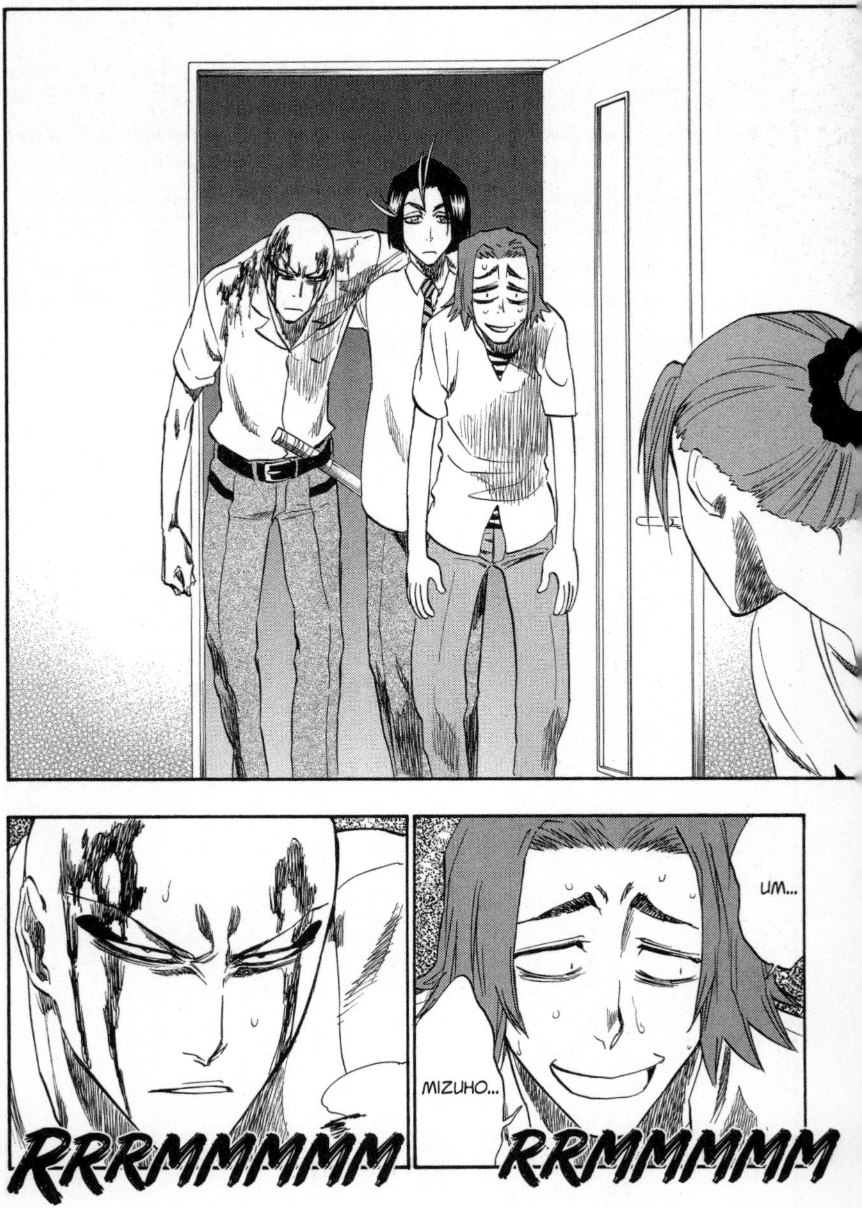
UM...
MIZUHO...
RRMMMMMM
RRRMMMMMM

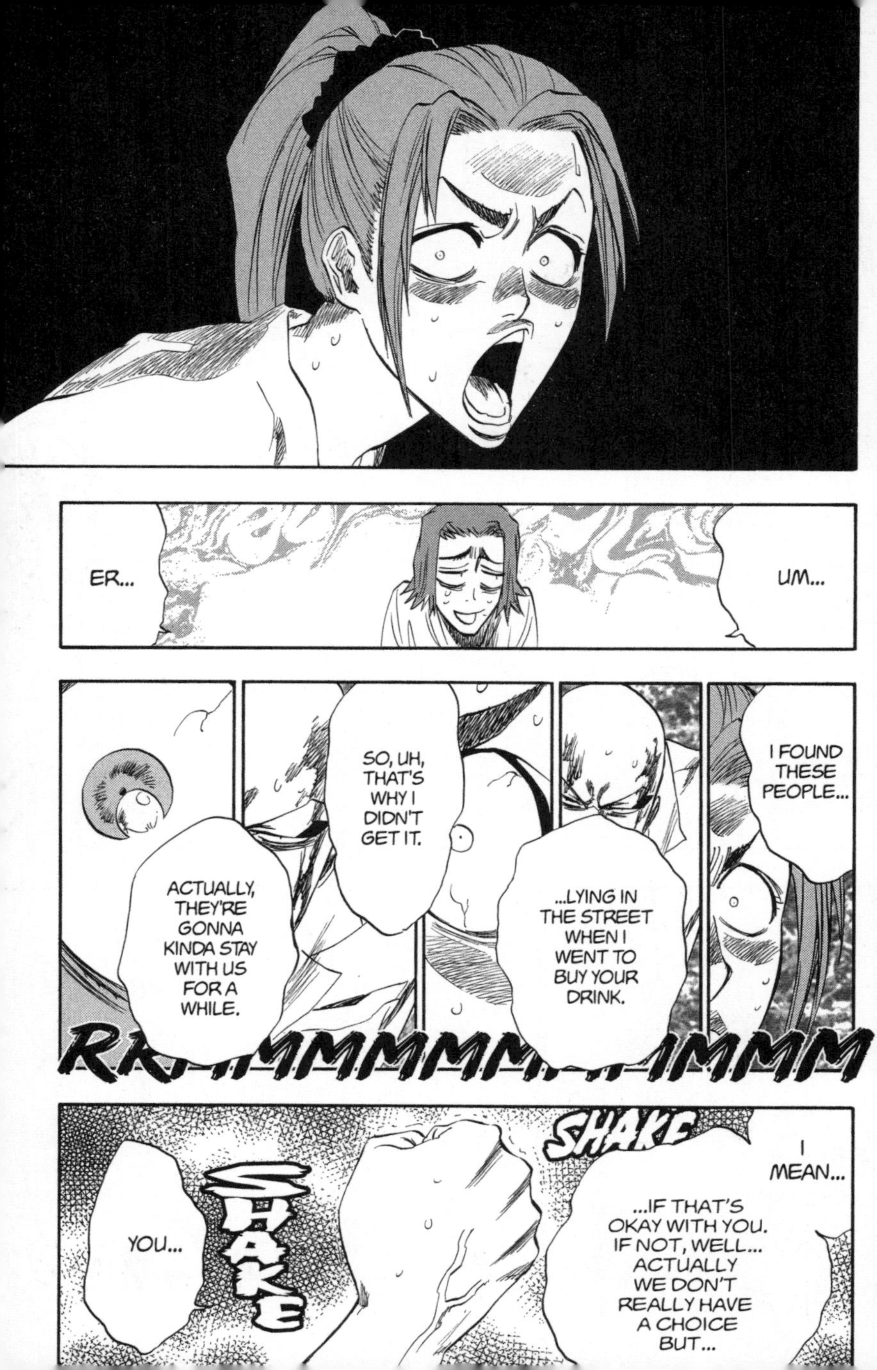
UM...
ER...
I FOUND THESE PEOPLE...
...LYING IN THE STREET WHEN I WENT TO BUY YOUR DRINK.
SO, UH, THAT'S WHY I DIDN'T GET IT.
ACTUALLY, THEY'RE GONNA KINDA STAY WITH US FOR A WHILE.
I MEAN...
...IF THAT'S OKAY WITH YOU. IF NOT, WELL... ACTUALLY WE DON'T REALLY HAVE A CHOICE BUT...
SHAKE
SHAKE
YOU...

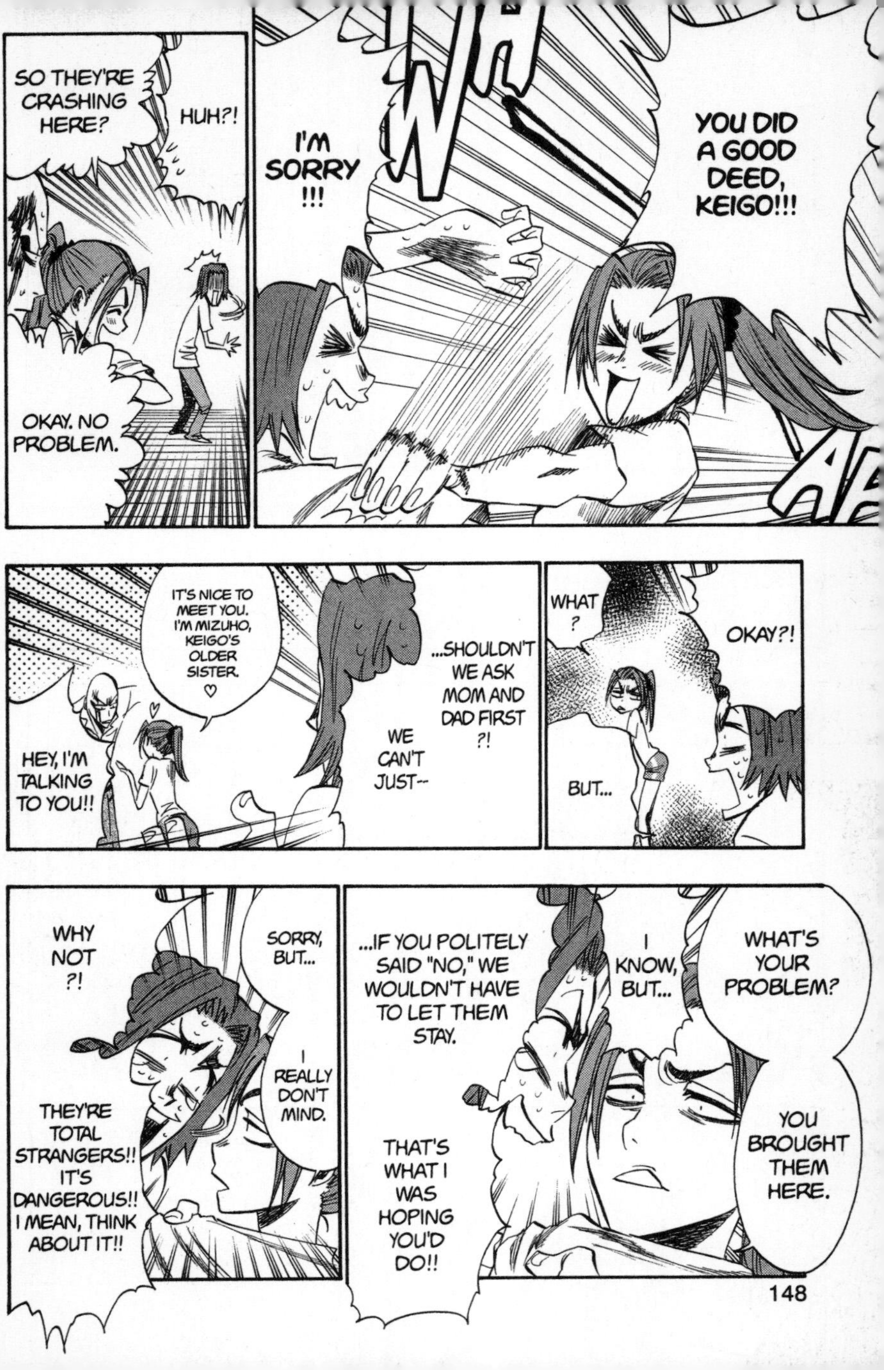
SO THEY'RE CRASHING HERE?
HUH?!
OKAY. NO PROBLEM.
I'M SORRY !!!
YOU DID A GOOD DEED, KEIGO!!!
IT'S NICE TO MEET YOU. I'M MIZUHO, KEIGO'S OLDER SISTER. ♡
HEY, I'M TALKING TO YOU!!
WE CAN'T JUST--
...SHOULDN'T WE ASK MOM AND DAD FIRST ?!
WHAT ?
OKAY?!
BUT...
WHY NOT ?!
SORRY, BUT...
I REALLY DON'T MIND.
THEY'RE TOTAL STRANGERS!! IT'S DANGEROUS!! I MEAN, THINK ABOUT IT!!
...IF YOU POLITELY SAID "NO," WE WOULDN'T HAVE TO LET THEM STAY.
THAT'S WHAT I WAS HOPING YOU'D DO!!
I KNOW, BUT...
WHAT'S YOUR PROBLEM?
YOU BROUGHT THEM HERE.

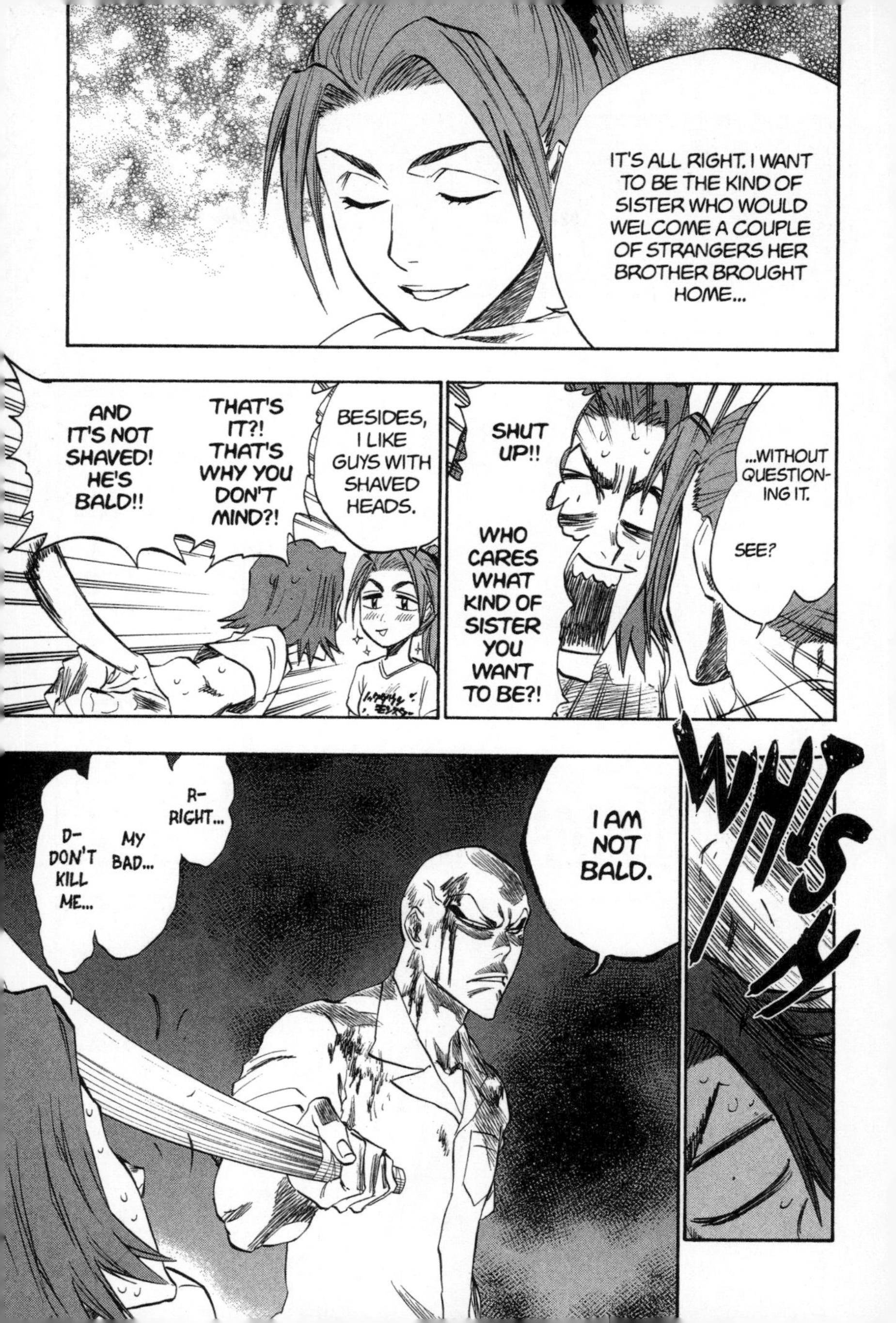
IT'S ALL RIGHT. I WANT TO BE THE KIND OF SISTER WHO WOULD WELCOME A COUPLE OF STRANGERS HER BROTHER BROUGHT HOME...
...WITHOUT QUESTIONING IT.
SEE?
SHUT UP!!
WHO CARES WHAT KIND OF SISTER YOU WANT TO BE?!
BESIDES, I LIKE GUYS WITH SHAVED HEADS.
THAT'S IT?! THAT'S WHY YOU DON'T MIND?!
AND IT'S NOT SHAVED! HE'S BALD!!
WHISH
I AM NOT BALD.
R-RIGHT...
MY BAD...
D-DON'T KILL ME...

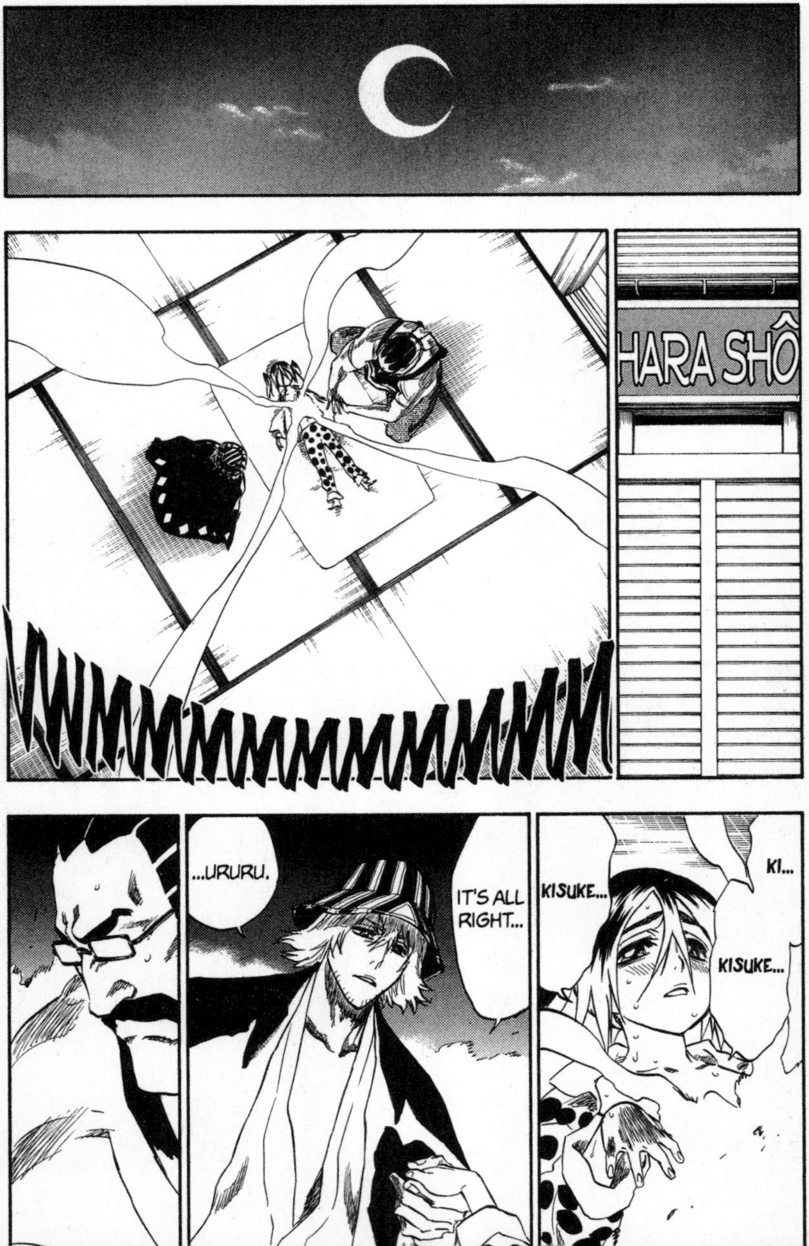
HARA SHÔ
VMMMMMMMMMMMMMMMM
KI...
KISUKE...
KISUKE...
...URURU.
IT'S ALL RIGHT...

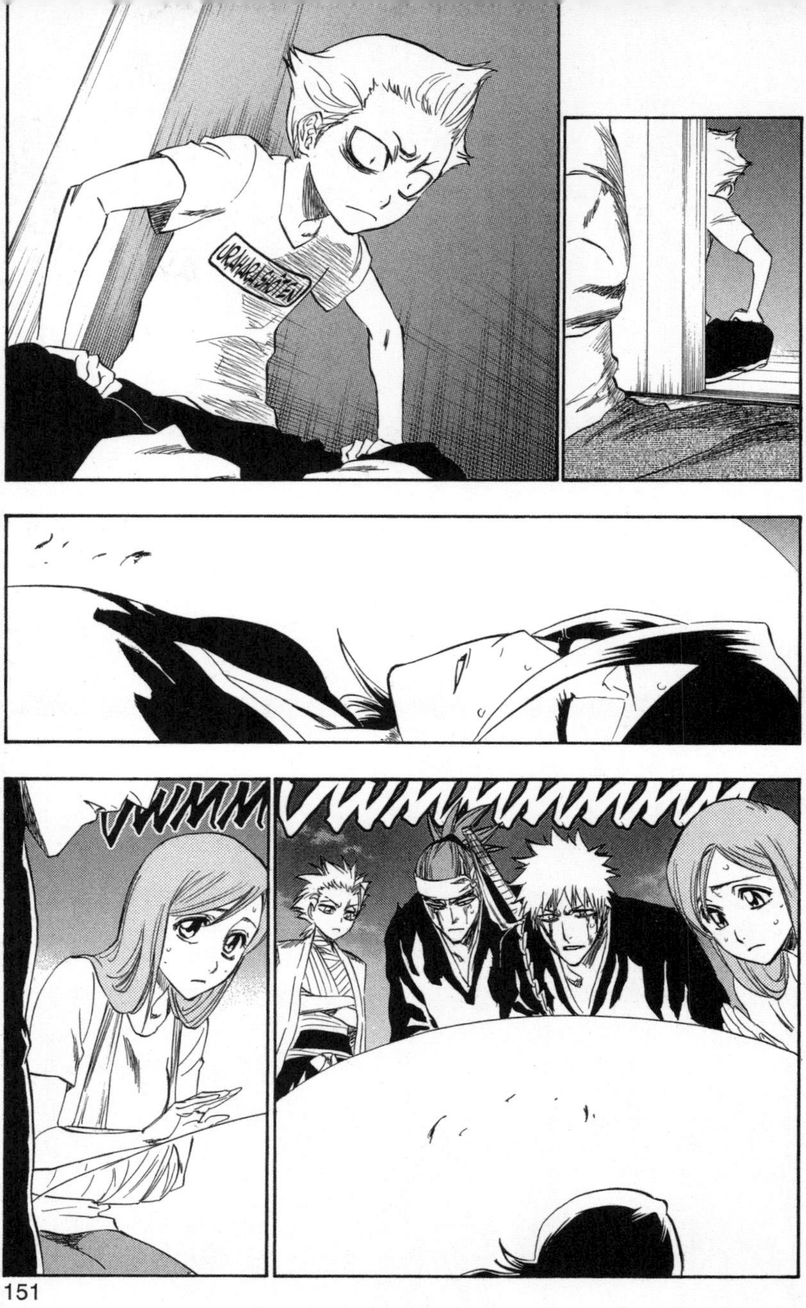
URAHARA SHOTEN
VWMM

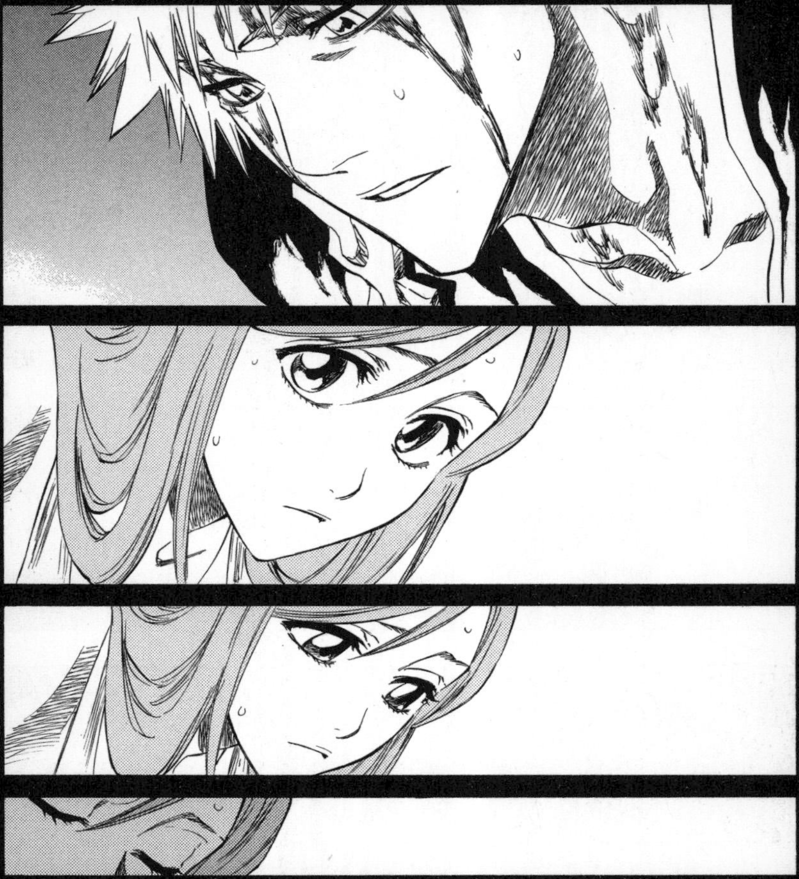

# 213. trifle

BLEACH

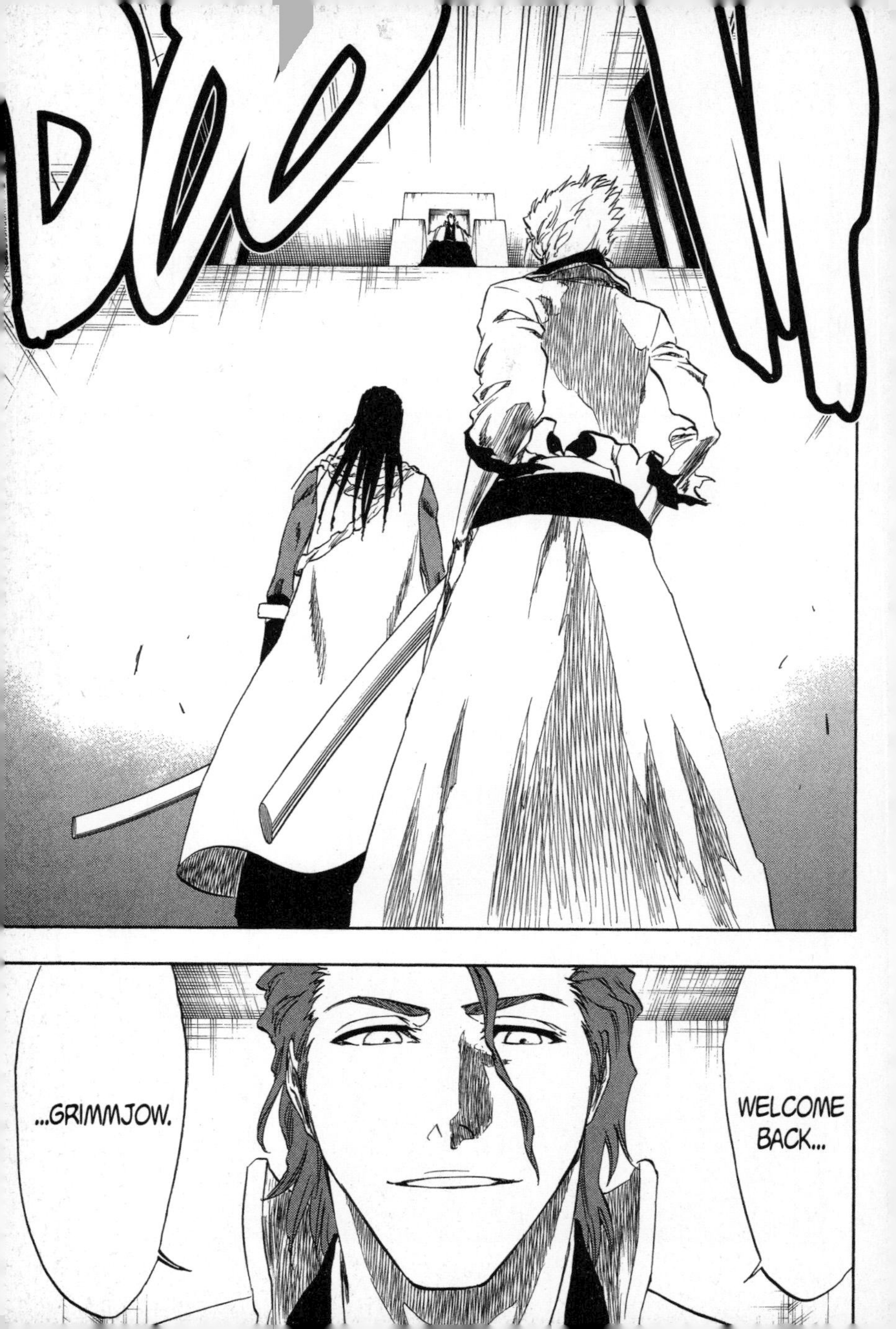
WELCOME BACK...
...GRIMMJOW.

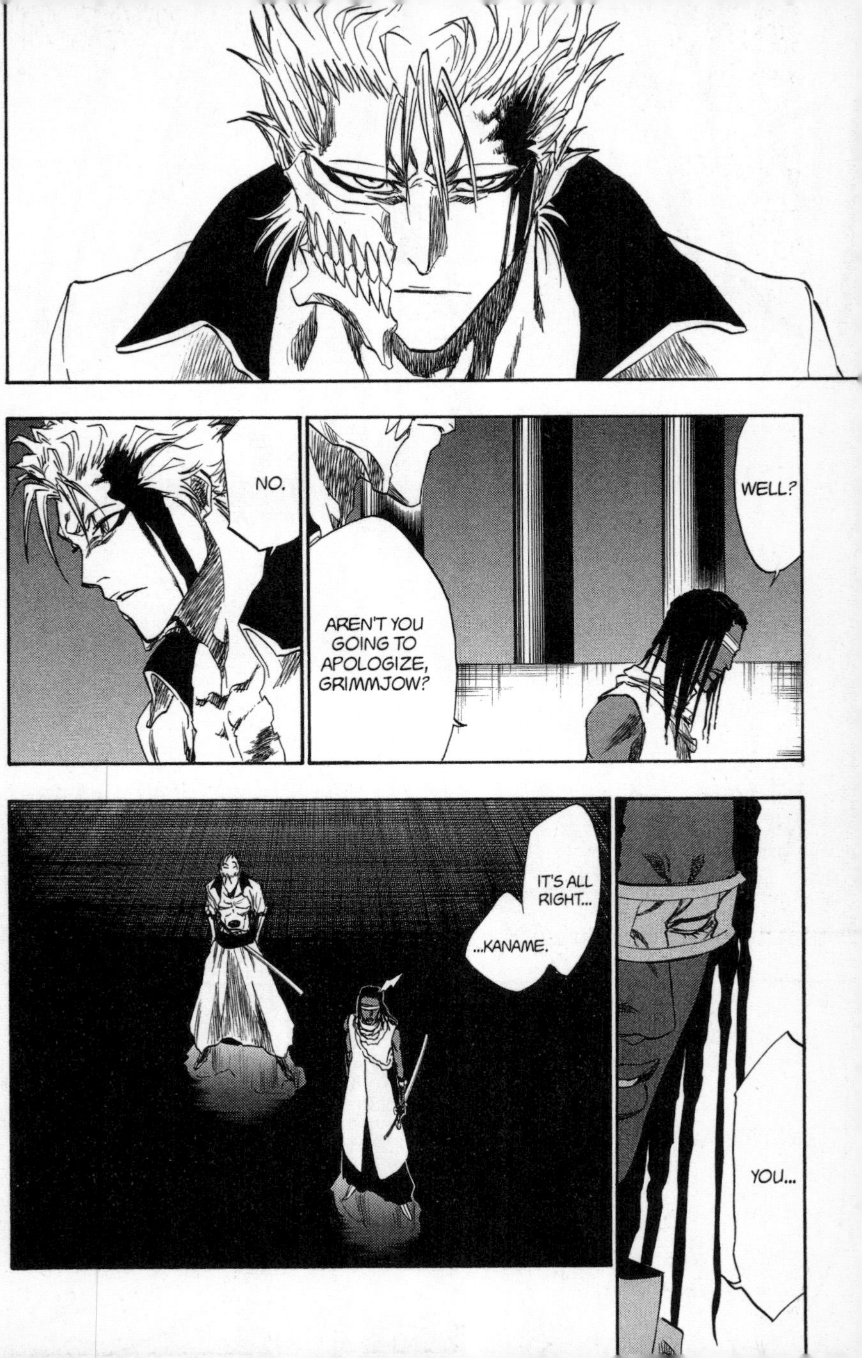
WELL?
AREN'T YOU GOING TO APOLOGIZE, GRIMMJOW?
NO.
YOU...
IT'S ALL RIGHT...
...KANAME.

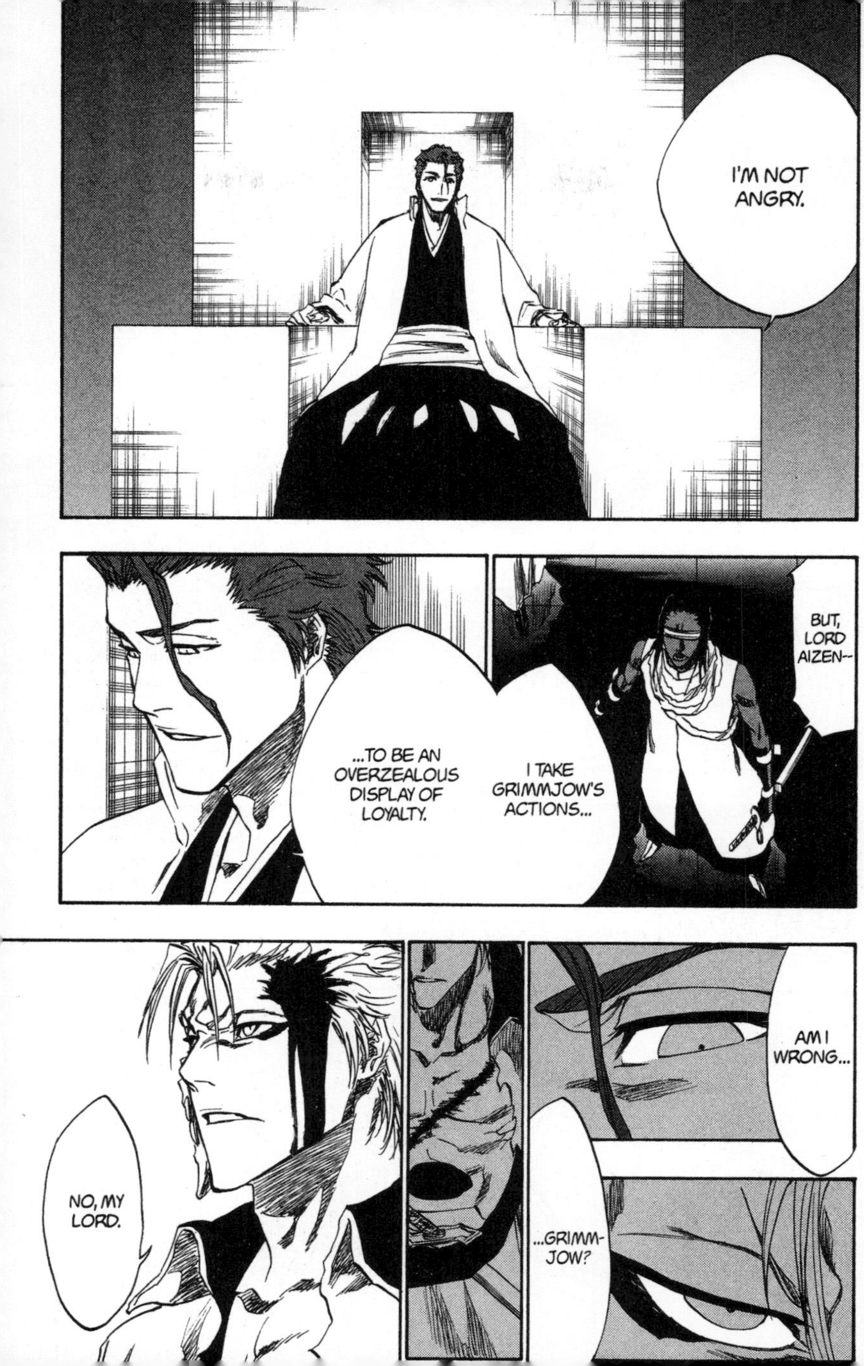
I'M NOT ANGRY.
BUT, LORD AIZEN--
I TAKE GRIMMJOW'S ACTIONS...
...TO BE AN OVERZEALOUS DISPLAY OF LOYALTY.
AM I WRONG...
...GRIMMJOW?
NO, MY LORD.

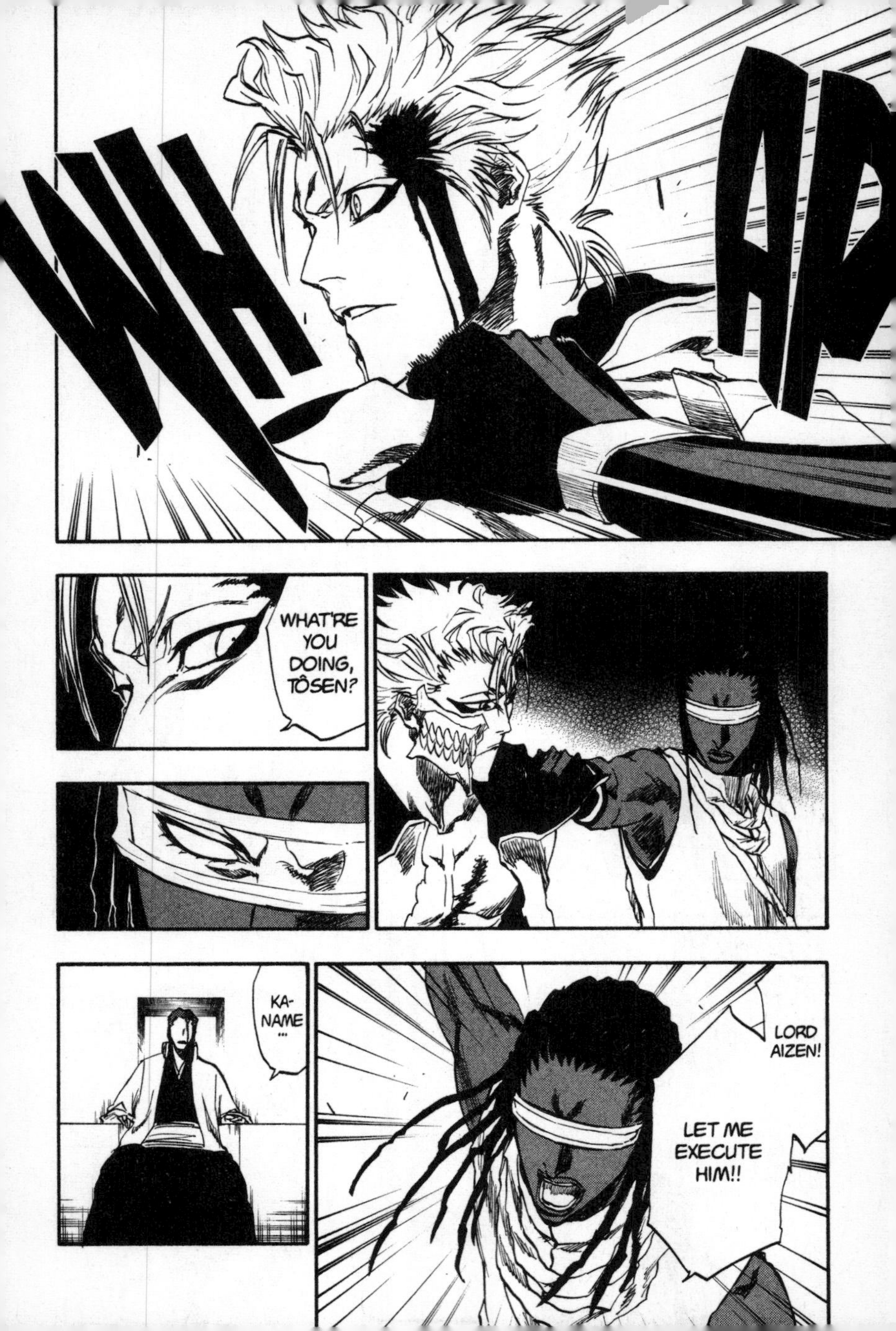
WHAP
WHAT'RE YOU DOING, TÔSEN?
LORD AIZEN!
LET ME EXECUTE HIM!!
KA-NAME...

READ THIS WAY

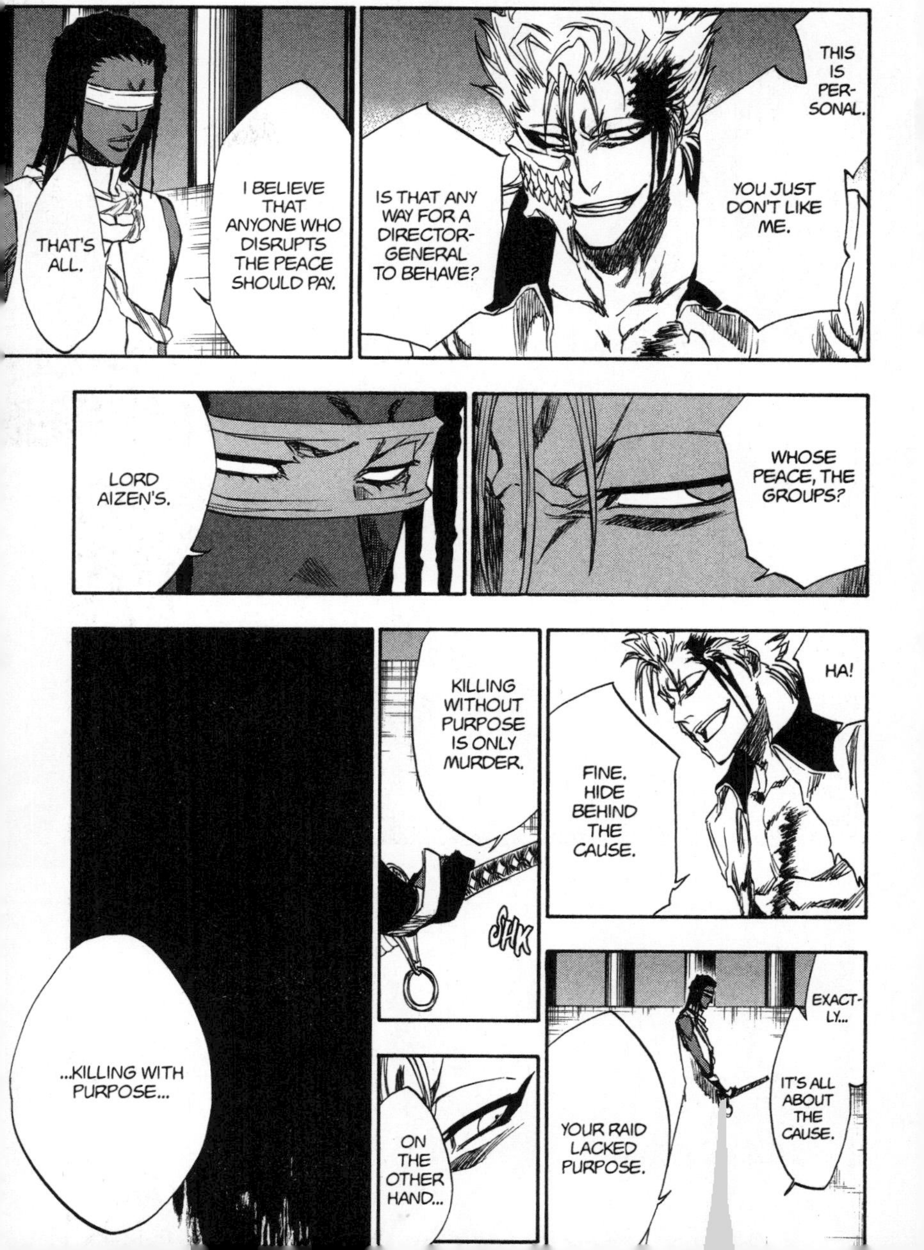
THIS IS PER-SONAL.
YOU JUST DON'T LIKE ME.
IS THAT ANY WAY FOR A DIRECTOR-GENERAL TO BEHAVE?
I BELIEVE THAT ANYONE WHO DISRUPTS THE PEACE SHOULD PAY.
THAT'S ALL.
WHOSE PEACE, THE GROUPS?
LORD AIZEN'S.
HA!
FINE. HIDE BEHIND THE CAUSE.
KILLING WITHOUT PURPOSE IS ONLY MURDER.
SHK
EXACT-LY...
IT'S ALL ABOUT THE CAUSE.
YOUR RAID LACKED PURPOSE.
ON THE OTHER HAND...
...KILLING WITH PURPOSE...

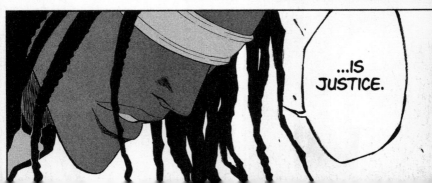

...IS
JUSTICE.

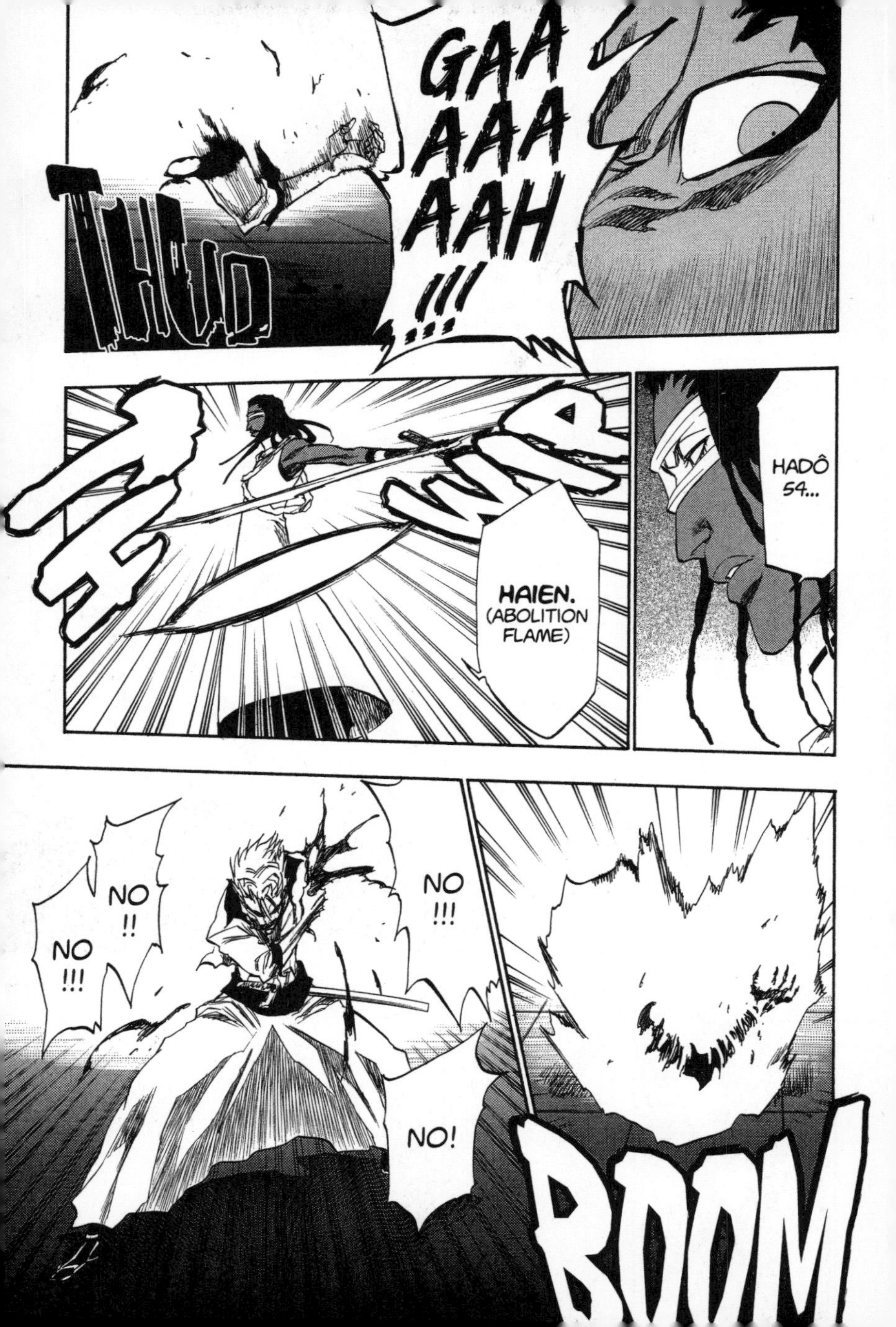
GAA AAA AAH !!!
THUD
HADÔ 54...
HAIEN. (ABOLITION FLAME)
BOOM
NO !!!
NO !!
NO !!!
NO!

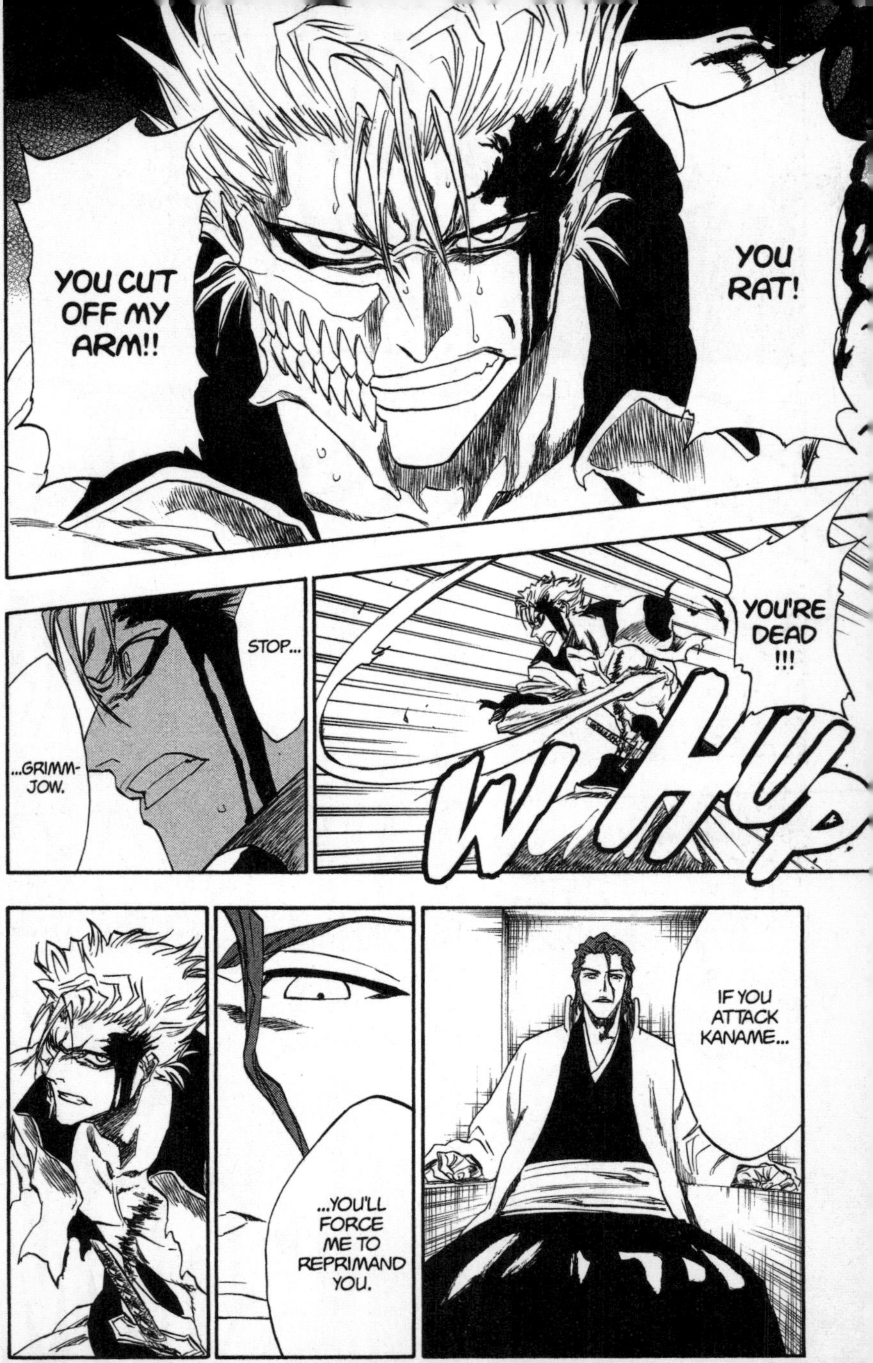
YOU RAT!
YOU CUT OFF MY ARM!!
YOU'RE DEAD !!!
WHUP
STOP...
...GRIMM-JOW.
IF YOU ATTACK KANAME...
...YOU'LL FORCE ME TO REPRIMAND YOU.

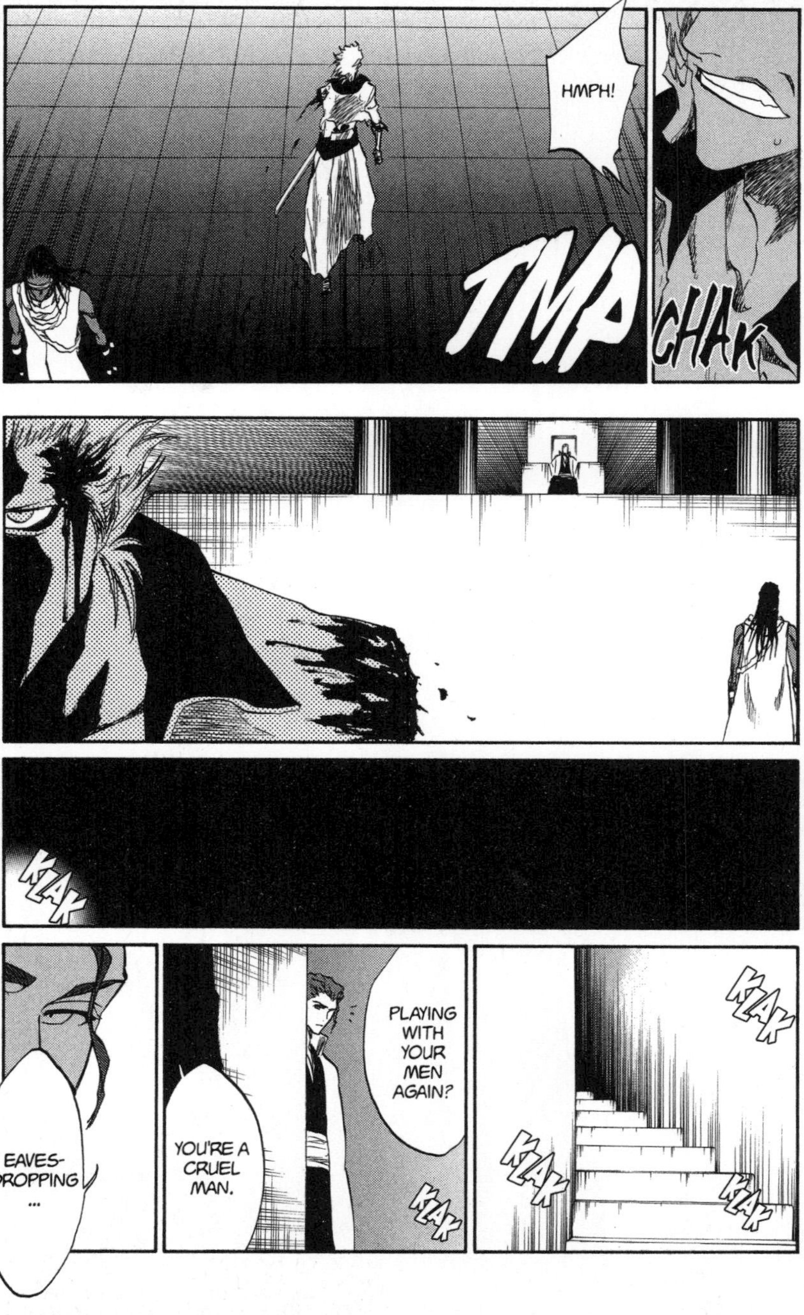
CHAK
HMPH!
TMP
KLAK
KLAK
KLAK
KLAK
PLAYING WITH YOUR MEN AGAIN?
YOU'RE A CRUEL MAN.
KLAK
EAVES-DROPPING ...

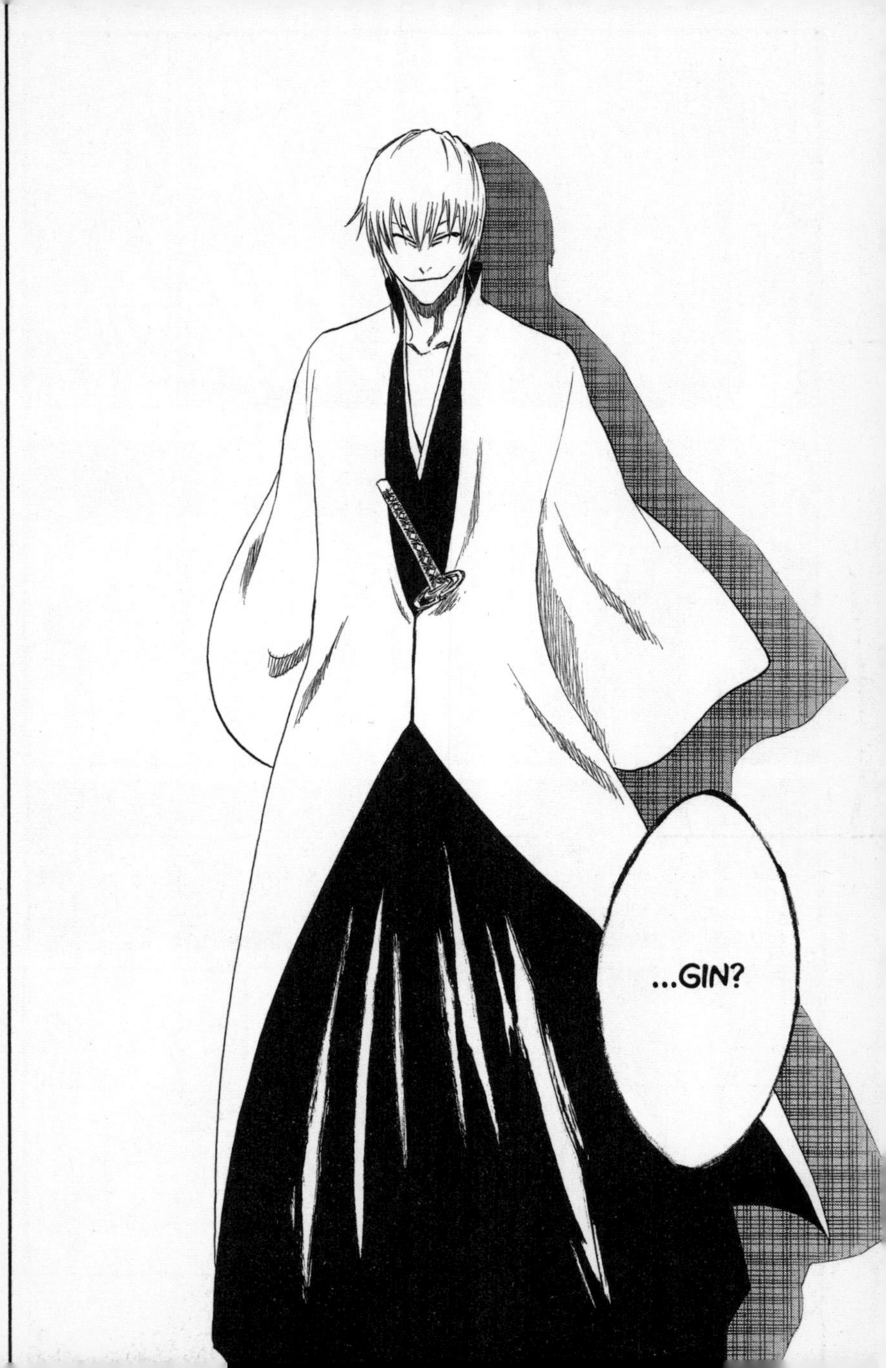
...GIN?

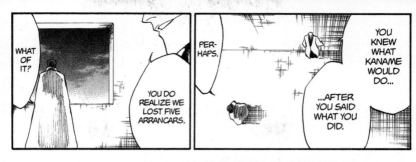

YOU KNEW WHAT KANAME WOULD DO...
...AFTER YOU SAID WHAT YOU DID.
PER-HAPS.
YOU DO REALIZE WE LOST FIVE ARRANCARS.
WHAT OF IT?
THEY WERE ONLY...
...GILLIANS.
IT WON'T AFFECT OUR PLAN IN THE LEAST.
ONCE WE'VE ASSEMBLED ENOUGH VASTO LORDES...
...AND THE ESPADAS ARE COMPLETE...

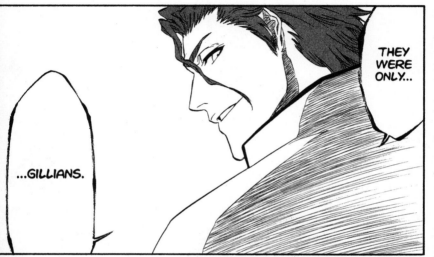

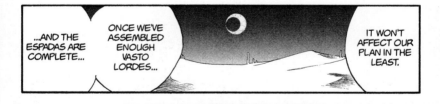

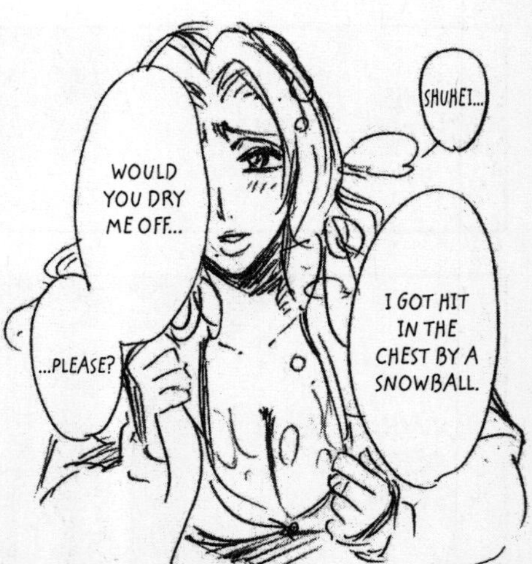
SHUHEI...
I GOT HIT IN THE CHEST BY A SNOWBALL.
WOULD YOU DRY ME OFF...
...PLEASE?

# 214. Immanent God Blues

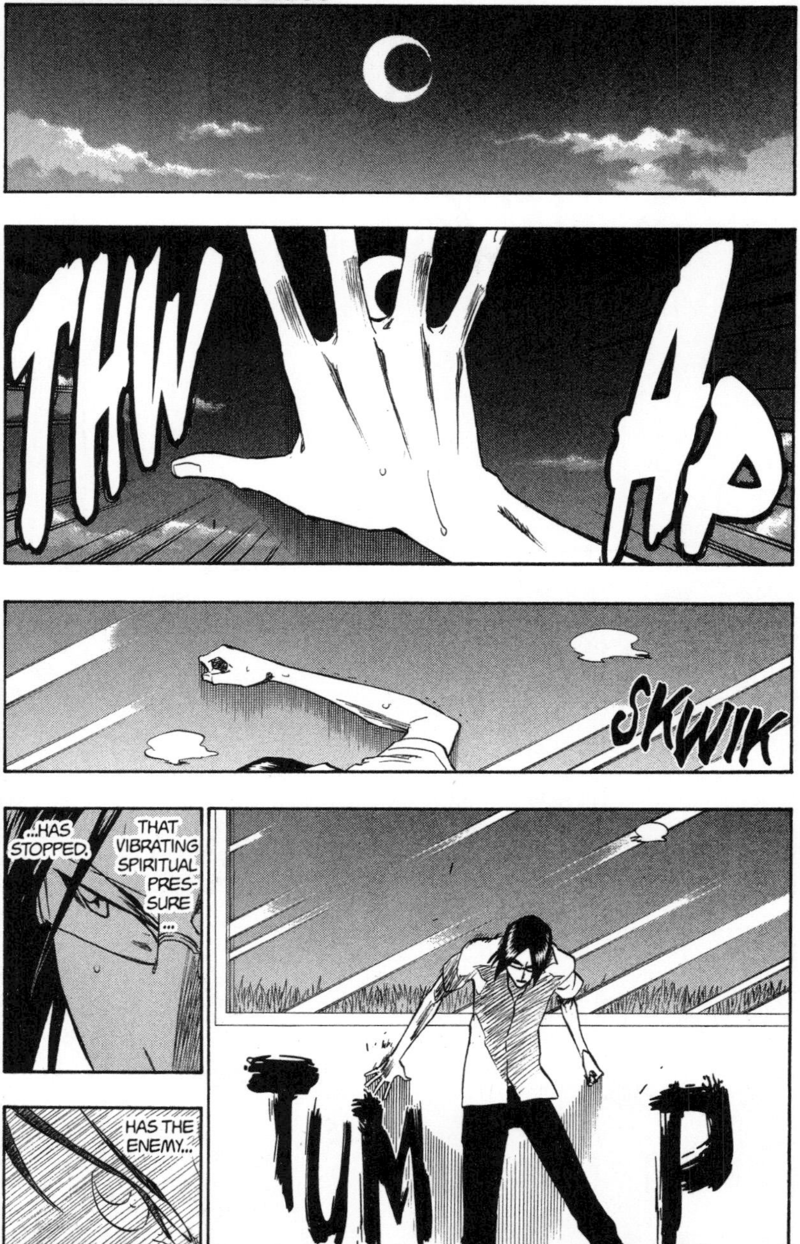
THWAP
SKWIK
TUMP
THAT VIBRATING SPIRITUAL PRES-SURE...
...HAS STOPPED.
HAS THE ENEMY...

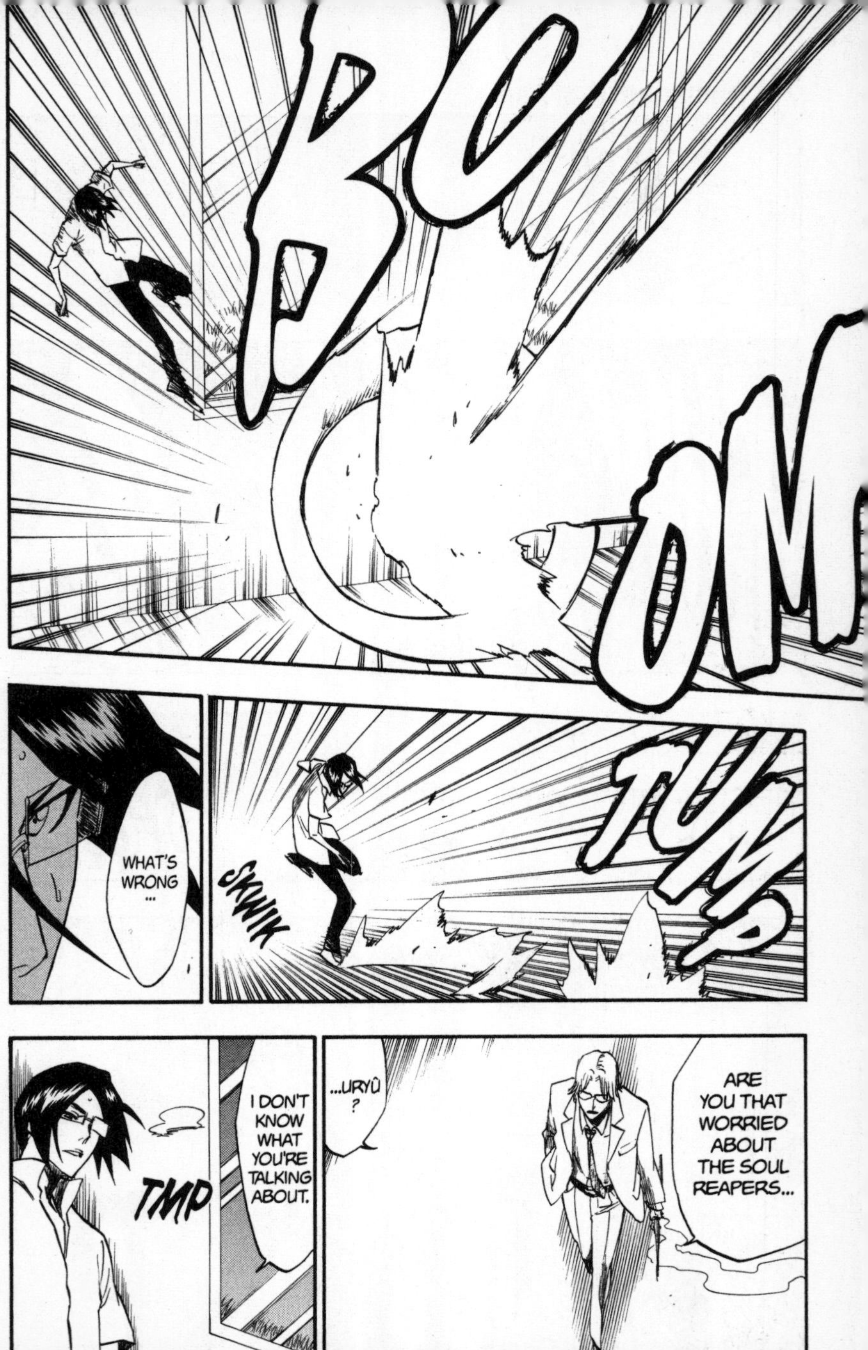
BOOM
TUMP
SKWIK
WHAT'S WRONG...
ARE YOU THAT WORRIED ABOUT THE SOUL REAPERS...
...URYÛ?
I DON'T KNOW WHAT YOU'RE TALKING ABOUT.
TMP

READ THIS WAY

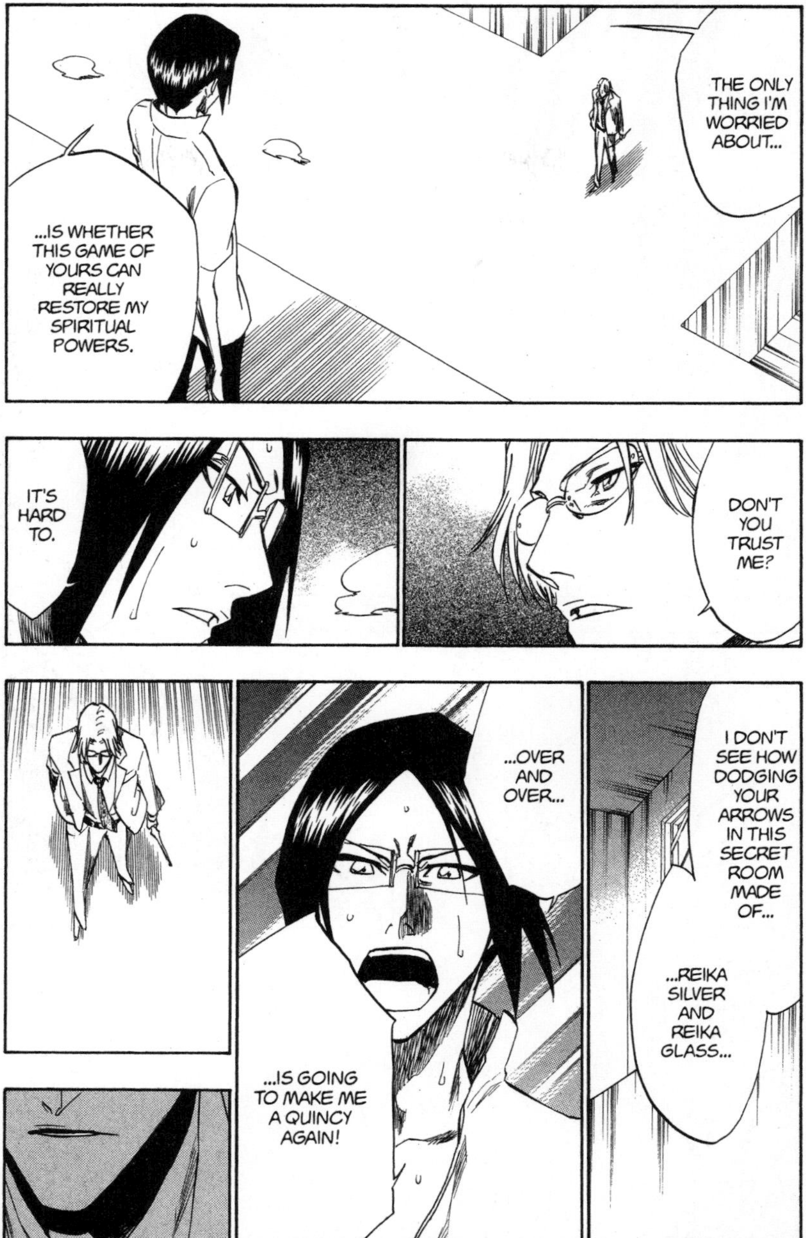
THE ONLY THING I'M WORRIED ABOUT...
...IS WHETHER THIS GAME OF YOURS CAN REALLY RESTORE MY SPIRITUAL POWERS.
DON'T YOU TRUST ME?
IT'S HARD TO.
I DON'T SEE HOW DODGING YOUR ARROWS IN THIS SECRET ROOM MADE OF...
...REIKA SILVER AND REIKA GLASS...
...OVER AND OVER...
...IS GOING TO MAKE ME A QUINCY AGAIN!

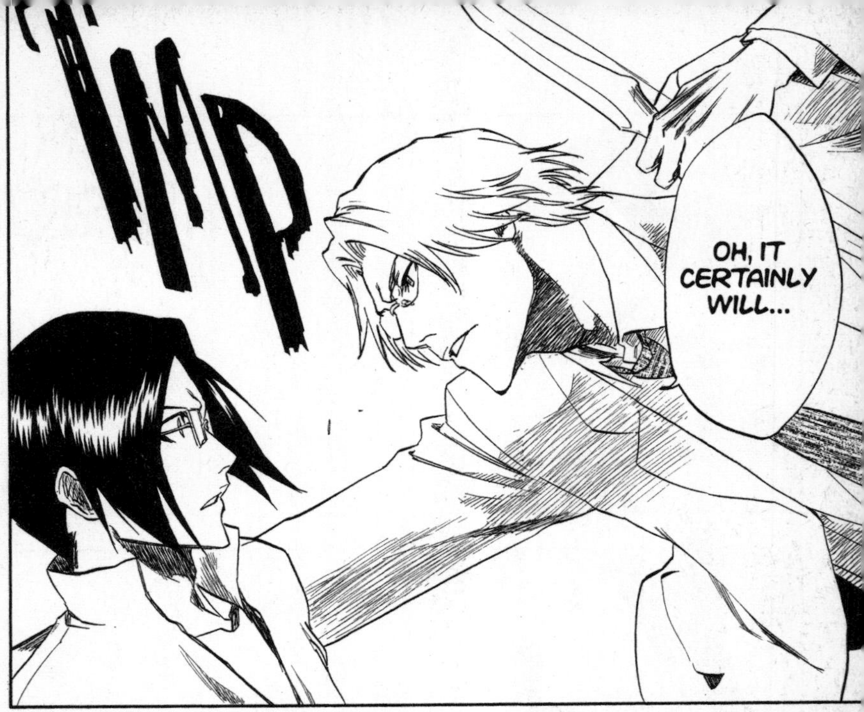
OH, IT CERTAINLY WILL...
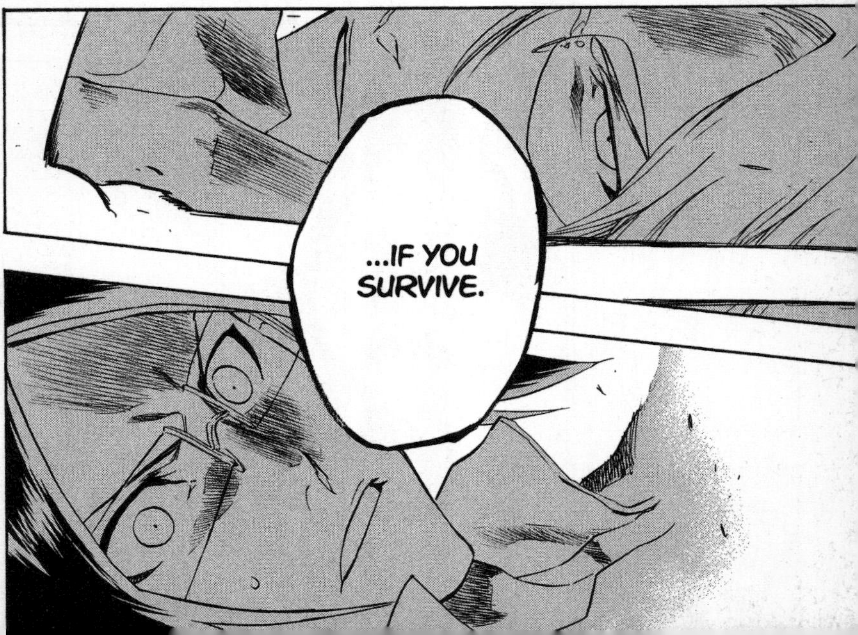
...IF YOU SURVIVE.

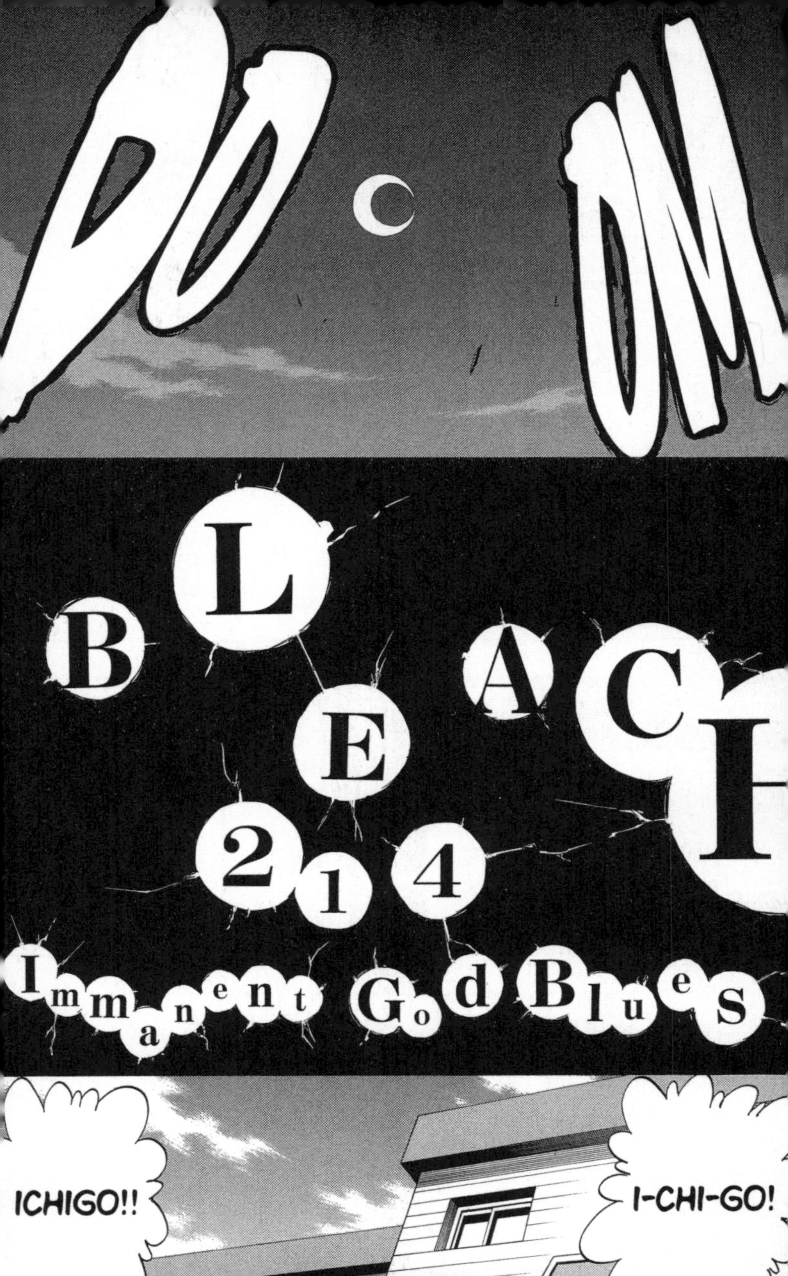
DO
OM
BLEACH
214
Immanent God Blues
I-CHI-GO!
ICHIGO!!

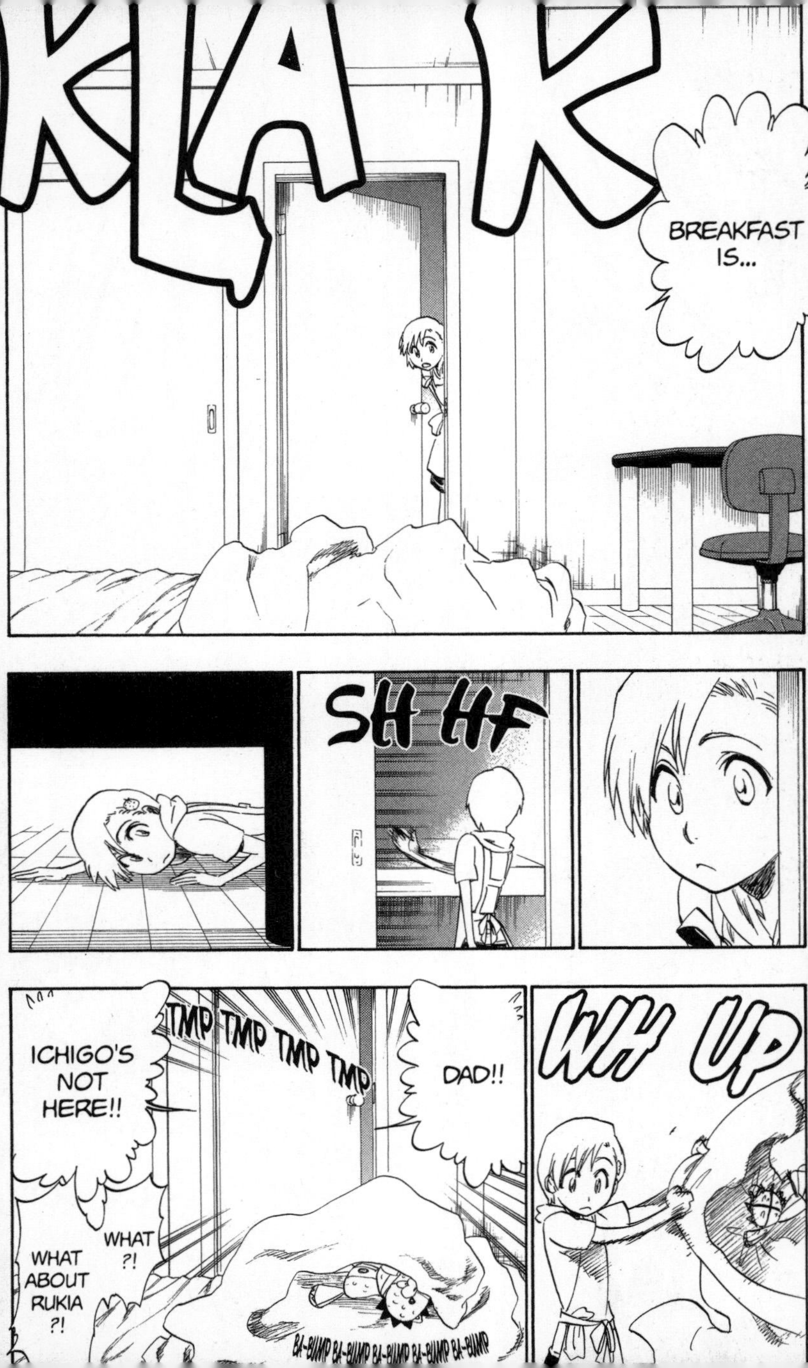
KLAK
BREAKFAST IS...
SHHF
WHUP
DAD!!
ICHIGO'S NOT HERE!!
TMP TMP TMP TMP
WHAT ?!
WHAT ABOUT RUKIA ?!
BA-BUMP BA-BUMP BA-BUMP BA-BUMP BA-BUMP

READ THIS WAY

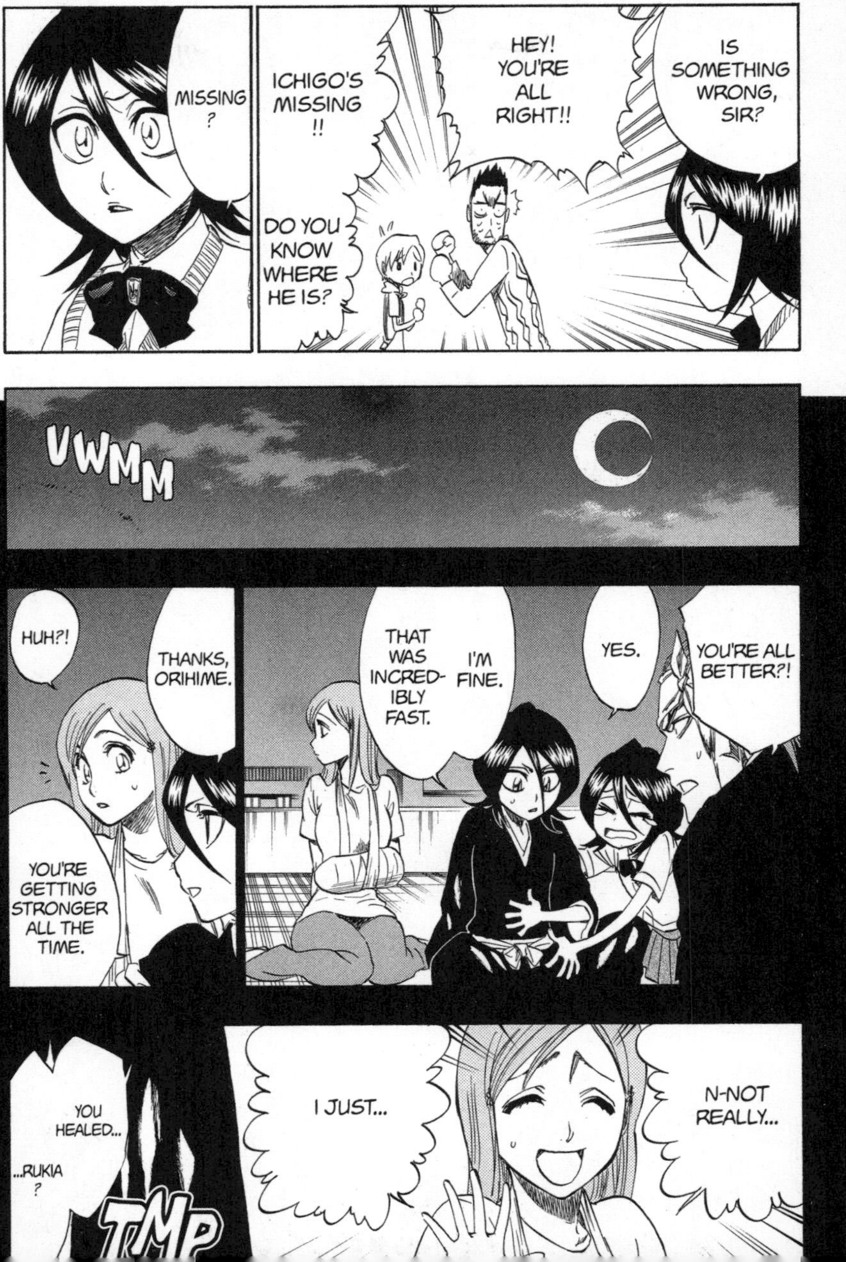
IS SOMETHING WRONG, SIR?
HEY! YOU'RE ALL RIGHT!!
ICHIGO'S MISSING!!
DO YOU KNOW WHERE HE IS?
MISSING?
VWMM
YOU'RE ALL BETTER?!
YES.
I'M FINE.
THAT WAS INCREDIBLY FAST.
THANKS, ORIHIME.
HUH?!
YOU'RE GETTING STRONGER ALL THE TIME.
N-NOT REALLY...
I JUST...
YOU HEALED...
...RUKIA?
TMP

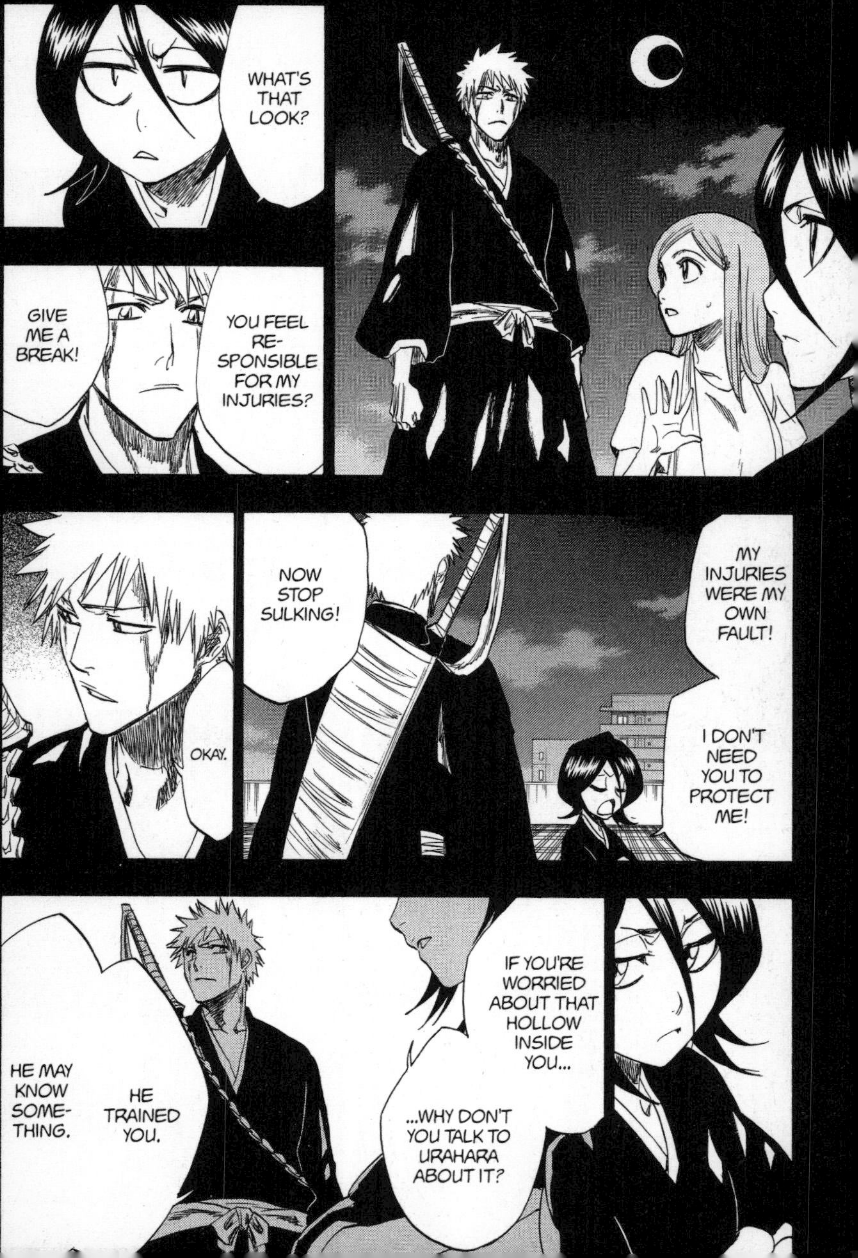
WHAT'S THAT LOOK?
YOU FEEL RE-SPONSIBLE FOR MY INJURIES?
GIVE ME A BREAK!
MY INJURIES WERE MY OWN FAULT!
I DON'T NEED YOU TO PROTECT ME!
NOW STOP SULKING!
OKAY.
IF YOU'RE WORRIED ABOUT THAT HOLLOW INSIDE YOU...
...WHY DON'T YOU TALK TO URAHARA ABOUT IT?
HE TRAINED YOU.
HE MAY KNOW SOME-THING.

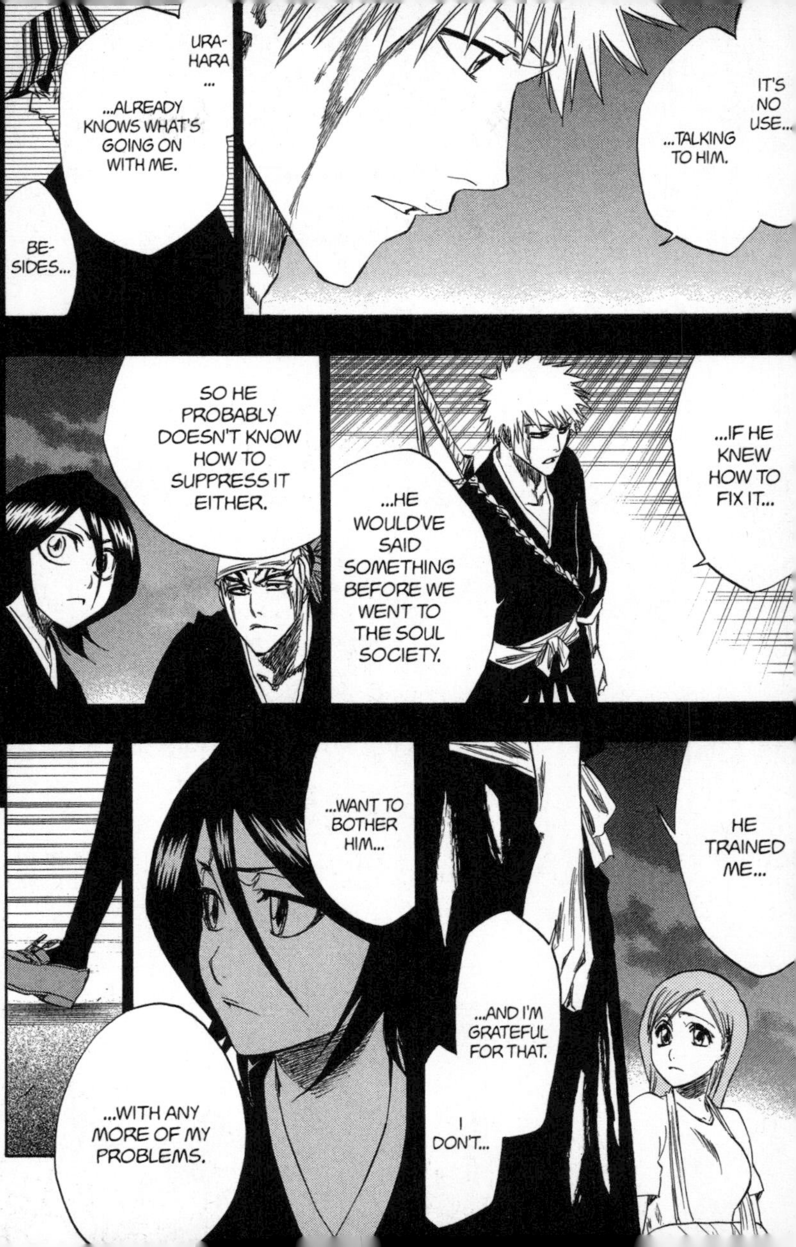
IT'S NO USE...
...TALKING TO HIM.
URA-HARA...
...ALREADY KNOWS WHAT'S GOING ON WITH ME.
BE-SIDES...
...IF HE KNEW HOW TO FIX IT...
...HE WOULD'VE SAID SOMETHING BEFORE WE WENT TO THE SOUL SOCIETY.
SO HE PROBABLY DOESN'T KNOW HOW TO SUPPRESS IT EITHER.
HE TRAINED ME...
...AND I'M GRATEFUL FOR THAT.
I DON'T...
...WANT TO BOTHER HIM...
...WITH ANY MORE OF MY PROBLEMS.

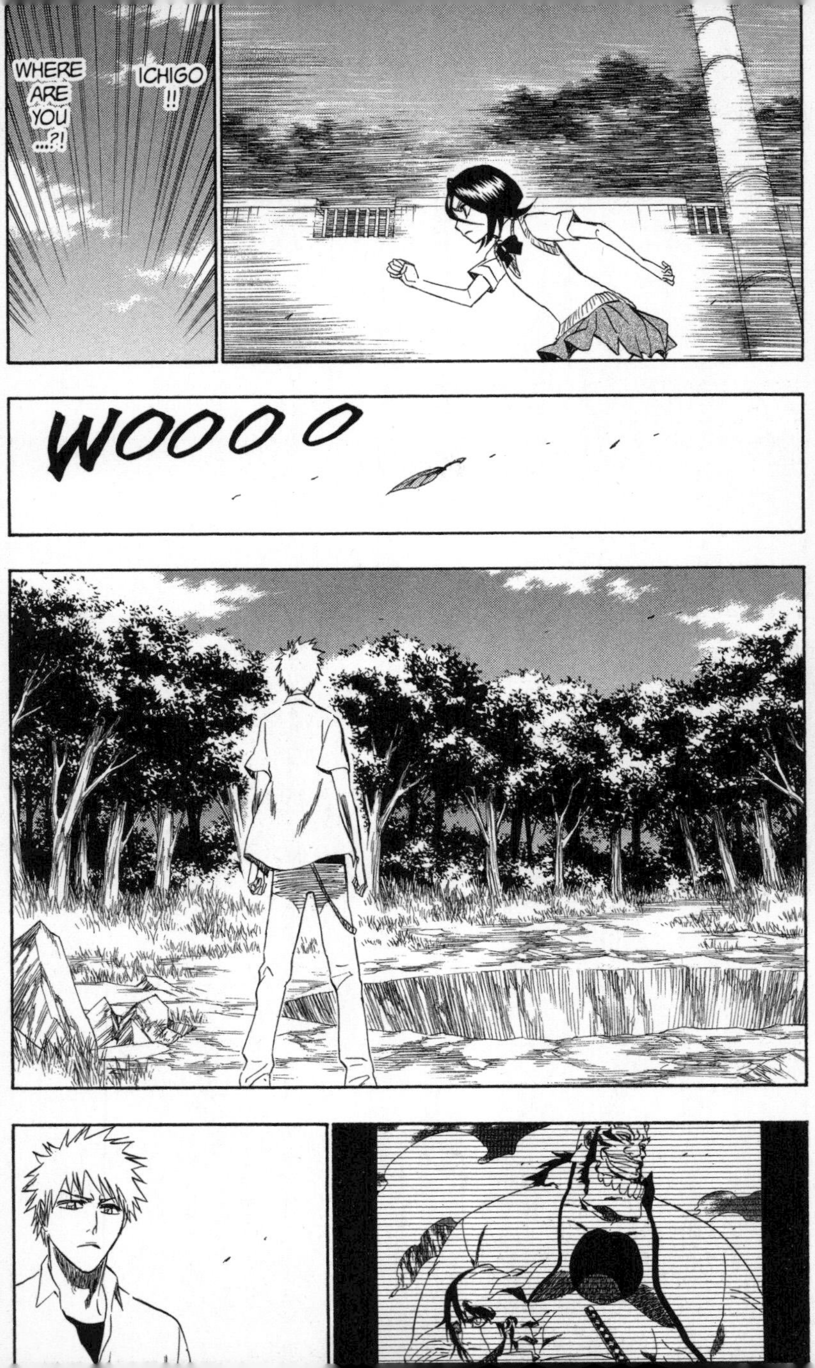
ICHIGO !!
WHERE ARE YOU ...?!
WOOOO

READ THIS WAY

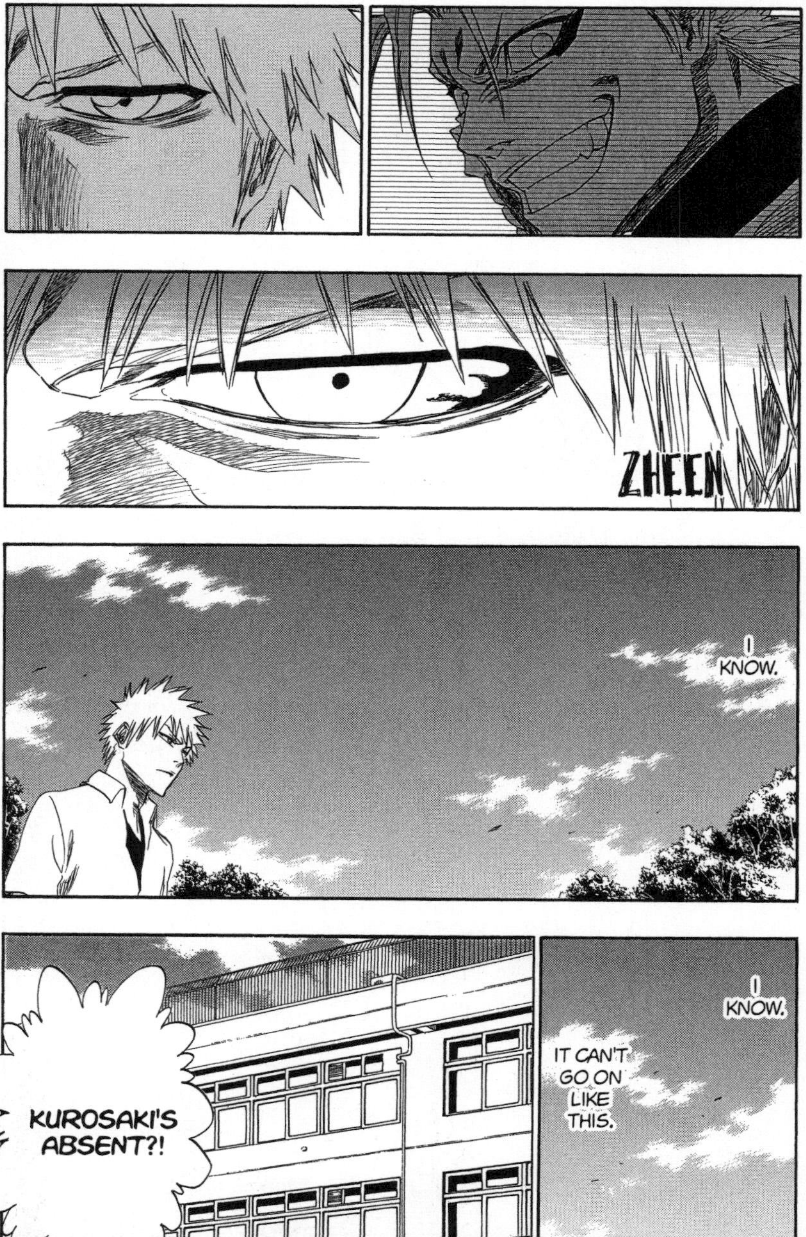
ZHEEN
I KNOW.
I KNOW.
IT CAN'T GO ON LIKE THIS.
KUROSAKI'S ABSENT?!

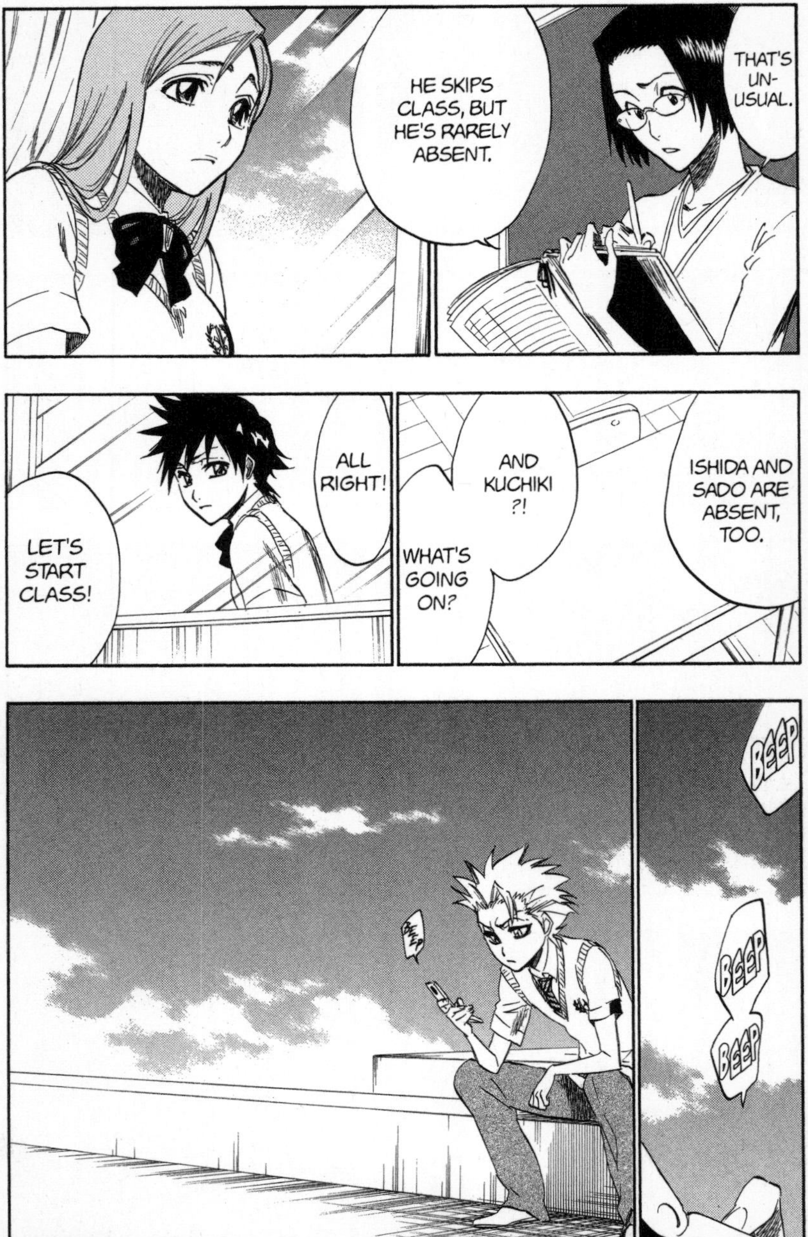
THAT'S UN- USUAL.
HE SKIPS CLASS, BUT HE'S RARELY ABSENT.
ISHIDA AND SADO ARE ABSENT, TOO.
AND KUCHIKI ?!
WHAT'S GOING ON?
ALL RIGHT!
LET'S START CLASS!
BEEP
BEEP
BEEP

READ THIS WAY

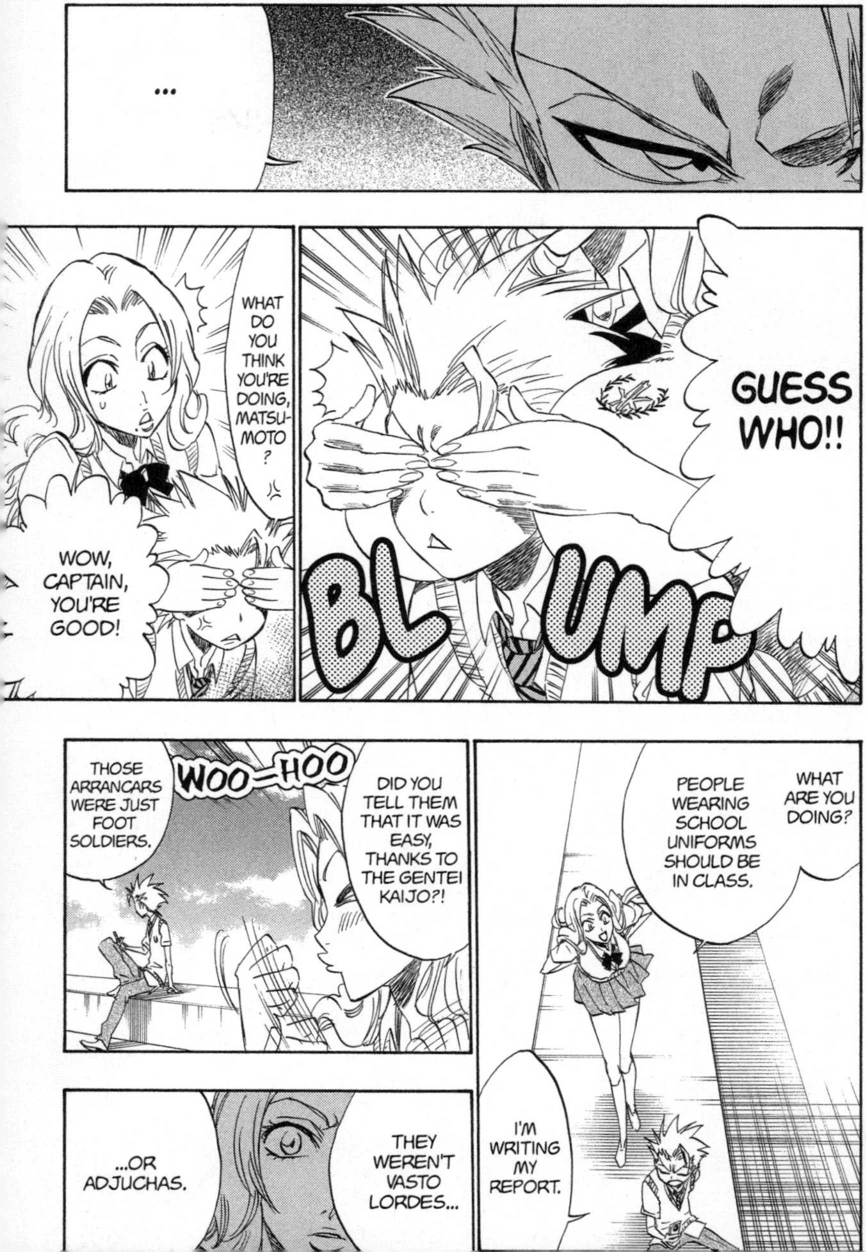
...
GUESS WHO!!
BLUMP
WHAT DO YOU THINK YOU'RE DOING, MATSU-MOTO?
WOW, CAPTAIN, YOU'RE GOOD!
WHAT ARE YOU DOING?
PEOPLE WEARING SCHOOL UNIFORMS SHOULD BE IN CLASS.
I'M WRITING MY REPORT.
DID YOU TELL THEM THAT IT WAS EASY, THANKS TO THE GENTEI KAIJO?!
WOO-HOO
THOSE ARRANCARS WERE JUST FOOT SOLDIERS.
THEY WEREN'T VASTO LORDES...
...OR ADJUCHAS.

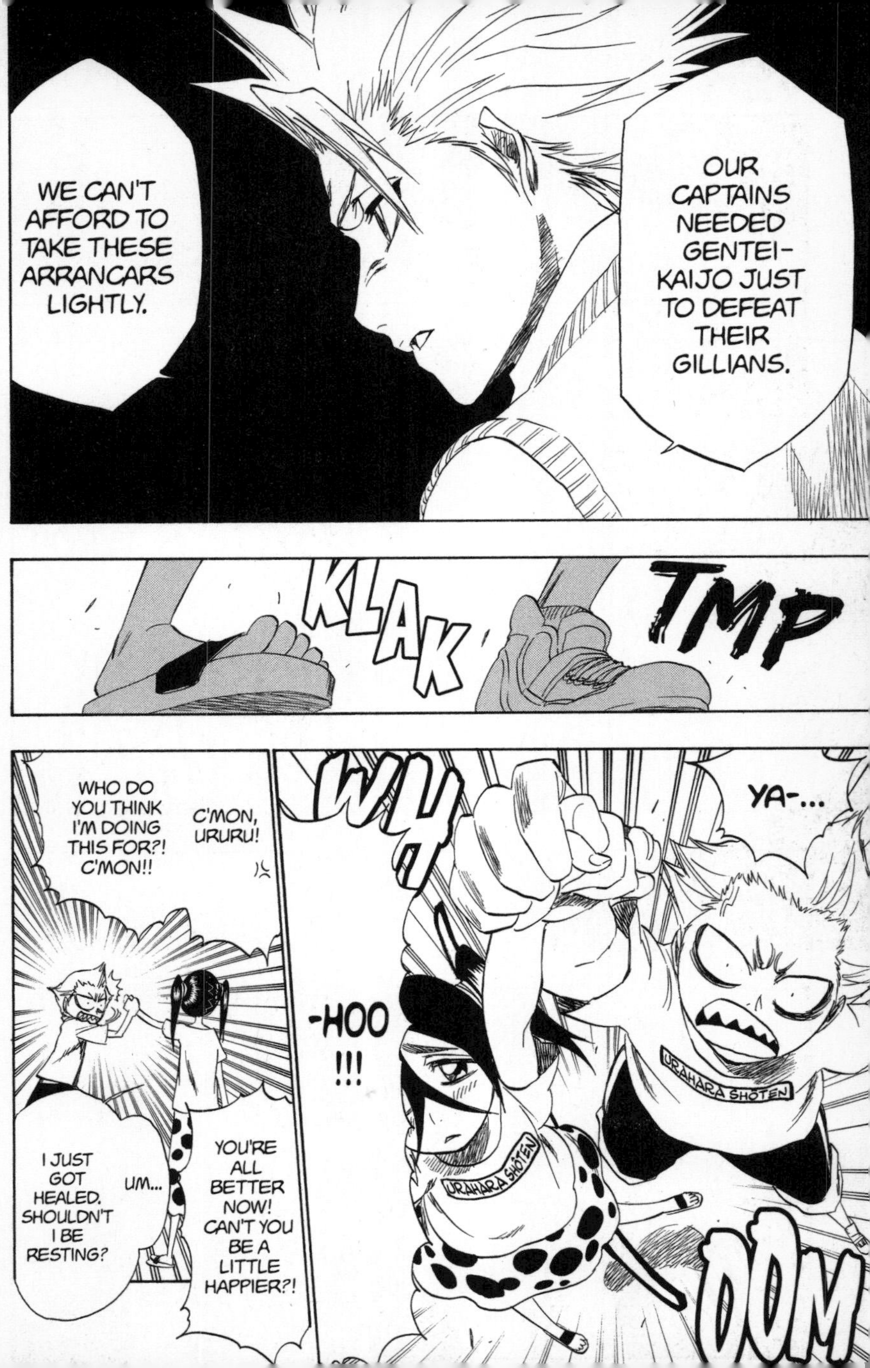
OUR CAPTAINS NEEDED GENTEI-KAIJO JUST TO DEFEAT THEIR GILLIANS.
WE CAN'T AFFORD TO TAKE THESE ARRANCARS LIGHTLY.
TMP
KLAK
YA-...
WH
-HOO !!!
URAHARA SHŌTEN
URAHARA SHŌTEN
DOM
C'MON, URURU!
WHO DO YOU THINK I'M DOING THIS FOR?! C'MON!!
YOU'RE ALL BETTER NOW! CAN'T YOU BE A LITTLE HAPPIER?!
UM...
I JUST GOT HEALED. SHOULDN'T I BE RESTING?

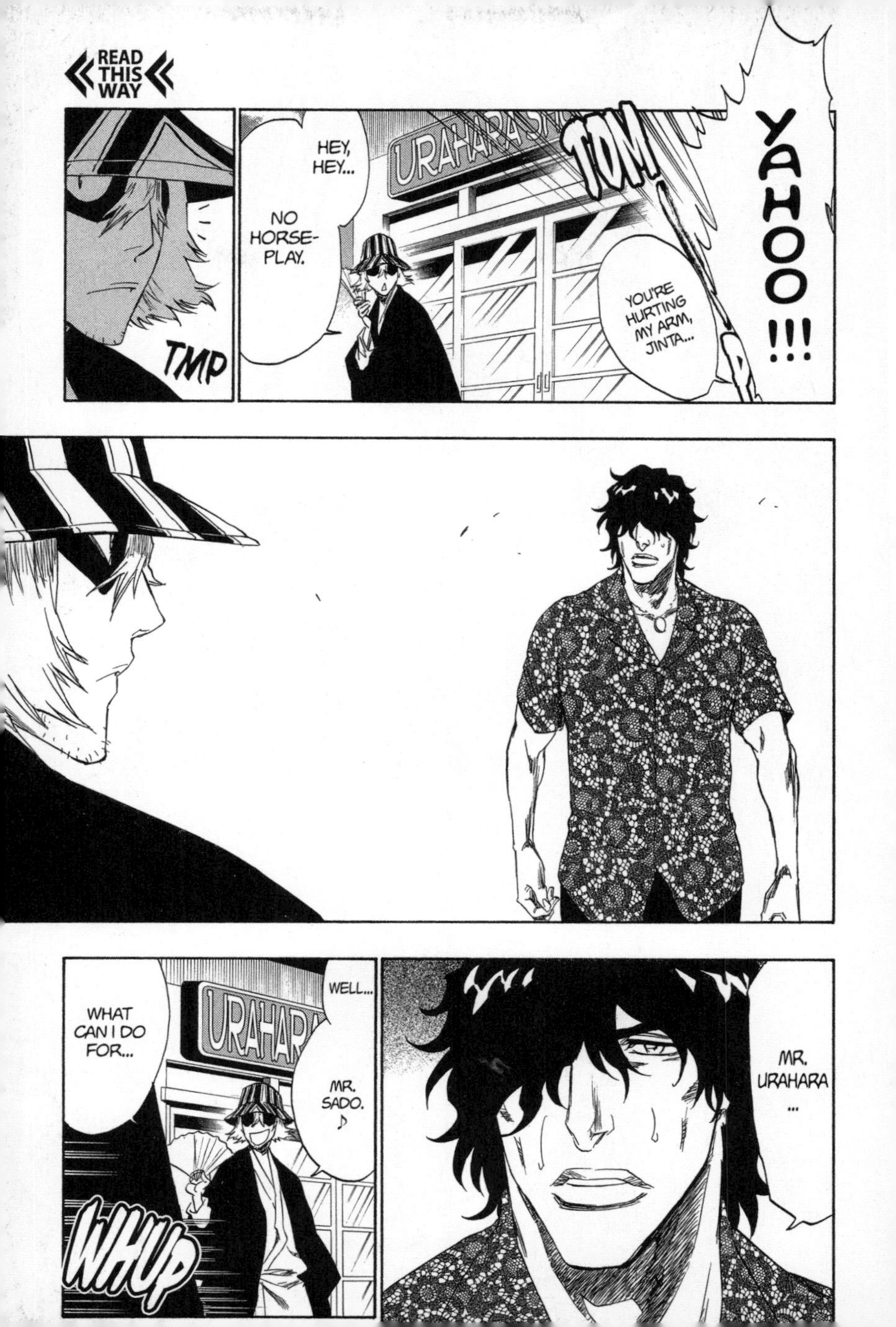
READ THIS WAY
YAHOO!!!
YOU'RE HURTING MY ARM, JINTA...
TOM
URAHARA SHO
HEY, HEY...
NO HORSE-PLAY.
TMP
MR. URAHARA ...
WELL...
WHAT CAN I DO FOR...
MR. SADO. ♪
URAHARA
WHUP

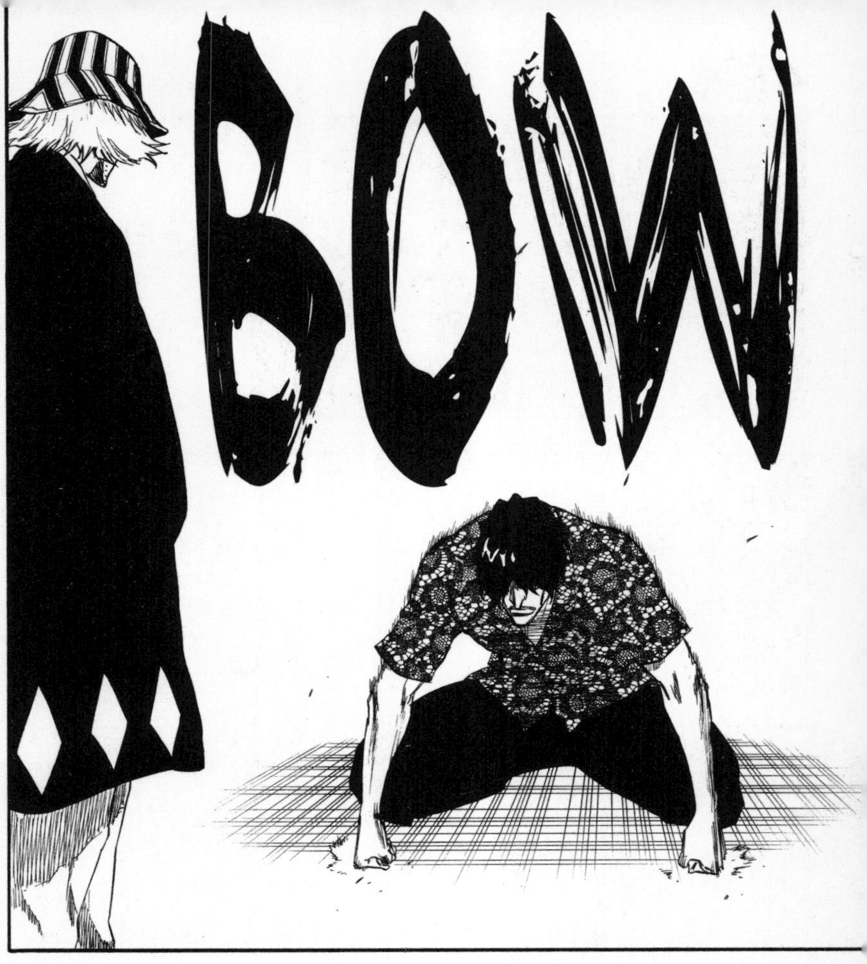
BOW

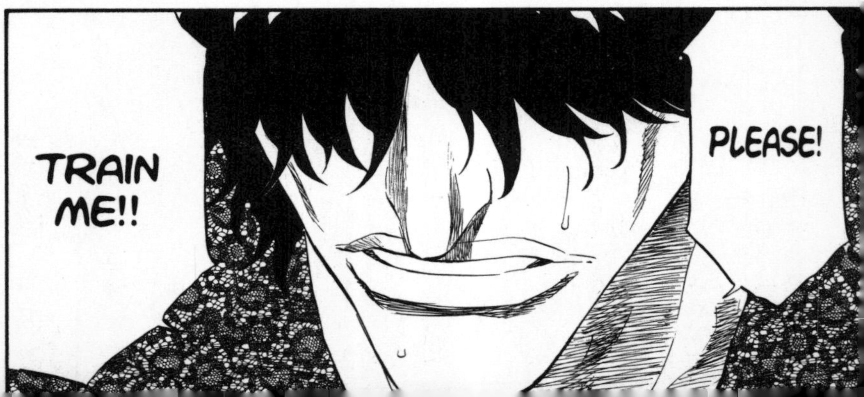
PLEASE!
TRAIN ME!!

READ THIS WAY

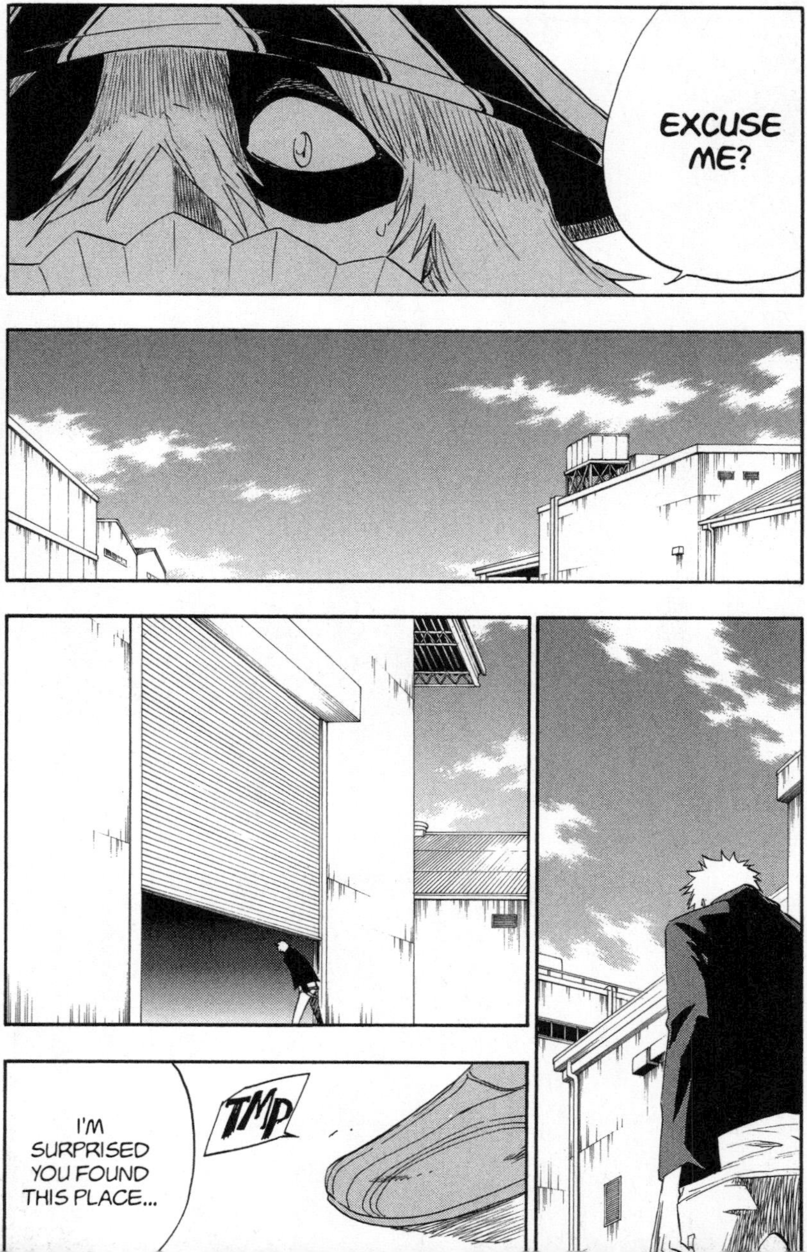
EXCUSE ME?
TMP
I'M SURPRISED YOU FOUND THIS PLACE...

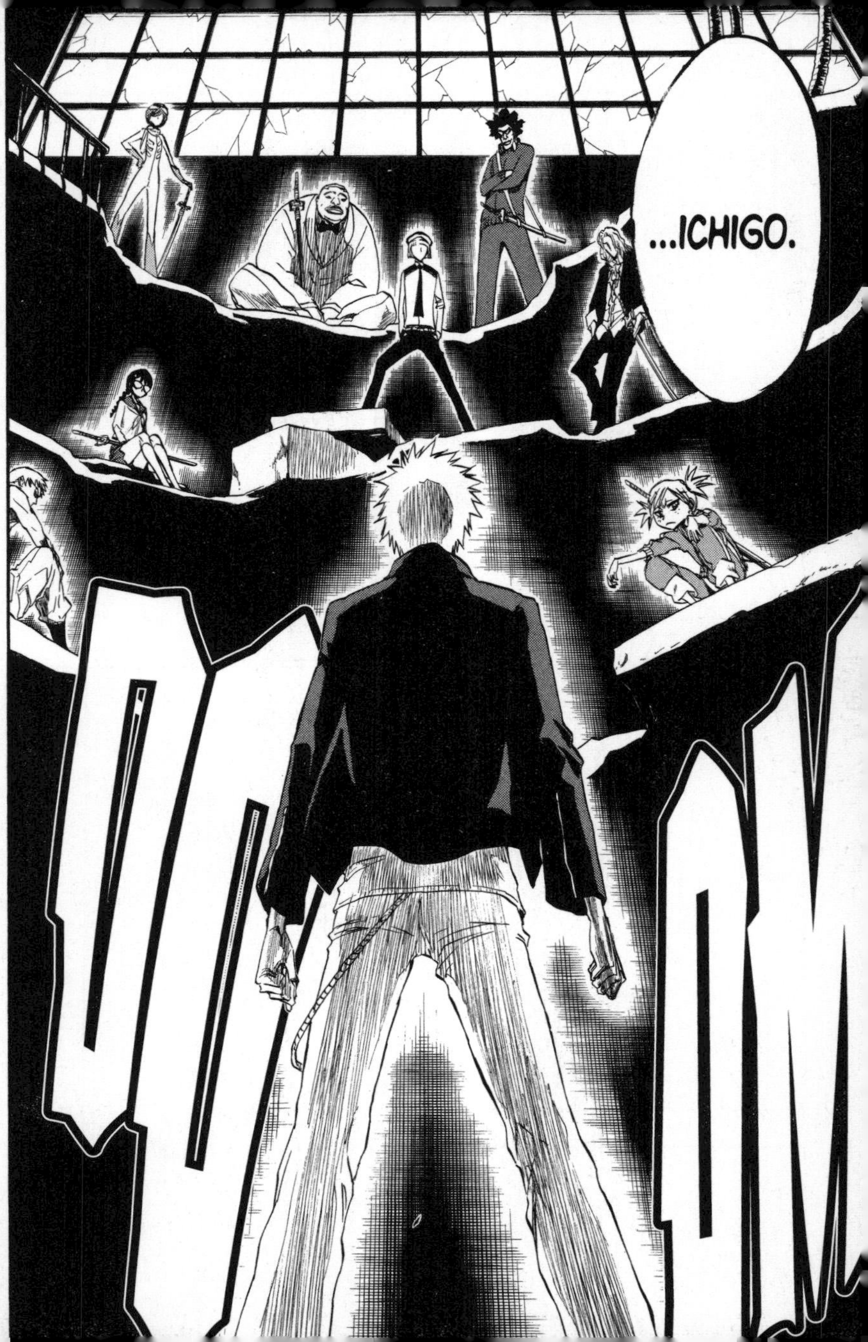
...ICHIGO.
DOOM

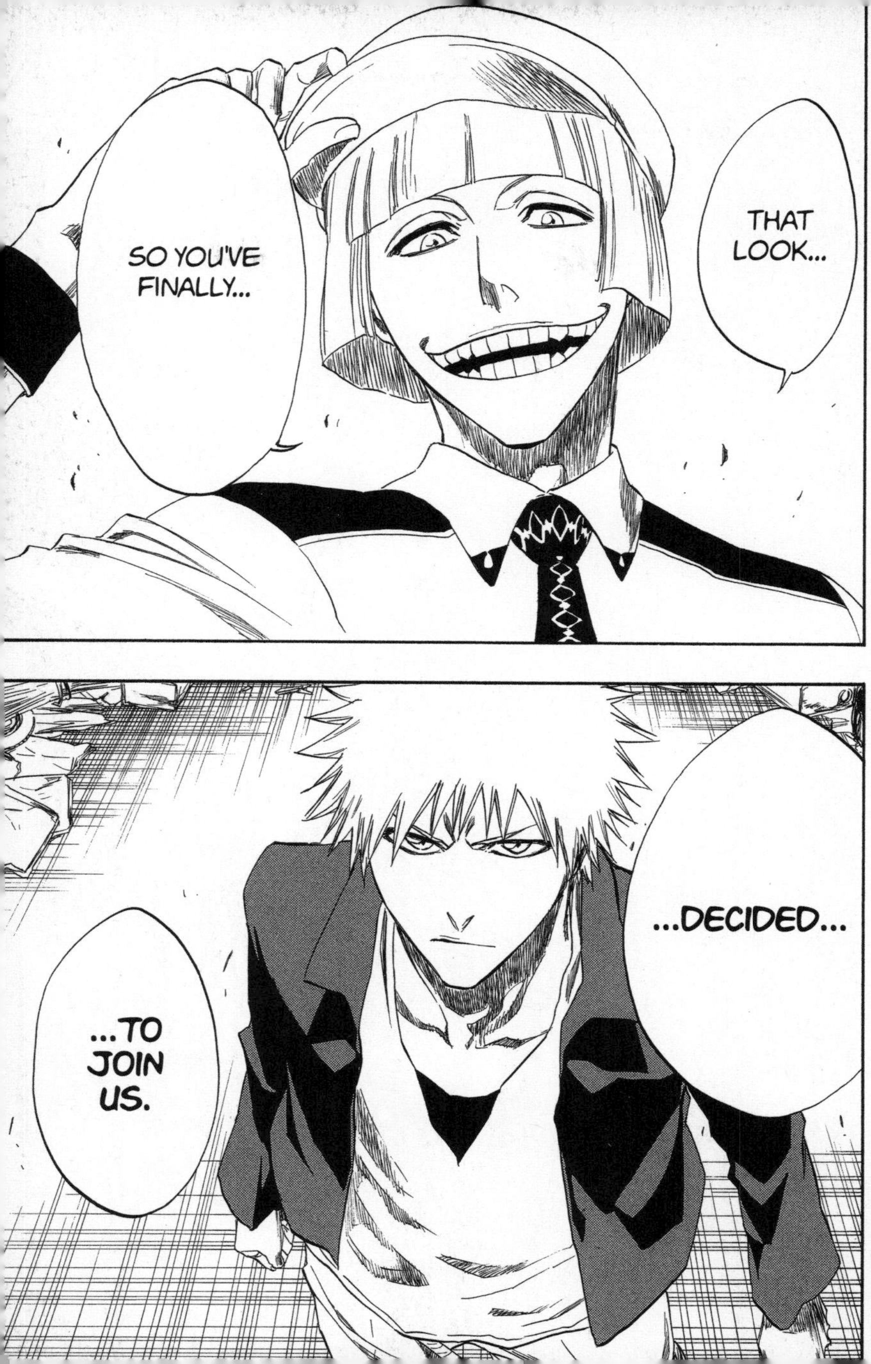
THAT LOOK...
SO YOU'VE FINALLY...
...DECIDED...
...TO JOIN US.

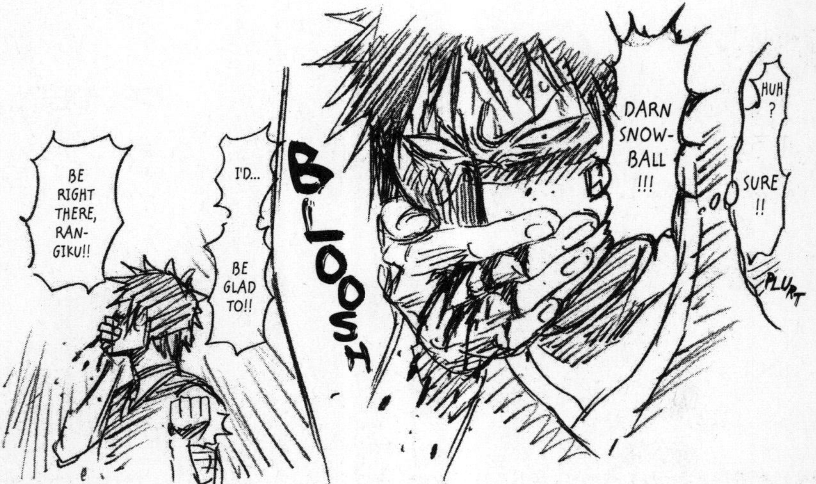
HUH? SURE!!
PLURT
DARN SNOW-BALL!!!
BLOOS!
I'D... BE GLAD TO!!
BE RIGHT THERE, RAN-GIKU!!

# BLEACH POPULARITY POLL 3

## DETAILED RESULTS!! THE COMPLETE LIST

## OVER 75,000 VOTES! THE THIRD CHARACTER POPULARITY POLL RESULTS!!

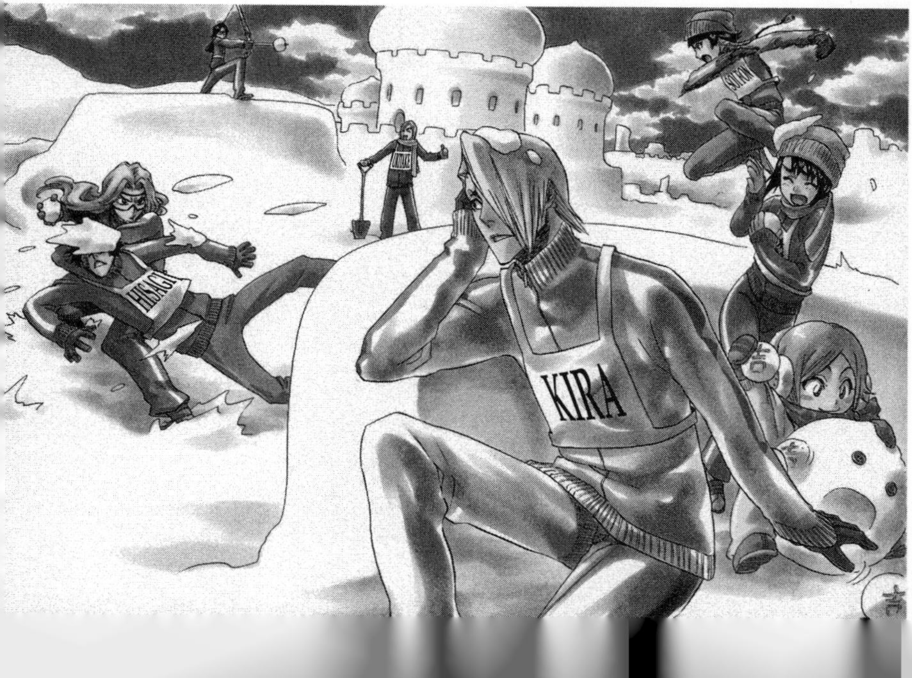
HISAGI
KIRA

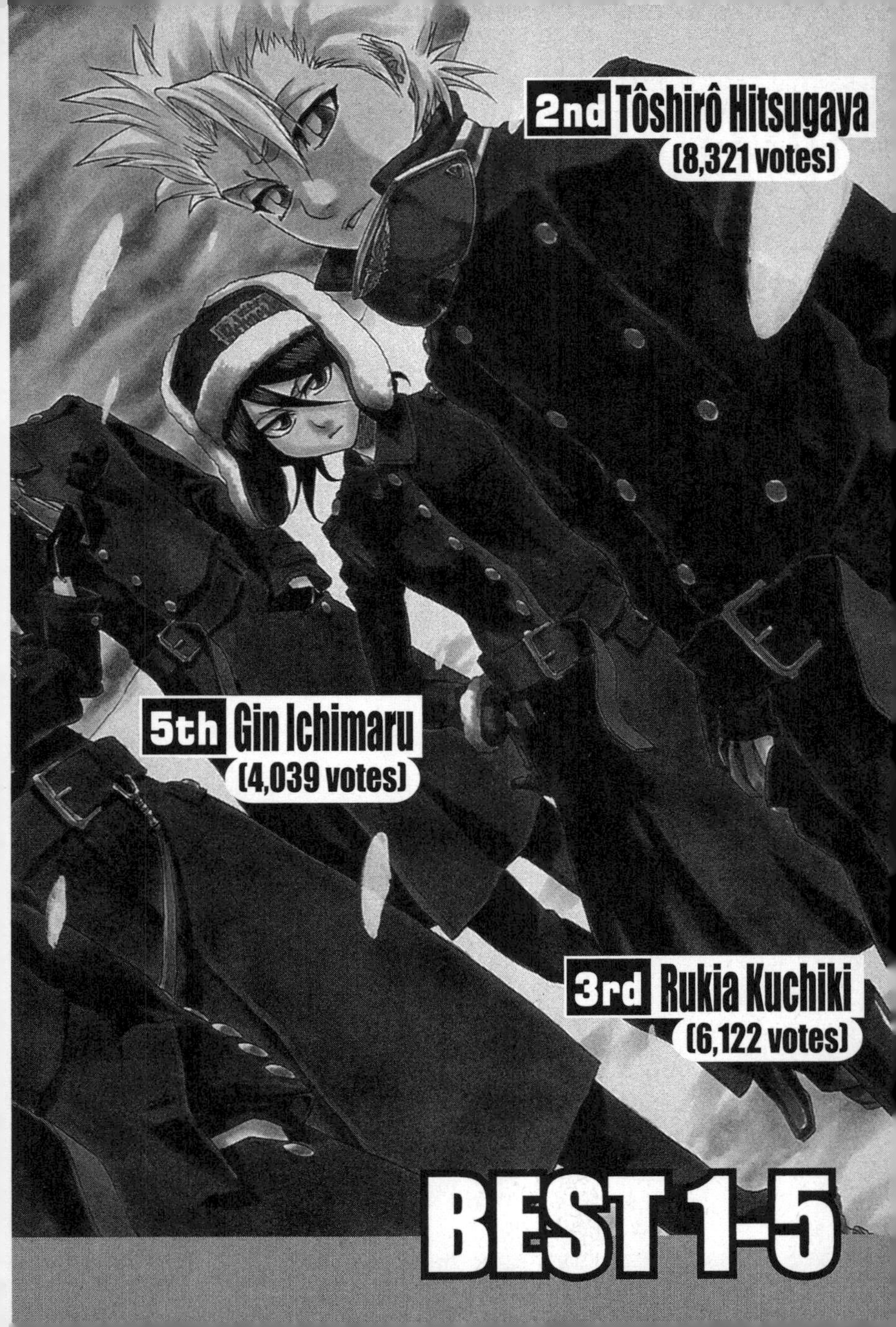
2nd Tôshirô Hitsugaya
(8,321 votes)
5th Gin Ichimaru
(4,039 votes)
3rd Rukia Kuchiki
(6,122 votes)
BEST 1-5

# BLEACH POPULARITY POLL 3

## DETAILED RESULTS!! THE COMPLETE LIST

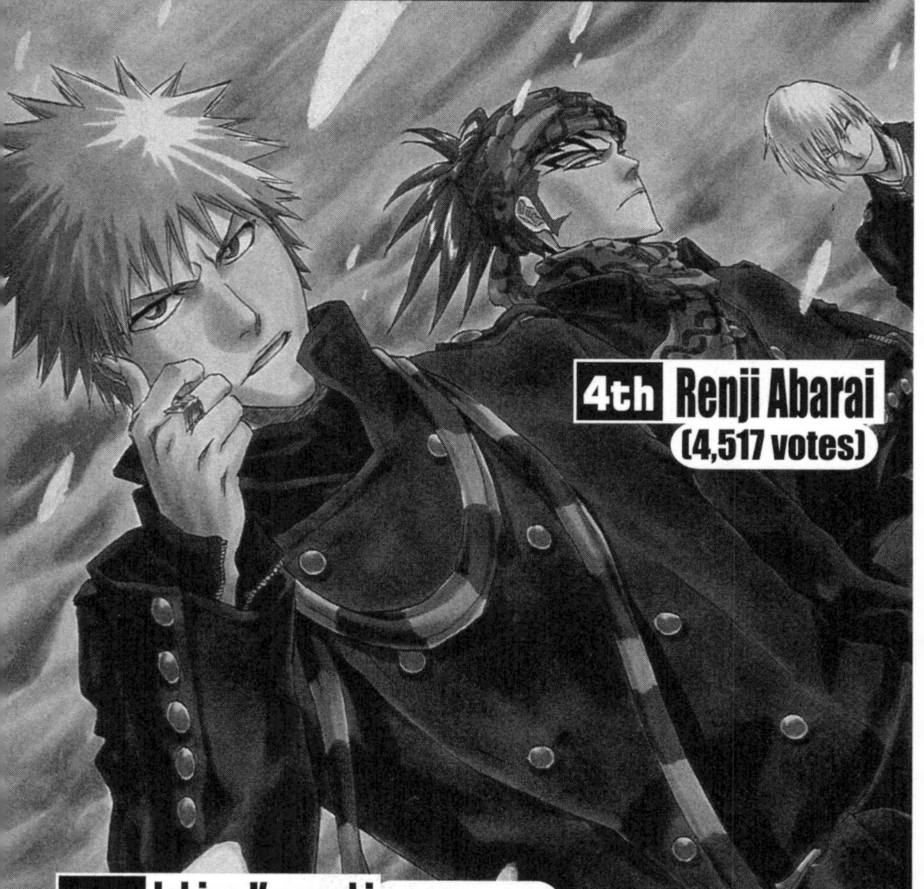
4th Renji Abarai
(4,517 votes)
1st Ichigo Kurosaki (8,370 votes)

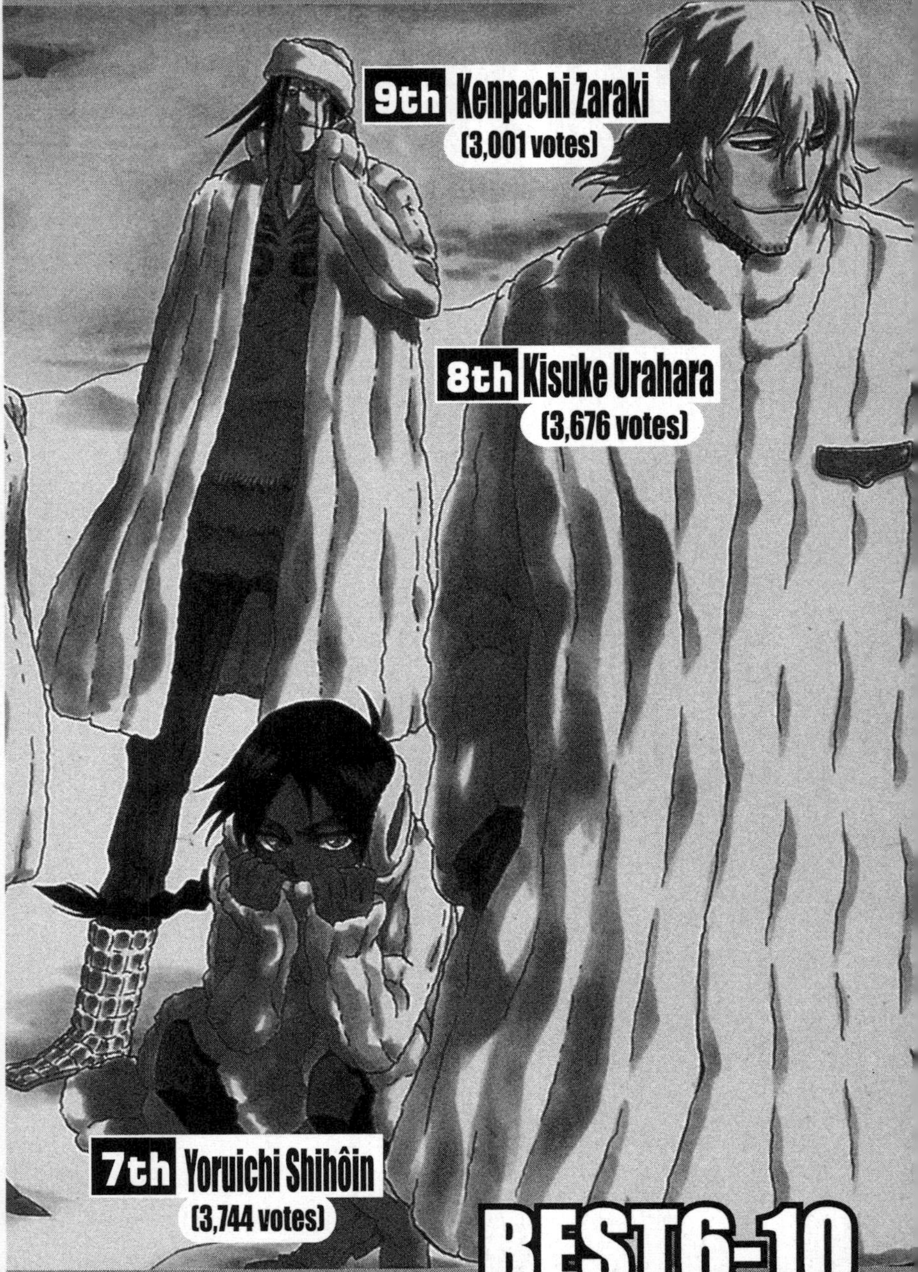
9th Kenpachi Zaraki
(3,001 votes)
8th Kisuke Urahara
(3,676 votes)
7th Yoruichi Shihôin
(3,744 votes)
BEST6-10

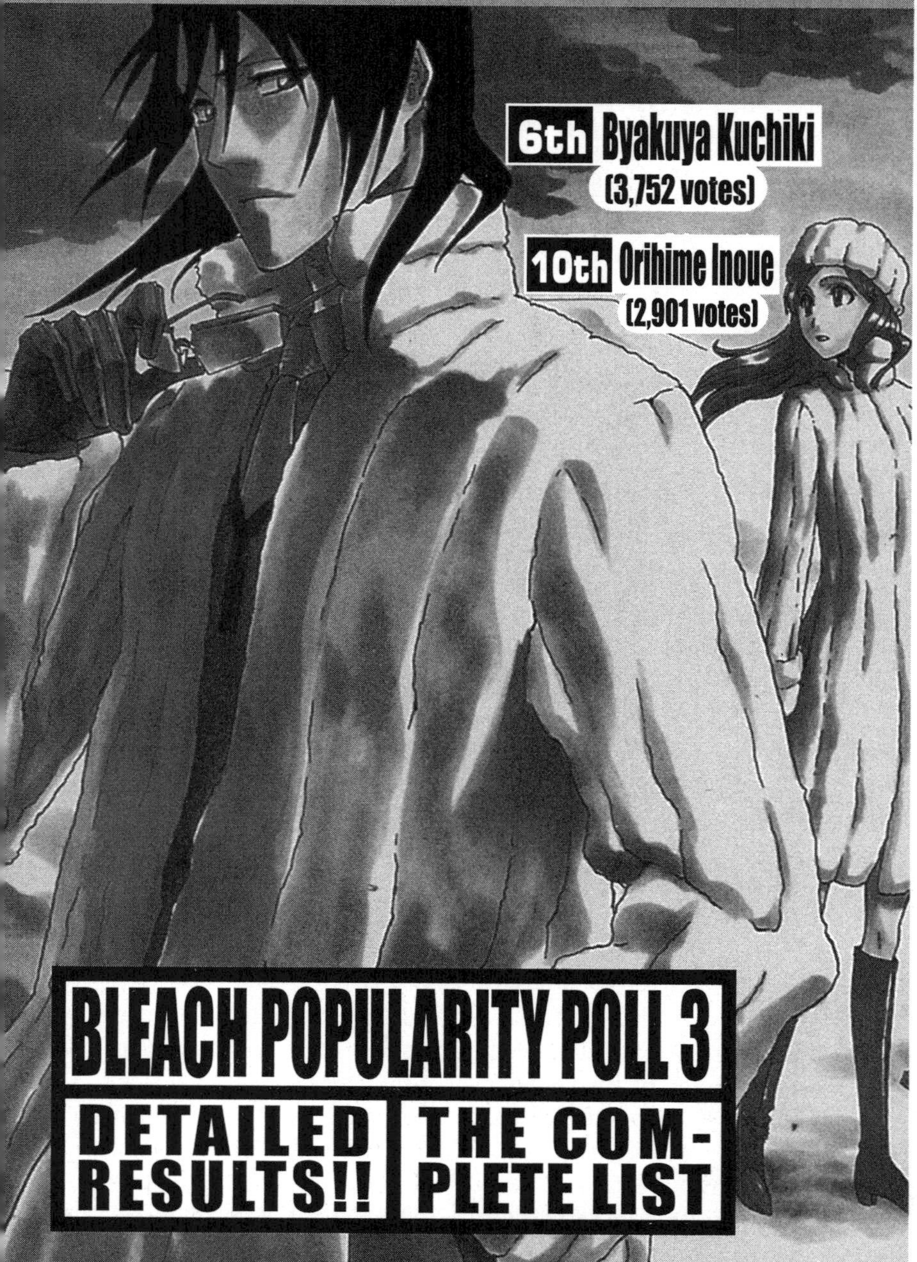
6th Byakuya Kuchiki
(3,752 votes)
10th Orihime Inoue
(2,901 votes)
BLEACH POPULARITY POLL 3
DETAILED RESULTS!!
THE COM-PLETE LIST

# BLEACH POPULARITY POLL 3

## DETAILED RESULTS!! THE COMPLETE LIST

**1st** (8,370 votes) Ichigo Kurosaki
**2nd** (8,321 votes) Tôshirô Hitsugaya
**3rd** (6,122 votes) Rukia Kuchiki
**4th** (4,517 votes) Renji Abarai
**5th** (4,039 votes) Gin Ichimaru
**6th** (3,752 votes) Byakuya Kuchiki
**7th** (3,744 votes) Yoruichi Shihôin
**8th** (3,676 votes) Kisuke Urahara
**9th** (3,001 votes) Kenpachi Zaraki
**10th** (2,901 votes) Orihime Inoue

**11th** (2,873 votes) Izuru Kira
**12th** (2,735 votes) Momo Hinamori
**13th** (2,317 votes) Shûhei Hisagi
**14th** (2,298 votes) Jûshiro Ukitake
**15th** (1,742 votes) Uryû Ishida
**16th** (1,628 votes) Soi Fon
**17th** (1,377 votes) Rangiku Matsumoto
**18th** (1,266 votes) Sôsuke Aizen
**19th** (1,244 votes) Yachiru Kusajishi
**20th** (737 votes) Ulquiorra
**21st** (641 votes) Yumichika Ayasegawa
**22nd** (609 votes) Nanao Ise
**23rd** (601 votes) Kon
**24th** (566 votes) Ururu Tsumugiya
**25th** (545 votes) Hanatarô Yamada
**26th** (519 votes) Tôsen Kaname
**27th** (456 votes) Ikkaku Madarame
**28th** (448 votes) Mayuri Kurotsuchi
**29th** (445 votes) Shunsui Kyoraku
**30th** (440 votes) Isshin Kurosaki
**31st** (370 votes) Yasutora Sado
**32nd** (346 votes) Isane Kotetsu
**33rd** (316 votes) Kaien Shiba
Akon
**35th** (258 votes) Zangetsu
**36th** (217 votes) Ganju Shiba
**37th** (202 votes) Nemu Kurotsuchi
**38th** (181 votes) Retsu Unohana
**39th** (175 votes) Sajin Komamura
**40th** (174 votes) Tatsuki Arisawa
**41st** (171 votes) Keigo Asano
**42nd** (155 votes) Shinji Hirako
**43rd** (151 votes) Hiyori Sarugaki
**44th** (145 votes) Ryûken Ishida
**45th** (142 votes) Chojiro Sasakibe
**46th** (137 votes) Hisana Kuchiki
**47th** (137 votes) Aizen's glasses
**48th** (129 votes) Rikichi
**49th** (109 votes) Kûkaku Shiba
**50th** (88 votes) Kiyone Kotetsu

# BEST 1-146

Horiuchi/Kenseikan/Pupples/The 12th Company member who was tricked by Kurotsuchi/Uryû's glasses/Kenpachi's Zanpaku-tô/The leaf Shunsui has in his mouth/Enraku/The cover with Kenpachi covered in blood that got nixed/Rukia's Zanpaku-tô/Isshin's charm/The button on Kon's belly/Reiichi Ohshima/Michiru's broken doll/Monshirochô/Yumichika's wig/Acidwire/Elwood

**146th** (1 vote) Sora Inoue/Chappy/Shunshun Rikka/Koganehiko/Mareyo Ohmaeda/Suzumebachi/Zangetsu's sunglasses/Gillian/Senzai-kyu/The Champs-Élysées/Melon & Cookie/Kurôemon Tsujishiro/Lord Baron/Ugendô/Matatabi?!/Tessai Deathcatch/Madame Akiyama/Mod Konpaku/Kurosaki Clinic/The Karakura High School guidebook/Kenpachi's eye patch/Comedian guidebook 2001/Konpaku in pain during Konsô/Asano's head cracking game/Kisuke's hat/Chain of Fate/Ginosuke/Chinamidama/Rangiku's memo with lips on it/Rukia's letter/ Hômonka/Shihôin Family Crest/Suzumushi/Tsuki Tsuki Dance/Hojiku-zai/Wasabi and Honey Taiyaki-style Ramen/Tokkuri Monaka from Kuriya/Kurotsuchi's detonation button/Dai-Kukaku-Wan/Marriane's older sister/Francois/The Hollow that could either be a cow or pig/Toshirin/Yama-chan/Assistant Captain Hirayama/Fujio/Onodera/Hitomi Victoria Odagiri/Gengoro Ohunabara/Hotarukazura/Lily/Kidô-shu/Numb Chandelier/Frozen Snow/Komamura's Tetsugasa/Shinji's Hollow mask/Tessai's Jûtai Glasses/Iba's sunglasses/The god who made Keigo stupid

★ Others: Around 100 votes for characters (can they be called that?) that couldn't fit due to lack of space.

**51st** (84 votes) Yuzu Kurosaki
**52nd** (72 votes) Karin Kurosaki
**53rd** (71 votes) Tite Kubo
**54th** (56 votes) Rin Tsubokura
**55th** (42 votes) Tetsuzaemon Iba
**56th** (40 votes) Hollowfied Ichigo
**57th** (37 votes) Genryûsai Shigekuni Yamamoto
**58th** (35 votes) Mizuiro Kojima
**59th** (21 votes) Don Kanonji
**60th** (19 votes) Harunobu Ogidô
**61st** (17 votes) Yasochika Iemura
**62nd** (16 votes) Chizuru Honshô
**63rd** (15 votes) Kizô Aramaki/Menos Grande
**65th** (14 votes) Minazuki
**66th** (13 votes) Marechiyo Ohmaeda/Zabimaru
**68th** (12 votes) Jinta Hanakari/Wabisuke/Editor Nakano
**71st** (11 votes) Tetsuo Momohara/Bulbous G
**73rd** (10 votes) Tessai Tsukabishi/Yammy
**75th** (9 votes) Kôkichiro Takezoe/Jidanbô/Benihime
**78th** (8 votes) Masaki Kurosaki/Tsubaki/Hyôrinmaru
**81st** (7 votes) Maremi Ohmaeda/Pictures Rukia drew/Kanisawa/Deputy Badge
**85th** (6 votes) Michiru Ogawa/Hiyosu/Hanataro's Energy Drink/Isshin's T-shirt/Yuichi Shibata
**90th** (5 votes) Misato Ochi/Ryo Kunieda/Bonnie/Kokujotengen Myoô/Hexapodus/The shark Kûkaku caught/Hitsugaya's grandmother/Shrieker
**98th** (4 votes) Miyako Shiba/Midoriko Tôno/Shunô/Kiko-oh/Kagekiyo Kira/bandana Soul Reaper in chapter 99/The training wheels on Yachiru's Zanpaku-tô/Renji's loincloth
**106th** (3 votes) Tatsuhusa Enjôji/Mahana Natsui/Tensa Zangetsu/Shizuka Kira/Jennifer/Ishida's fitting room/Zabimaru that became a woman in its fantasy/Oil rice cracker/Denrei Shinki/Tobiume/The bell in Kenpachi's hair/Edible Denrei Shinki
**118th** (2 votes) Kaiwan/Ayame/Yokochin/Bostov/Hell Butterfly/Fishbone D/Gamma Akutabi/Shiroganehiko/Heita Tôjôin/Tomohiro Conrad Odagiri/Hironari

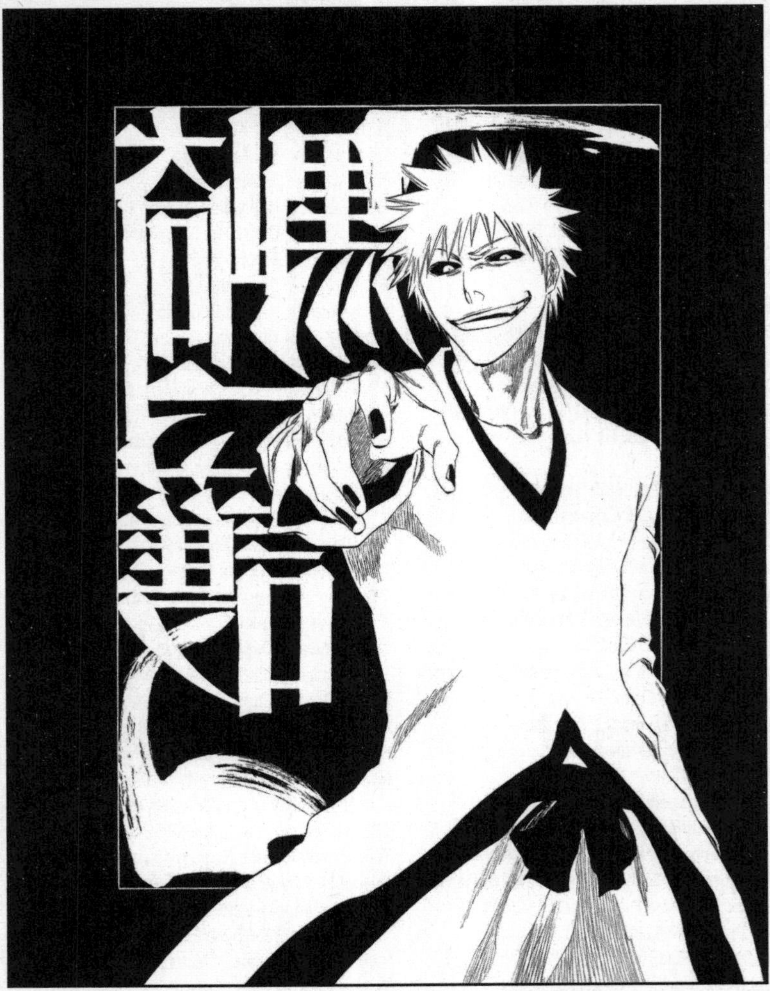

To have any hope of defeating Aizen and his army of Arrancars, Ichigo

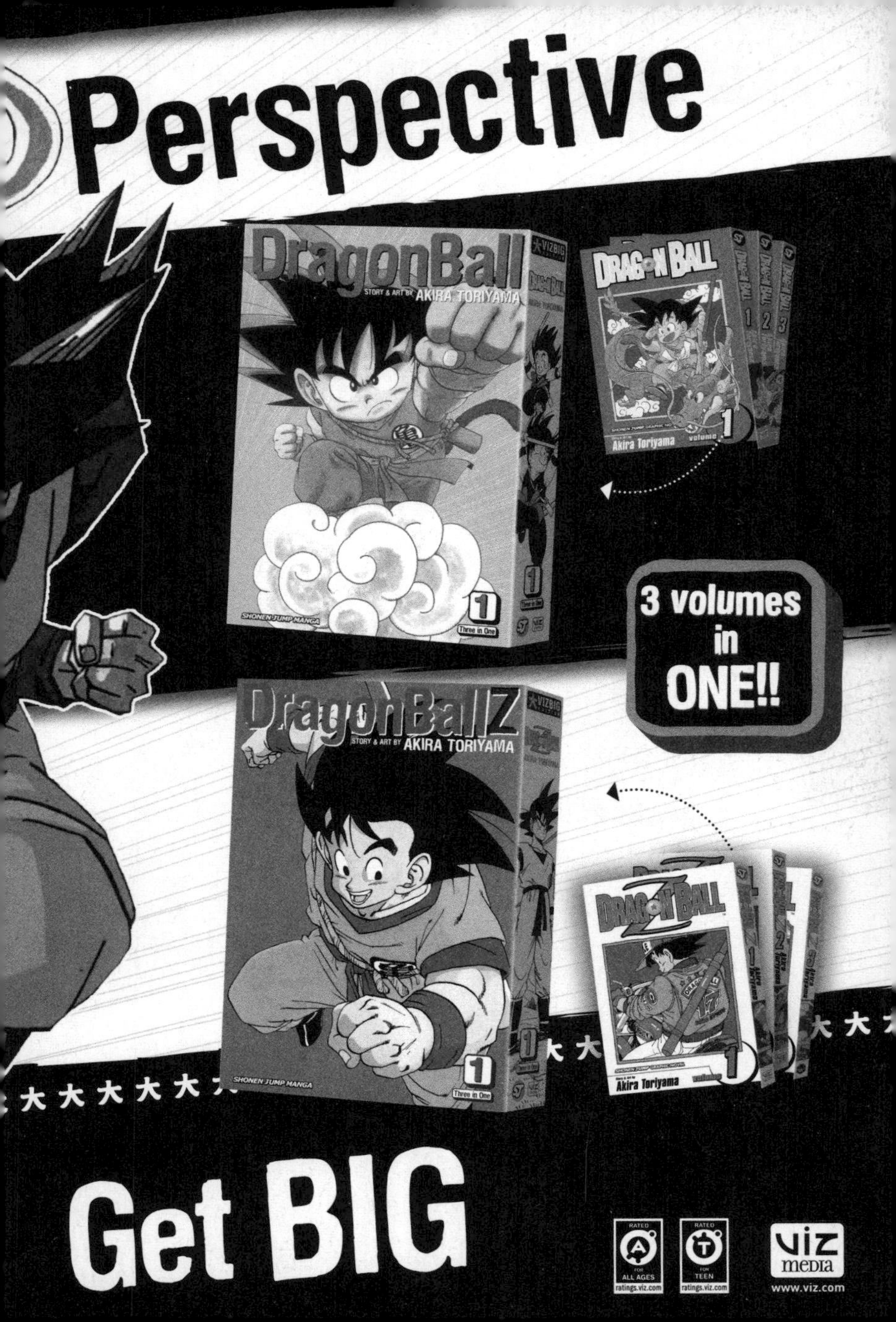
Perspective
DragonBall
STORY & ART BY AKIRA TORIYAMA
SHONEN JUMP MANGA
Three in One
DRAGON BALL
Akira Toriyama
3 volumes in ONE!!
DragonBall Z
STORY & ART BY AKIRA TORIYAMA
SHONEN JUMP MANGA
Three in One
DRAGON BALL Z
Akira Toriyama
大大大大大
Get BIG
RATED A FOR ALL AGES ratings.viz.com
RATED T FOR TEEN ratings.viz.com
VIZ media
www.viz.com

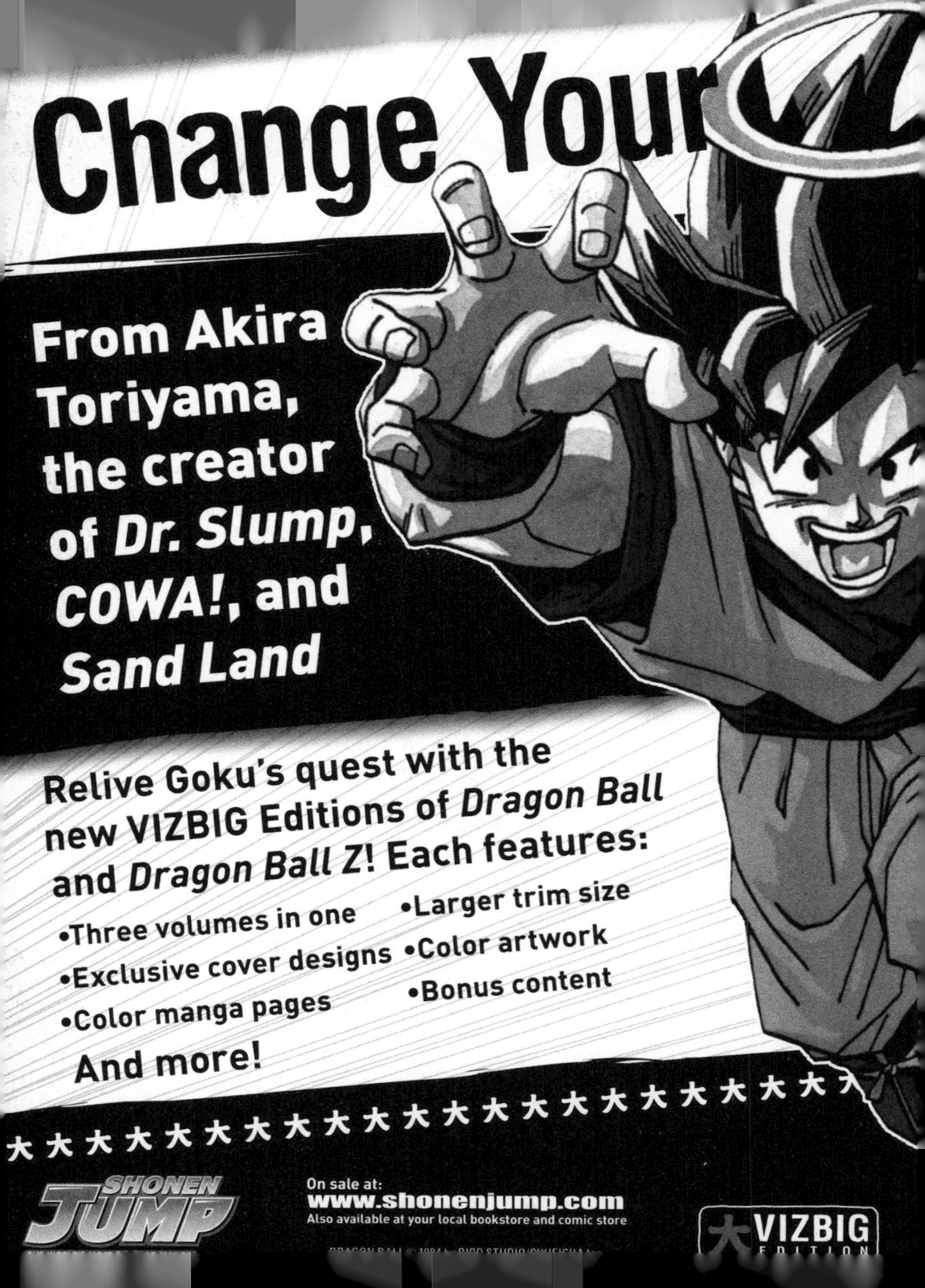

Change Your
From Akira Toriyama, the creator of Dr. Slump, COWA!, and Sand Land
Relive Goku's quest with the new VIZBIG Editions of Dragon Ball and Dragon Ball Z! Each features:
•Three volumes in one
•Exclusive cover designs
•Color manga pages
•Larger trim size
•Color artwork
•Bonus content
And more!
SHONEN JUMP
On sale at:
www.shonenjump.com
Also available at your local bookstore and comic store
VIZBIG EDITION

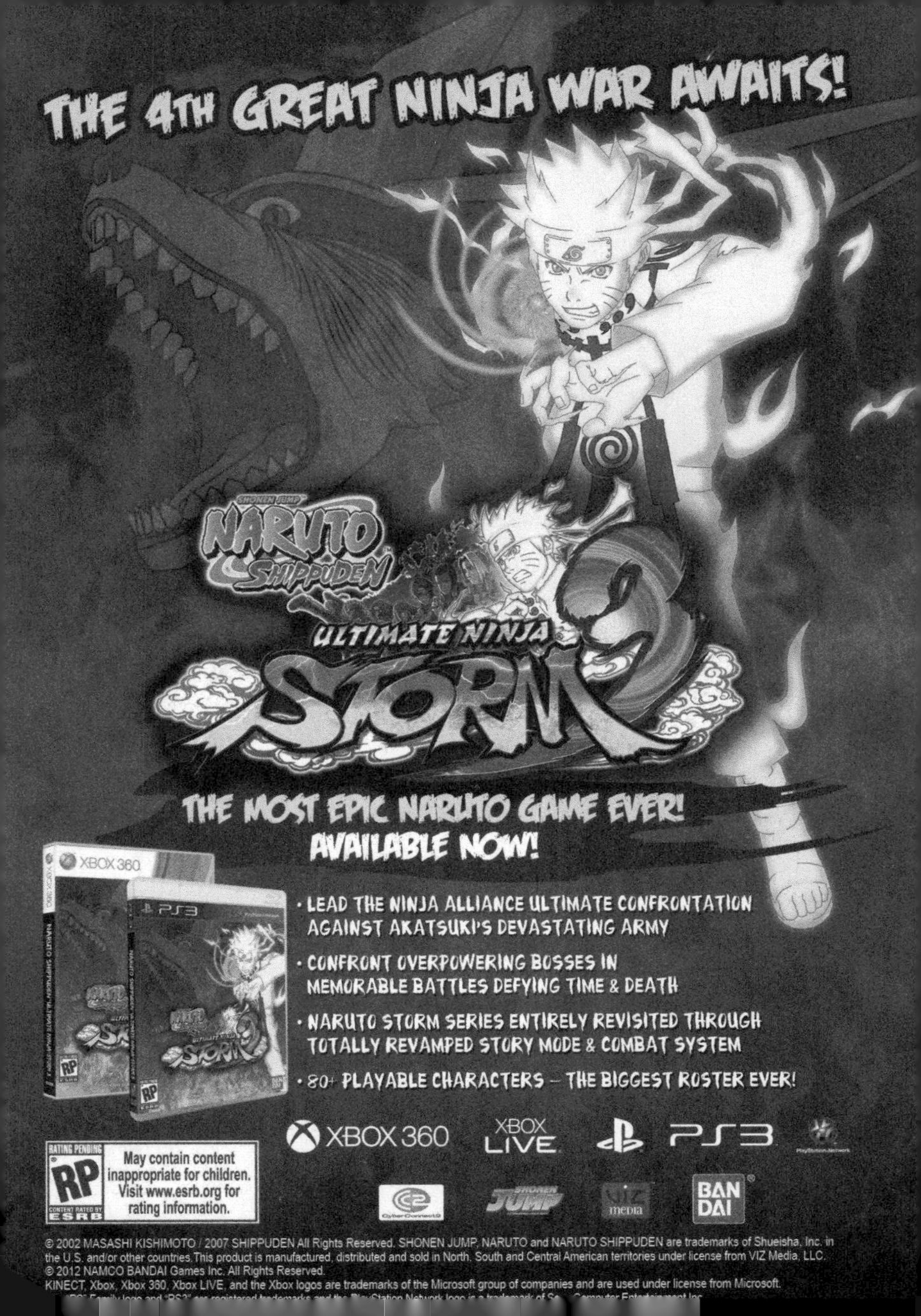
THE 4TH GREAT NINJA WAR AWAITS!
SHONEN JUMP
NARUTO SHIPPUDEN
ULTIMATE NINJA STORM 3
THE MOST EPIC NARUTO GAME EVER!
AVAILABLE NOW!
• LEAD THE NINJA ALLIANCE ULTIMATE CONFRONTATION AGAINST AKATSUKI'S DEVASTATING ARMY
• CONFRONT OVERPOWERING BOSSES IN MEMORABLE BATTLES DEFYING TIME & DEATH
• NARUTO STORM SERIES ENTIRELY REVISITED THROUGH TOTALLY REVAMPED STORY MODE & COMBAT SYSTEM
• 80+ PLAYABLE CHARACTERS – THE BIGGEST ROSTER EVER!
XBOX 360
XBOX LIVE
PS3
RATING PENDING
RP
CONTENT RATED BY ESRB
May contain content inappropriate for children. Visit www.esrb.org for rating information.
CyberConnect2
SHONEN JUMP
VIZ media
BANDAI
© 2002 MASASHI KISHIMOTO / 2007 SHIPPUDEN All Rights Reserved. SHONEN JUMP, NARUTO and NARUTO SHIPPUDEN are trademarks of Shueisha, Inc. in the U.S. and/or other countries. This product is manufactured, distributed and sold in North, South and Central American territories under license from VIZ Media, LLC.
© 2012 NAMCO BANDAI Games Inc. All Rights Reserved.
KINECT, Xbox, Xbox 360, Xbox LIVE, and the Xbox logos are trademarks of the Microsoft group of companies and are used under license from Microsoft.

# A BRUSH WITH THE AFTERLIFE

## All Colour But The Black
### THE ART OF BLEACH
**By Tite Kubo, creator of ZOMBIEPOWDER.**

**EXPLORE THE WORLD OF** *BLEACH* **THROUGH THIS HIGH-QUALITY ART BOOK SHOWCASING ARTWORK FROM TITE KUBO'S POPULAR MANGA SERIES, WHICH INCLUDES:**

- Vibrant illustrations, including art from volumes 1-19
- An annotated art guide
- Extra character information

**PLUS, AN EXCLUSIVE POSTER!**

**COMPLETE YOUR** *BLEACH* **COLLECTION WITH** ***THE ART OF BLEACH: ALL COLOUR BUT THE BLACK—* GET YOURS TODAY!**

On sale at
www.shonenjump.com
Also available at your local
bookstore and comic store.

www.shonenjump.com    www.viz.com

# DISCOVER ANIME
## IN A WHOLE NEW WAY!

# www.neonalley.com

## What it is...

- Streaming anime delivered 24/7 straight to your TV via your connected video game console
- All English dubbed content
- Anime, martial arts movies, and more

Go to **neonalley.com** for news, updates and to see if Neon Alley is available in your area.

NEON ALLEY is a trademark or service mark of VIZ Media, LLC

# You're Reading in the Wrong Direction!!

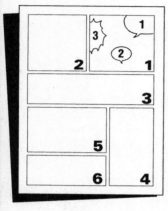

**W**hoops! Guess what? You're starting at the wrong end of the comic!

...It's true! In keeping with the original Japanese format, **Bleach** is meant to be read from right to left, starting in the upper-right corner.

Unlike English, which is read from left to right, Japanese is read from right to left, meaning that action, sound effects and word-balloon order are completely reversed... something which can make readers unfamiliar with Japanese feel pretty backwards themselves. For this reason, manga or Japanese comics published in the U.S. in English have sometimes been published "flopped"—that is, printed in exact reverse order, as though seen from the other side of a mirror.

By flopping pages, U.S. publishers can avoid confusing readers, but the compromise is not without its downside. For one thing, a character in a flopped manga series who once wore in the original Japanese version a T-shirt emblazoned with "M A Y" (as in "the merry month of") now wears one which reads "Y A M"! Additionally, many manga creators in Japan are themselves unhappy with the process, as some feel the mirror-imaging of their art skews their original intentions.

We are proud to bring you Tite Kubo's **Bleach** in the original unflopped format. For now, though, turn to the other side of the book and let the adventure begin...!

—Editor